Viz Graphic Novel

# FLAME OF RECCA™

## Vol. 7

Story & Art by Nobuyuki Anzai

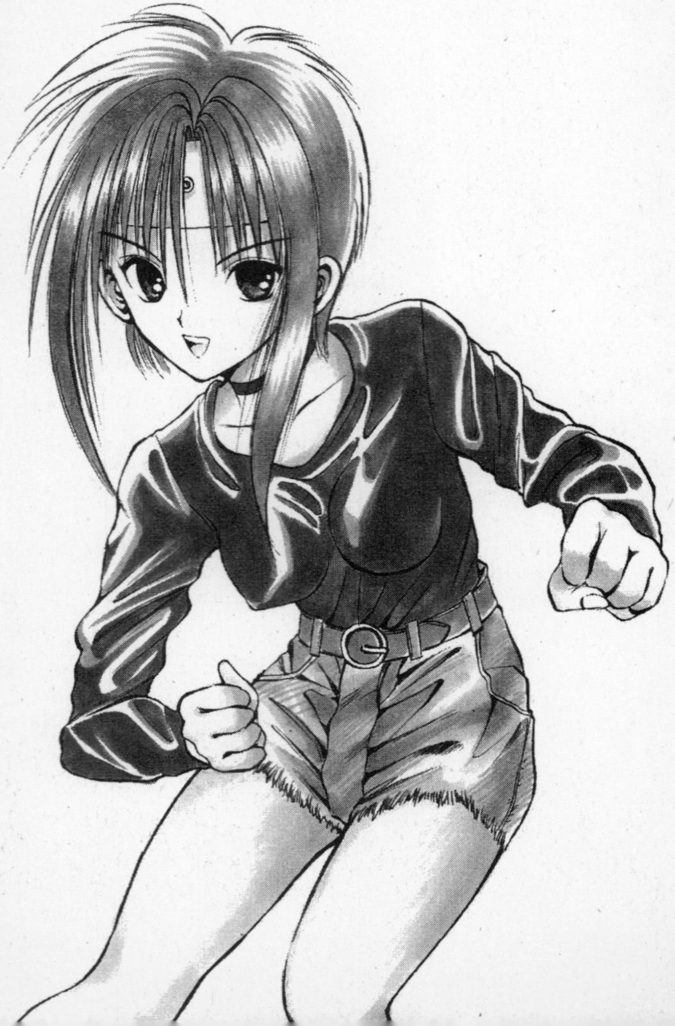

# Contents






Flame of Recca
Vol. 7
Action Edition

Story and Art by
Nobuyuki Anzai

English Adaptation/Lance Caselman
Translation/Joe Yamazaki
Touch-Up & Lettering/Jim Keefe
Graphics & Cover Design/Sean Lee
Editor/Eric Searleman

Managing Editior/Annette Roman
Editor-in-Chief/Alvin Lu
Production Manager/Noboru Watanabe
Sr. Director of Licensing & Acquisitions/Rika Inouye
Vice President of Marketing/Liza Coppola
Executive Vice President/Hyoe Narita
Publisher/Seiji Horibuchi

Flame of Recca is rated "T+" and is recommended for readers ages 13 and above. This book contains strong language and violence.





Printed in Canada

Published by VIZ, LLC
P.O. Box 77064
San Francisco, CA 94107

Action Edition
10 9 8 7 6 5 4 3 2 1
First Published, July 2004

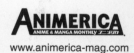

# Part Sixty:
# The Mad Illusionist's Feast
# (5) Stone Cold

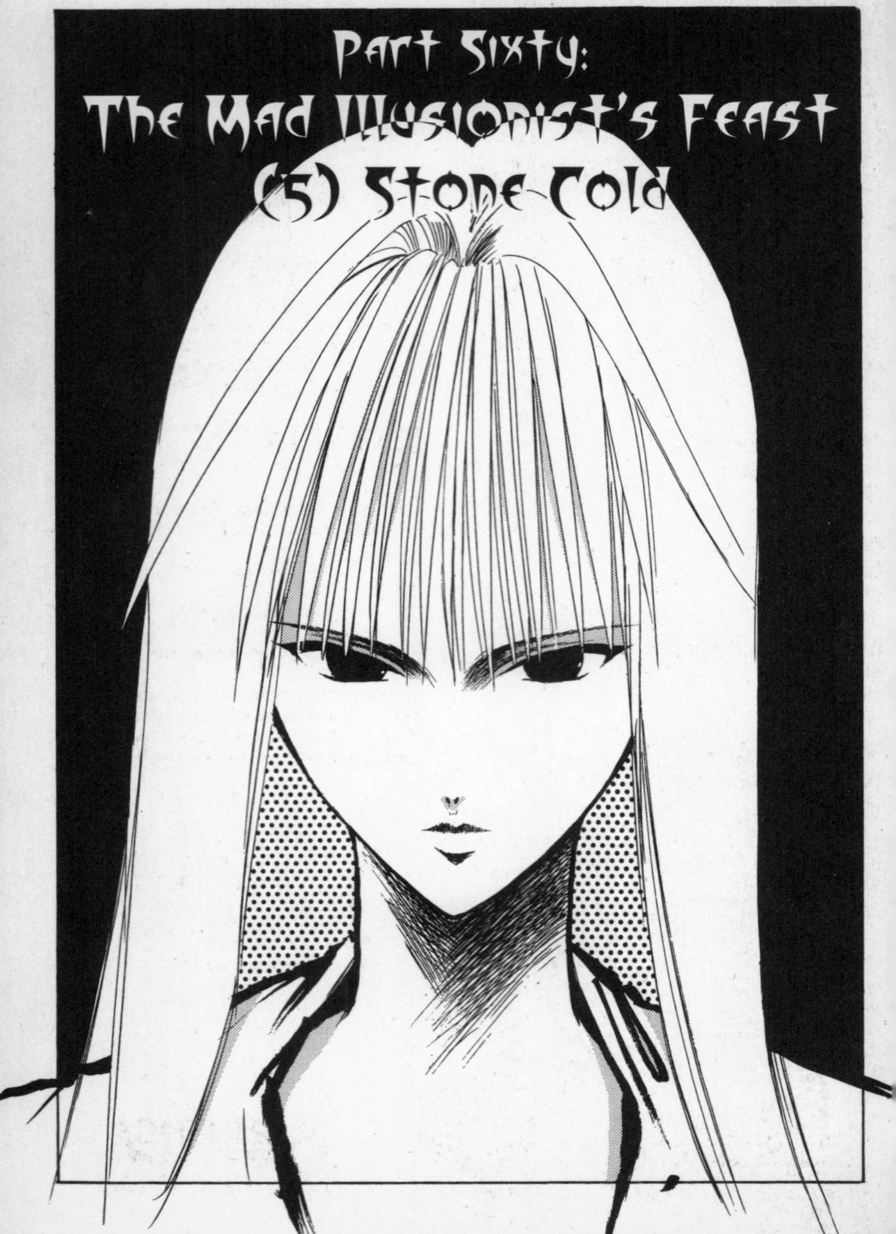

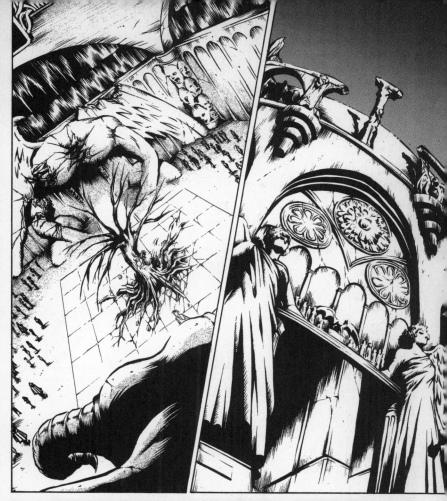

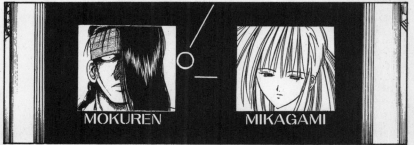

MOKUREN                    MIKAGAMI

4

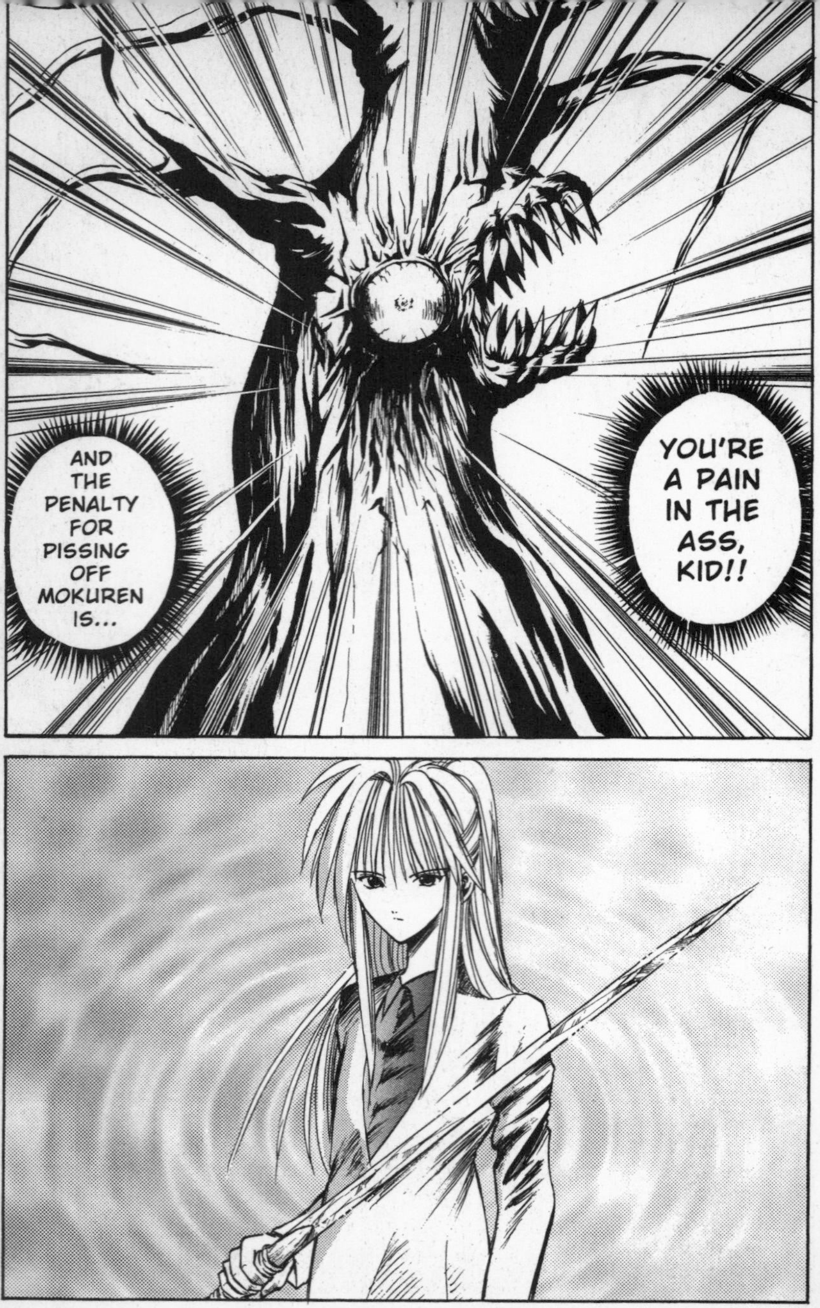
YOU'RE A PAIN IN THE ASS, KID!!
AND THE PENALTY FOR PISSING OFF MOKUREN IS...

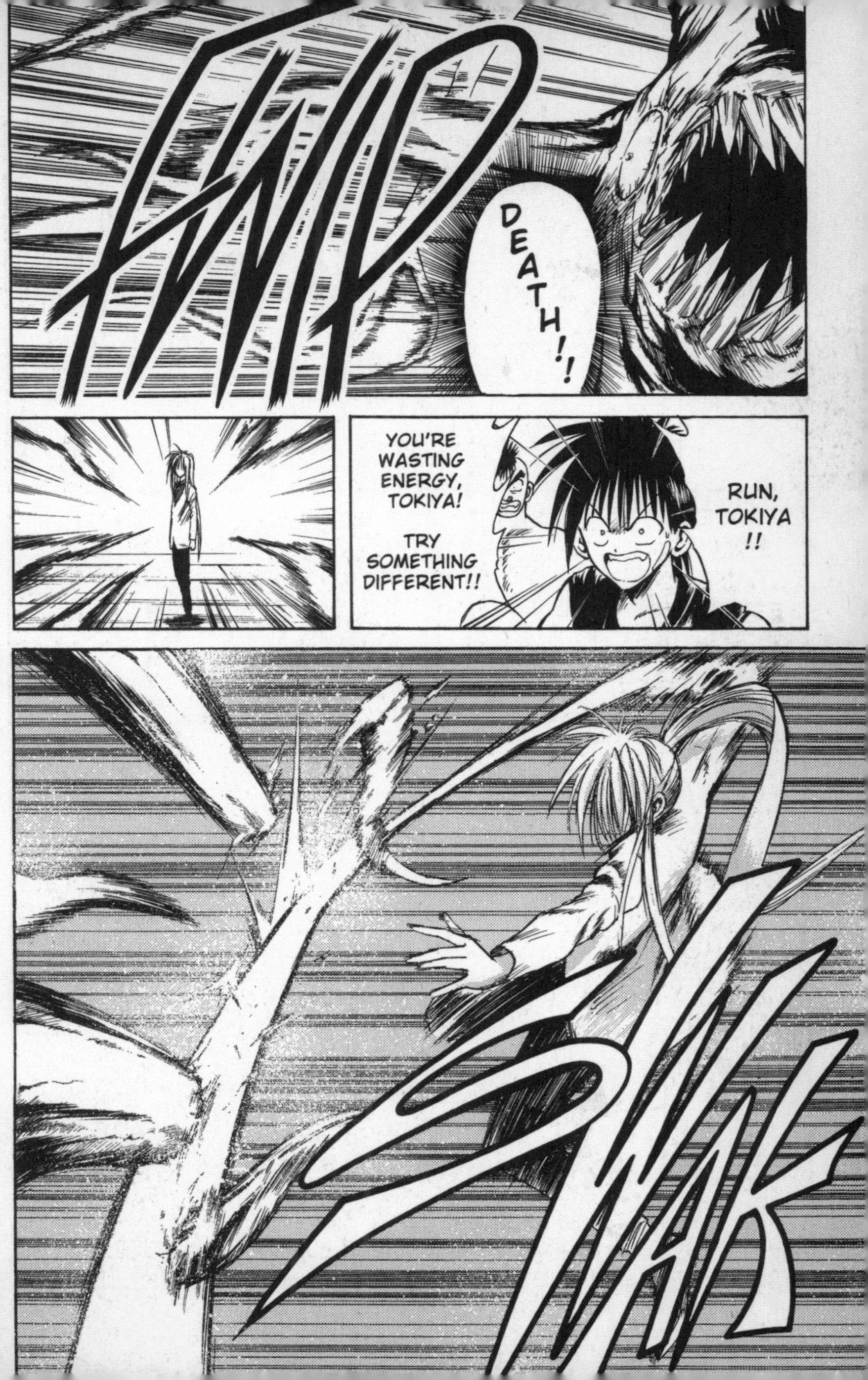
DEATH!!
RUN, TOKIYA!!
YOU'RE WASTING ENERGY, TOKIYA!
TRY SOMETHING DIFFERENT!!

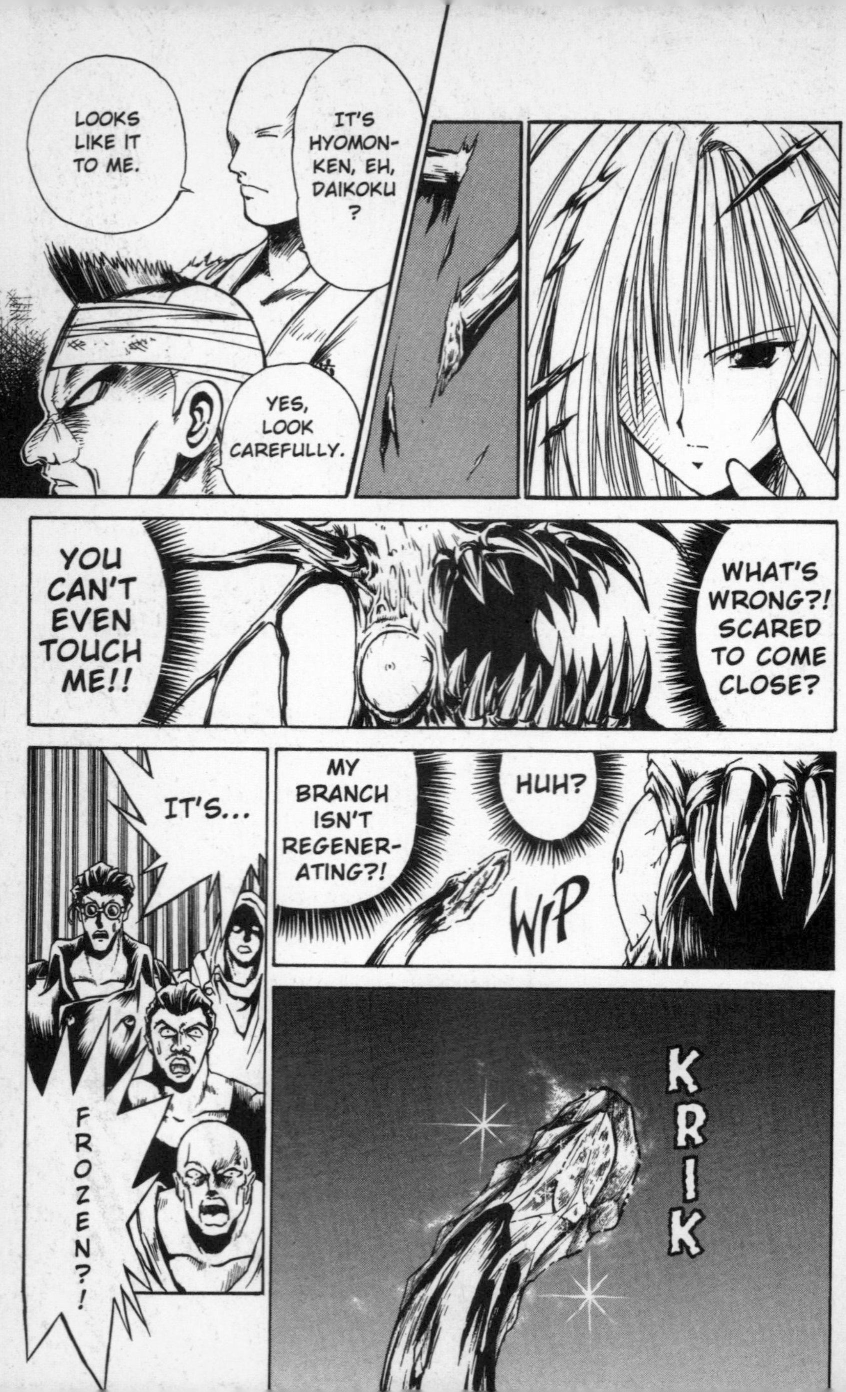
IT'S HYOMON-KEN, EH, DAIKOKU?
LOOKS LIKE IT TO ME.
YES, LOOK CAREFULLY.
WHAT'S WRONG?! SCARED TO COME CLOSE?
YOU CAN'T EVEN TOUCH ME!!
HUH?
MY BRANCH ISN'T REGENER-ATING?!
WIP
KRIK
IT'S...
FROZEN?!

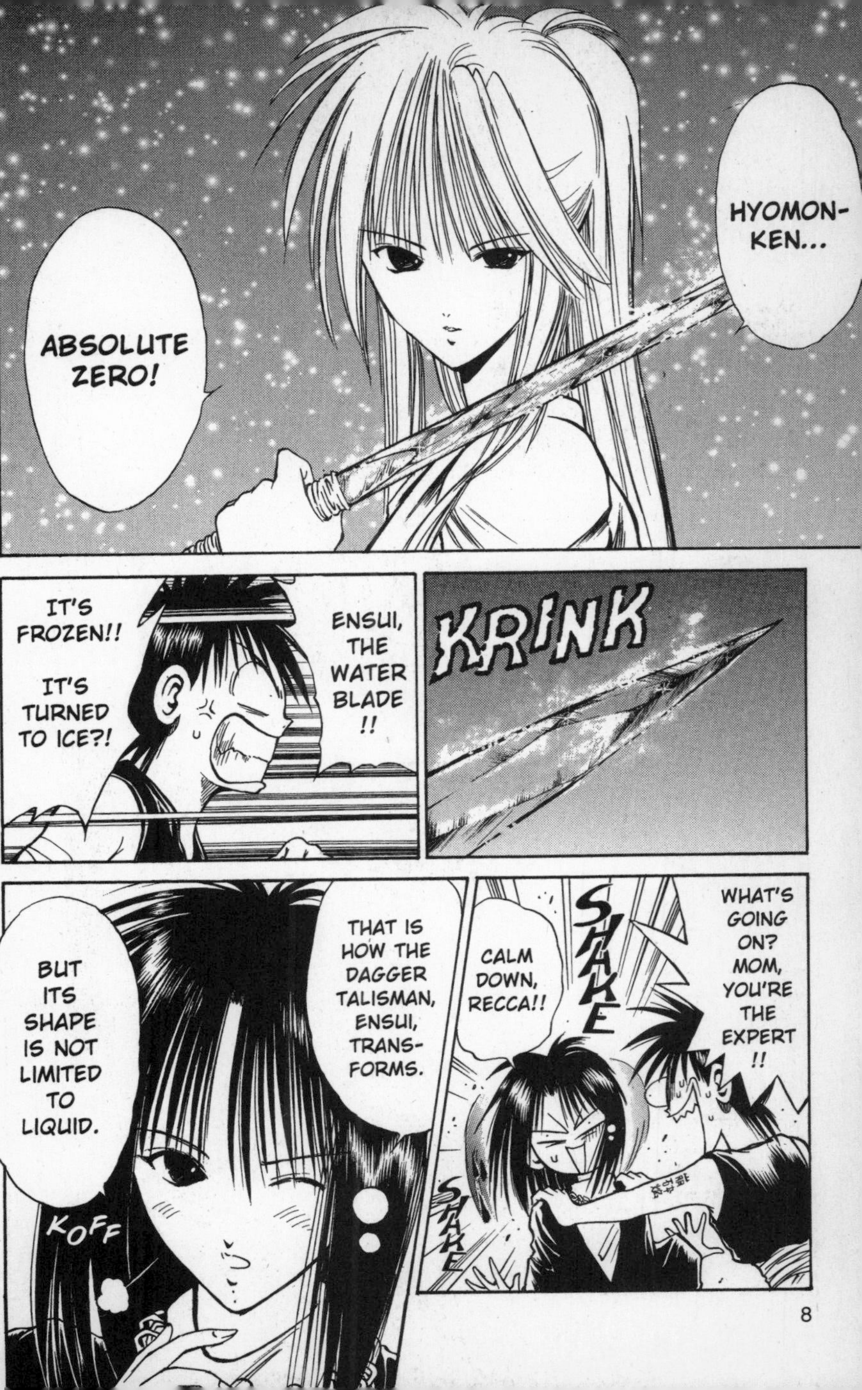
HYOMON-KEN...
ABSOLUTE ZERO!
KRINK
ENSUI, THE WATER BLADE!!
IT'S FROZEN!!
IT'S TURNED TO ICE?!
WHAT'S GOING ON? MOM, YOU'RE THE EXPERT!!
SHAKE
CALM DOWN, RECCA!!
SHAKE
THAT IS HOW THE DAGGER TALISMAN, ENSUI, TRANS-FORMS.
BUT ITS SHAPE IS NOT LIMITED TO LIQUID.
KOFF

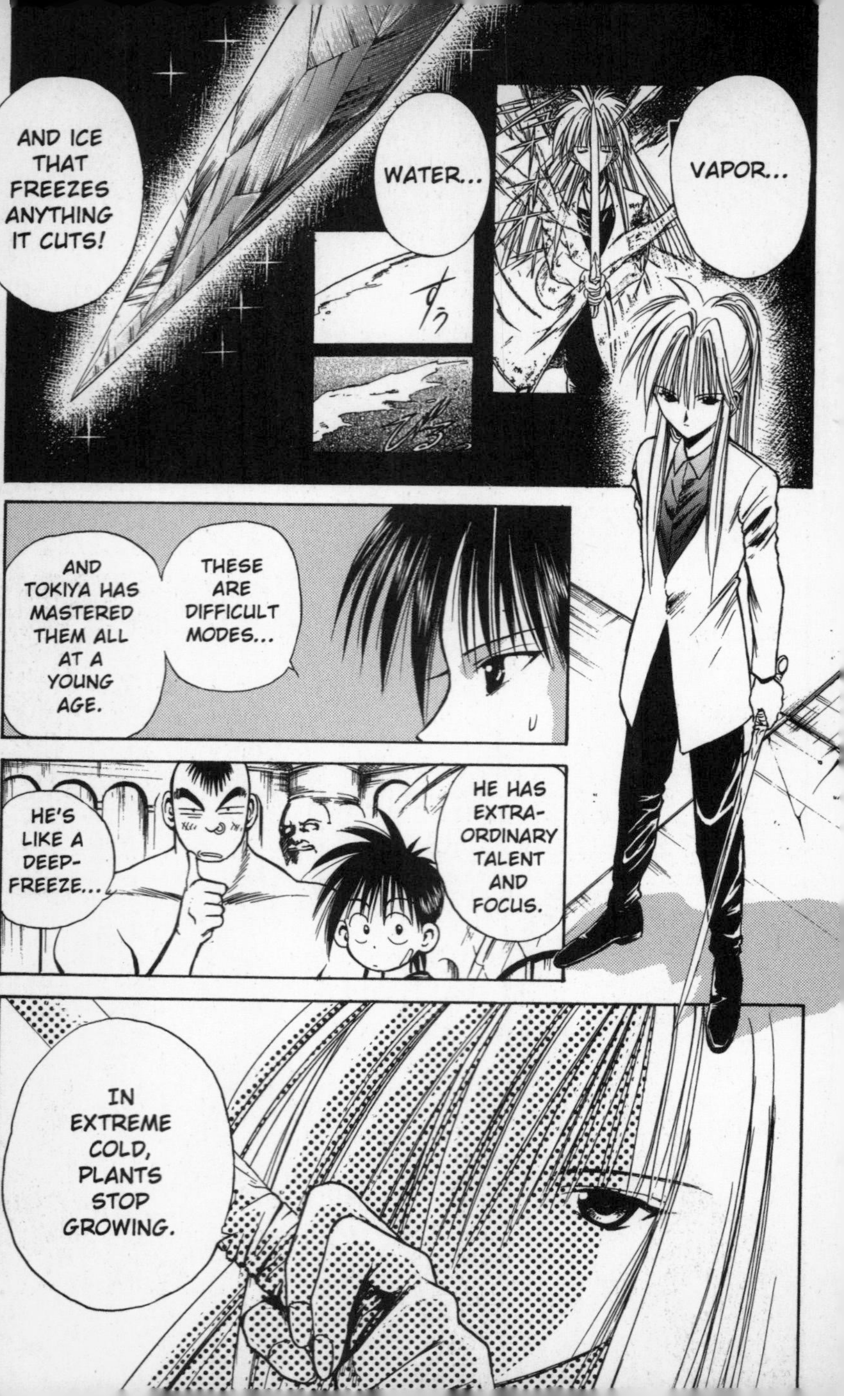
VAPOR...
WATER...
AND ICE THAT FREEZES ANYTHING IT CUTS!
THESE ARE DIFFICULT MODES...
AND TOKIYA HAS MASTERED THEM ALL AT A YOUNG AGE.
HE HAS EXTRA-ORDINARY TALENT AND FOCUS.
HE'S LIKE A DEEP-FREEZE...
IN EXTREME COLD, PLANTS STOP GROWING.

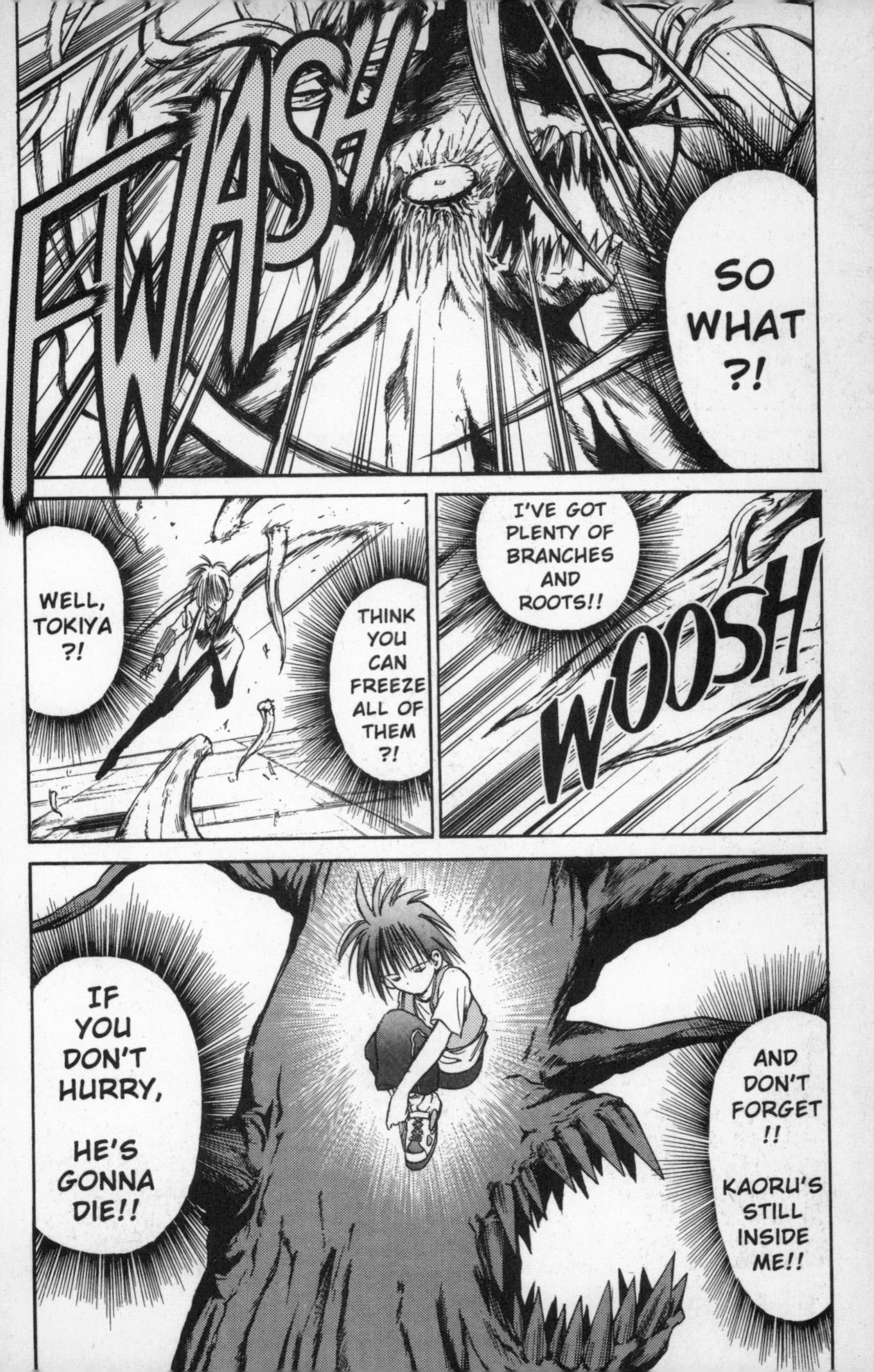
SO WHAT ?!
FWASH
I'VE GOT PLENTY OF BRANCHES AND ROOTS!!
WOOSH
WELL, TOKIYA ?!
THINK YOU CAN FREEZE ALL OF THEM ?!
AND DON'T FORGET !!
KAORU'S STILL INSIDE ME!!
IF YOU DON'T HURRY,
HE'S GONNA DIE!!

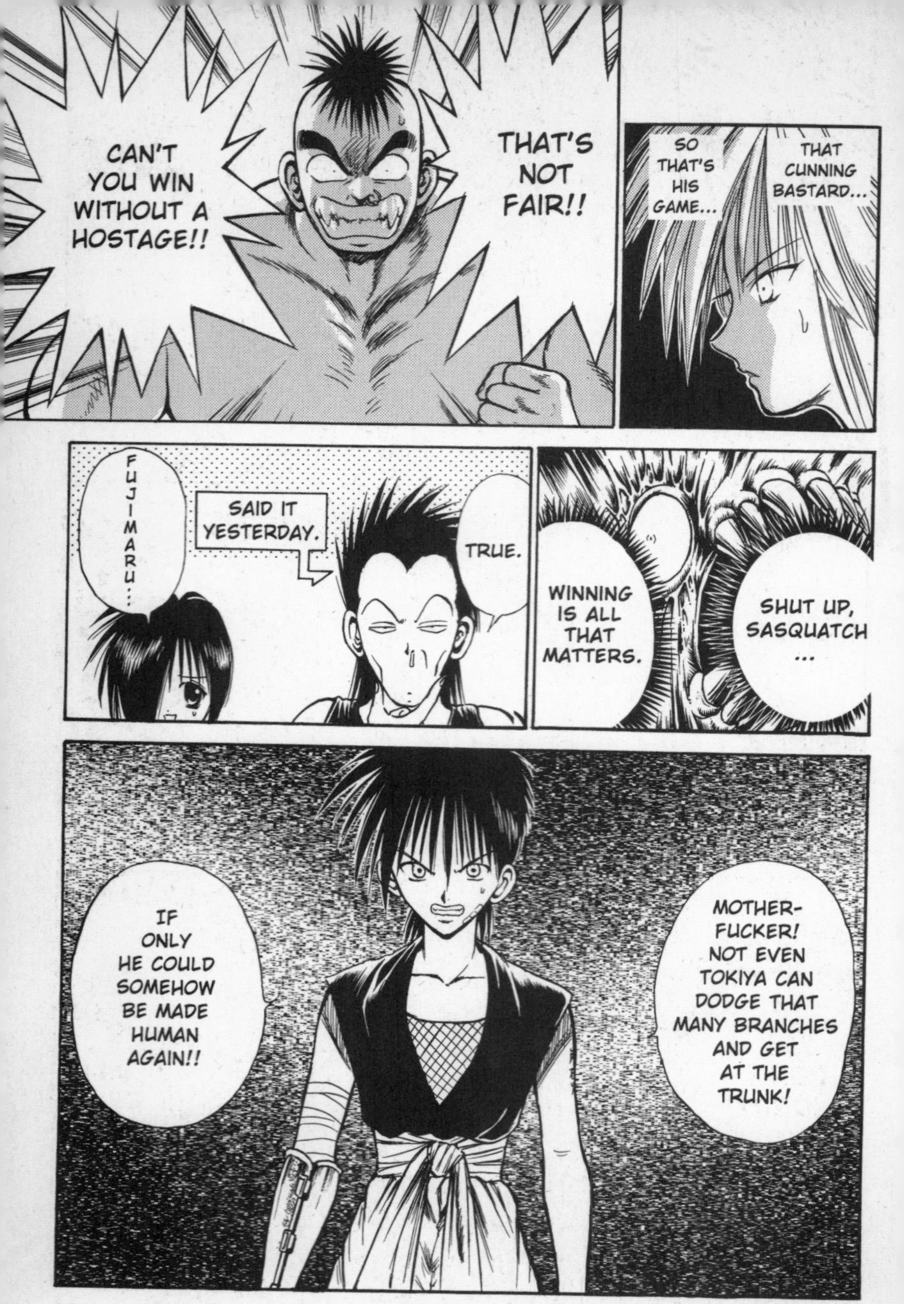

THAT CUNNING BASTARD...
SO THAT'S HIS GAME...
THAT'S NOT FAIR!!
CAN'T YOU WIN WITHOUT A HOSTAGE!!
SHUT UP, SASQUATCH ...
WINNING IS ALL THAT MATTERS.
TRUE.
SAID IT YESTERDAY.
FUJIMARU...
MOTHER-FUCKER! NOT EVEN TOKIYA CAN DODGE THAT MANY BRANCHES AND GET AT THE TRUNK!
IF ONLY HE COULD SOMEHOW BE MADE HUMAN AGAIN!!

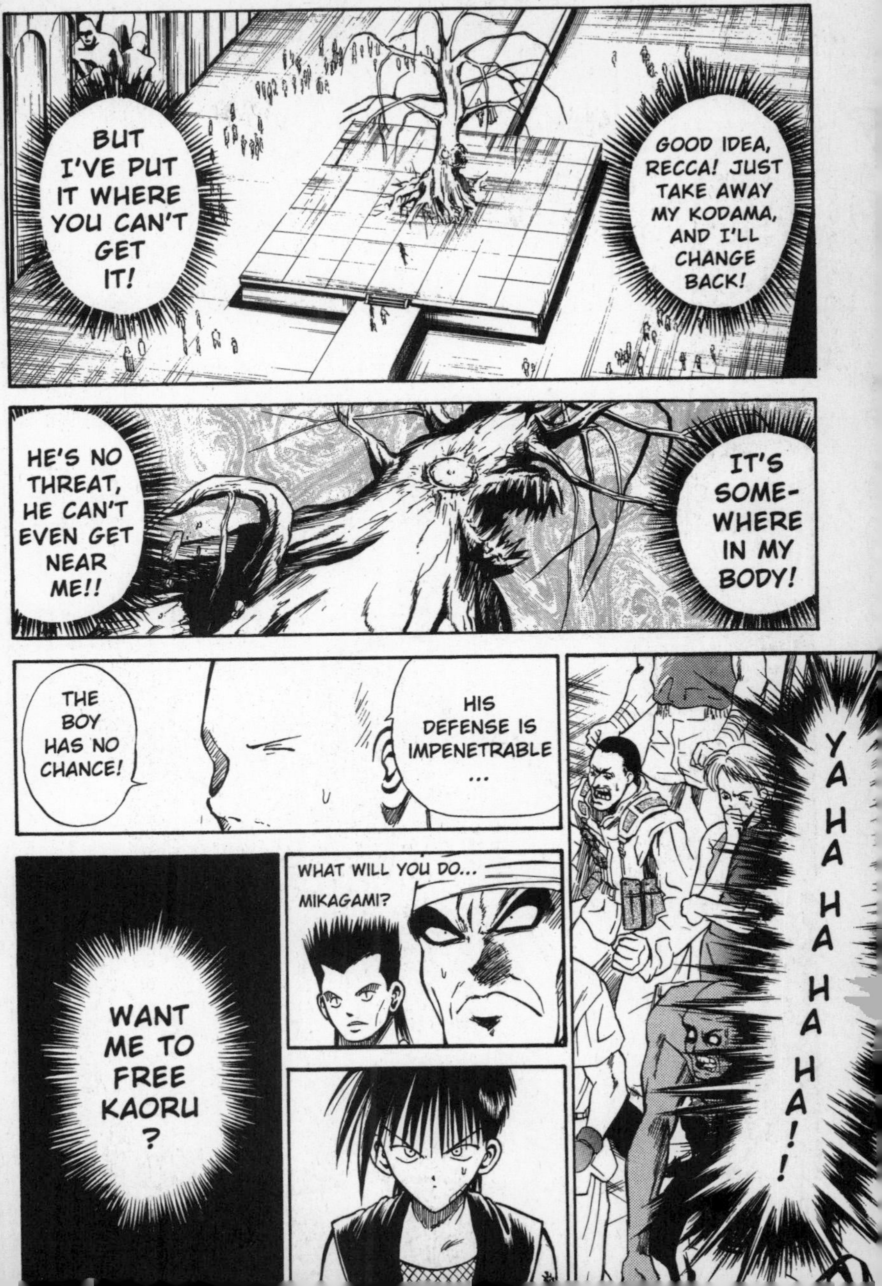
GOOD IDEA, RECCA! JUST TAKE AWAY MY KODAMA, AND I'LL CHANGE BACK!
BUT I'VE PUT IT WHERE YOU CAN'T GET IT!
IT'S SOME-WHERE IN MY BODY!
HE'S NO THREAT, HE CAN'T EVEN GET NEAR ME!!
YA HA HA HA HA HA!!
HIS DEFENSE IS IMPENETRABLE ...
THE BOY HAS NO CHANCE!
WHAT WILL YOU DO... MIKAGAMI?
WANT ME TO FREE KAORU ?

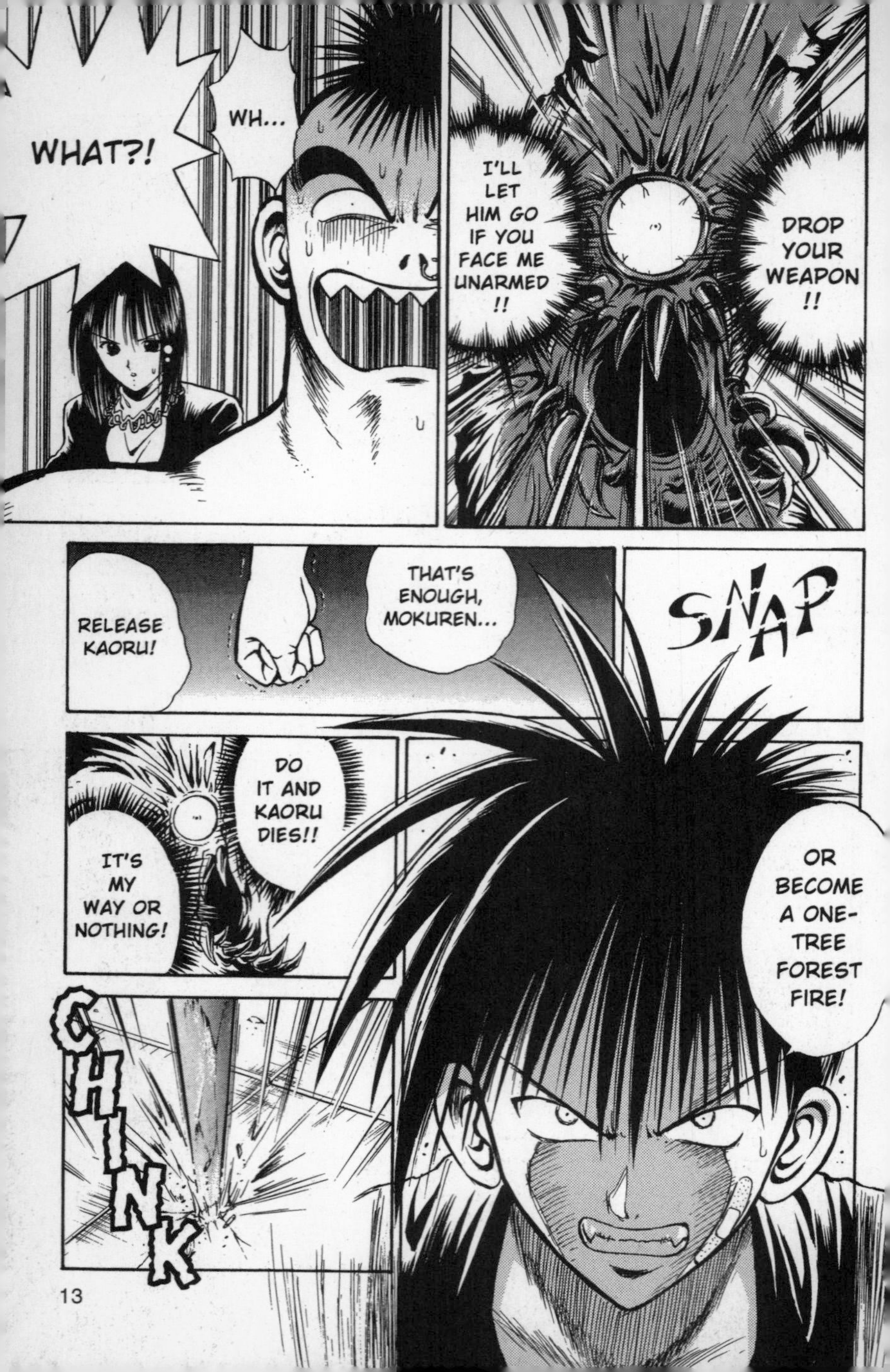

DROP YOUR WEAPON!!
I'LL LET HIM GO IF YOU FACE ME UNARMED!!
WH...
WHAT?!
SNAP
THAT'S ENOUGH, MOKUREN...
RELEASE KAORU!
OR BECOME A ONE-TREE FOREST FIRE!
DO IT AND KAORU DIES!!
IT'S MY WAY OR NOTHING!
CHINK

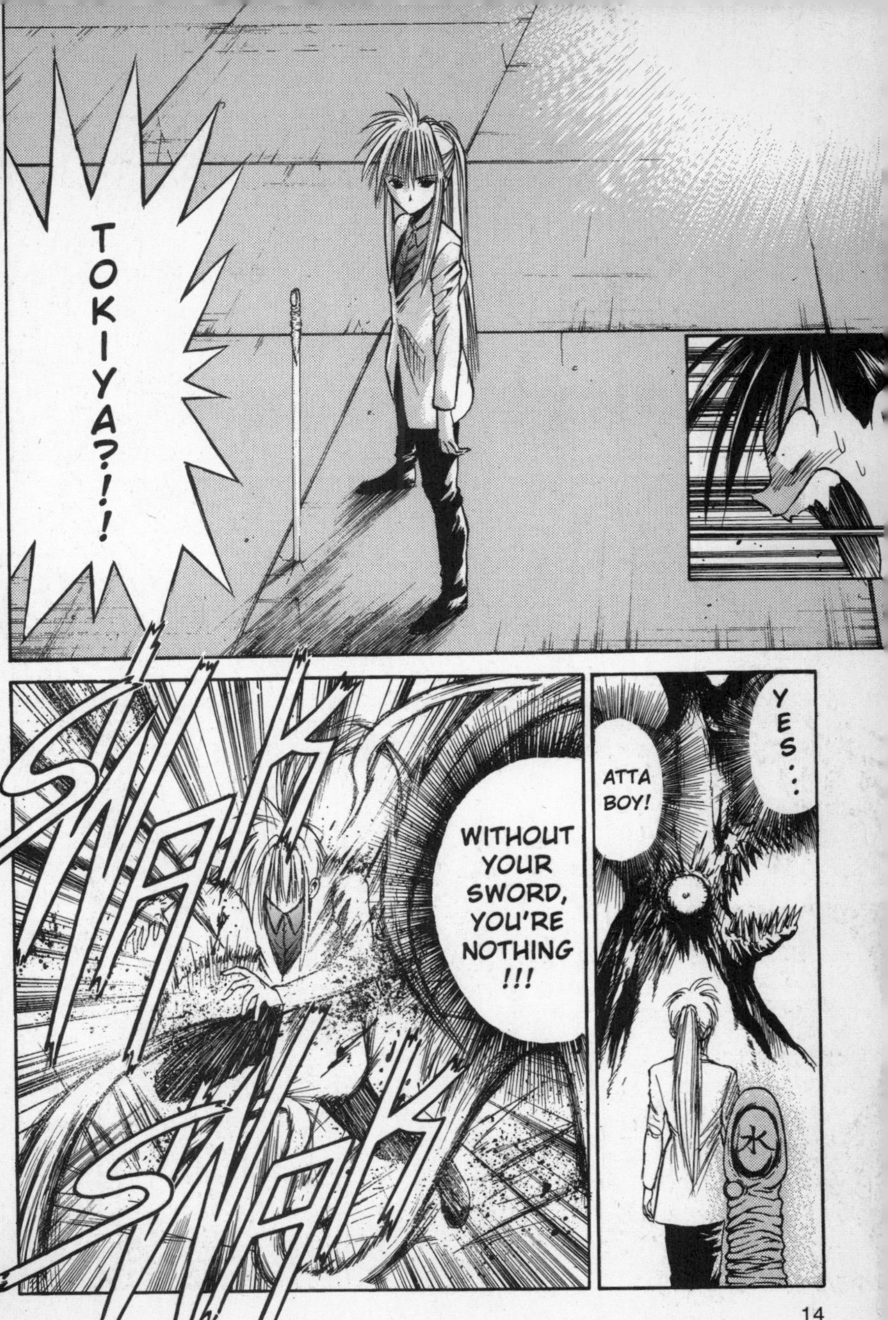
TOKIYA?!!
YES...
ATTA BOY!
WITHOUT YOUR SWORD, YOU'RE NOTHING !!!
SHAK SHAK

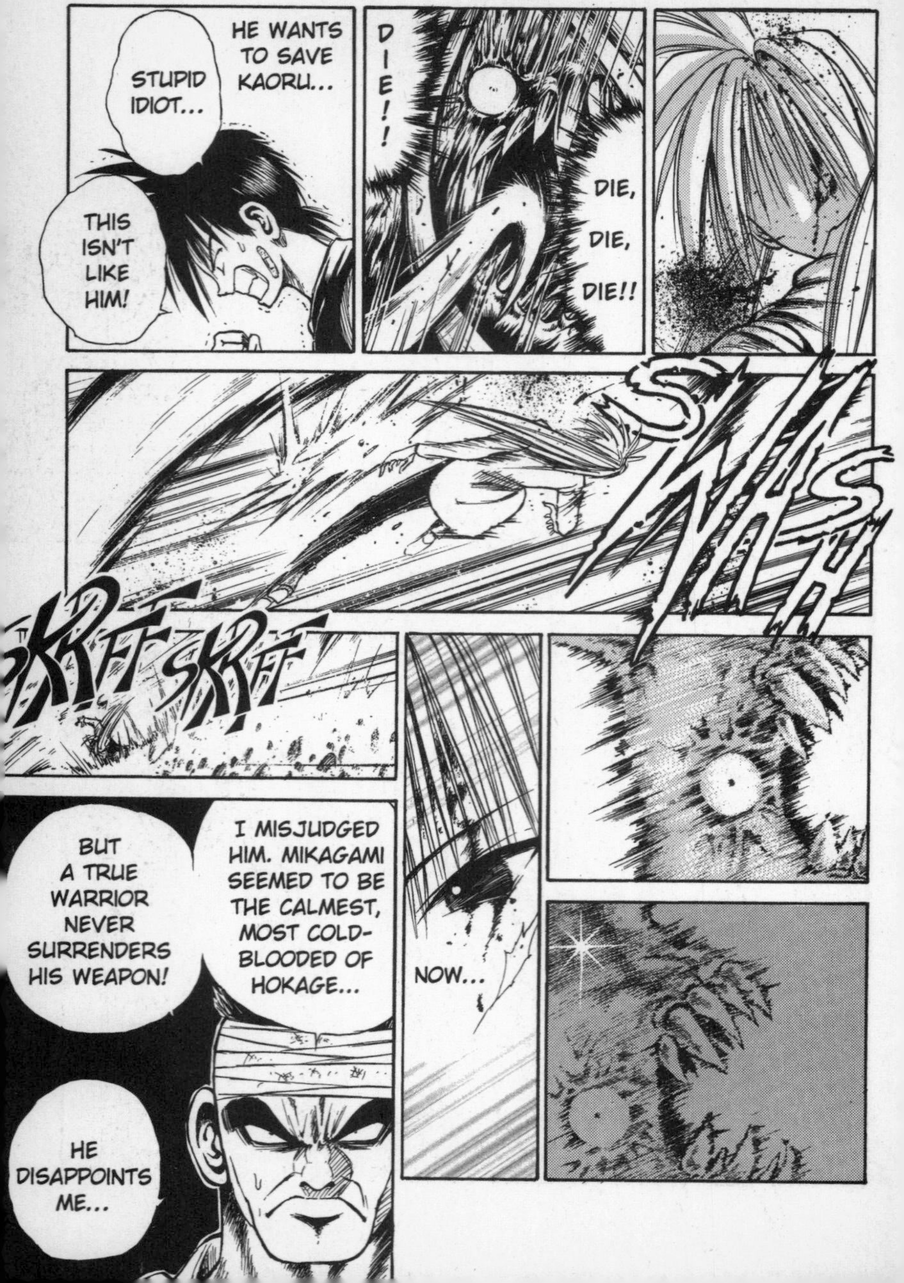
DIE!!
DIE,
DIE,
DIE!!
HE WANTS TO SAVE KAORU...
STUPID IDIOT...
THIS ISN'T LIKE HIM!
SWASH
SKRFF SKRFF
NOW...
I MISJUDGED HIM. MIKAGAMI SEEMED TO BE THE CALMEST, MOST COLD-BLOODED OF HOKAGE...
BUT A TRUE WARRIOR NEVER SURRENDERS HIS WEAPON!
HE DISAPPOINTS ME...

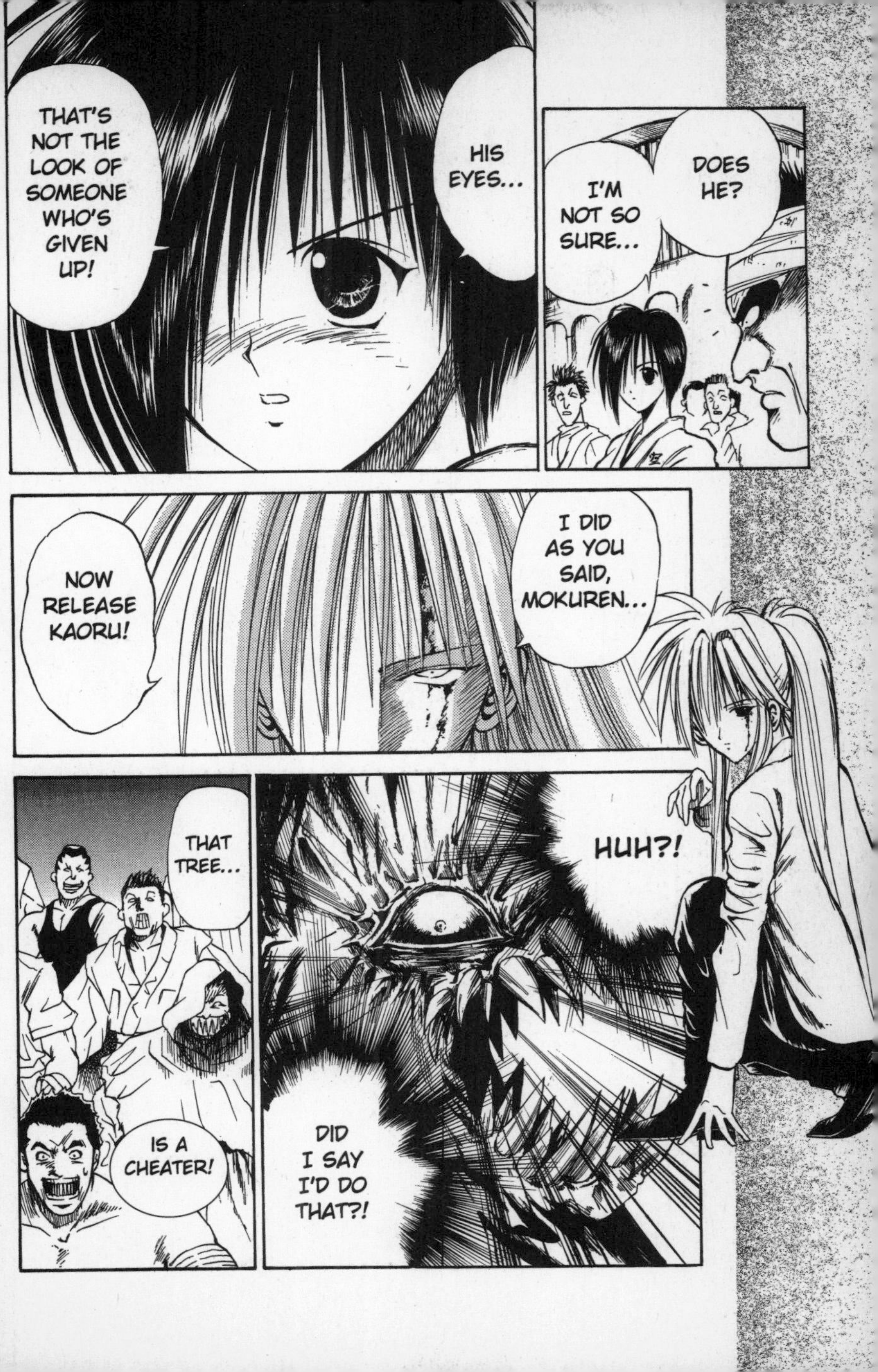
DOES HE?
I'M NOT SO SURE...
HIS EYES...
THAT'S NOT THE LOOK OF SOMEONE WHO'S GIVEN UP!
I DID AS YOU SAID, MOKUREN...
NOW RELEASE KAORU!
HUH?!
DID I SAY I'D DO THAT?!
THAT TREE...
IS A CHEATER!

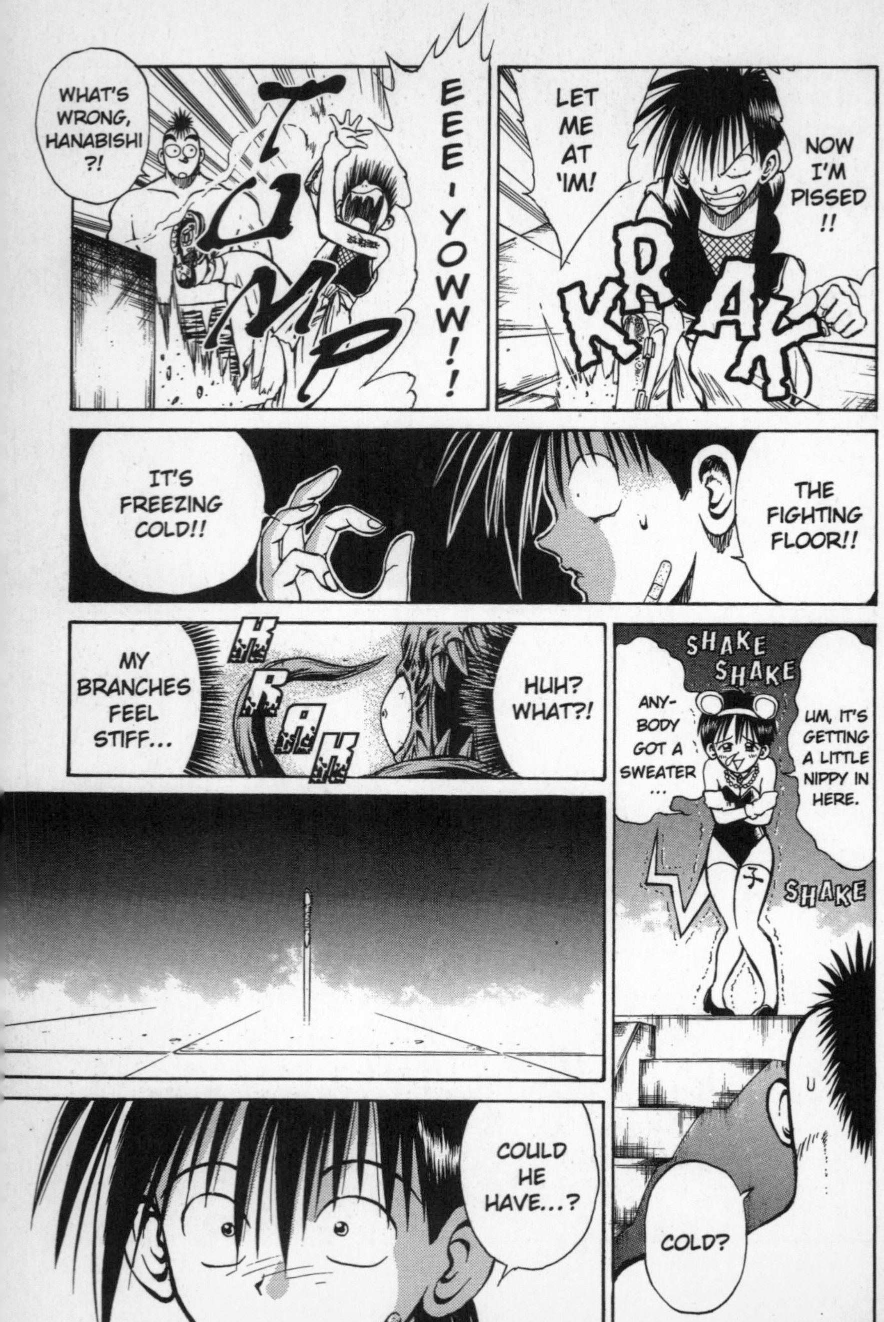
NOW I'M PISSED!!
LET ME AT 'IM!
KRAK
EEE-YOWW!!
TUMP
WHAT'S WRONG, HANABISHI?!
THE FIGHTING FLOOR!!
IT'S FREEZING COLD!!
SHAKE SHAKE
UM, IT'S GETTING A LITTLE NIPPY IN HERE.
ANY-BODY GOT A SWEATER...
SHAKE
HUH? WHAT?!
KRAK
MY BRANCHES FEEL STIFF...
COLD?
COULD HE HAVE...?

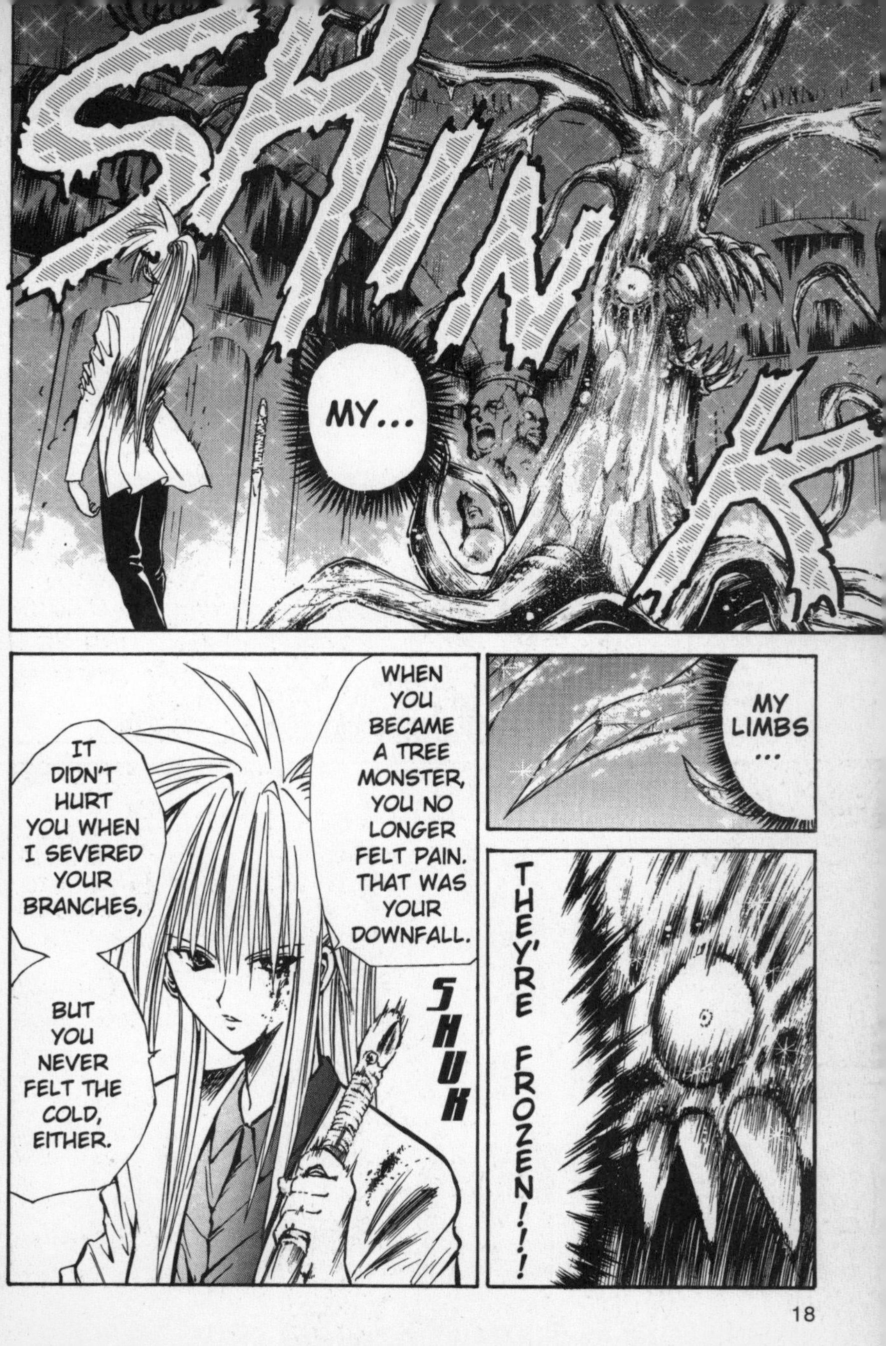
SHINK
MY...
MY LIMBS ...
THEY'RE FROZEN!!!
WHEN YOU BECAME A TREE MONSTER, YOU NO LONGER FELT PAIN. THAT WAS YOUR DOWNFALL.
IT DIDN'T HURT YOU WHEN I SEVERED YOUR BRANCHES,
SHUK
BUT YOU NEVER FELT THE COLD, EITHER.

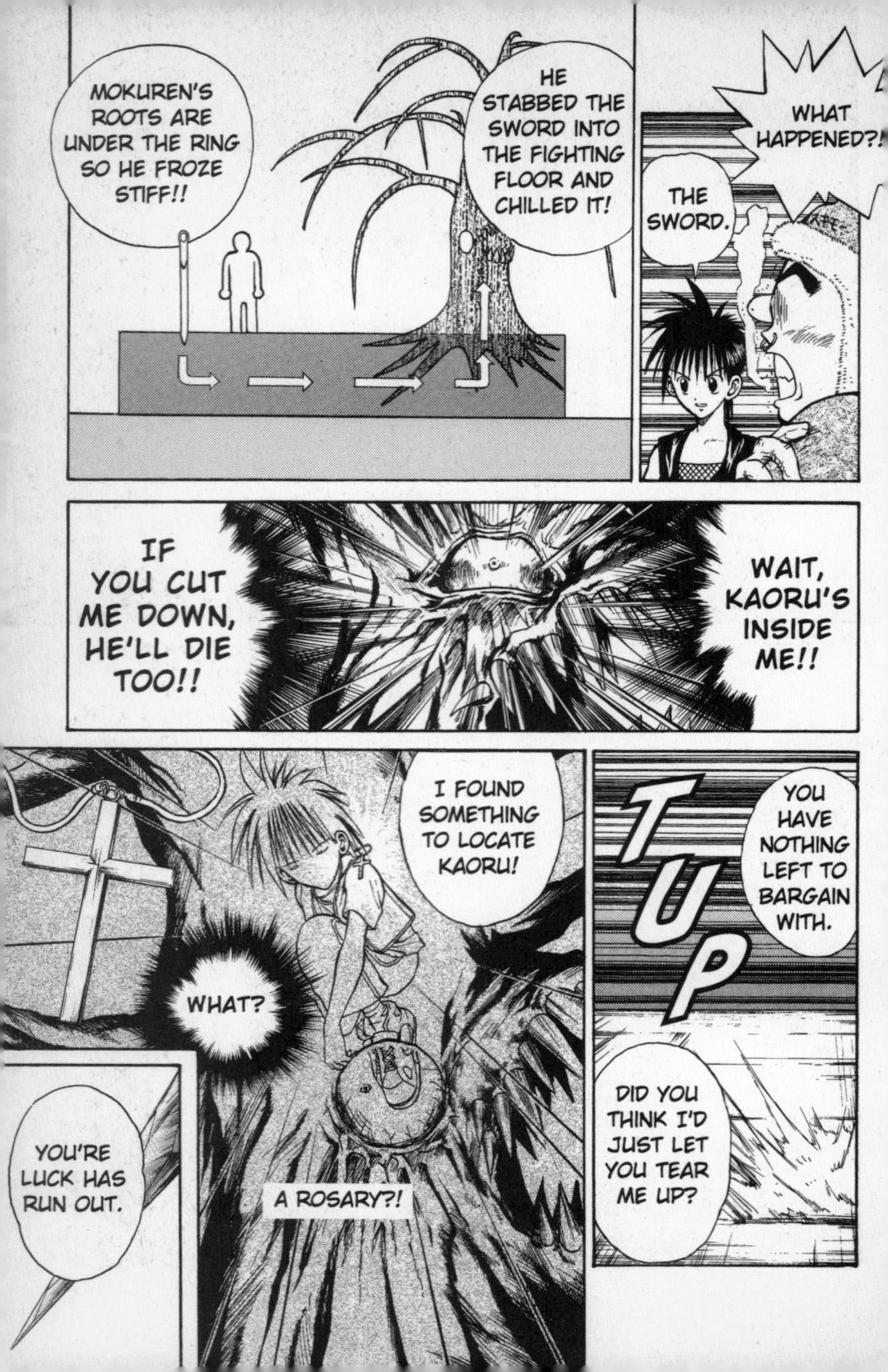
WHAT HAPPENED?!
THE SWORD.
HE STABBED THE SWORD INTO THE FIGHTING FLOOR AND CHILLED IT!
MOKUREN'S ROOTS ARE UNDER THE RING SO HE FROZE STIFF!!
WAIT, KAORU'S INSIDE ME!!
IF YOU CUT ME DOWN, HE'LL DIE TOO!!
TUP
YOU HAVE NOTHING LEFT TO BARGAIN WITH.
DID YOU THINK I'D JUST LET YOU TEAR ME UP?
I FOUND SOMETHING TO LOCATE KAORU!
WHAT?
A ROSARY?!
YOU'RE LUCK HAS RUN OUT.

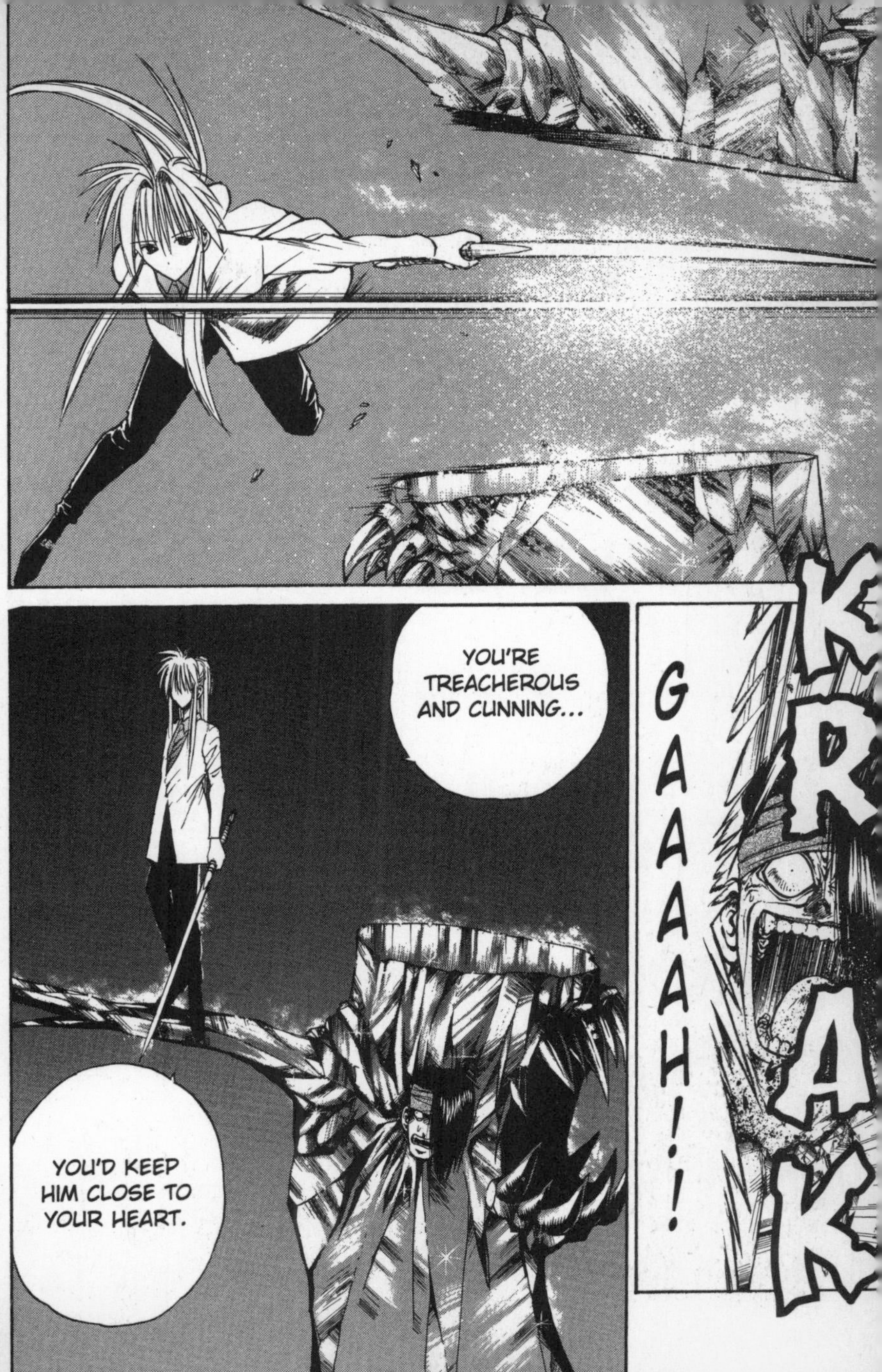
KRAK
GAAAAH!!
YOU'RE TREACHEROUS AND CUNNING...
YOU'D KEEP HIM CLOSE TO YOUR HEART.

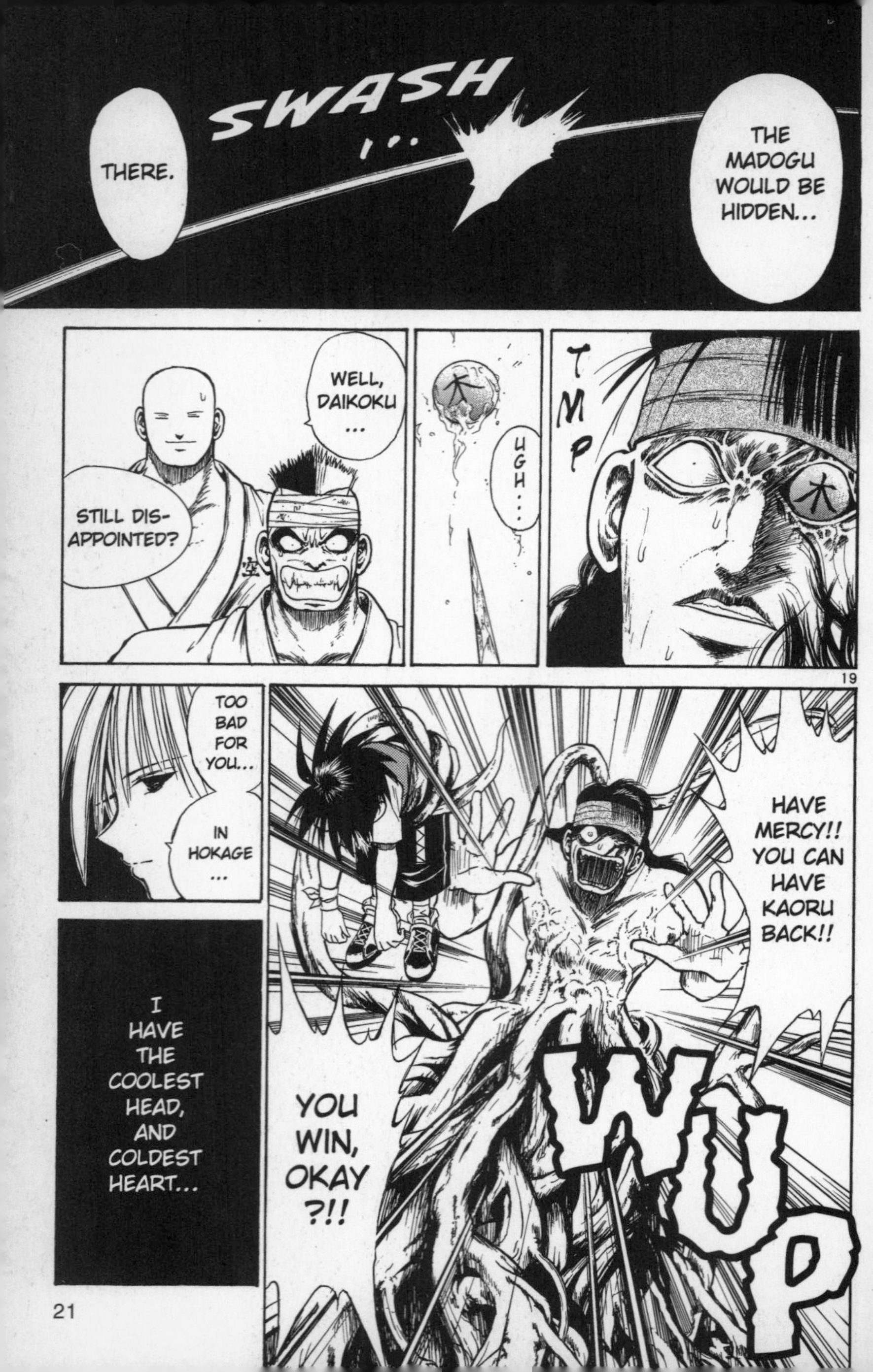
THE MADOGU WOULD BE HIDDEN...
SWASH
THERE.
TMP
UGH...
WELL, DAIKOKU ...
STILL DIS-APPOINTED?
HAVE MERCY!! YOU CAN HAVE KAORU BACK!!
YOU WIN, OKAY ?!!
WUP
TOO BAD FOR YOU...
IN HOKAGE ...
I HAVE THE COOLEST HEAD, AND COLDEST HEART...
19

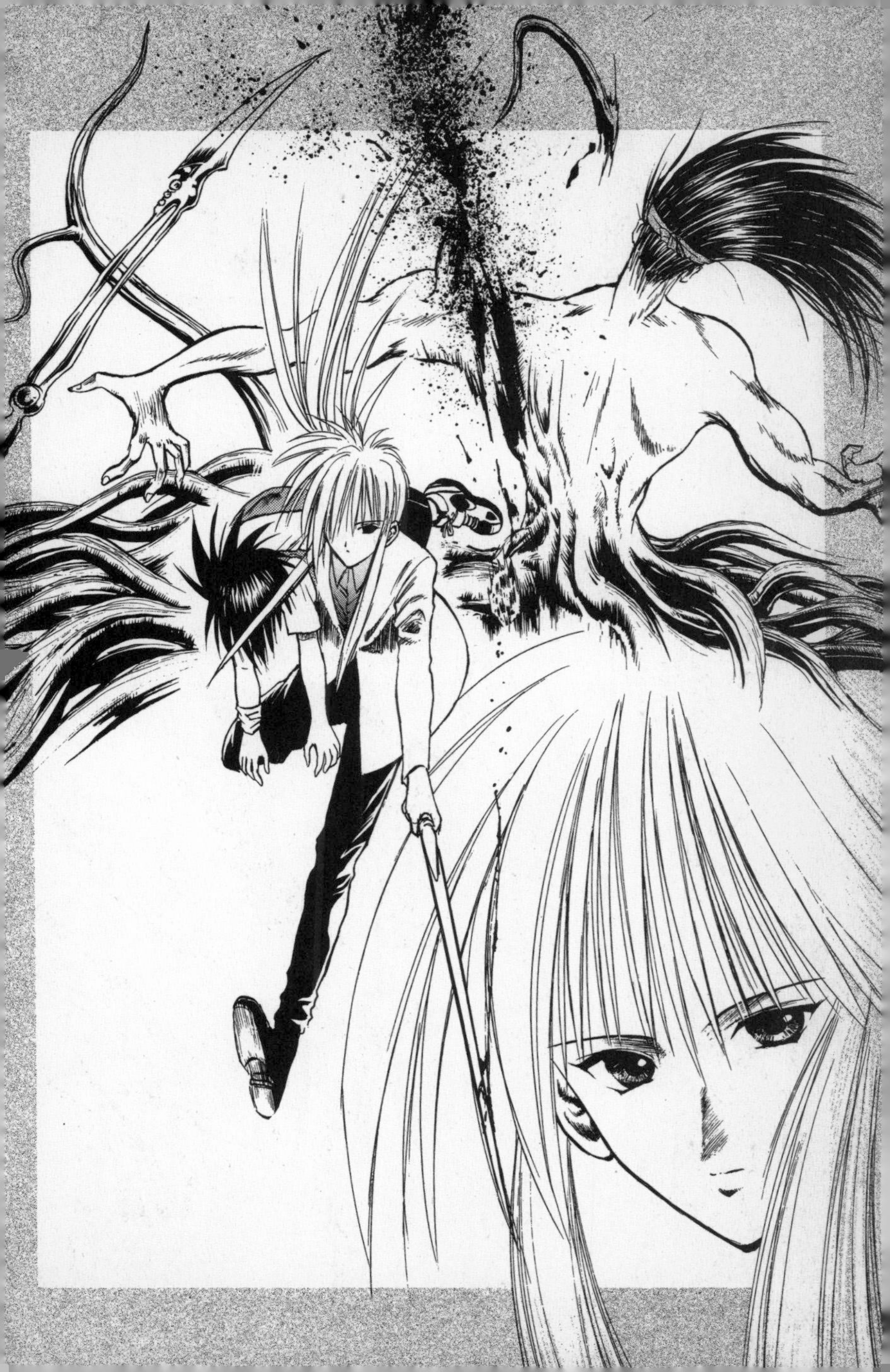

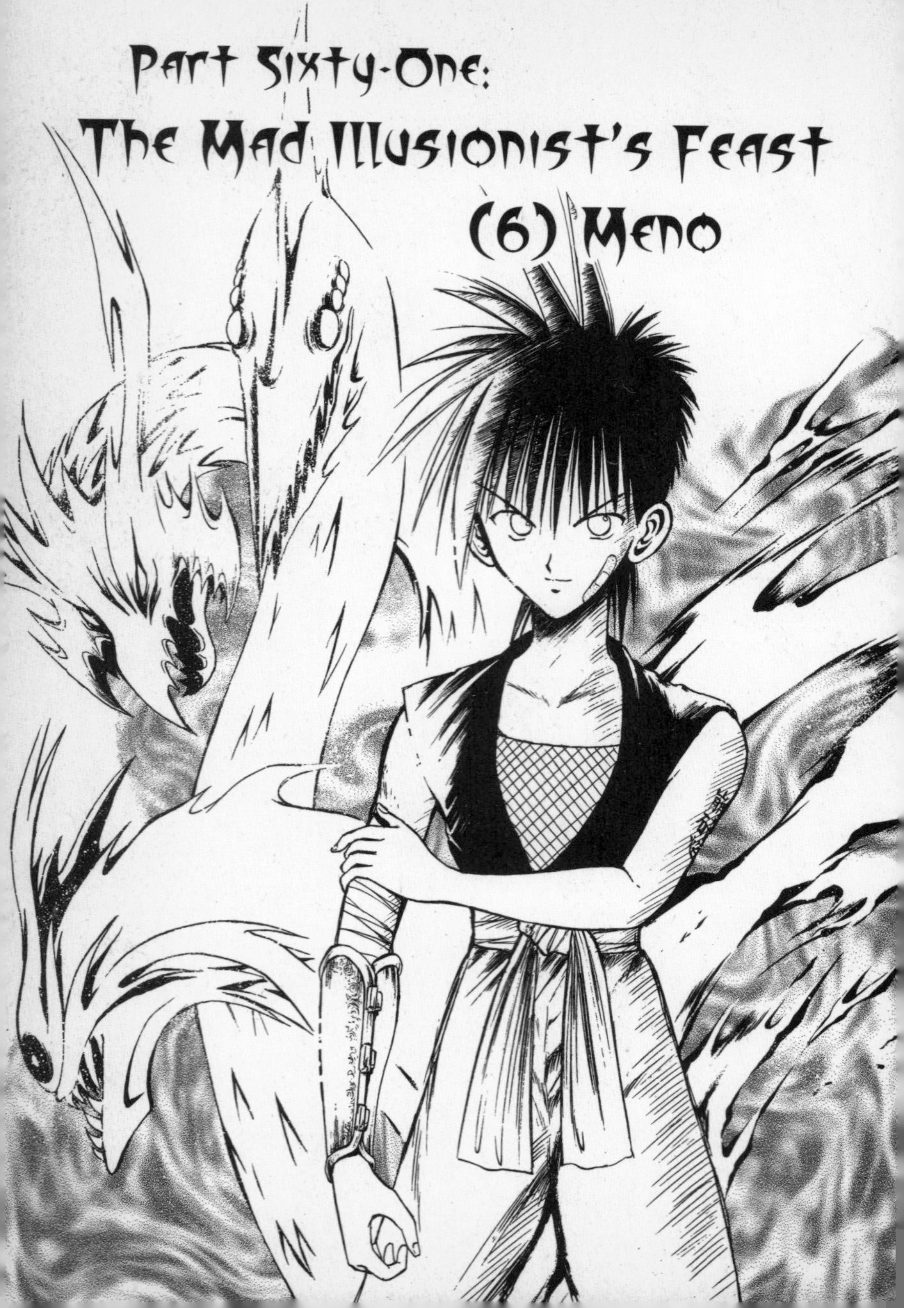
Part Sixty-One:
The Mad Illusionist's Feast
(6) Meno

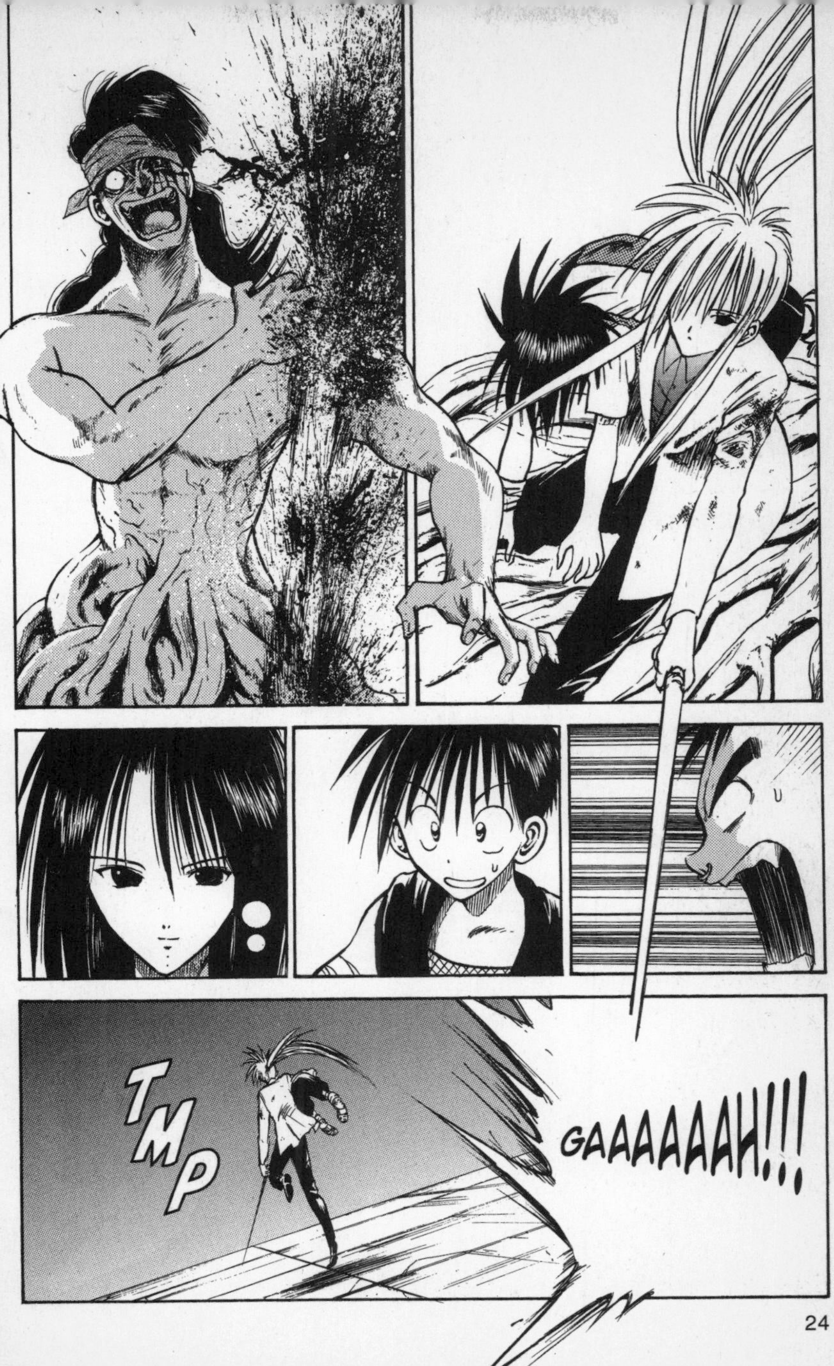
GAAAAAAH!!!
TMP

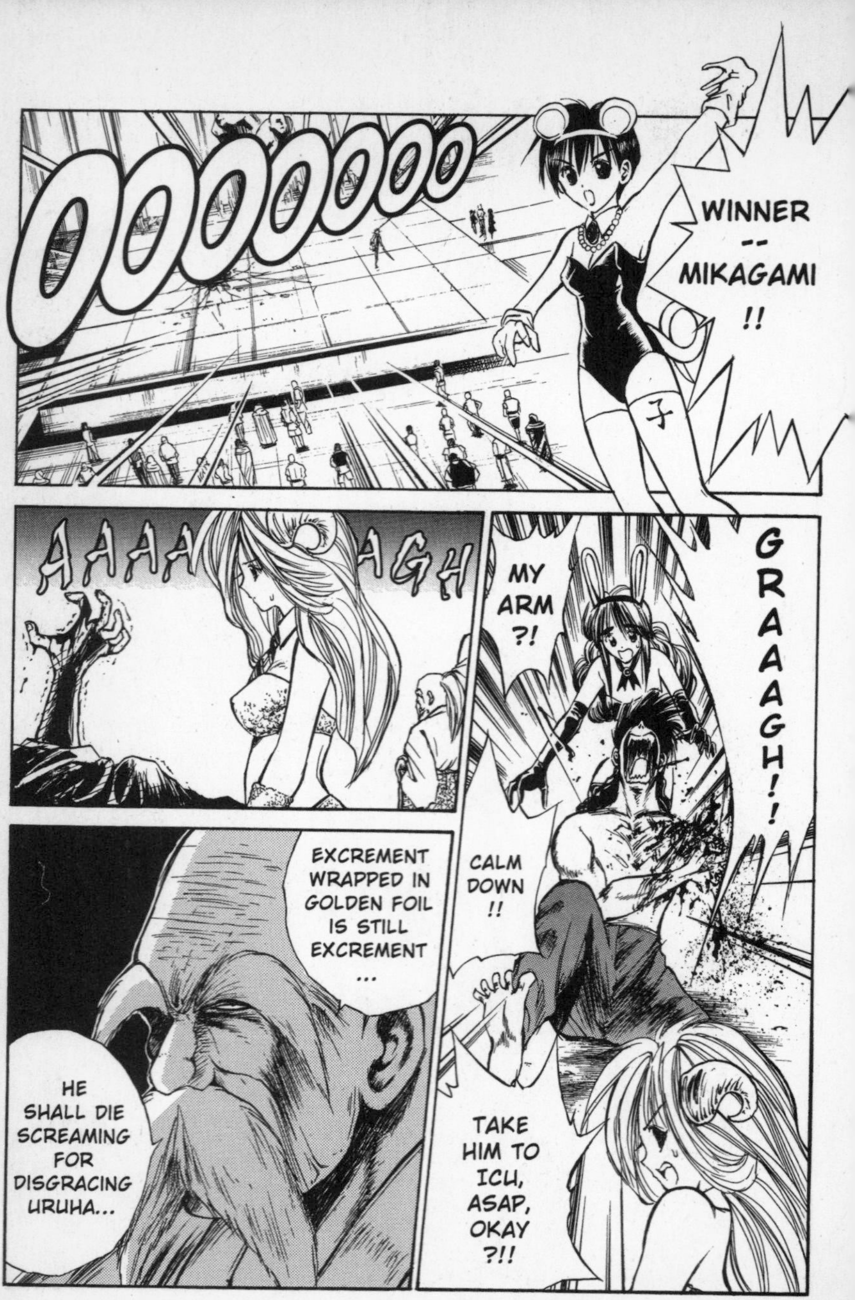
WINNER -- MIKAGAMI !!
OOOOOOO
GRAAAGH!!
MY ARM ?!
CALM DOWN !!
TAKE HIM TO ICU, ASAP, OKAY ?!!
AAAA AGH
EXCREMENT WRAPPED IN GOLDEN FOIL IS STILL EXCREMENT ...
HE SHALL DIE SCREAMING FOR DISGRACING URUHA...

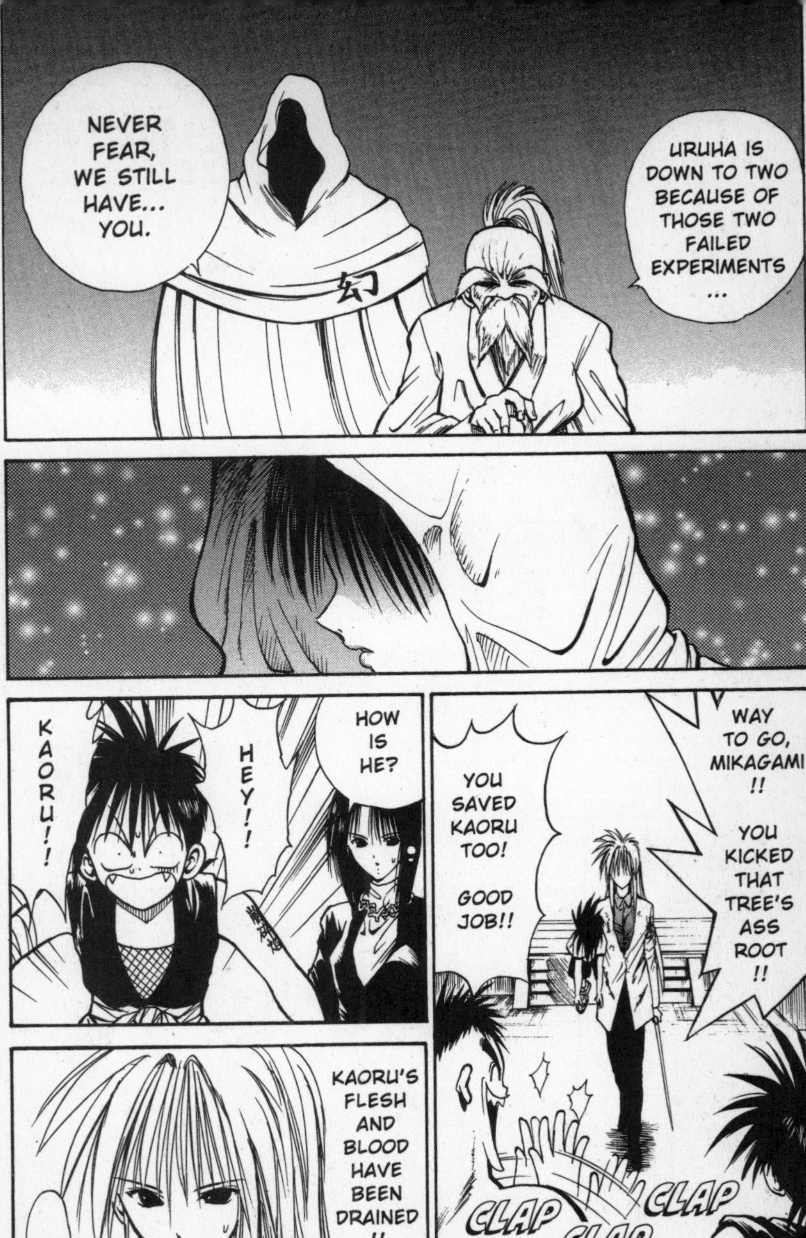
URUHA IS DOWN TO TWO BECAUSE OF THOSE TWO FAILED EXPERIMENTS ...
NEVER FEAR, WE STILL HAVE... YOU.
WAY TO GO, MIKAGAMI !!
YOU KICKED THAT TREE'S ASS ROOT !!
YOU SAVED KAORU TOO!
GOOD JOB!!
CLAP
CLAP
CLAP
HOW IS HE?
HEY!!
KAORU!!
KAORU'S FLESH AND BLOOD HAVE BEEN DRAINED !!
...

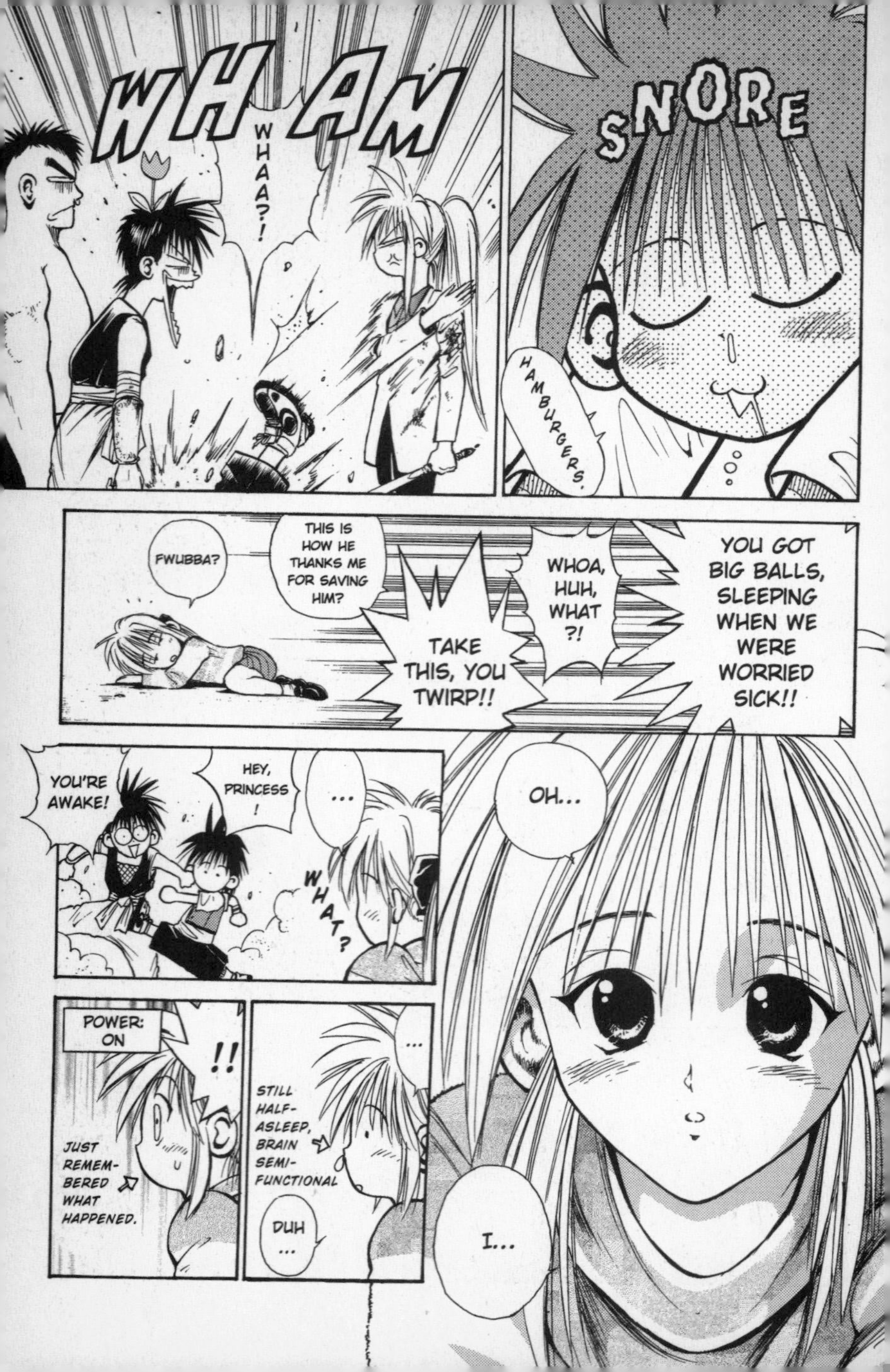
SNORE
HAMBURGERS.
WHAM
WHAAA?!
YOU GOT BIG BALLS, SLEEPING WHEN WE WERE WORRIED SICK!!
WHOA, HUH, WHAT?!
TAKE THIS, YOU TWIRP!!
THIS IS HOW HE THANKS ME FOR SAVING HIM?
FWUBBA?
OH...
I...
...
HEY, PRINCESS!
YOU'RE AWAKE!
WHAT?
...
STILL HALF-ASLEEP, BRAIN SEMI-FUNCTIONAL
DUH ...
POWER: ON
!!
JUST REMEMBERED WHAT HAPPENED.

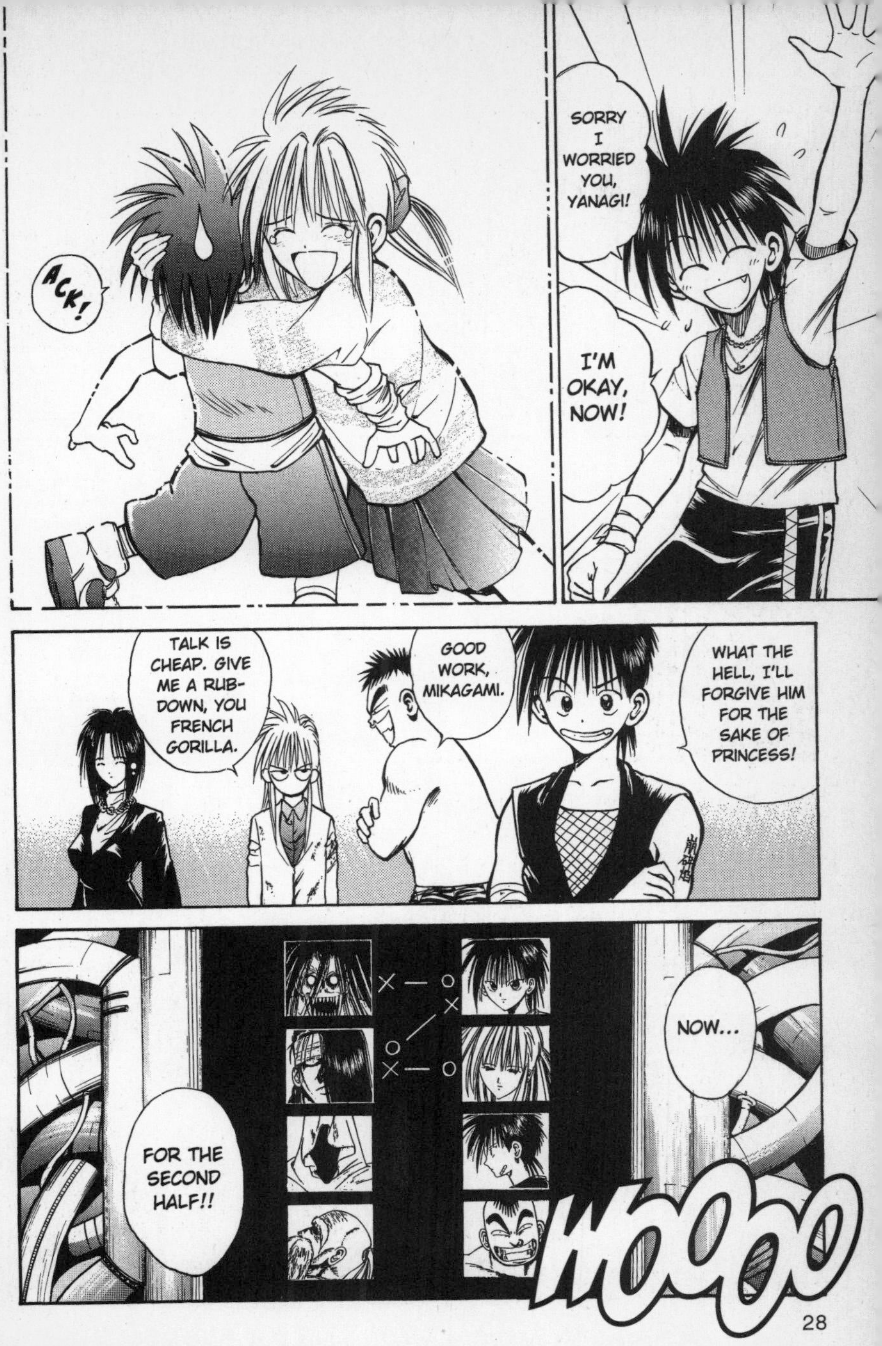
SORRY I WORRIED YOU, YANAGI!
I'M OKAY, NOW!
ACK!
WHAT THE HELL, I'LL FORGIVE HIM FOR THE SAKE OF PRINCESS!
GOOD WORK, MIKAGAMI.
TALK IS CHEAP. GIVE ME A RUB-DOWN, YOU FRENCH GORILLA.
NOW...
FOR THE SECOND HALF!!
WOOOO

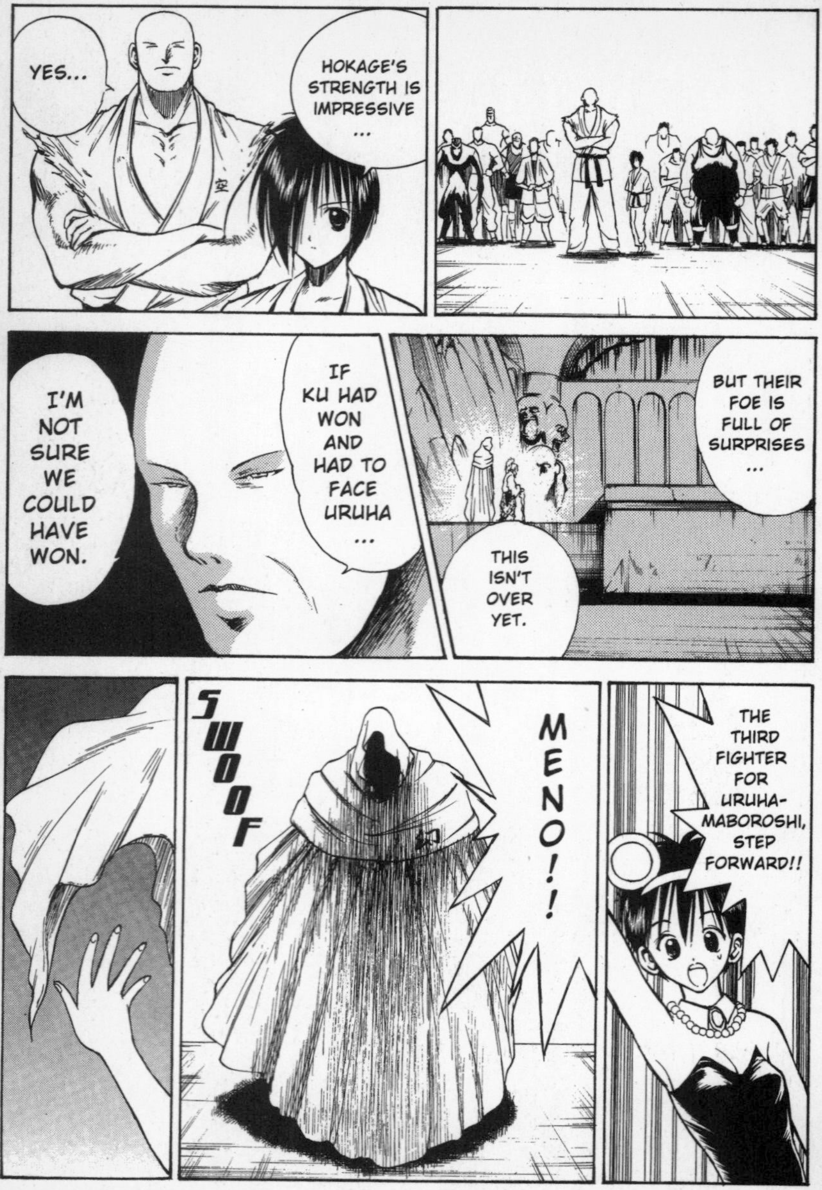
HOKAGE'S STRENGTH IS IMPRESSIVE ...
YES...
BUT THEIR FOE IS FULL OF SURPRISES ...
THIS ISN'T OVER YET.
IF KU HAD WON AND HAD TO FACE URUHA ...
I'M NOT SURE WE COULD HAVE WON.
THE THIRD FIGHTER FOR URUHA-MABOROSHI, STEP FORWARD!!
MENO!!
SWOOOF

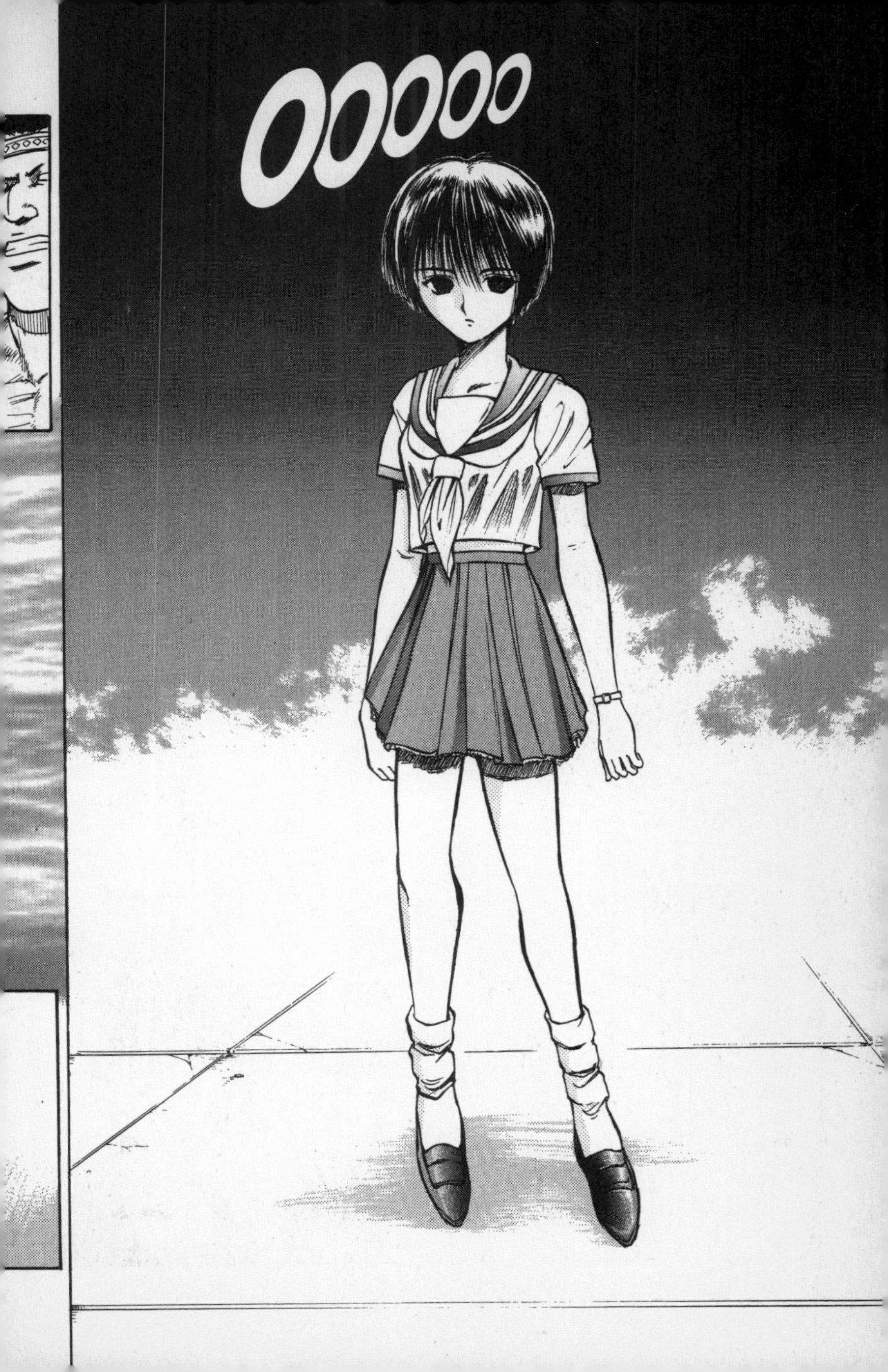
OOOOO

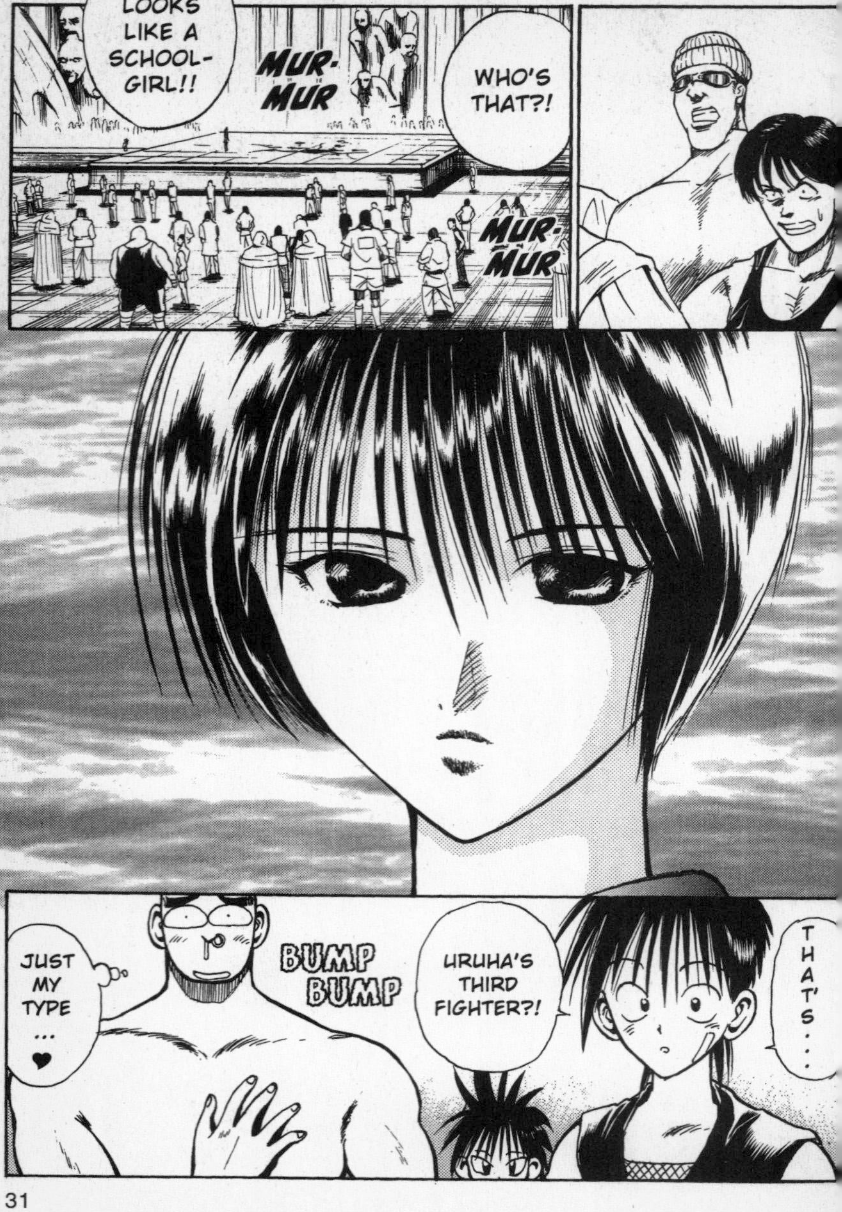
WHO'S THAT?!
SHE LOOKS LIKE A SCHOOL-GIRL!!
MUR-MUR
MUR-MUR
THAT'S...
URUHA'S THIRD FIGHTER?!
BUMP BUMP
JUST MY TYPE... ♥

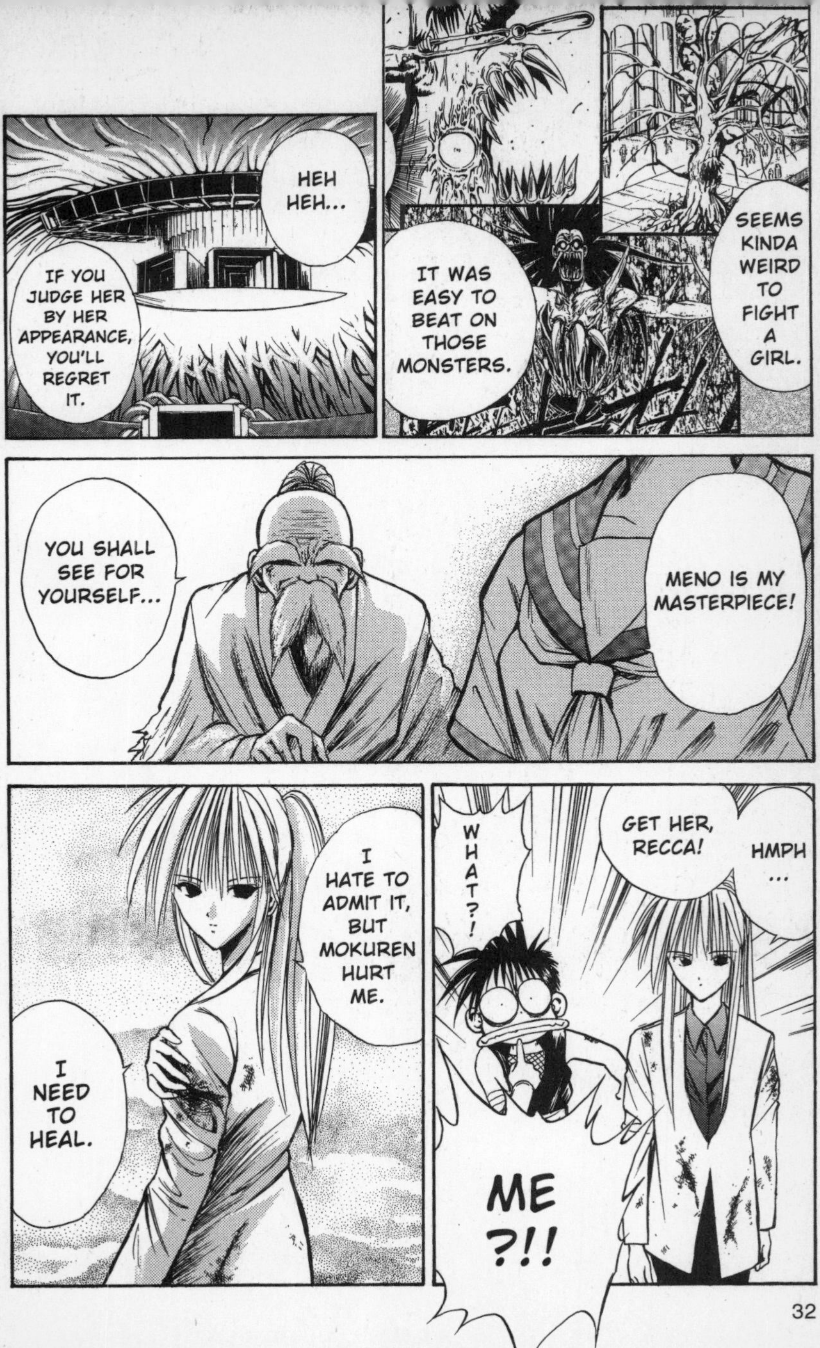
SEEMS KINDA WEIRD TO FIGHT A GIRL.
IT WAS EASY TO BEAT ON THOSE MONSTERS.
HEH HEH...
IF YOU JUDGE HER BY HER APPEARANCE, YOU'LL REGRET IT.
MENO IS MY MASTERPIECE!
YOU SHALL SEE FOR YOURSELF...
HMPH ...
GET HER, RECCA!
WHAT?!
ME ?!!
I HATE TO ADMIT IT, BUT MOKUREN HURT ME.
I NEED TO HEAL.

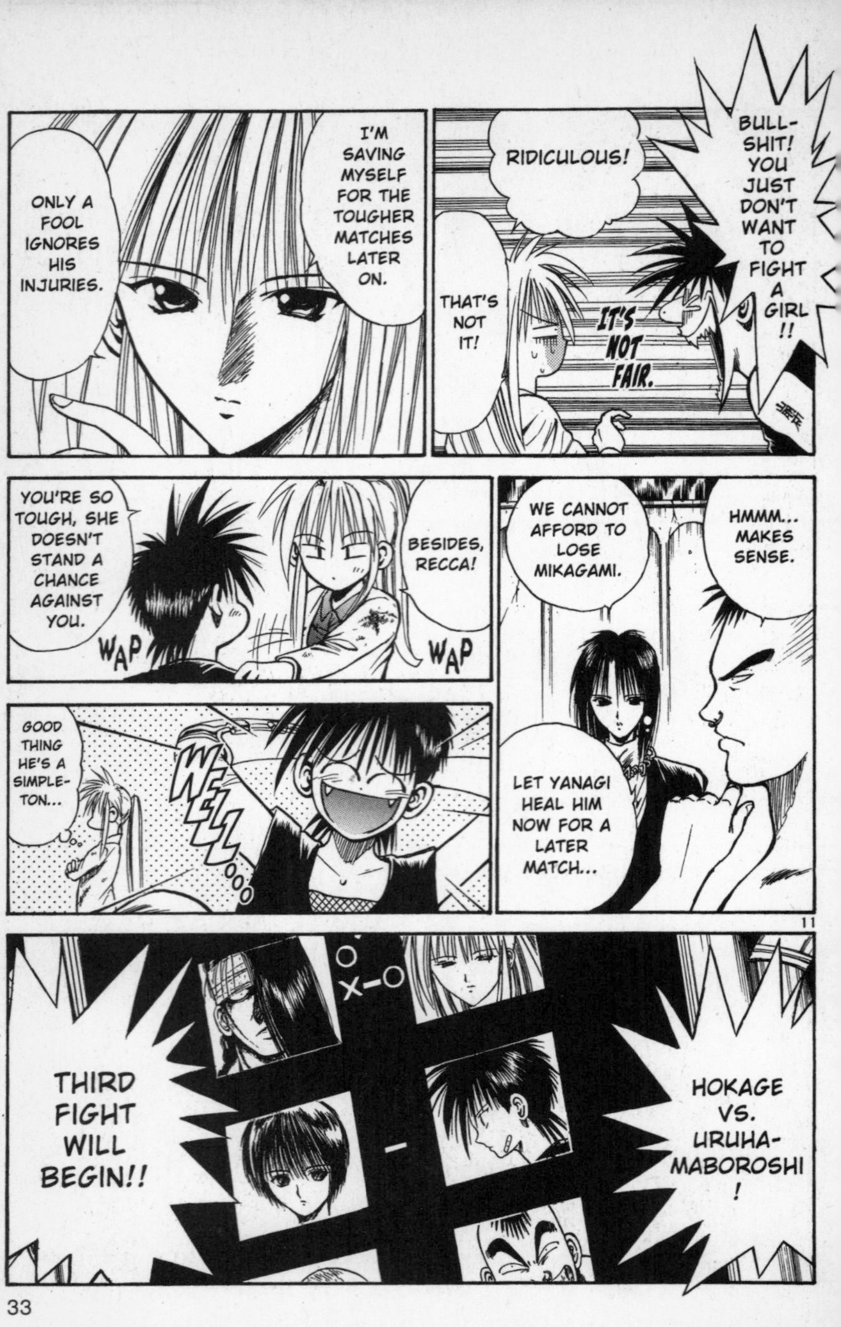
BULL-SHIT! YOU JUST DON'T WANT TO FIGHT A GIRL!!
RIDICULOUS!
IT'S NOT FAIR.
THAT'S NOT IT!
I'M SAVING MYSELF FOR THE TOUGHER MATCHES LATER ON.
ONLY A FOOL IGNORES HIS INJURIES.
HMMM... MAKES SENSE.
WE CANNOT AFFORD TO LOSE MIKAGAMI.
LET YANAGI HEAL HIM NOW FOR A LATER MATCH...
BESIDES, RECCA!
WAP
YOU'RE SO TOUGH, SHE DOESN'T STAND A CHANCE AGAINST YOU.
WAP
WELLooo
GOOD THING HE'S A SIMPLETON...
HOKAGE VS. URUHA-MABOROSHI!
THIRD FIGHT WILL BEGIN!!

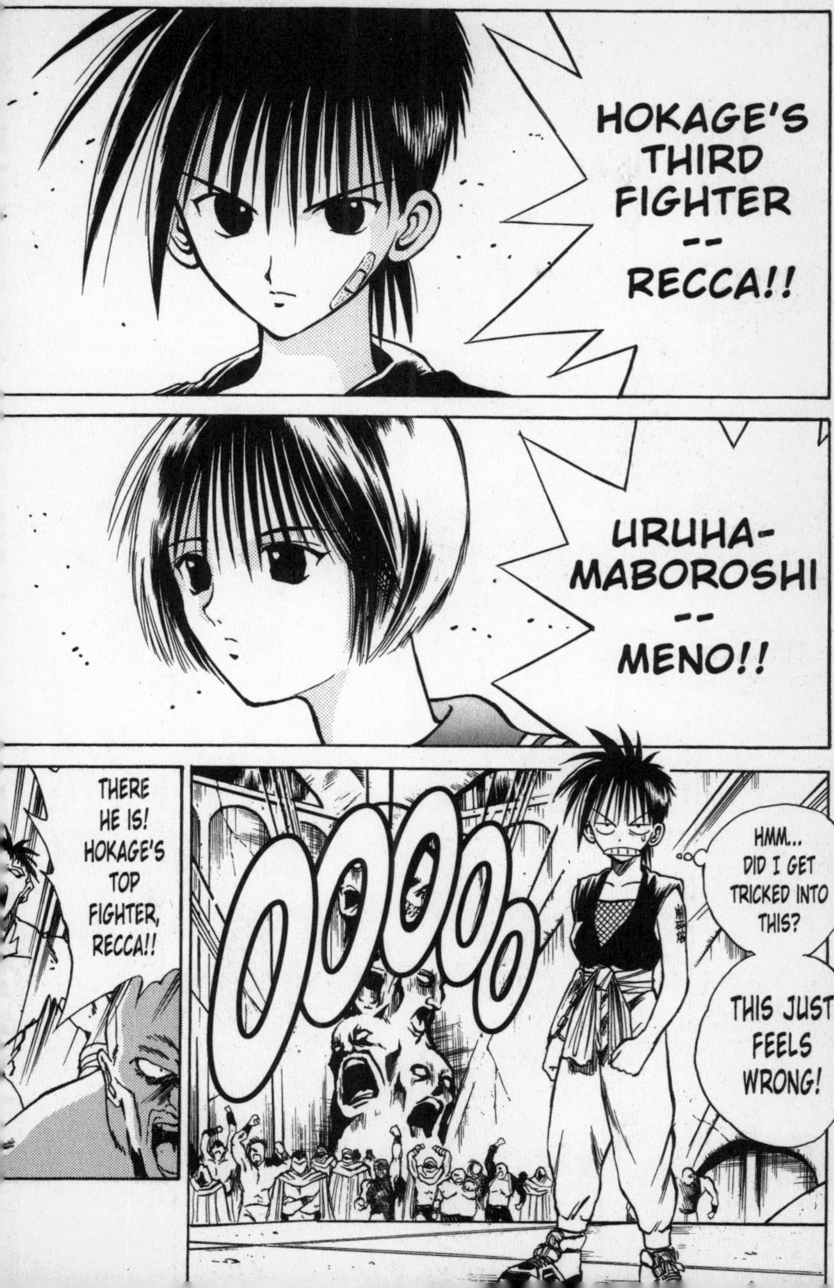
HOKAGE'S THIRD FIGHTER -- RECCA!!
URUHA-MABOROSHI -- MENO!!
OOOOOO
HMM... DID I GET TRICKED INTO THIS?
THIS JUST FEELS WRONG!
THERE HE IS! HOKAGE'S TOP FIGHTER, RECCA!!

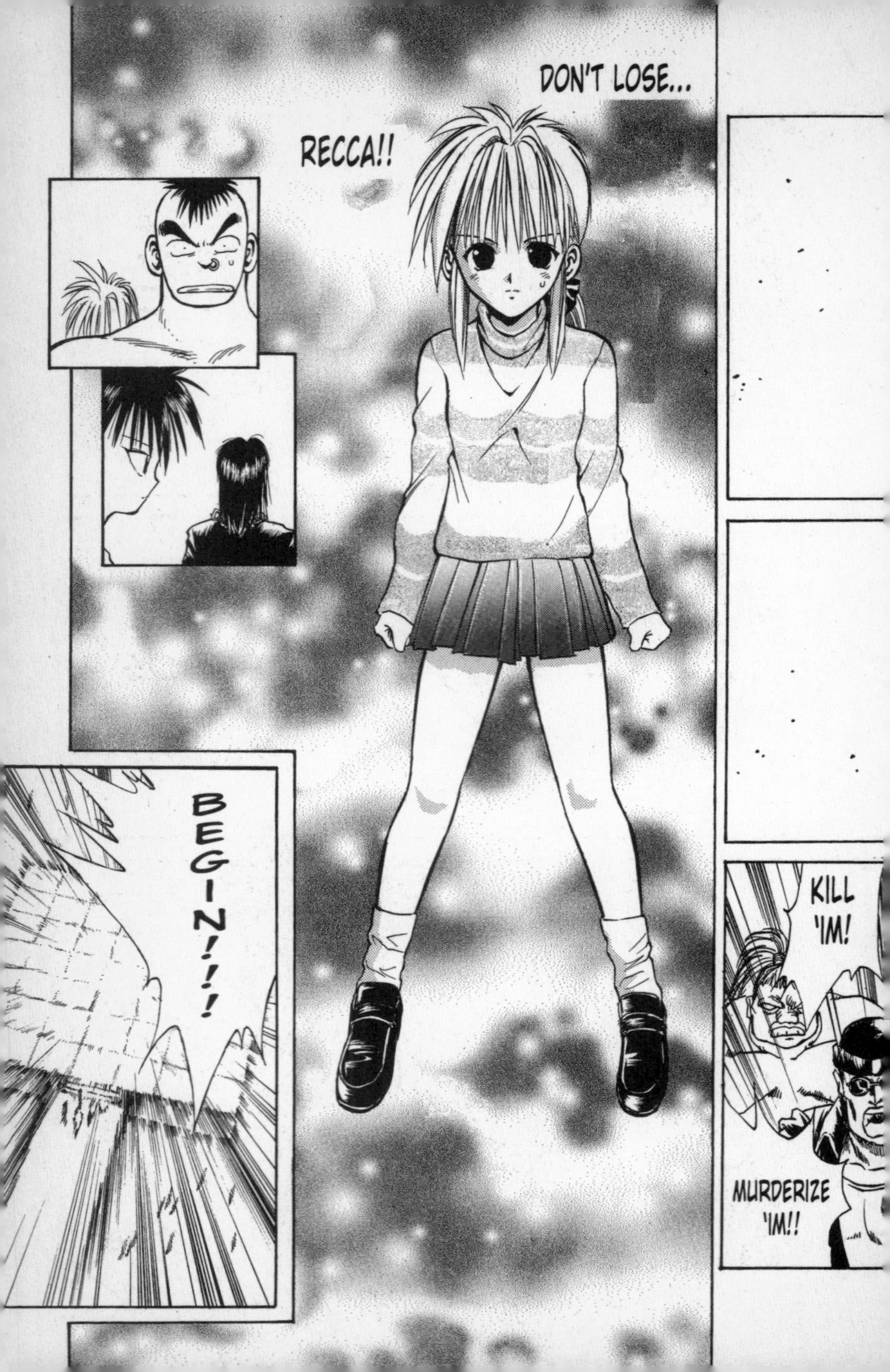
KILL 'IM!
MURDERIZE 'IM!!
DON'T LOSE...
RECCA!!
BEGIN!!!

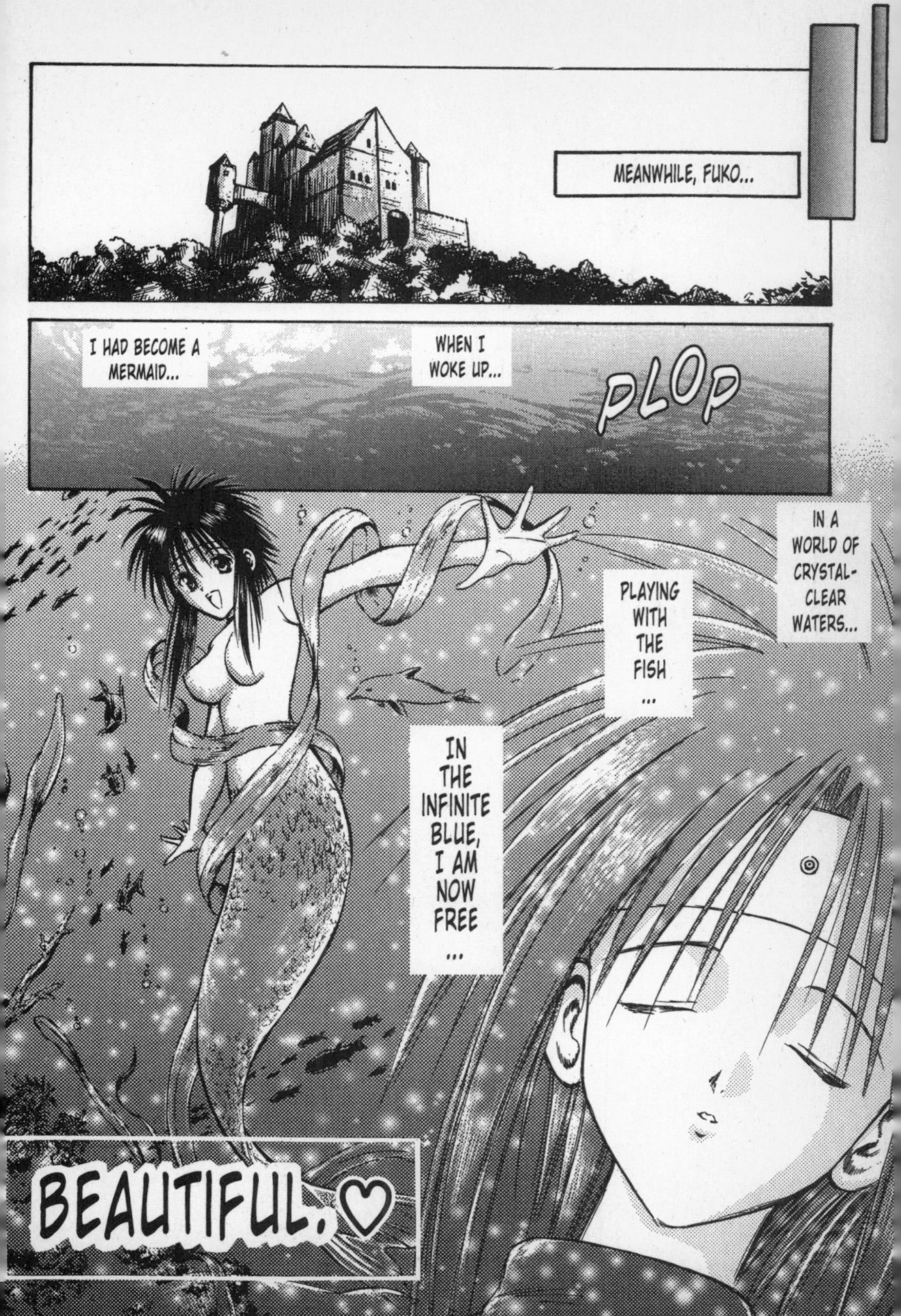

MEANWHILE, FUKO...
WHEN I WOKE UP...
I HAD BECOME A MERMAID...
PLOP
IN A WORLD OF CRYSTAL-CLEAR WATERS...
PLAYING WITH THE FISH ...
IN THE INFINITE BLUE, I AM NOW FREE ...
BEAUTIFUL.♡

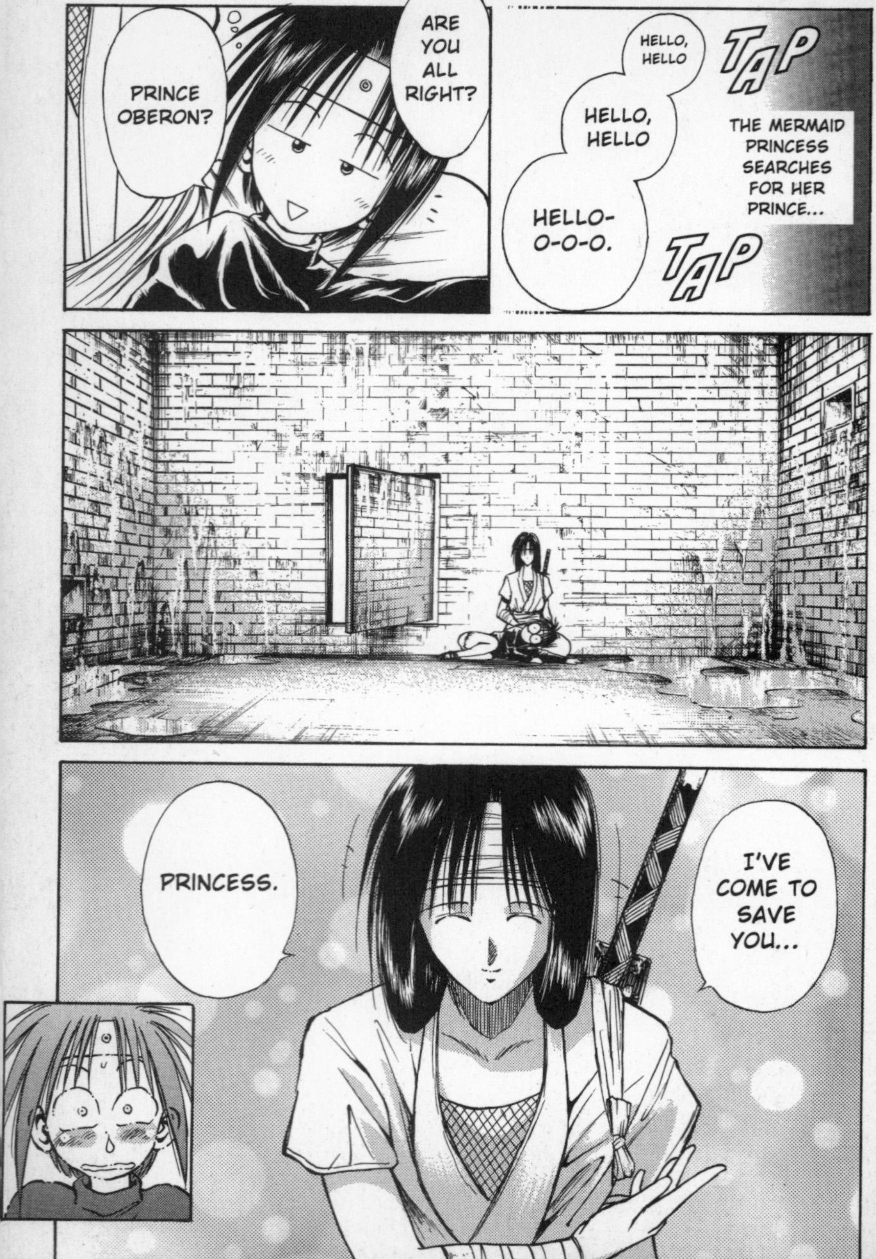
TAP
THE MERMAID PRINCESS SEARCHES FOR HER PRINCE...
HELLO, HELLO
HELLO, HELLO
TAP
HELLO-O-O-O.
ARE YOU ALL RIGHT?
PRINCE OBERON?
I'VE COME TO SAVE YOU...
PRINCESS.

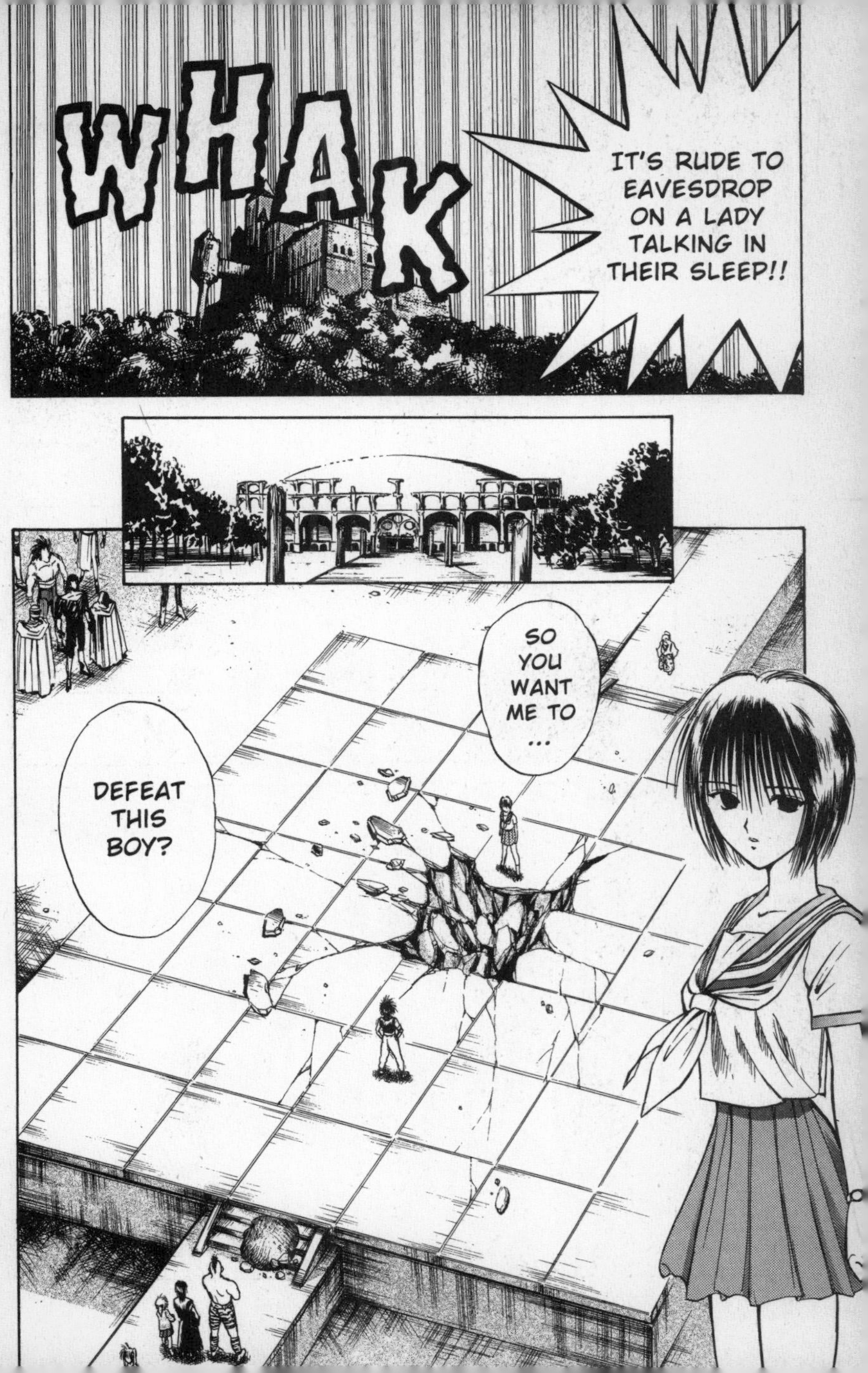
IT'S RUDE TO EAVESDROP ON A LADY TALKING IN THEIR SLEEP!!
WHAK
SO YOU WANT ME TO ...
DEFEAT THIS BOY?

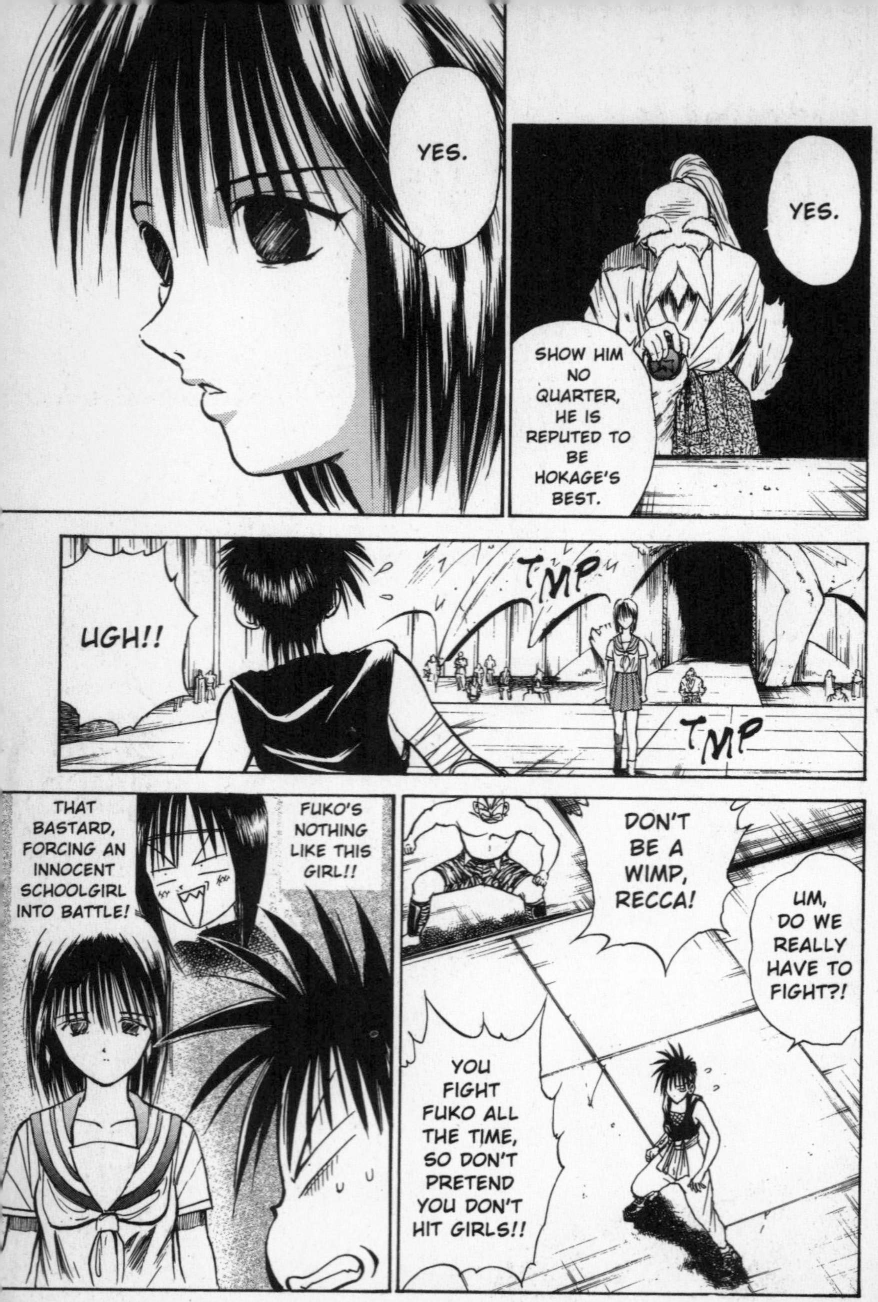
YES.
SHOW HIM NO QUARTER, HE IS REPUTED TO BE HOKAGE'S BEST.
YES.
TMP
TMP
UGH!!
UM, DO WE REALLY HAVE TO FIGHT?!
DON'T BE A WIMP, RECCA!
YOU FIGHT FUKO ALL THE TIME, SO DON'T PRETEND YOU DON'T HIT GIRLS!!
FUKO'S NOTHING LIKE THIS GIRL!!
THAT BASTARD, FORCING AN INNOCENT SCHOOLGIRL INTO BATTLE!

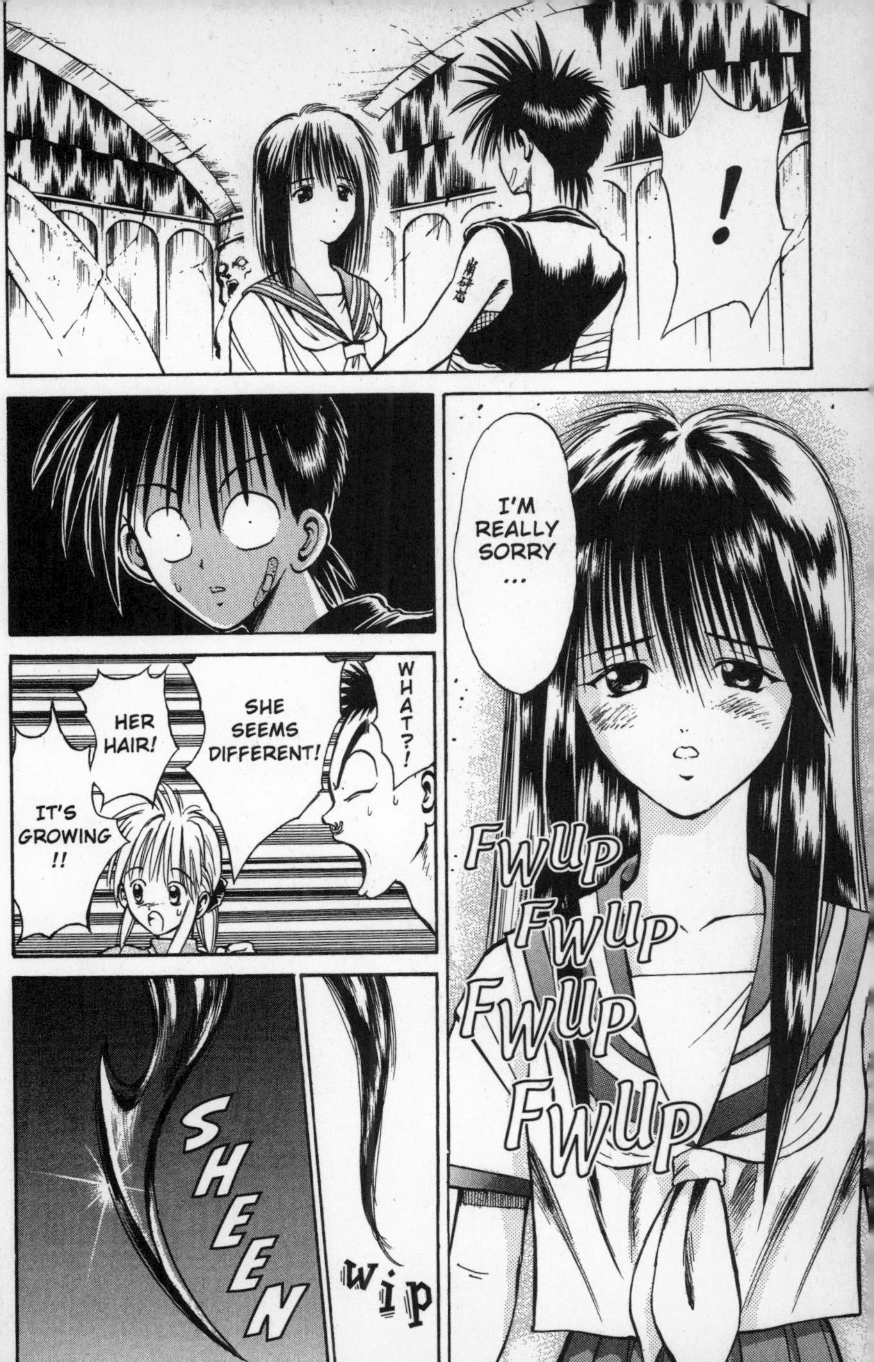
!
I'M REALLY SORRY ...
FWUP FWUP FWUP FWUP
WHAT?!
SHE SEEMS DIFFERENT!
HER HAIR!
IT'S GROWING !!
wip
SHEEN

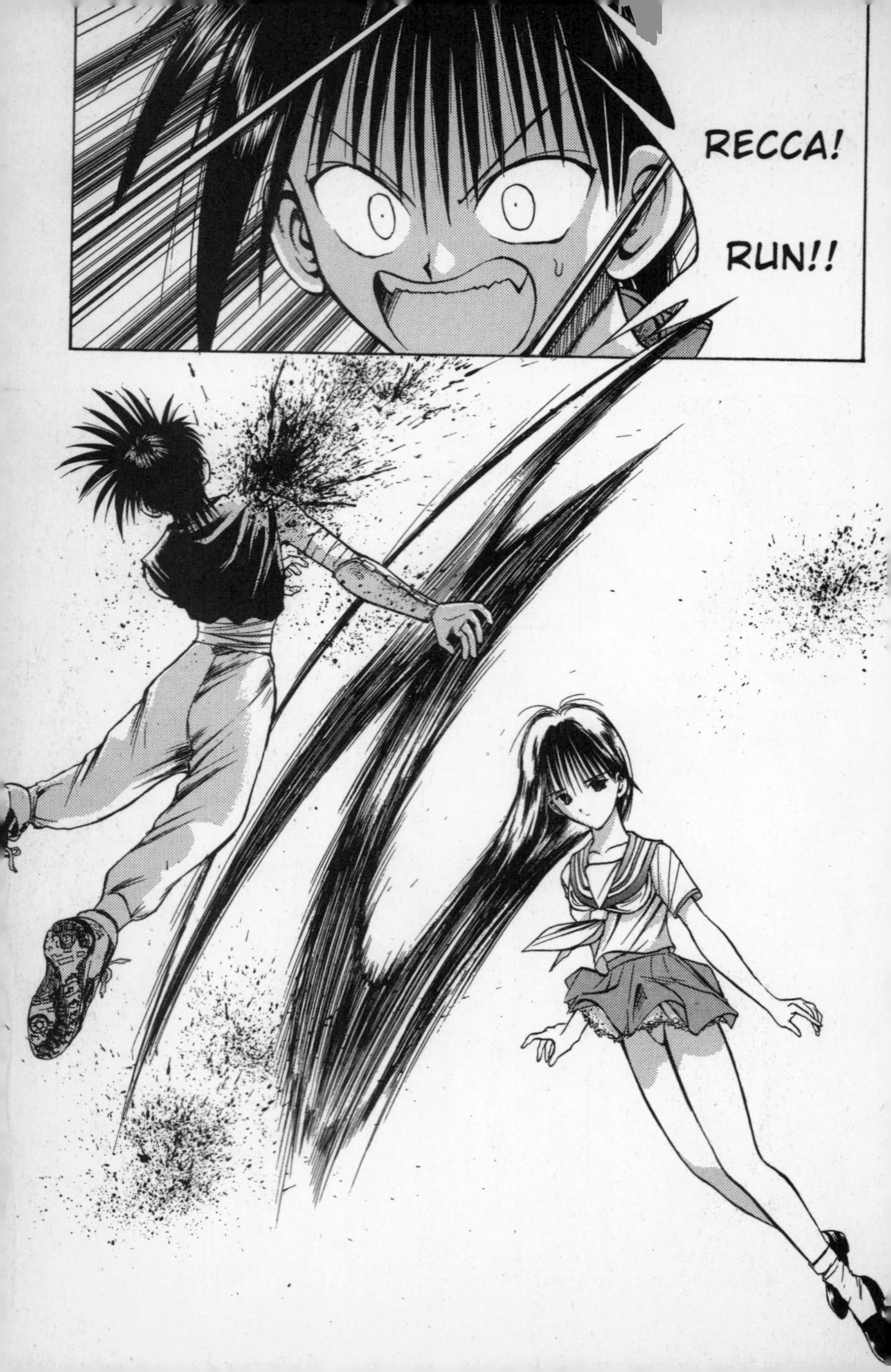
RECCA!
RUN!!

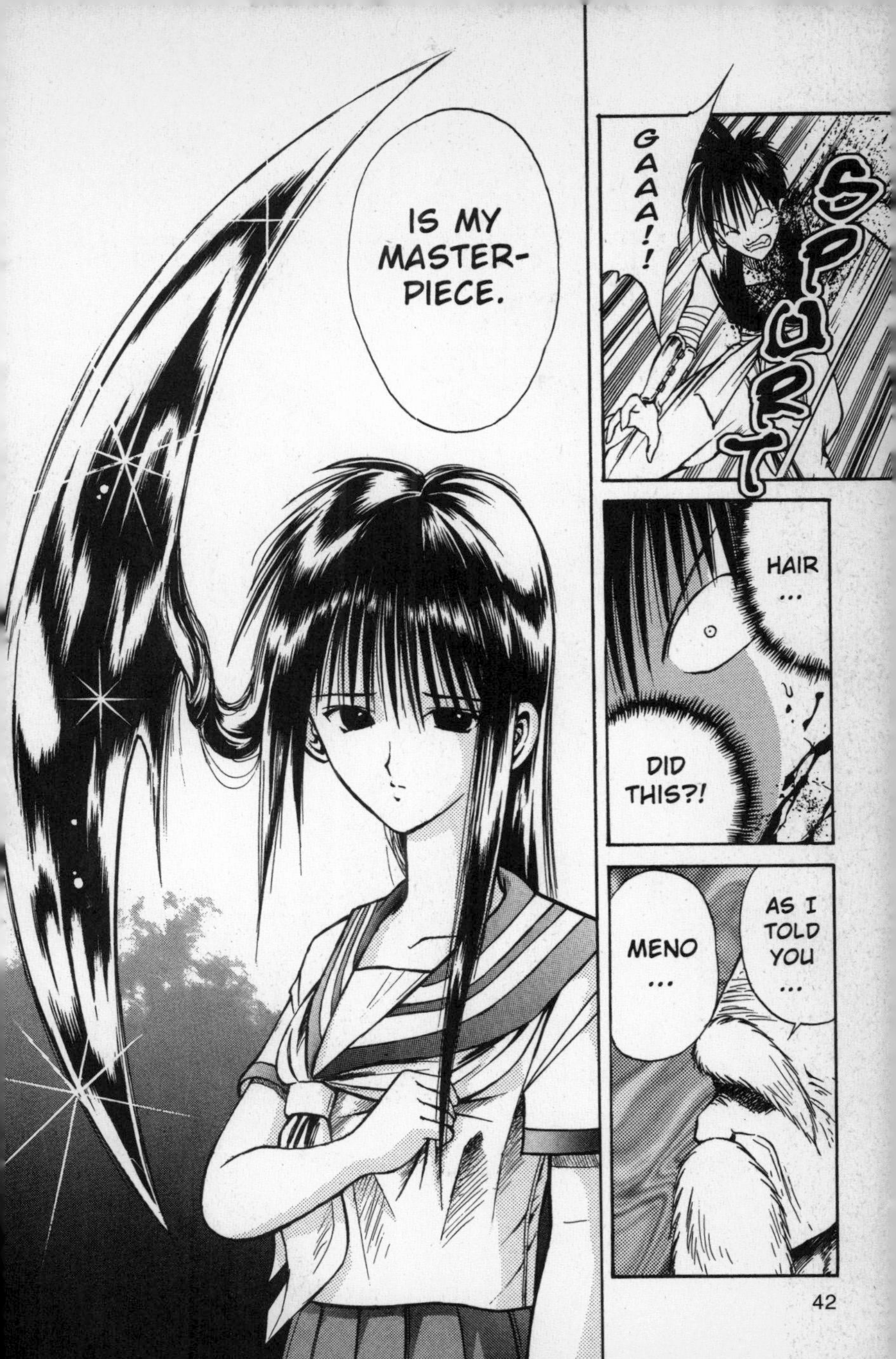
GAAAA!!
SPURT
HAIR...
DID THIS?!
AS I TOLD YOU...
MENO...
IS MY MASTER-PIECE.

# art Sixty-Two:
# he Mad Illusionist's Feast
# (7) The Sad-Faced Girl

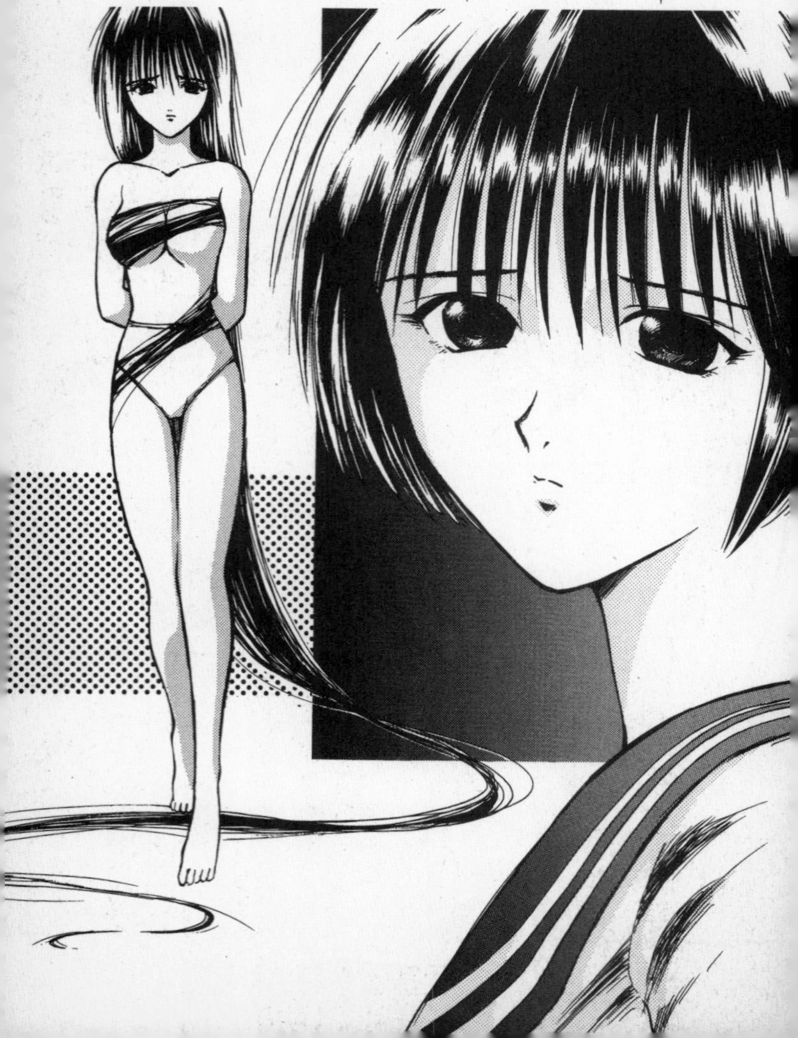

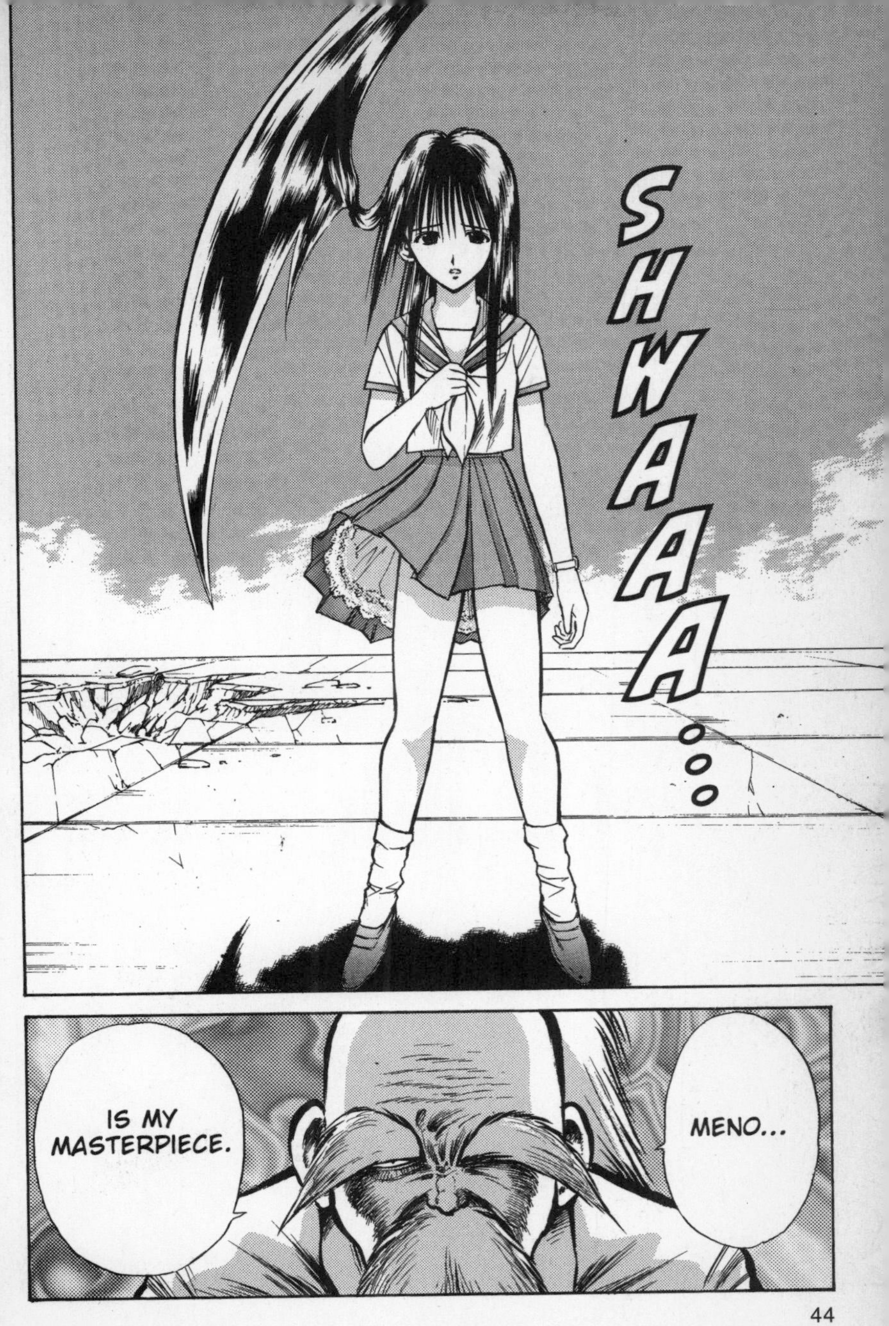
SHWAAAA...
MENO...
IS MY MASTERPIECE.

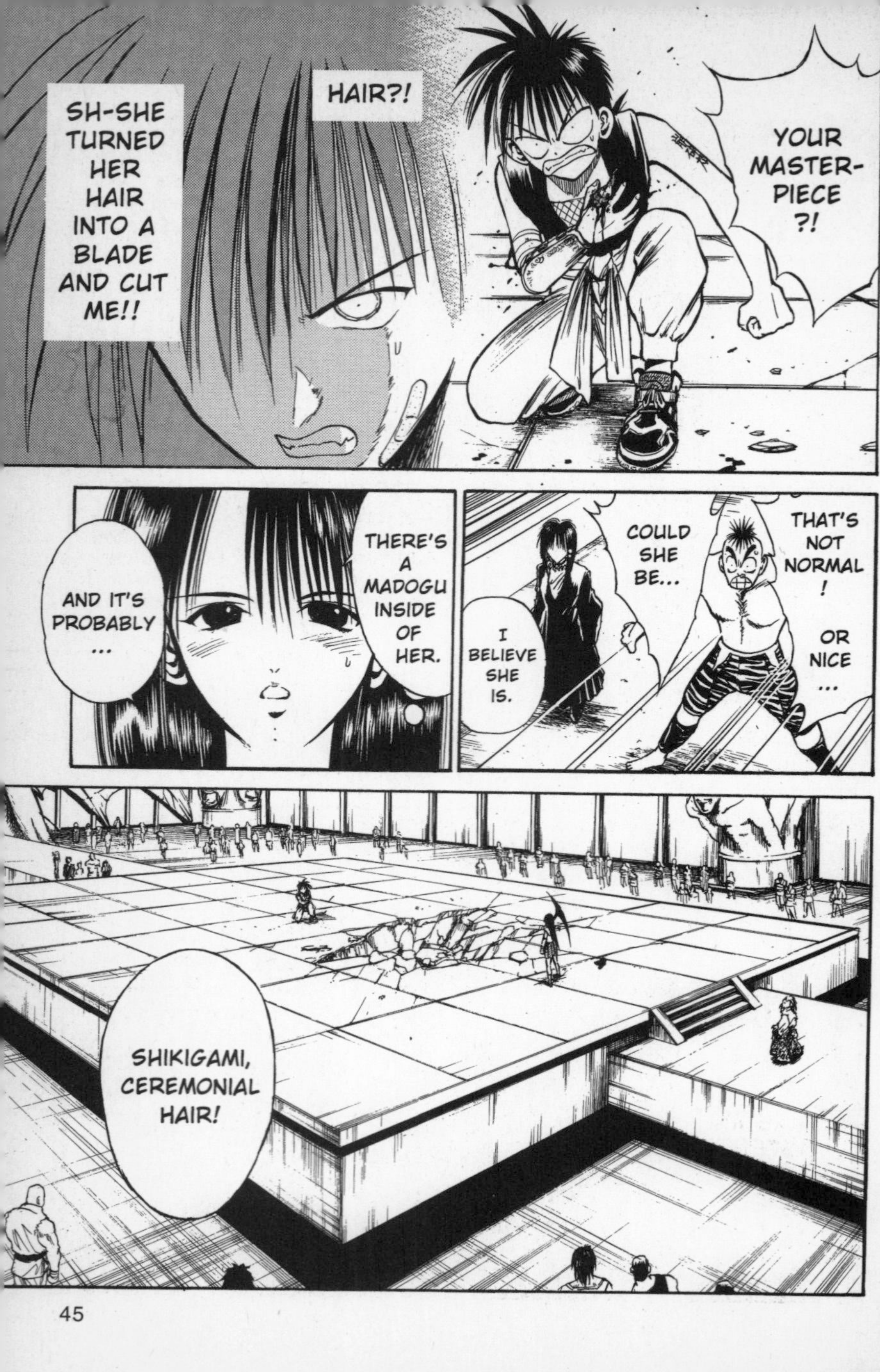
YOUR MASTER-PIECE?!
HAIR?!
SH-SHE TURNED HER HAIR INTO A BLADE AND CUT ME!!
THAT'S NOT NORMAL!
COULD SHE BE...
OR NICE...
I BELIEVE SHE IS.
THERE'S A MADOGU INSIDE OF HER.
AND IT'S PROBABLY...
SHIKIGAMI, CEREMONIAL HAIR!

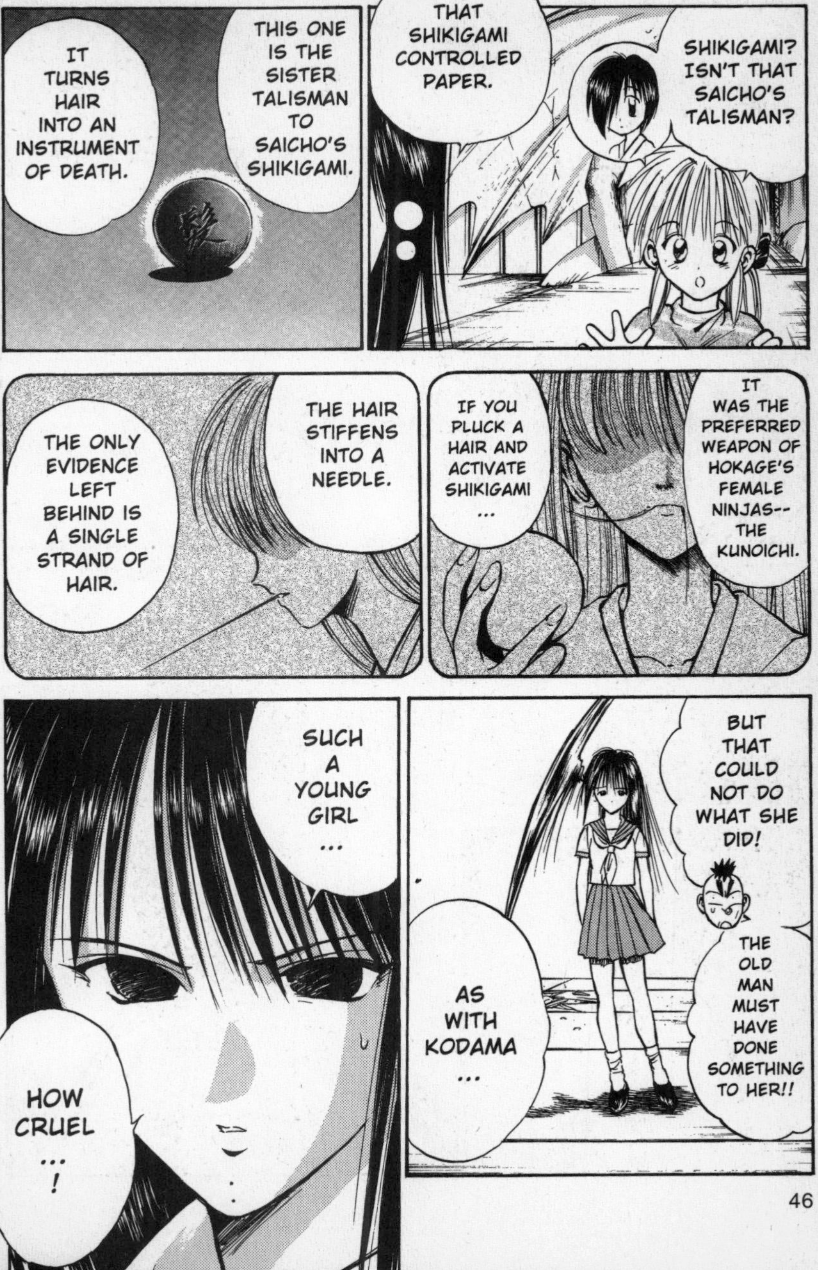
SHIKIGAMI? ISN'T THAT SAICHO'S TALISMAN?
THAT SHIKIGAMI CONTROLLED PAPER.
THIS ONE IS THE SISTER TALISMAN TO SAICHO'S SHIKIGAMI.
IT TURNS HAIR INTO AN INSTRUMENT OF DEATH.
IT WAS THE PREFERRED WEAPON OF HOKAGE'S FEMALE NINJAS-- THE KUNOICHI.
IF YOU PLUCK A HAIR AND ACTIVATE SHIKIGAMI ...
THE HAIR STIFFENS INTO A NEEDLE.
THE ONLY EVIDENCE LEFT BEHIND IS A SINGLE STRAND OF HAIR.
BUT THAT COULD NOT DO WHAT SHE DID!
THE OLD MAN MUST HAVE DONE SOMETHING TO HER!!
AS WITH KODAMA ...
SUCH A YOUNG GIRL ...
HOW CRUEL ... !

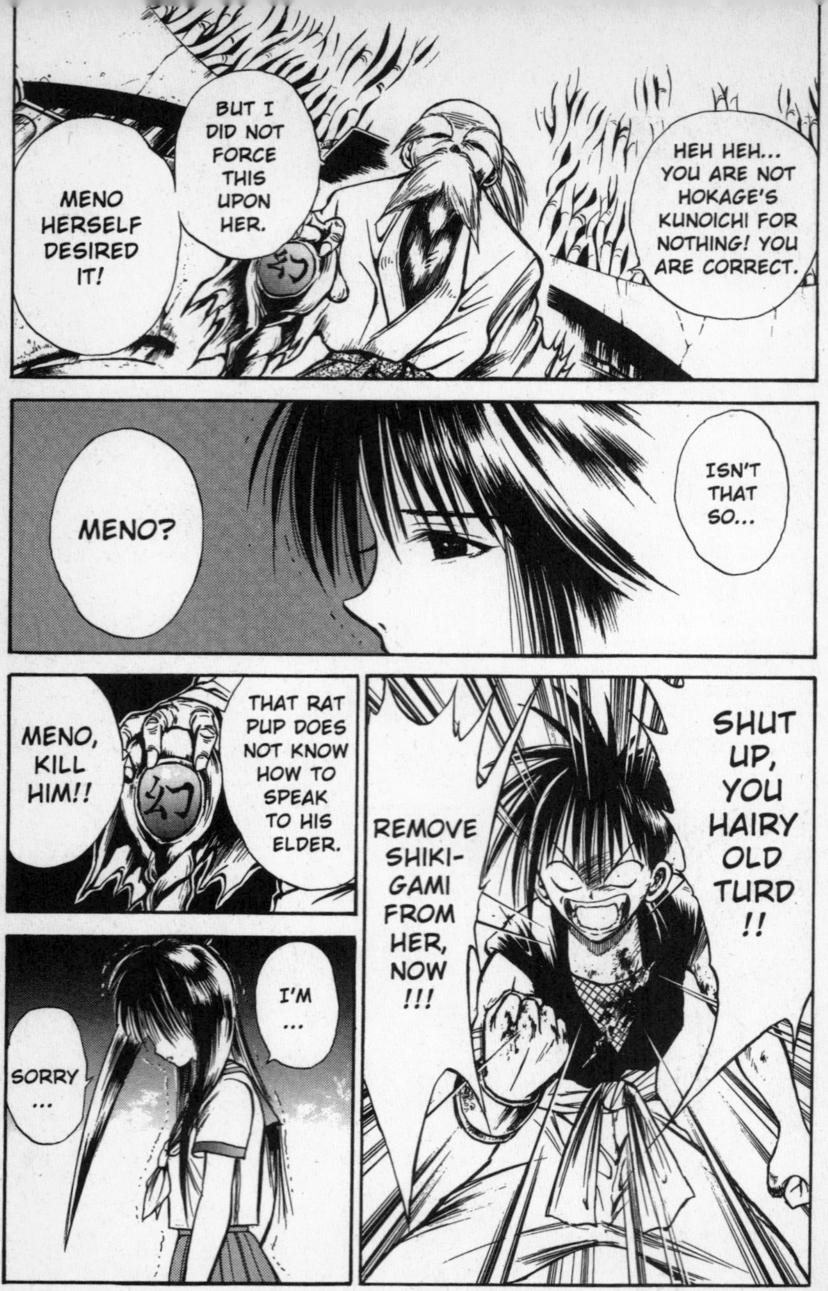
HEH HEH... YOU ARE NOT HOKAGE'S KUNOICHI FOR NOTHING! YOU ARE CORRECT.
BUT I DID NOT FORCE THIS UPON HER.
MENO HERSELF DESIRED IT!
ISN'T THAT SO...
MENO?
SHUT UP, YOU HAIRY OLD TURD!!
REMOVE SHIKI-GAMI FROM HER, NOW!!!
THAT RAT PUP DOES NOT KNOW HOW TO SPEAK TO HIS ELDER.
MENO, KILL HIM!!
I'M...
SORRY...

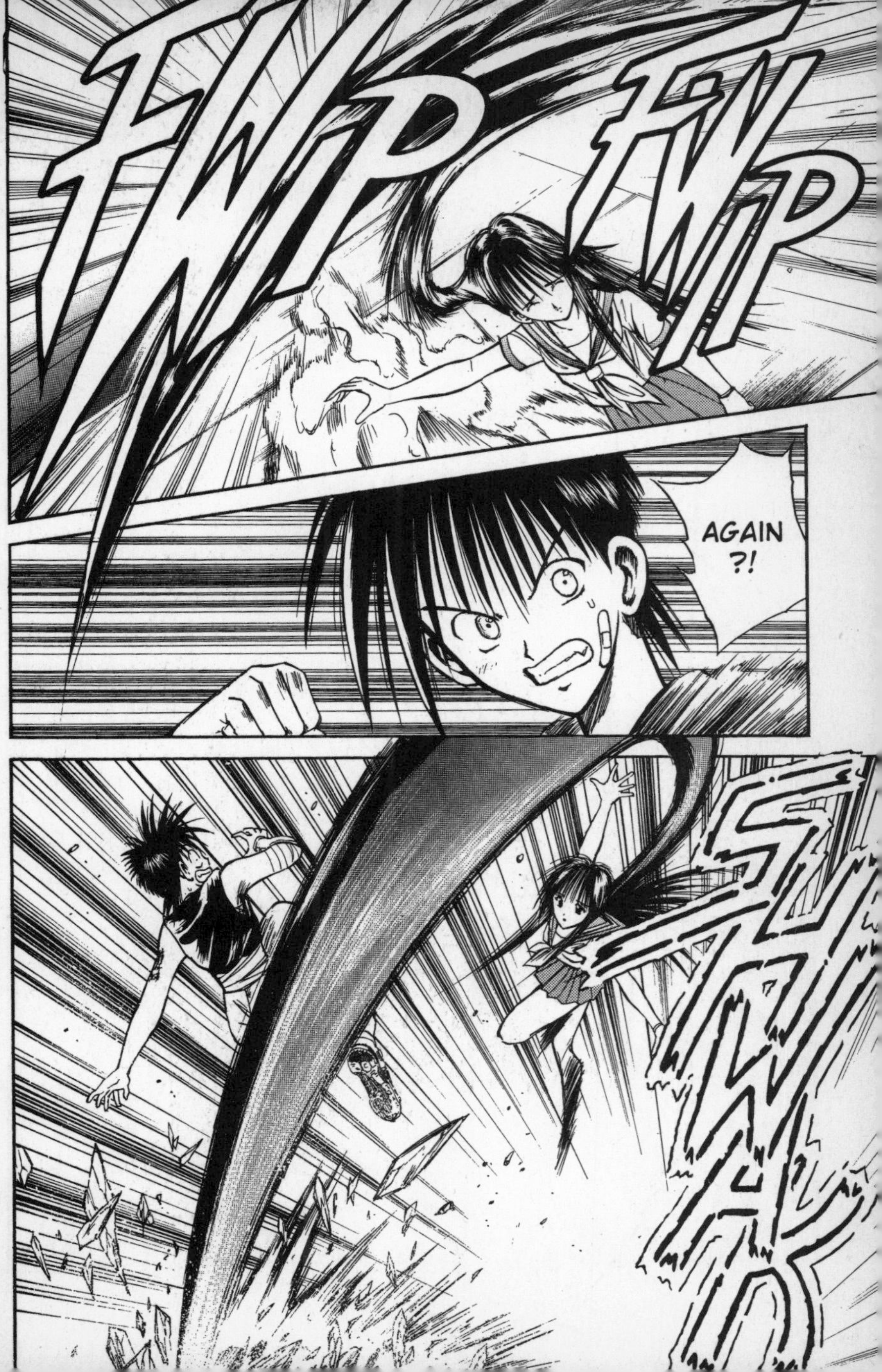
FWIP
FWIP
AGAIN ?!

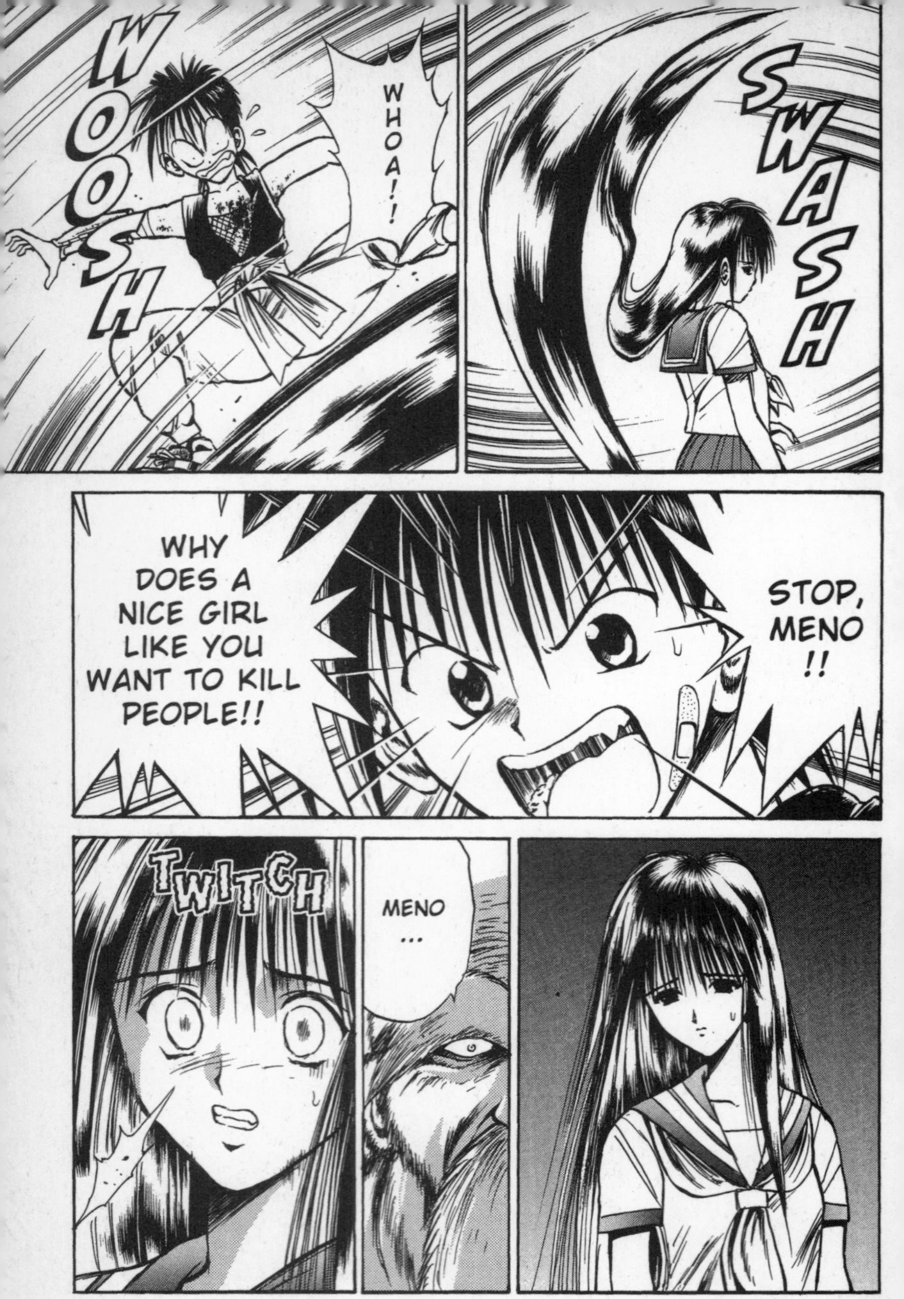
SWASH
WOOOSH
WHOA!!
STOP, MENO!!
WHY DOES A NICE GIRL LIKE YOU WANT TO KILL PEOPLE!!
MENO...
TWITCH

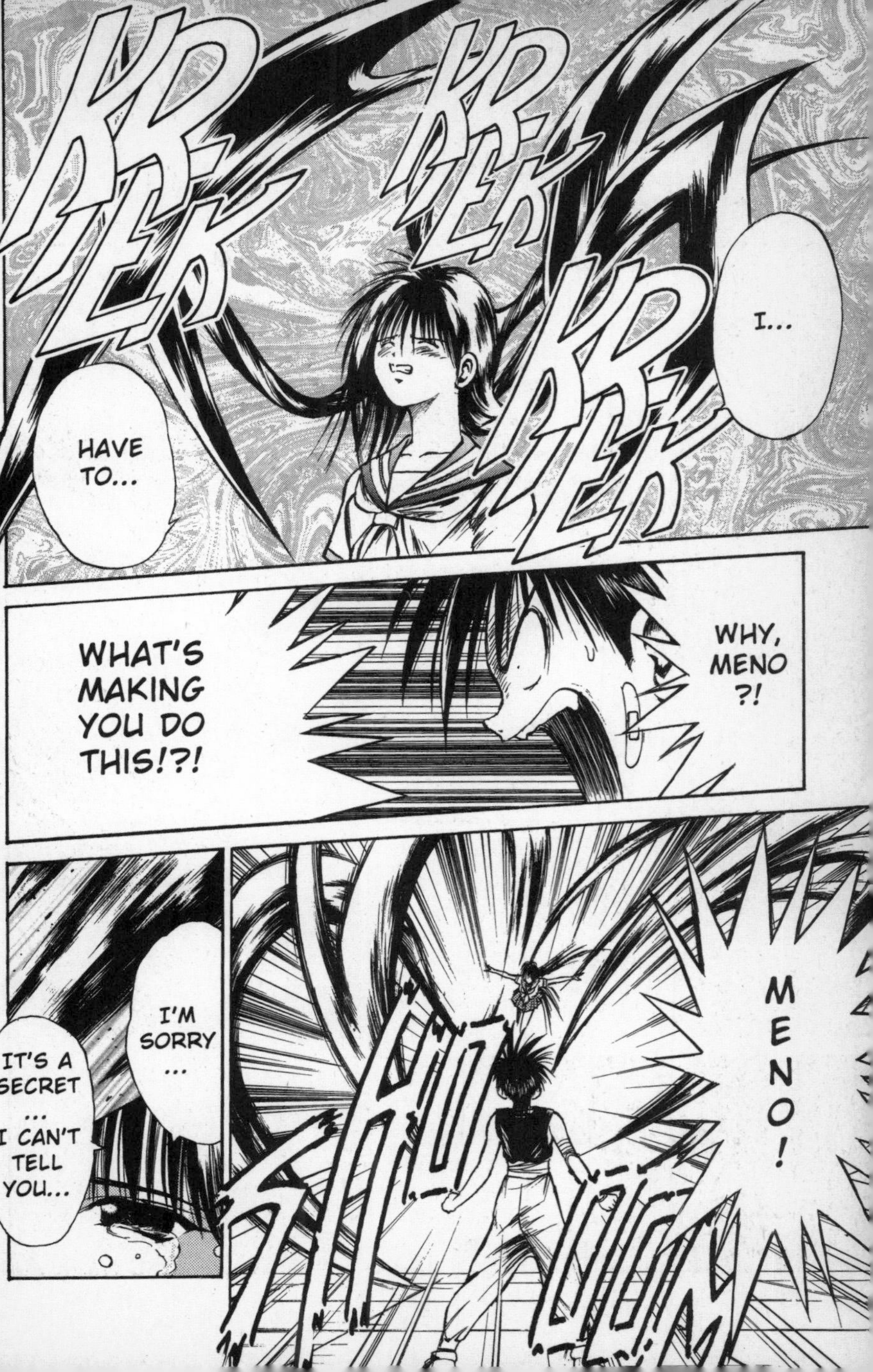
I...
HAVE TO...
WHY, MENO ?!
WHAT'S MAKING YOU DO THIS!?!
MENO!
I'M SORRY ...
IT'S A SECRET ... I CAN'T TELL YOU...

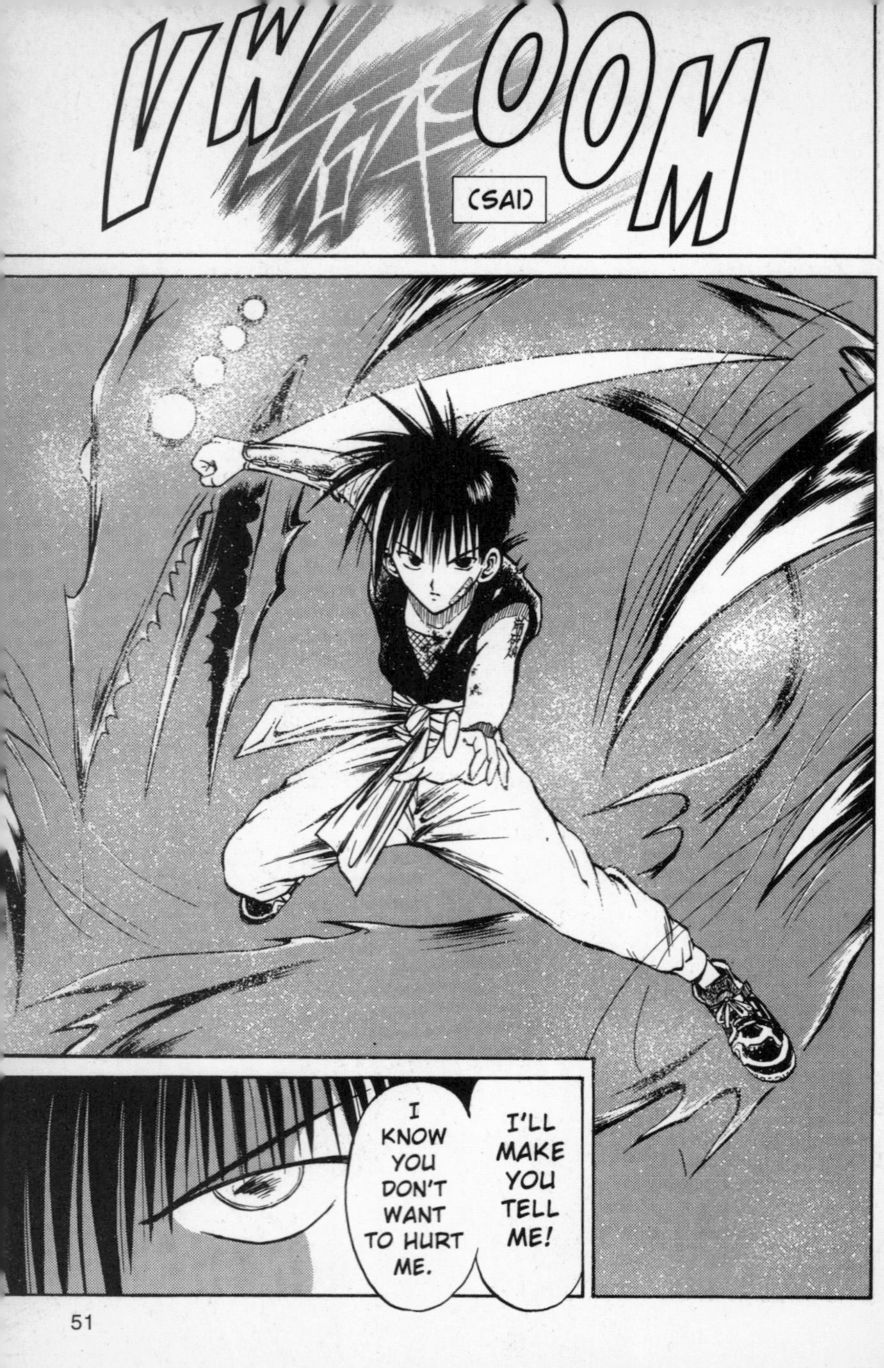
VWOOOM
(SAI)
I'LL MAKE YOU TELL ME!
I KNOW YOU DON'T WANT TO HURT ME.

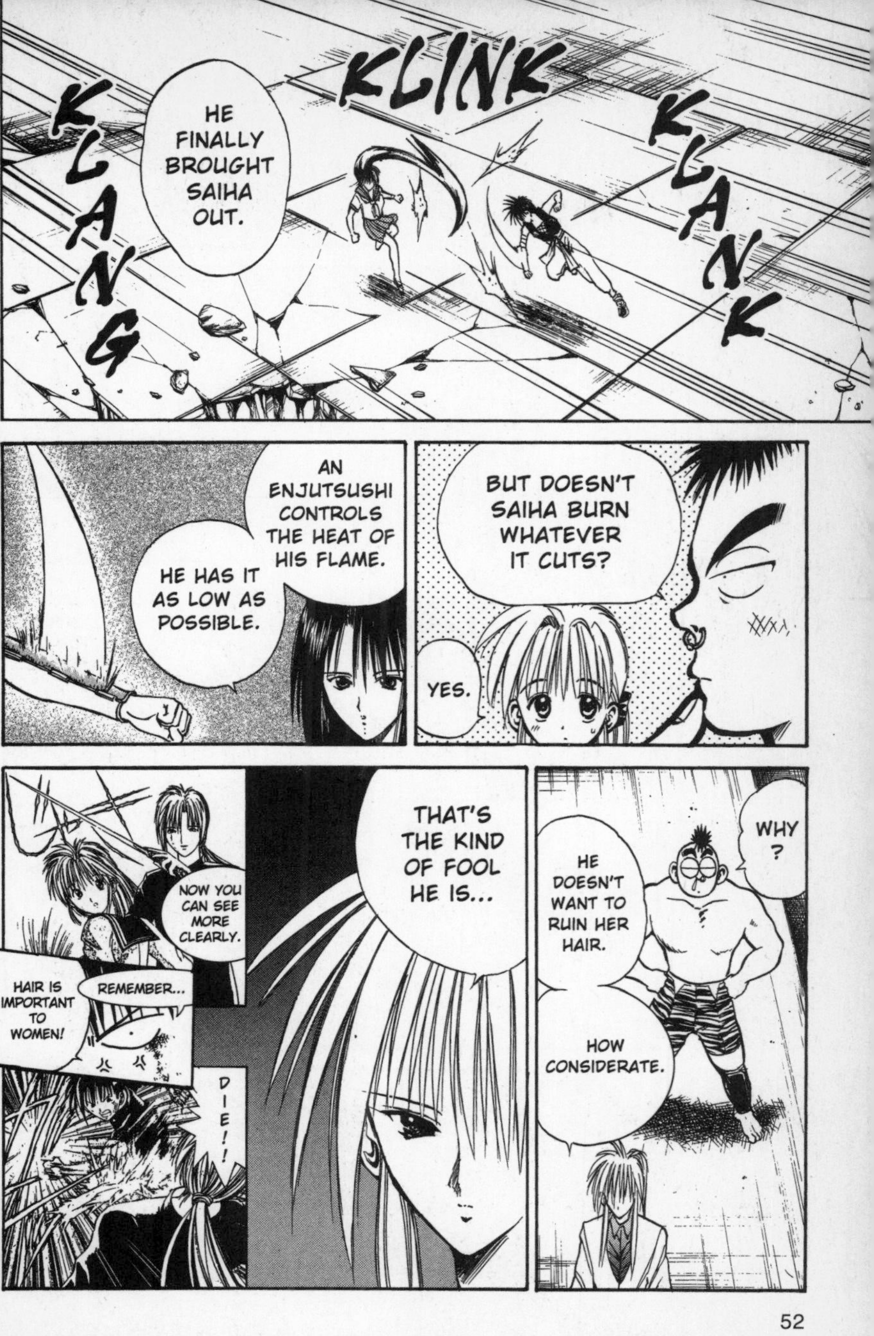
KLINK
KLANK
HE FINALLY BROUGHT SAIHA OUT.
KLANG
BUT DOESN'T SAIHA BURN WHATEVER IT CUTS?
YES.
AN ENJUTSUSHI CONTROLS THE HEAT OF HIS FLAME.
HE HAS IT AS LOW AS POSSIBLE.
WHY?
HE DOESN'T WANT TO RUIN HER HAIR.
HOW CONSIDERATE.
THAT'S THE KIND OF FOOL HE IS...
NOW YOU CAN SEE MORE CLEARLY.
REMEMBER...
HAIR IS IMPORTANT TO WOMEN!
DIE!!

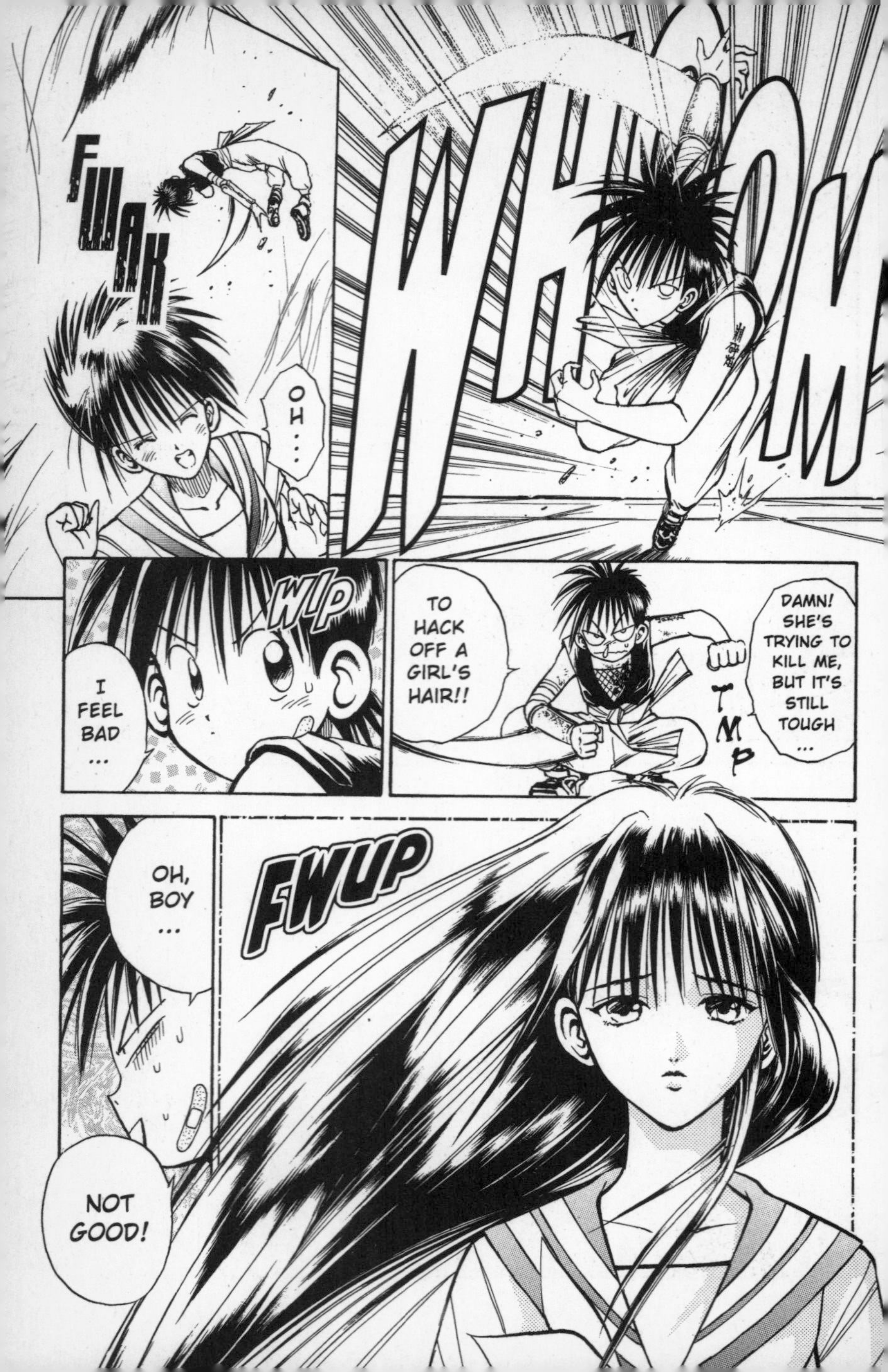
FWAK
OH...
DAMN! SHE'S TRYING TO KILL ME, BUT IT'S STILL TOUGH ...
TMP
TO HACK OFF A GIRL'S HAIR!!
WIP
I FEEL BAD ...
FWUP
OH, BOY ...
NOT GOOD!

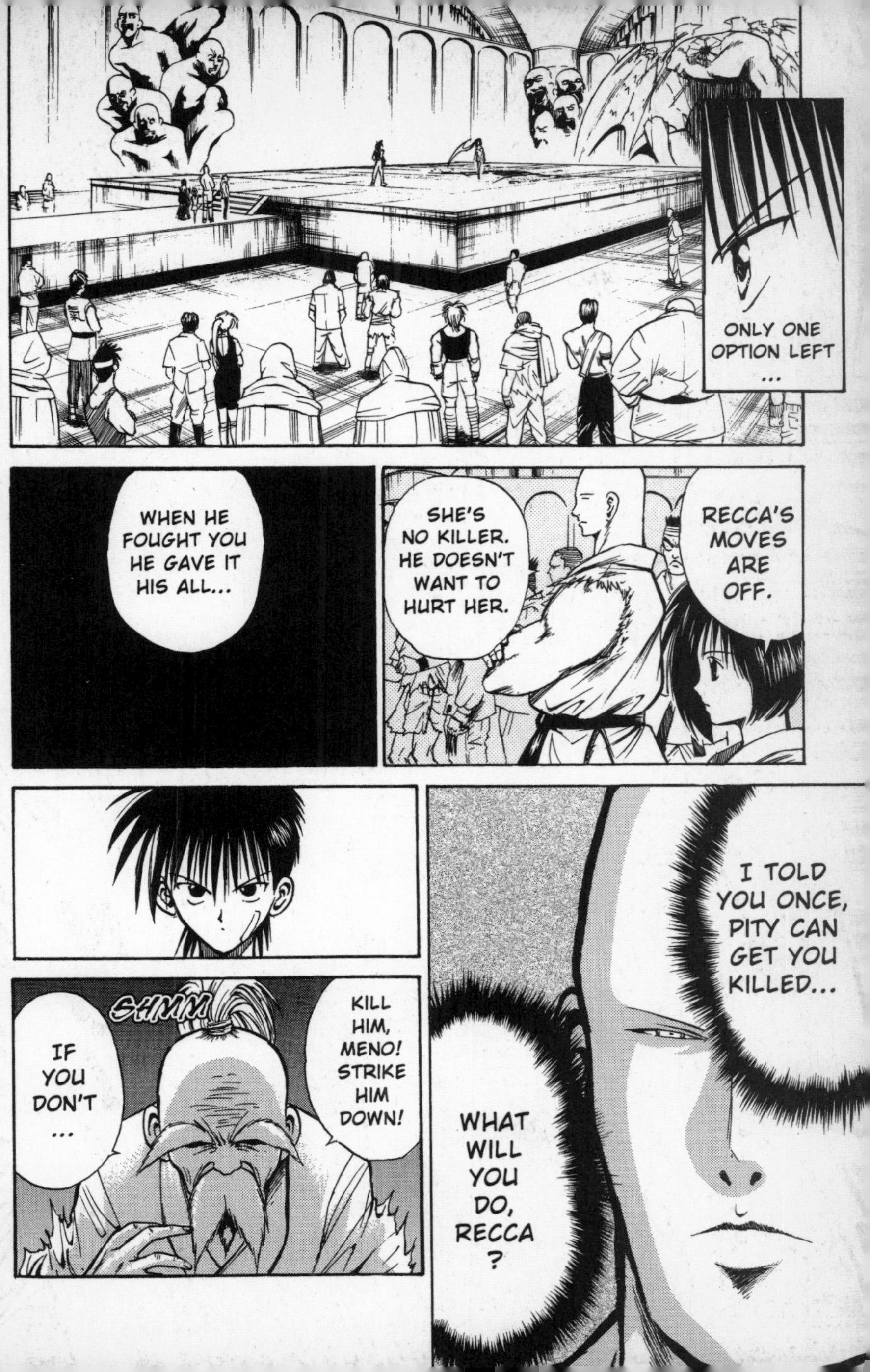
ONLY ONE OPTION LEFT ...
RECCA'S MOVES ARE OFF.
SHE'S NO KILLER. HE DOESN'T WANT TO HURT HER.
WHEN HE FOUGHT YOU HE GAVE IT HIS ALL...
I TOLD YOU ONCE, PITY CAN GET YOU KILLED...
WHAT WILL YOU DO, RECCA ?
SHMM
KILL HIM, MENO! STRIKE HIM DOWN!
IF YOU DON'T ...

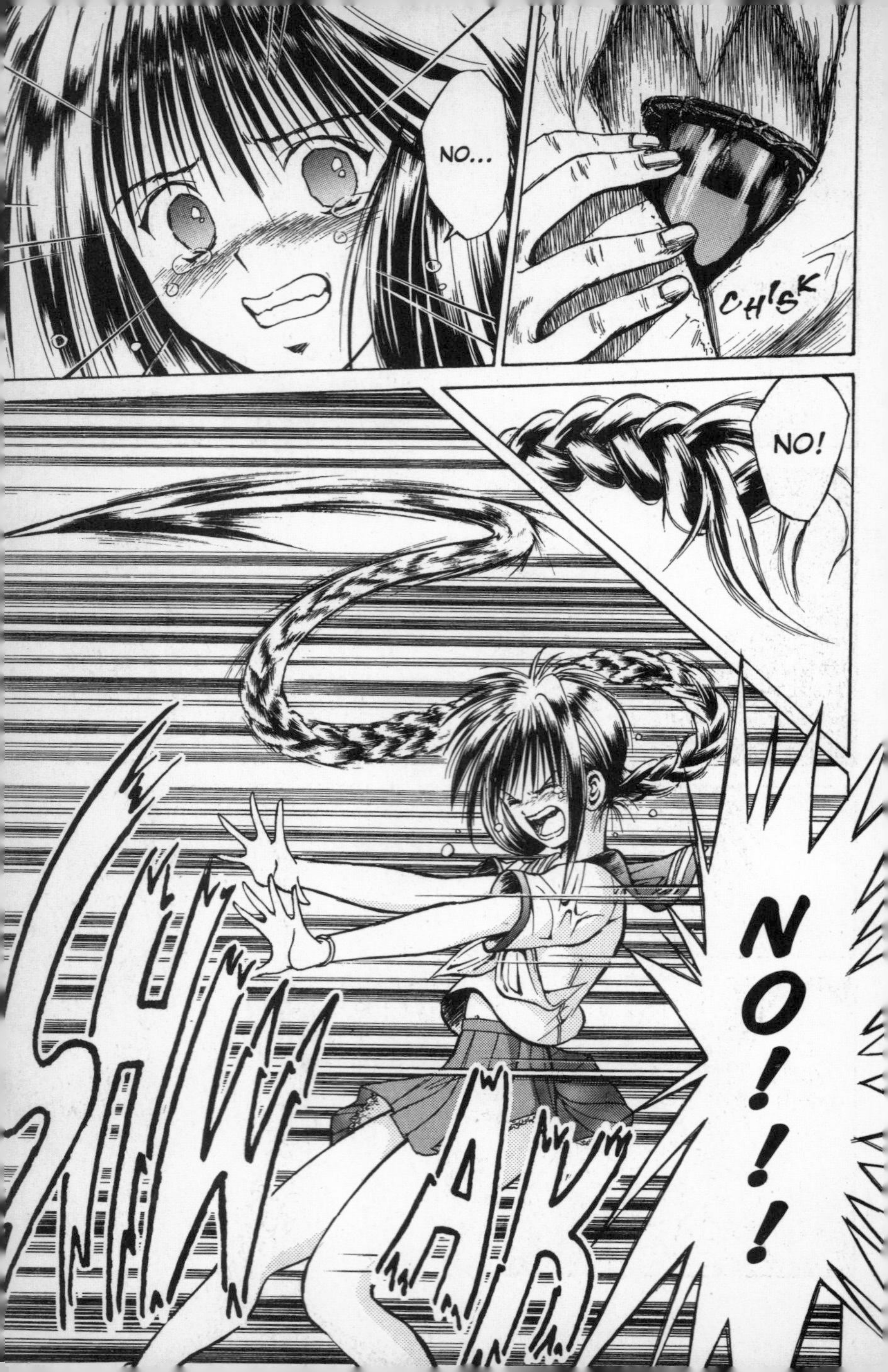
CH'SK
NO...
NO!
NO!!!!
SHWAK

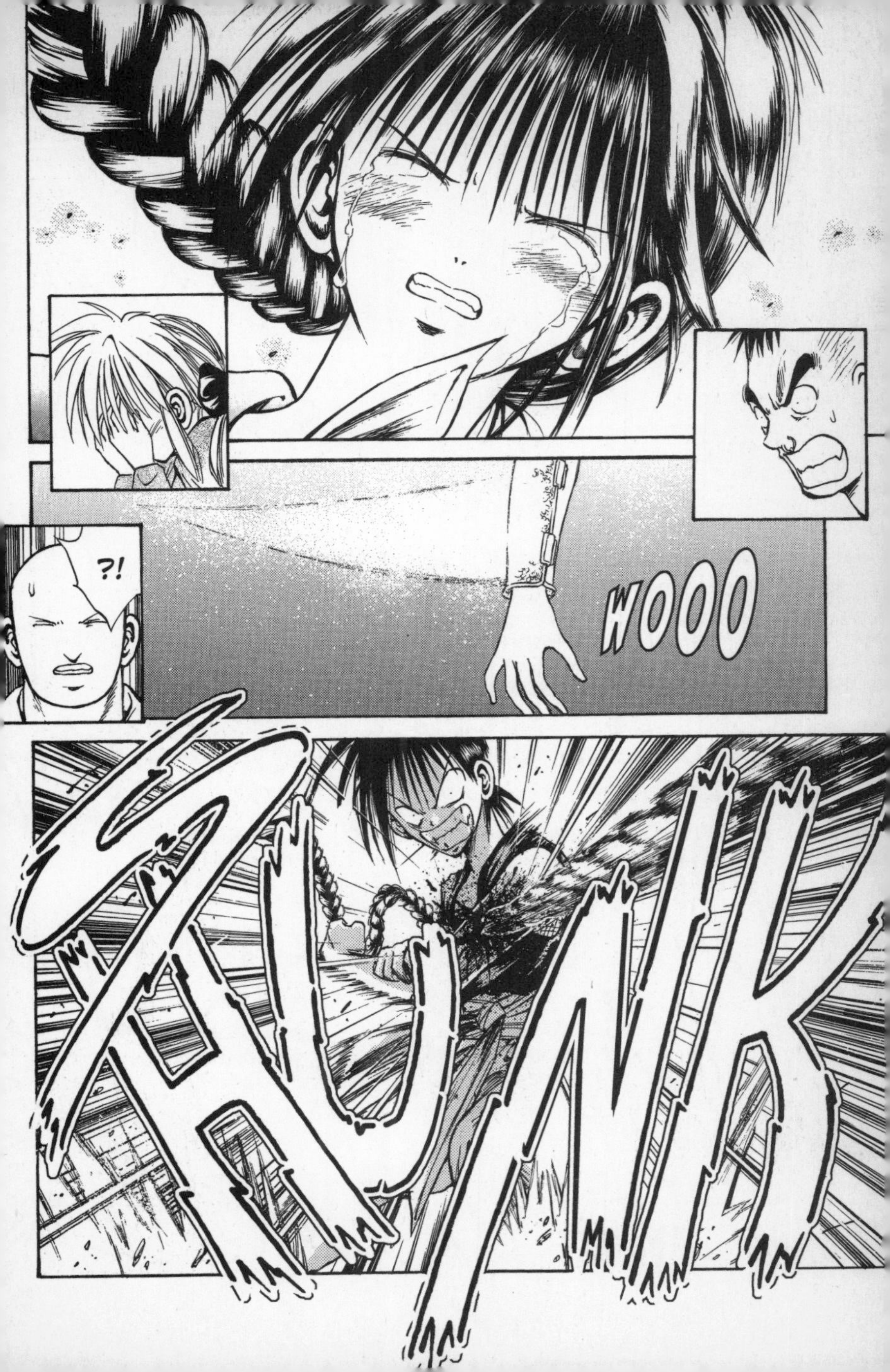
?!
WOOO
SHUNK

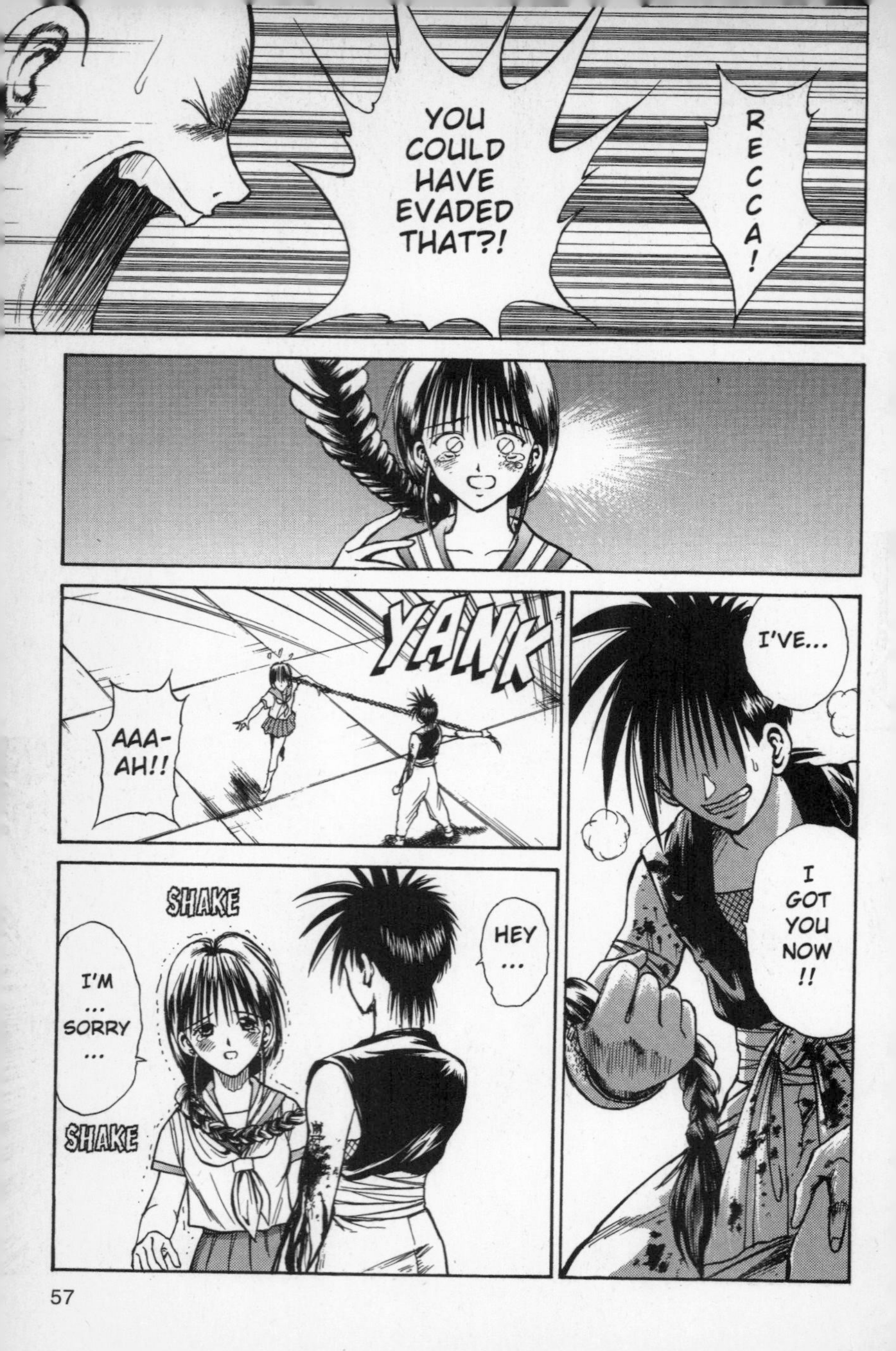
RECCA!
YOU COULD HAVE EVADED THAT?!
I'VE...
I GOT YOU NOW!!
YANK
AAA-AH!!
HEY...
SHAKE
I'M... SORRY...
SHAKE

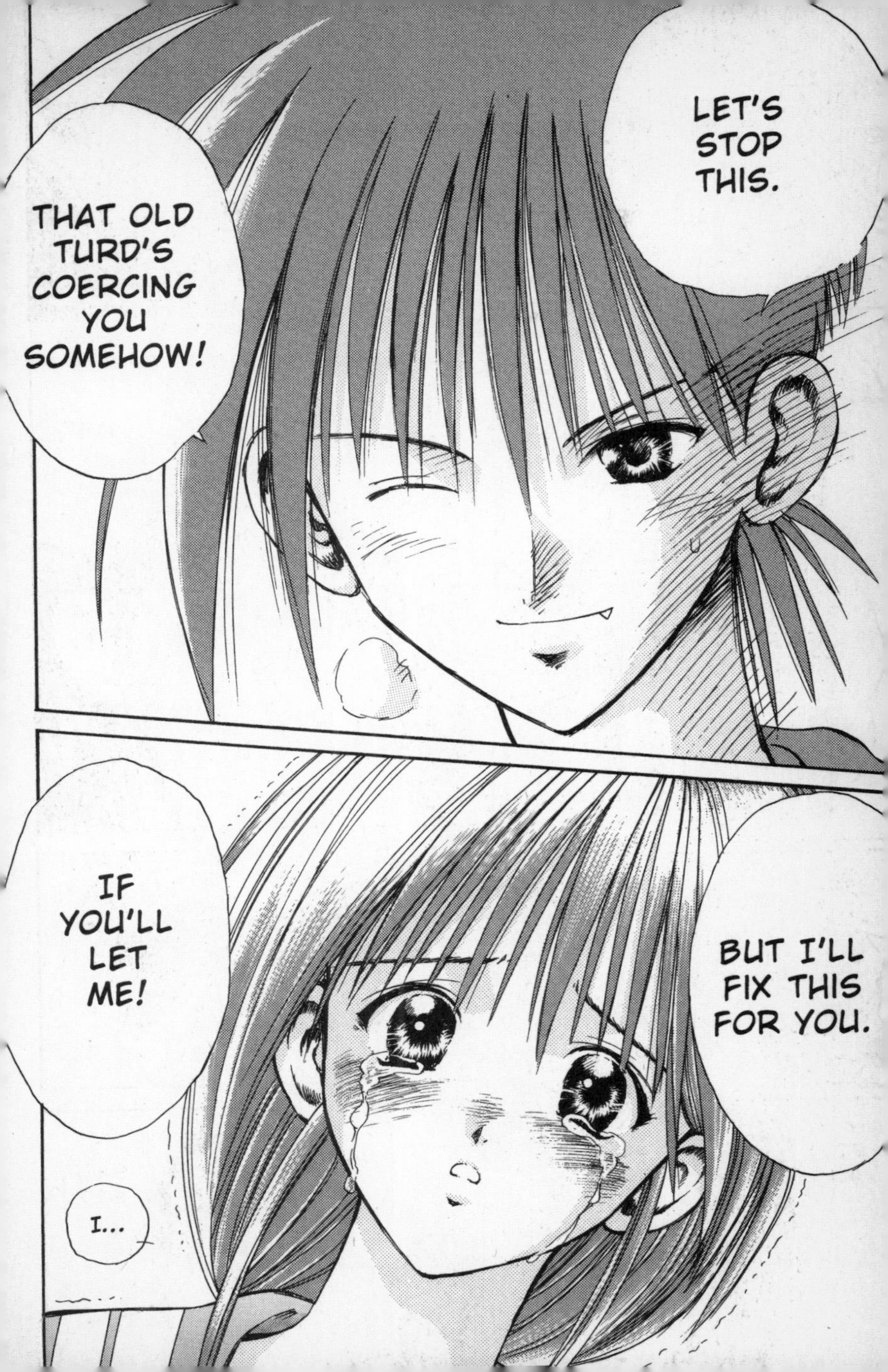
LET'S STOP THIS.
THAT OLD TURD'S COERCING YOU SOMEHOW!
BUT I'LL FIX THIS FOR YOU.
IF YOU'LL LET ME!
I...

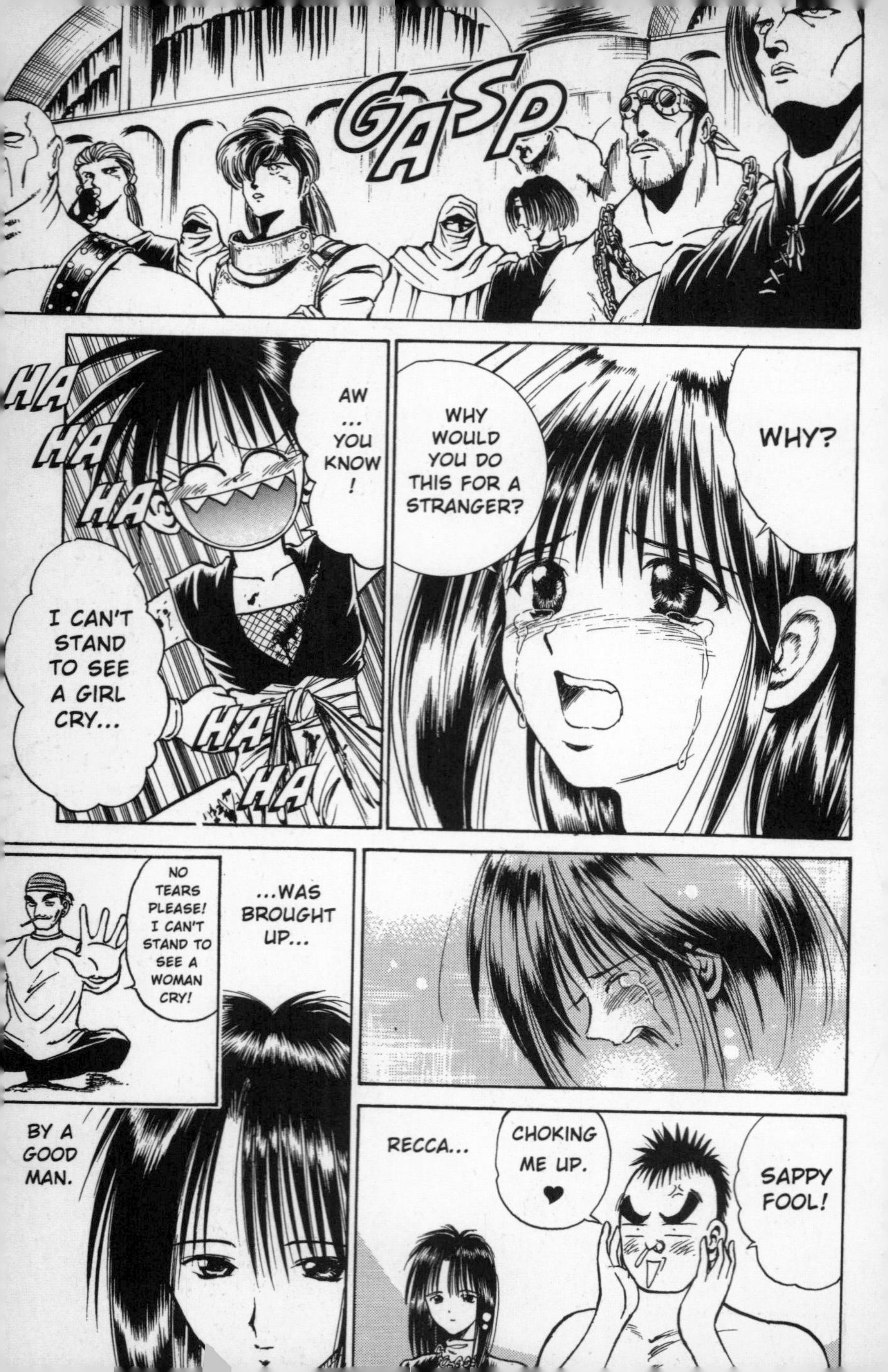
GASP
WHY?
WHY WOULD YOU DO THIS FOR A STRANGER?
AW ... YOU KNOW!
HA HA HA
I CAN'T STAND TO SEE A GIRL CRY...
HA HA
SAPPY FOOL!
CHOKING ME UP. ♥
RECCA...
...WAS BROUGHT UP...
NO TEARS PLEASE! I CAN'T STAND TO SEE A WOMAN CRY!
BY A GOOD MAN.

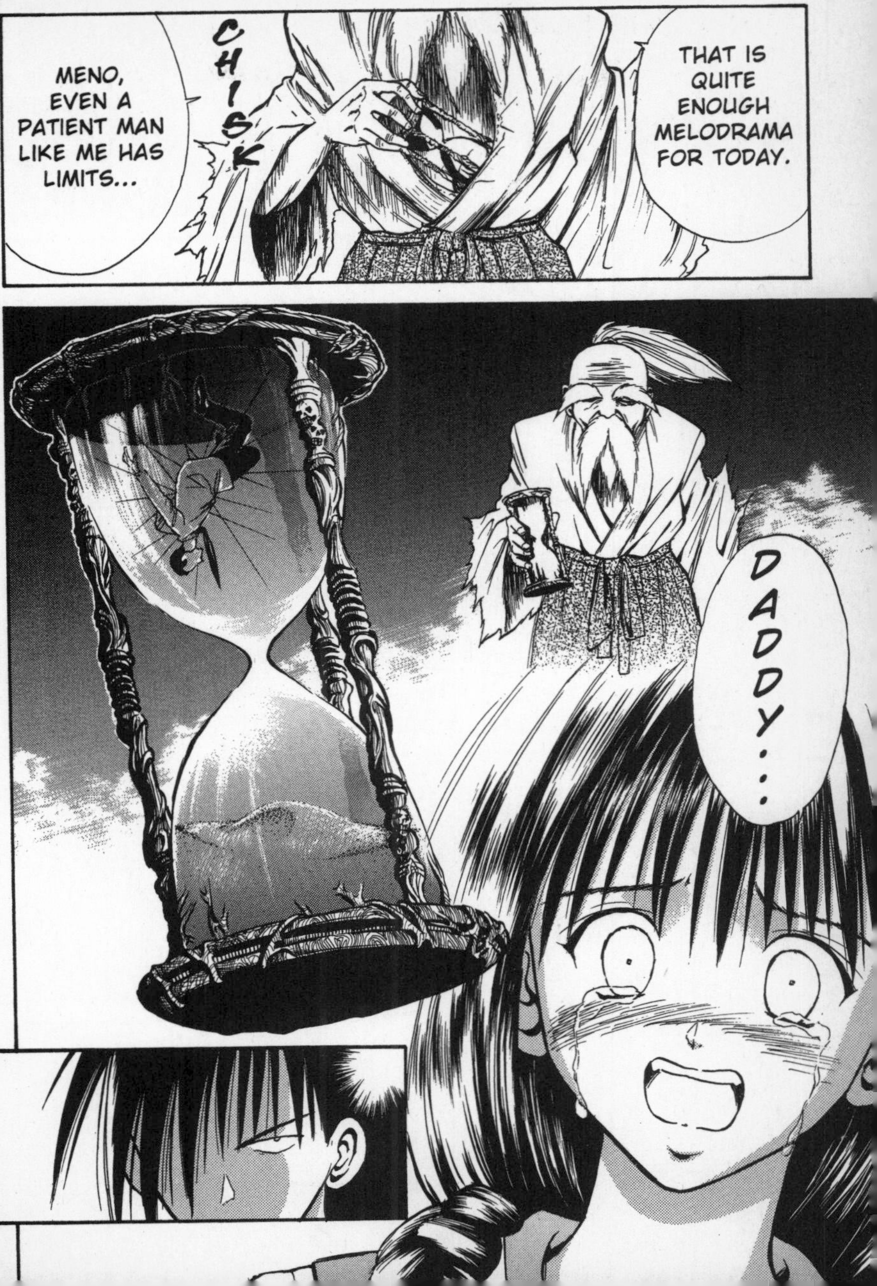
THAT IS QUITE ENOUGH MELODRAMA FOR TODAY.
CHISK
MENO, EVEN A PATIENT MAN LIKE ME HAS LIMITS...
DADDY...

# Part Sixty-Three:
# The Mad Illusionist's Feast (8) Hourglass Prison

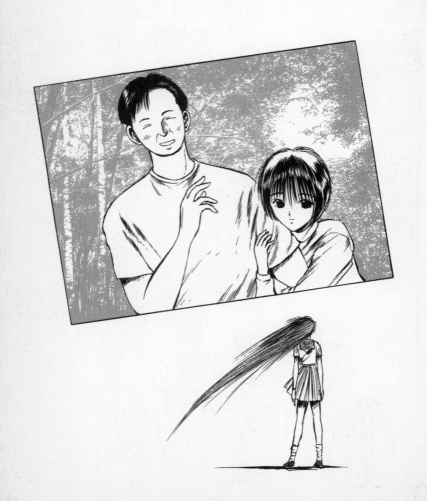

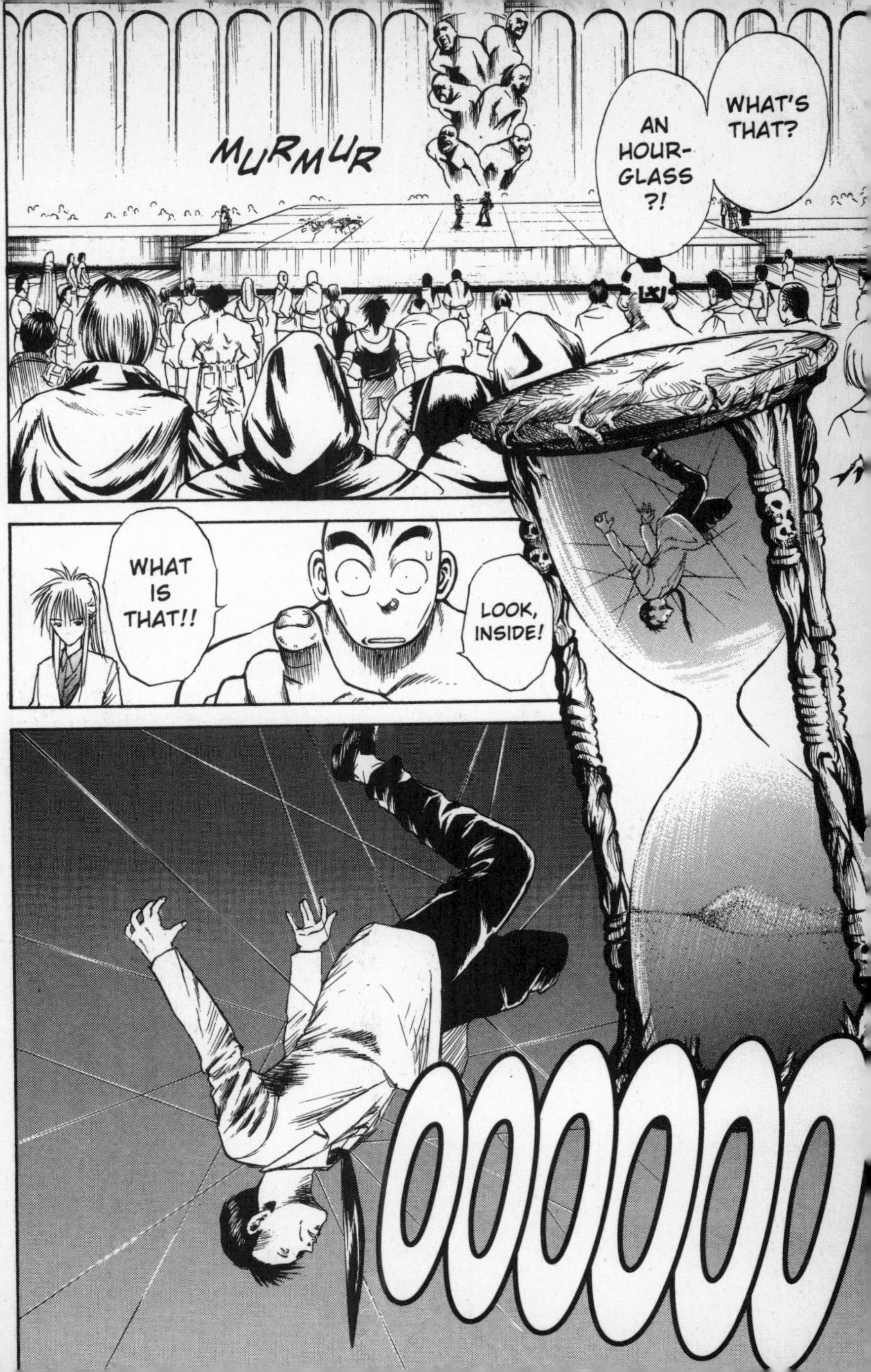
WHAT'S THAT?
AN HOUR-GLASS ?!
MURMUR
LOOK, INSIDE!
WHAT IS THAT!!
OOOOOOOO

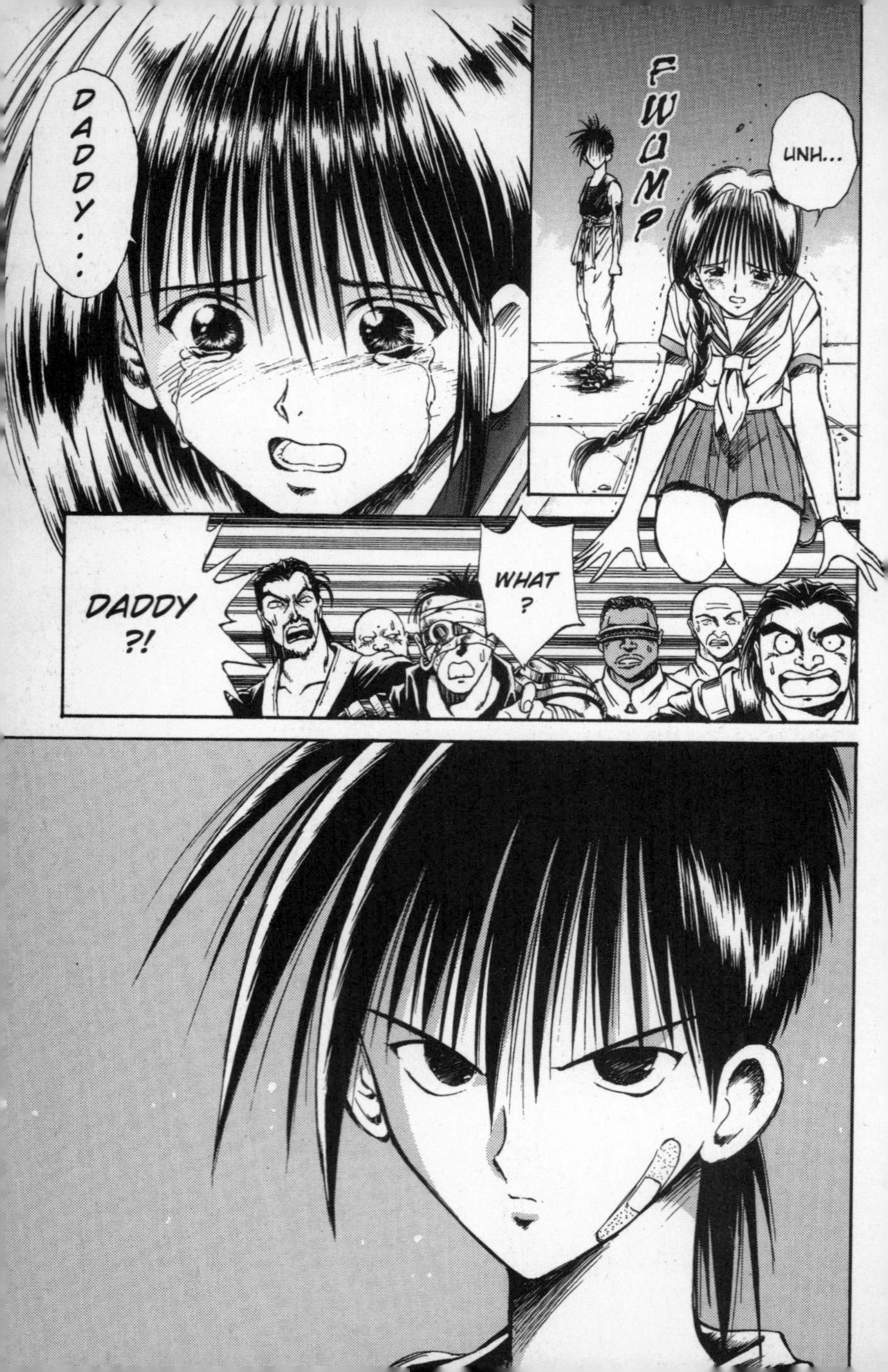
UNH...
FWUMP
DADDY...
WHAT?
DADDY?!

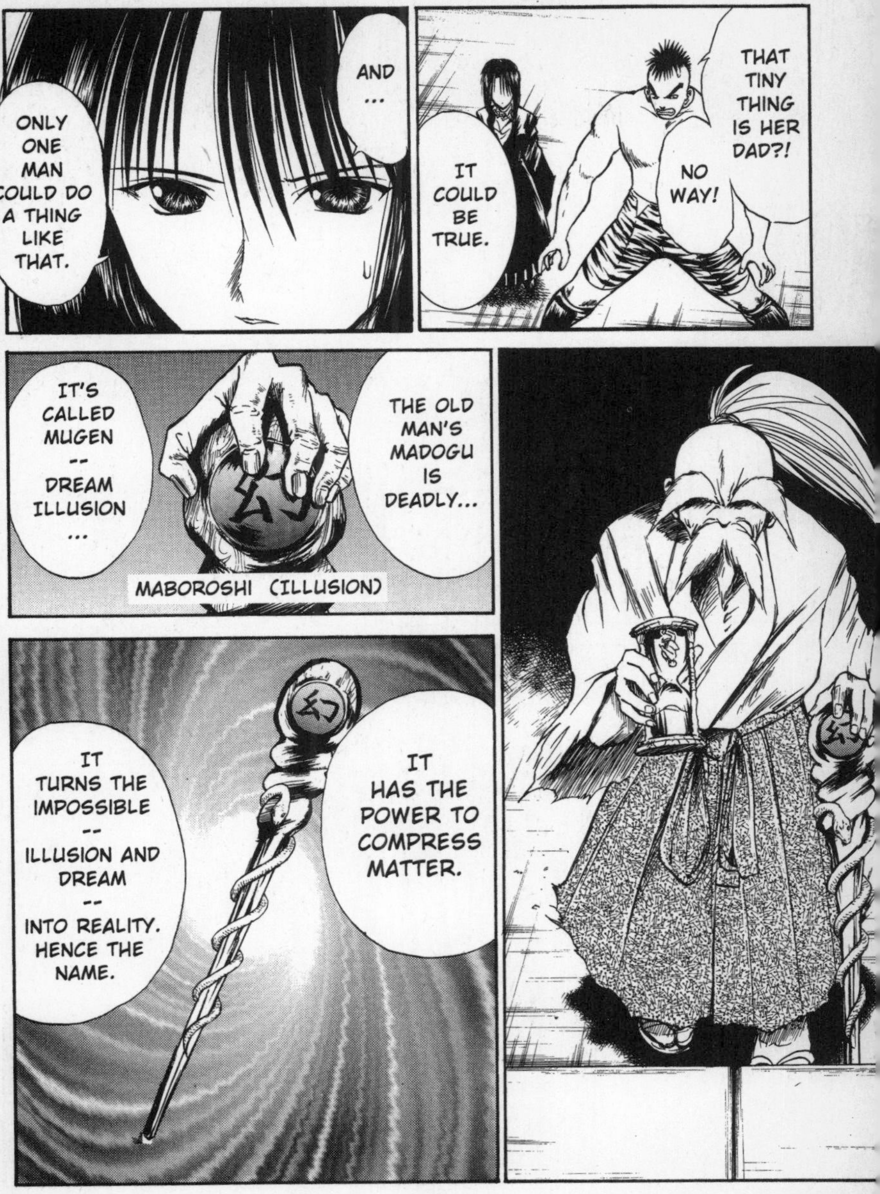
THAT TINY THING IS HER DAD?!
NO WAY!
IT COULD BE TRUE.
AND ...
ONLY ONE MAN COULD DO A THING LIKE THAT.
THE OLD MAN'S MADOGU IS DEADLY...
IT'S CALLED MUGEN -- DREAM ILLUSION ...
MABOROSHI (ILLUSION)
IT HAS THE POWER TO COMPRESS MATTER.
IT TURNS THE IMPOSSIBLE -- ILLUSION AND DREAM -- INTO REALITY. HENCE THE NAME.

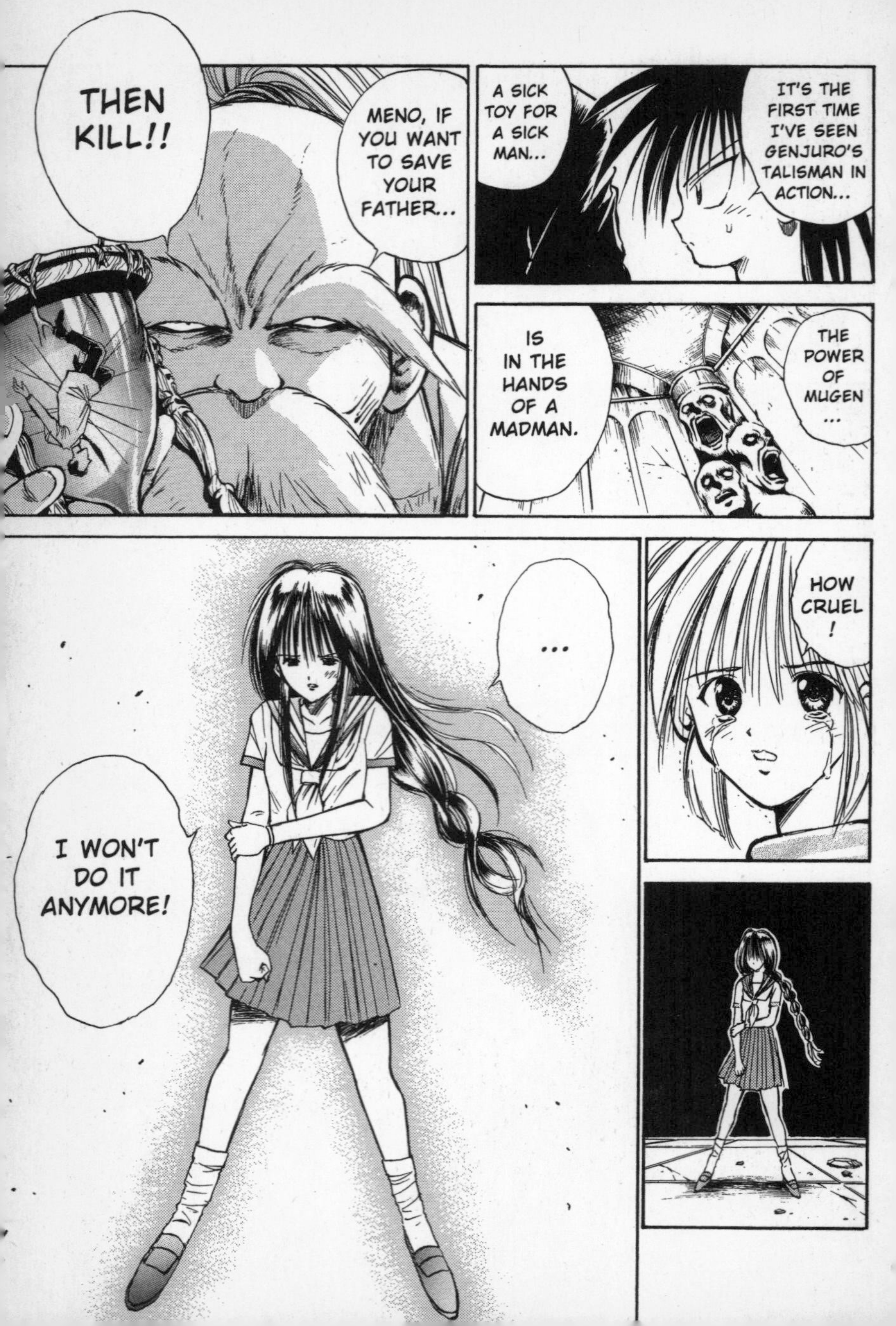
IT'S THE FIRST TIME I'VE SEEN GENJURO'S TALISMAN IN ACTION...
A SICK TOY FOR A SICK MAN...
THE POWER OF MUGEN...
IS IN THE HANDS OF A MADMAN.
MENO, IF YOU WANT TO SAVE YOUR FATHER...
THEN KILL!!
HOW CRUEL!
...
I WON'T DO IT ANYMORE!

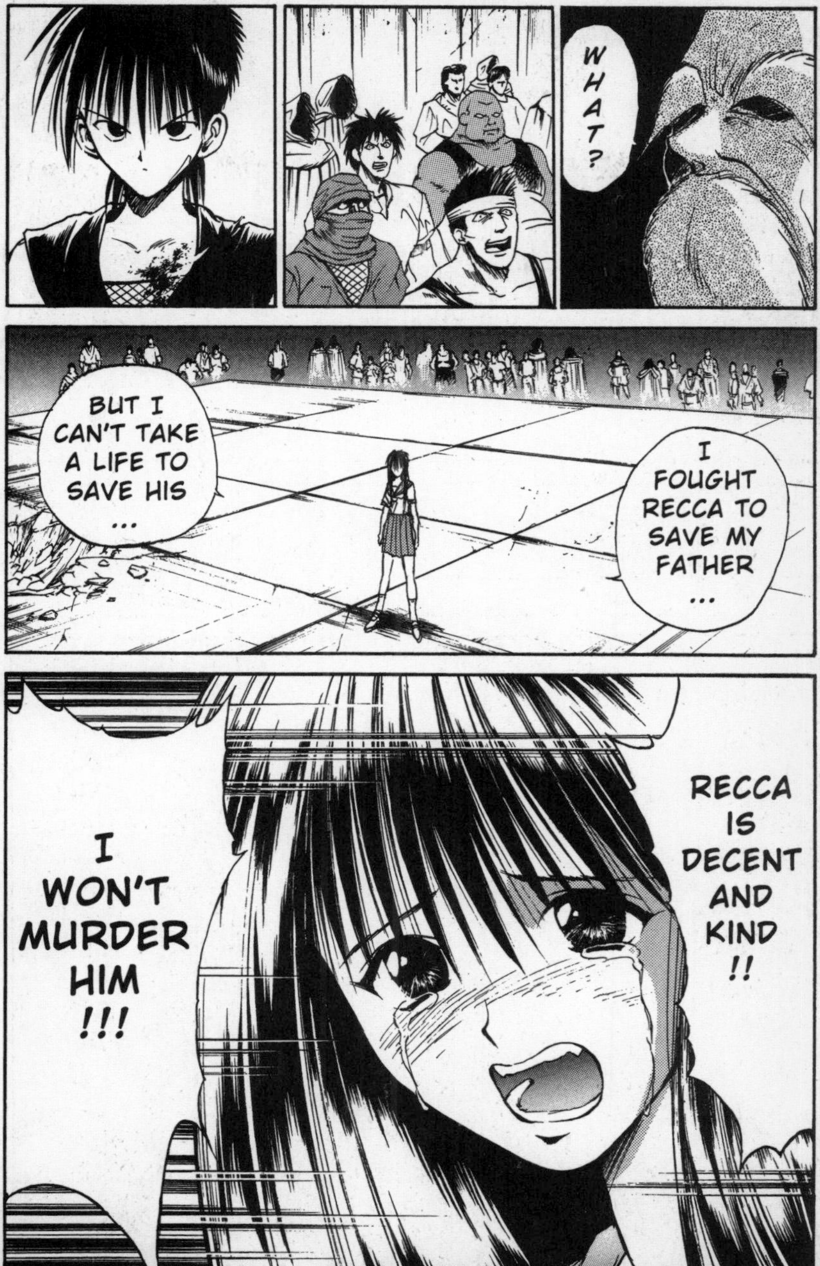

WHAT?
I FOUGHT RECCA TO SAVE MY FATHER ...
BUT I CAN'T TAKE A LIFE TO SAVE HIS ...
RECCA IS DECENT AND KIND !!
I WON'T MURDER HIM !!!

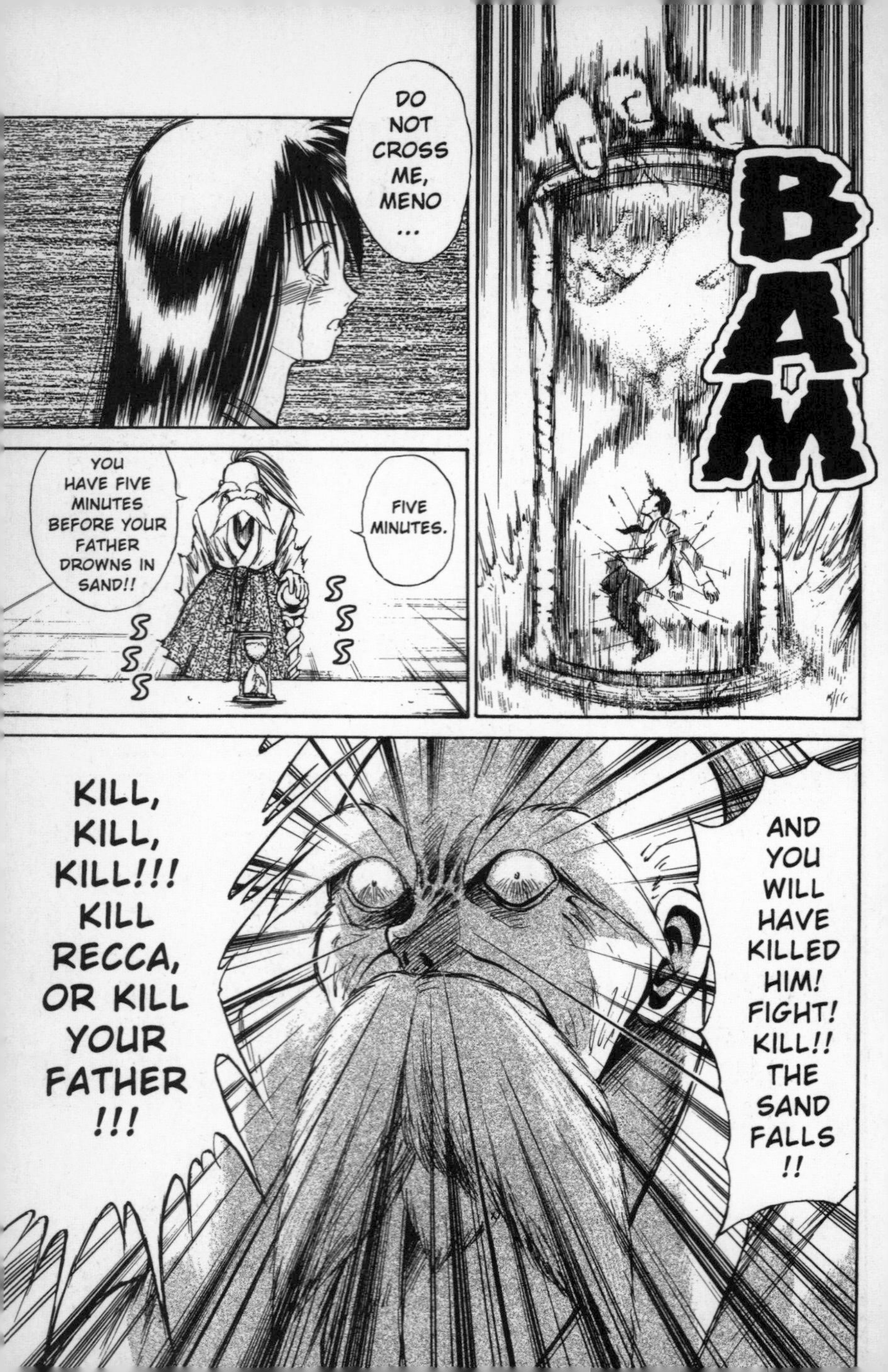
BAM
DO NOT CROSS ME, MENO ...
FIVE MINUTES.
YOU HAVE FIVE MINUTES BEFORE YOUR FATHER DROWNS IN SAND!!
S S S
S S S
AND YOU WILL HAVE KILLED HIM! FIGHT! KILL!! THE SAND FALLS !!
KILL, KILL, KILL!!! KILL RECCA, OR KILL YOUR FATHER !!!

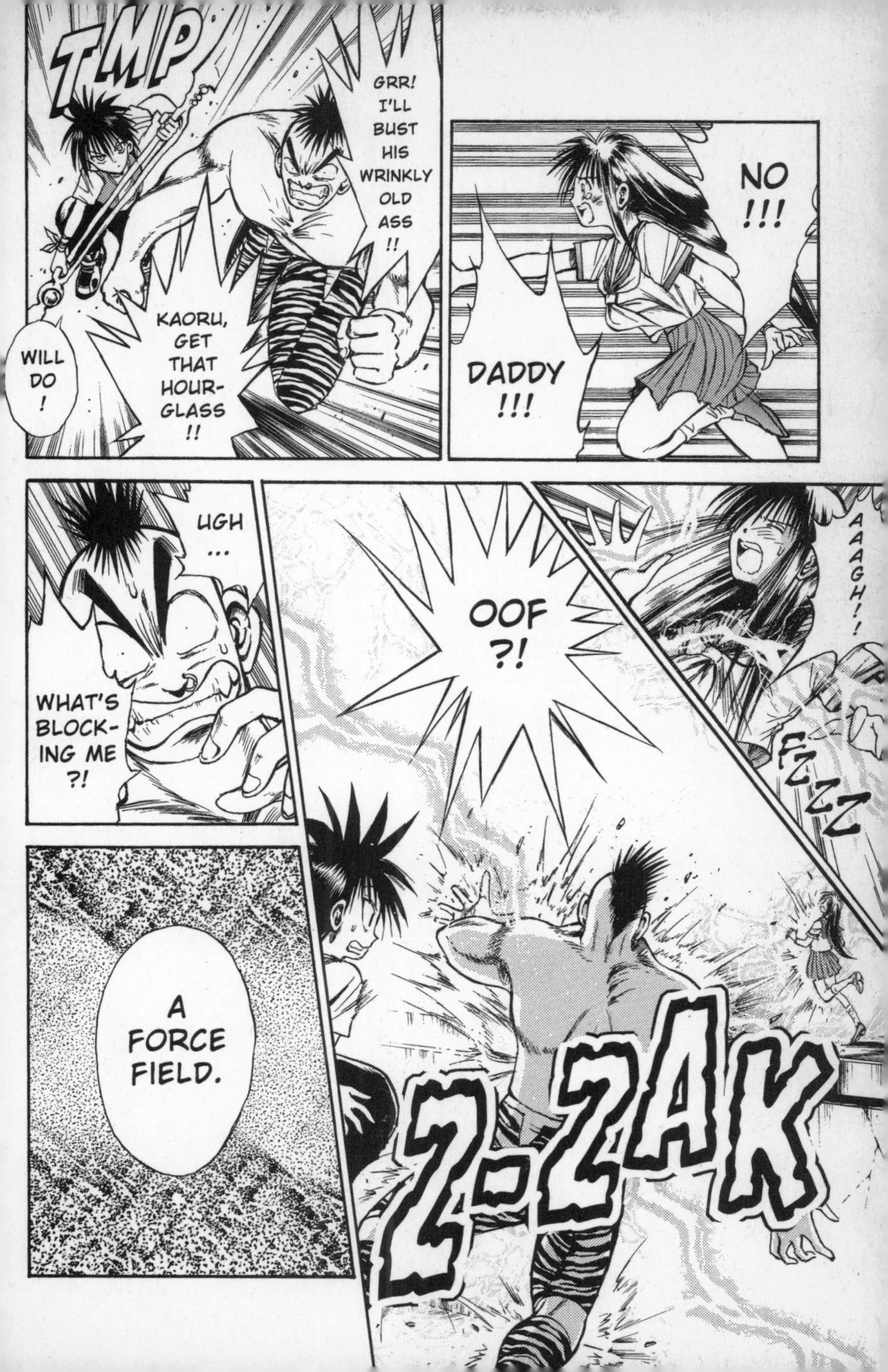
NO !!!
DADDY !!!
GRR! I'LL BUST HIS WRINKLY OLD ASS !!
TMP
KAORU, GET THAT HOURGLASS !!
WILL DO !
AAAGH!!
FZZZ
OOF ?!
Z-ZAK
UGH ...
WHAT'S BLOCKING ME ?!
A FORCE FIELD.

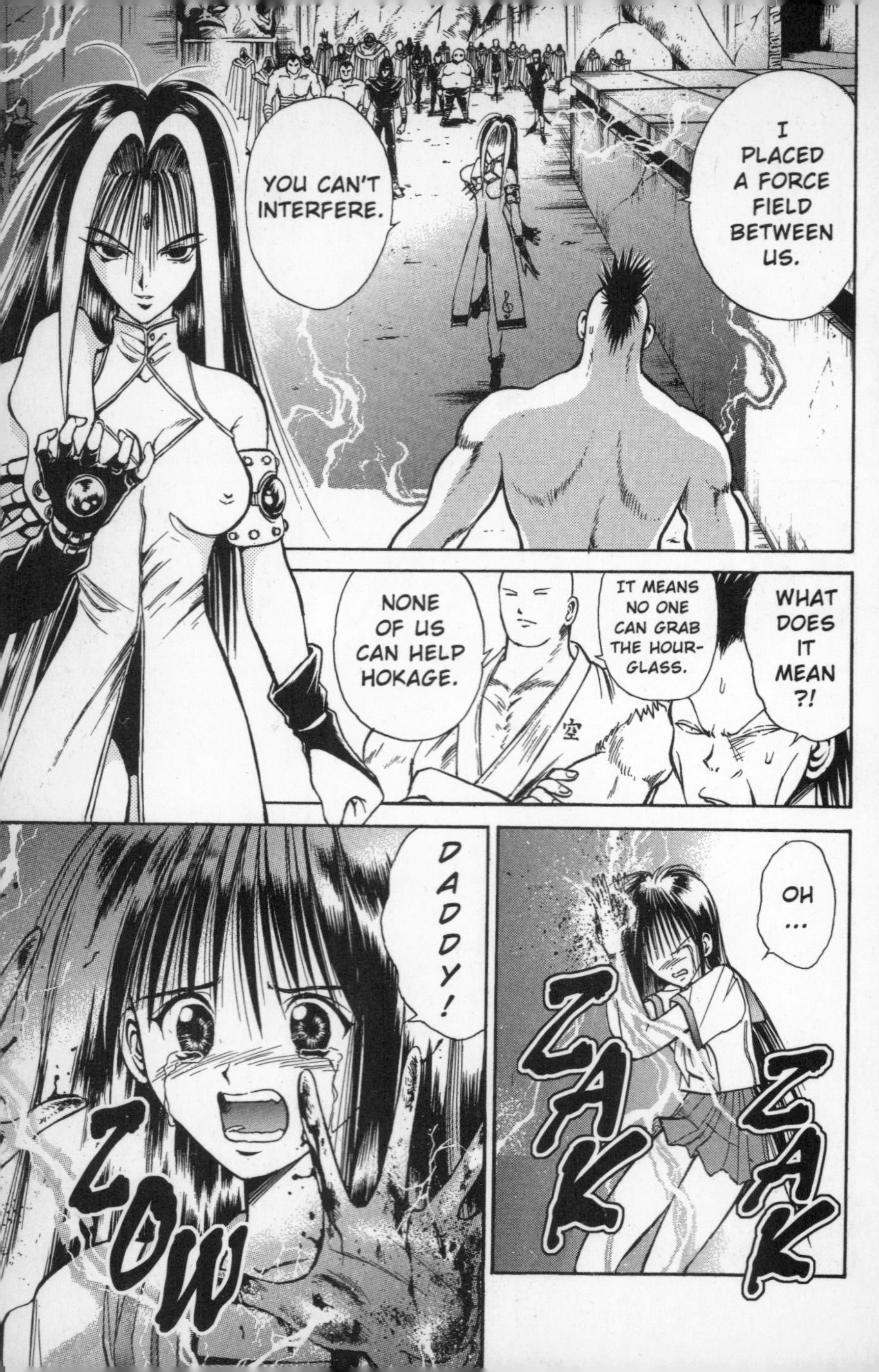
I PLACED A FORCE FIELD BETWEEN US.
YOU CAN'T INTERFERE.
WHAT DOES IT MEAN ?!
IT MEANS NO ONE CAN GRAB THE HOUR-GLASS.
NONE OF US CAN HELP HOKAGE.
OH ...
ZAK ZAK
DADDY!
ZOW

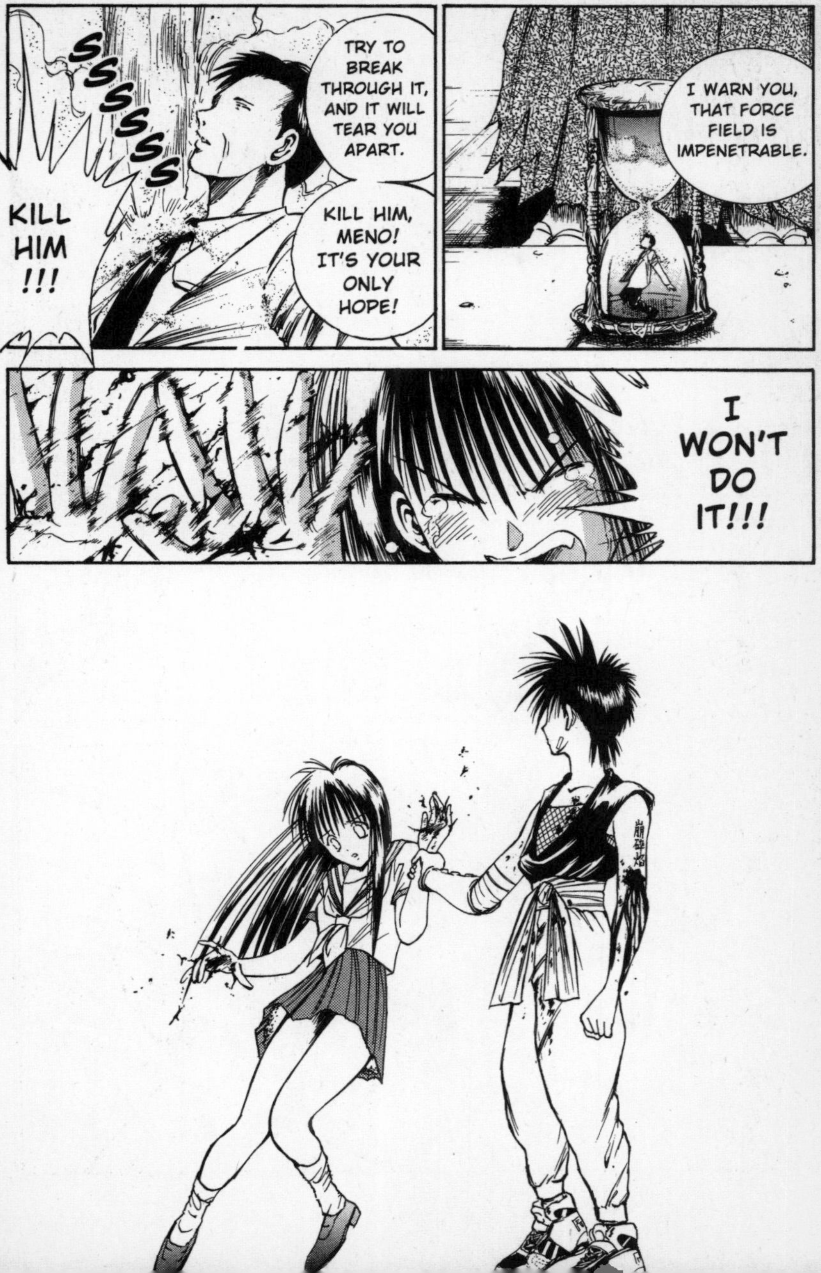
I WARN YOU, THAT FORCE FIELD IS IMPENETRABLE.
TRY TO BREAK THROUGH IT, AND IT WILL TEAR YOU APART.
KILL HIM, MENO! IT'S YOUR ONLY HOPE!
SSSSSS
KILL HIM !!!
I WON'T DO IT!!!

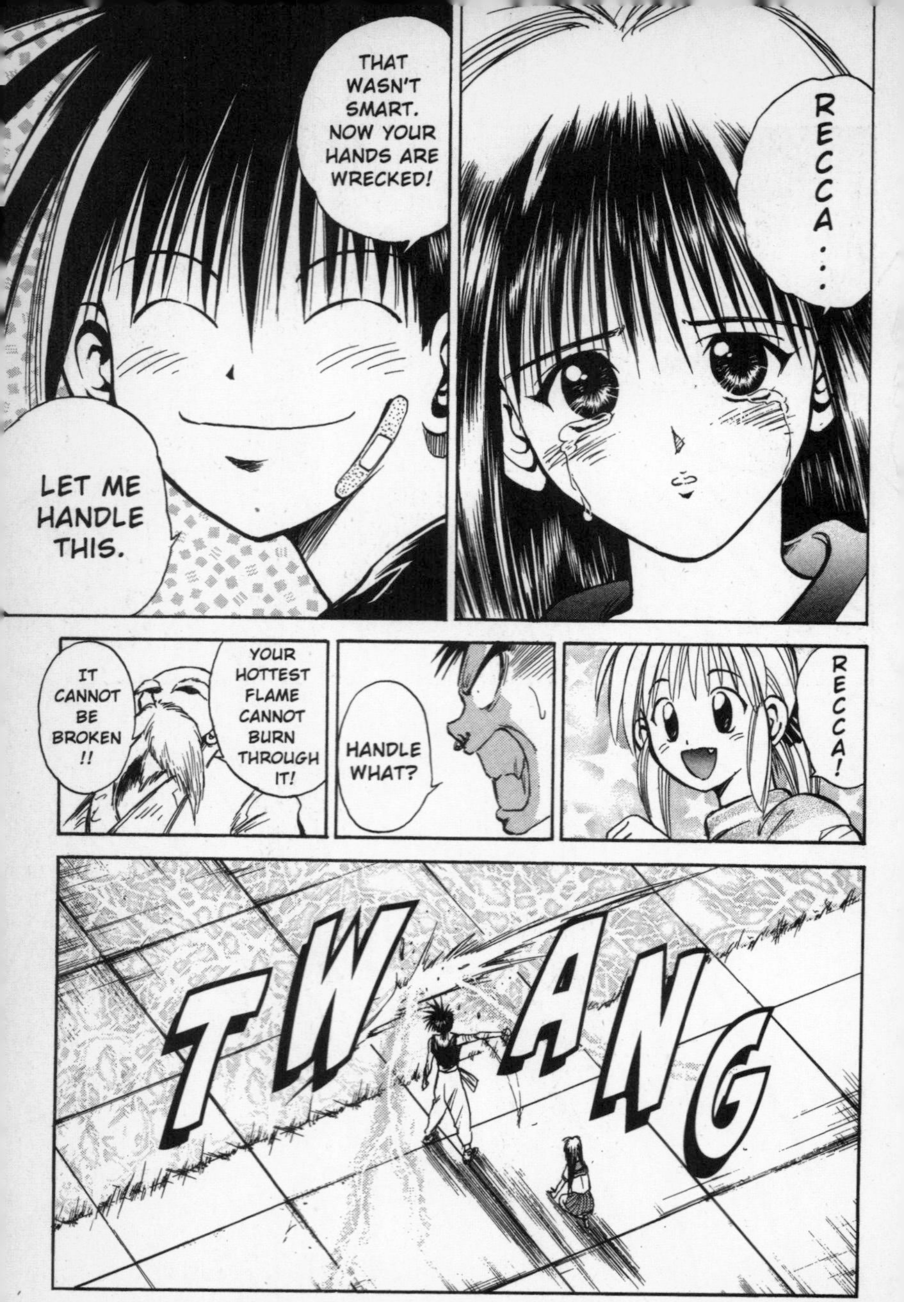
RECCA...
THAT WASN'T SMART. NOW YOUR HANDS ARE WRECKED!
LET ME HANDLE THIS.
RECCA!
HANDLE WHAT?
YOUR HOTTEST FLAME CANNOT BURN THROUGH IT!
IT CANNOT BE BROKEN!!
TWANG

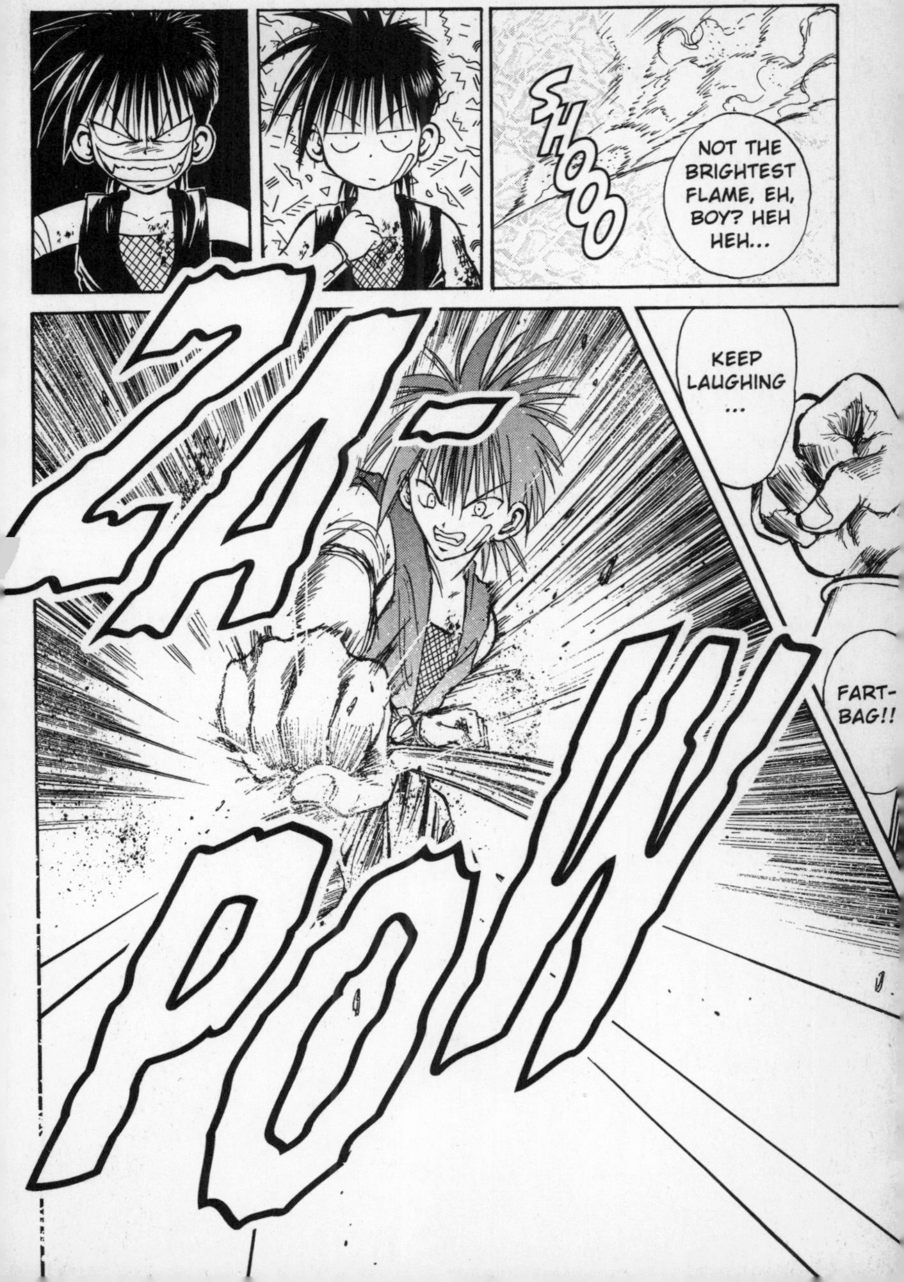
SHOOO
NOT THE BRIGHTEST FLAME, EH, BOY? HEH HEH...
KEEP LAUGHING ...
FART-BAG!!
ZA-POW

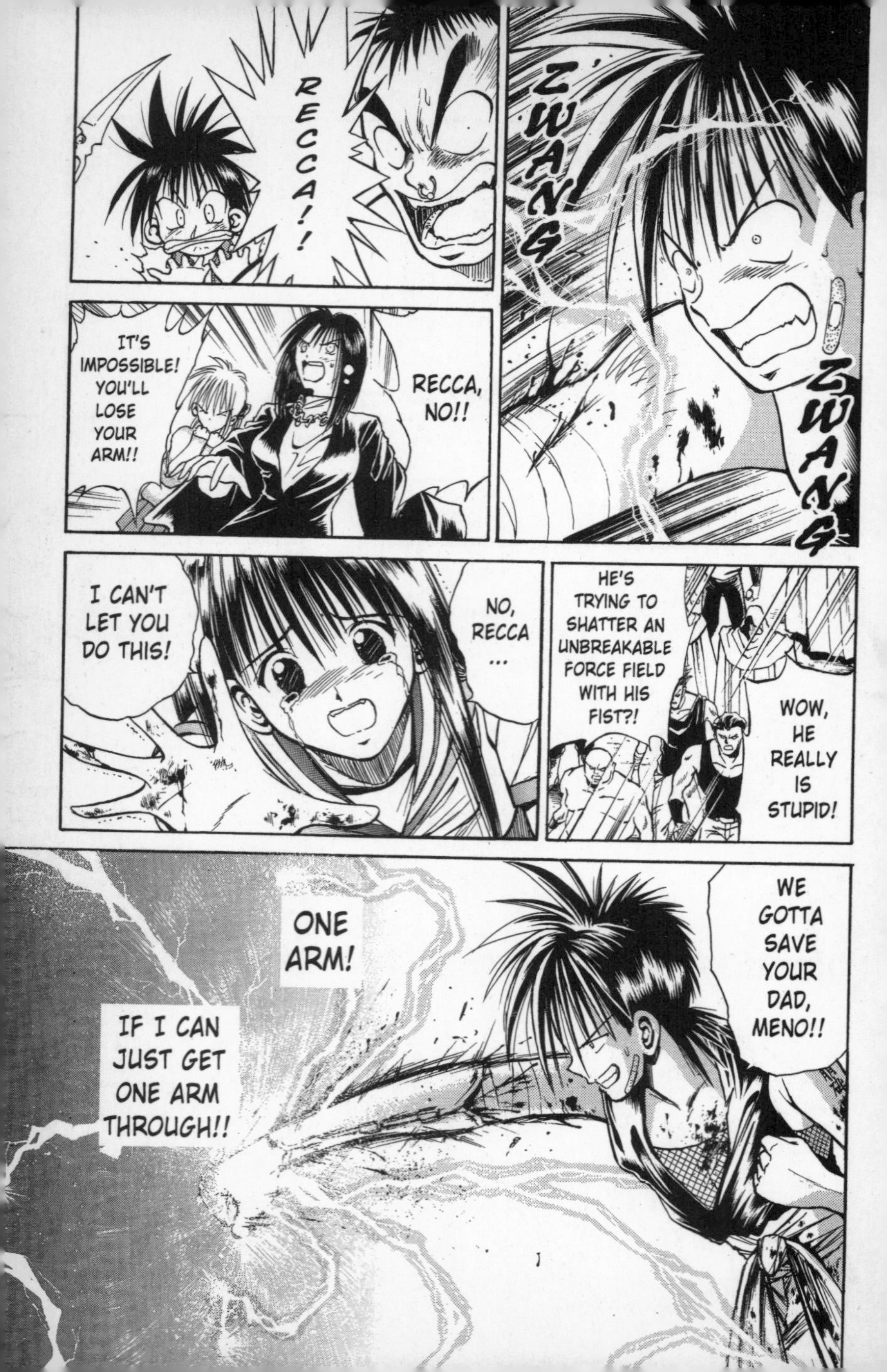
ZWANG
ZWANG
RECCA!!
RECCA, NO!!
IT'S IMPOSSIBLE! YOU'LL LOSE YOUR ARM!!
HE'S TRYING TO SHATTER AN UNBREAKABLE FORCE FIELD WITH HIS FIST?!
WOW, HE REALLY IS STUPID!
NO, RECCA ...
I CAN'T LET YOU DO THIS!
WE GOTTA SAVE YOUR DAD, MENO!!
ONE ARM!
IF I CAN JUST GET ONE ARM THROUGH!!

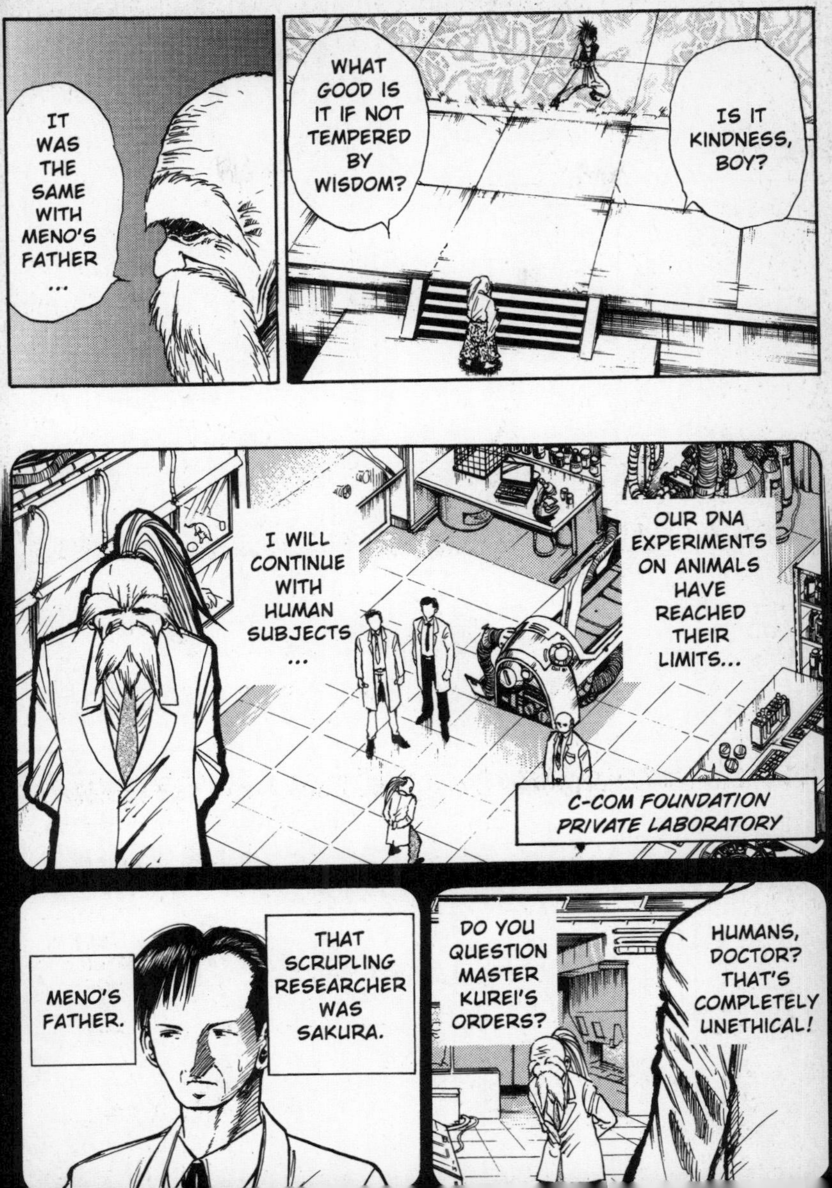
IS IT KINDNESS, BOY?
WHAT GOOD IS IT IF NOT TEMPERED BY WISDOM?
IT WAS THE SAME WITH MENO'S FATHER ...
OUR DNA EXPERIMENTS ON ANIMALS HAVE REACHED THEIR LIMITS...
I WILL CONTINUE WITH HUMAN SUBJECTS ...
C-COM FOUNDATION PRIVATE LABORATORY
HUMANS, DOCTOR? THAT'S COMPLETELY UNETHICAL!
DO YOU QUESTION MASTER KUREI'S ORDERS?
THAT SCRUPLING RESEARCHER WAS SAKURA.
MENO'S FATHER.

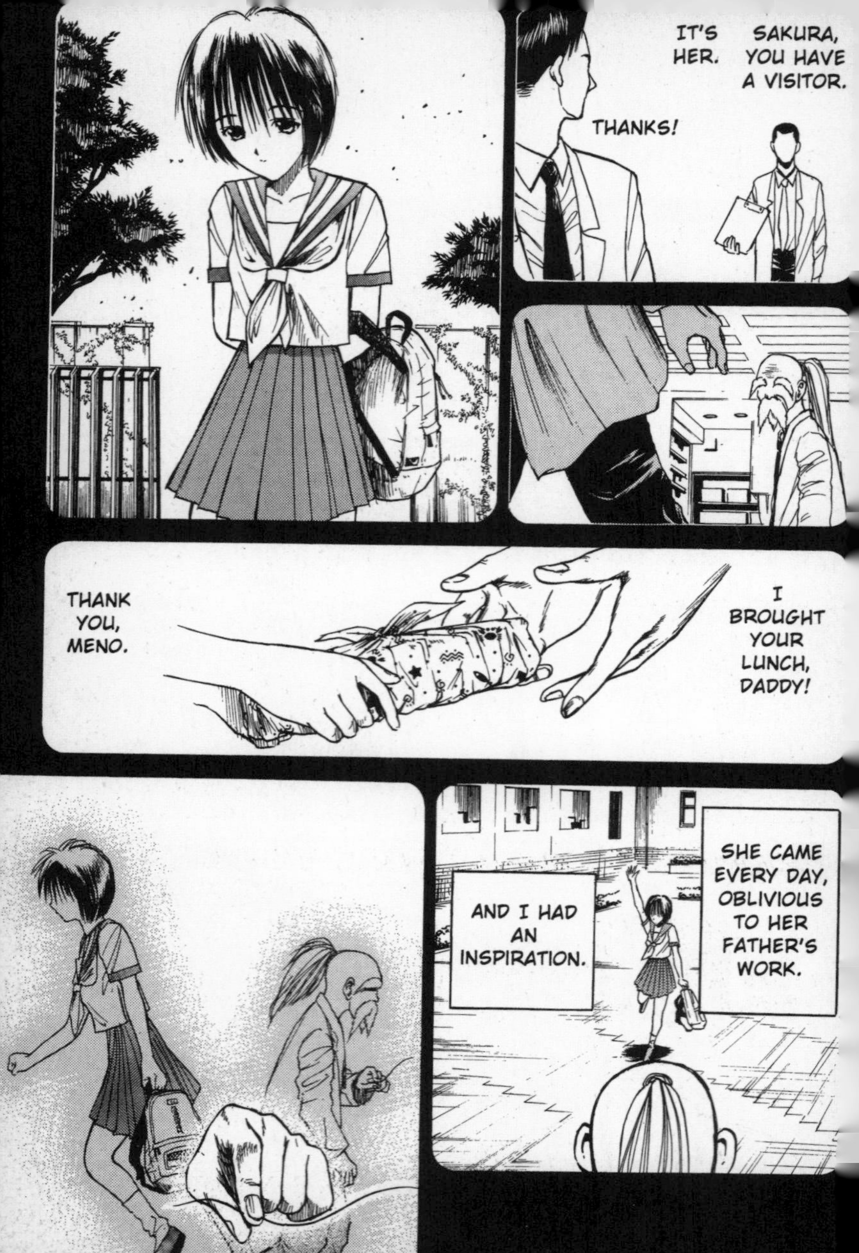
SAKURA, YOU HAVE A VISITOR.
IT'S HER.
THANKS!
I BROUGHT YOUR LUNCH, DADDY!
THANK YOU, MENO.
SHE CAME EVERY DAY, OBLIVIOUS TO HER FATHER'S WORK.
AND I HAD AN INSPIRATION.

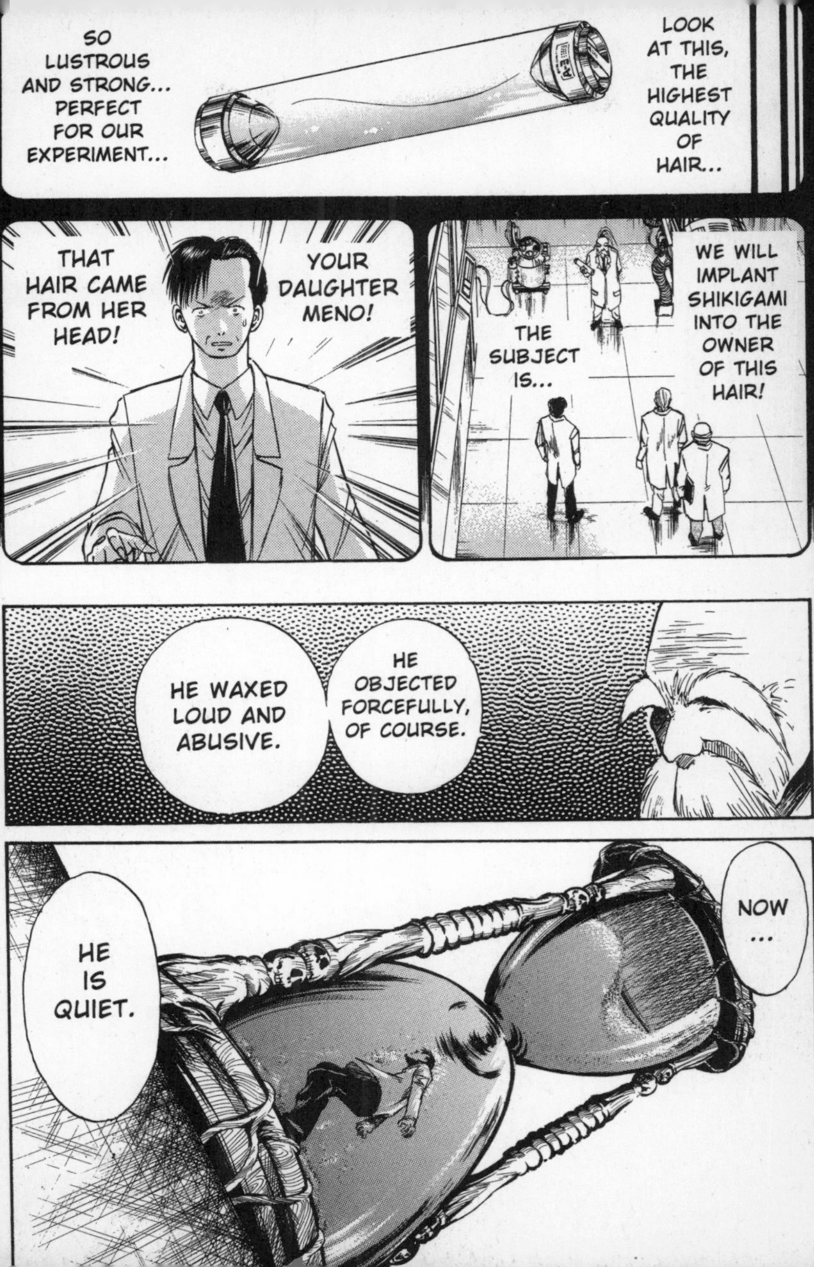

LOOK AT THIS, THE HIGHEST QUALITY OF HAIR...
SO LUSTROUS AND STRONG... PERFECT FOR OUR EXPERIMENT...
WE WILL IMPLANT SHIKIGAMI INTO THE OWNER OF THIS HAIR!
THE SUBJECT IS...
YOUR DAUGHTER MENO!
THAT HAIR CAME FROM HER HEAD!
HE OBJECTED FORCEFULLY, OF COURSE.
HE WAXED LOUD AND ABUSIVE.
NOW...
HE IS QUIET.

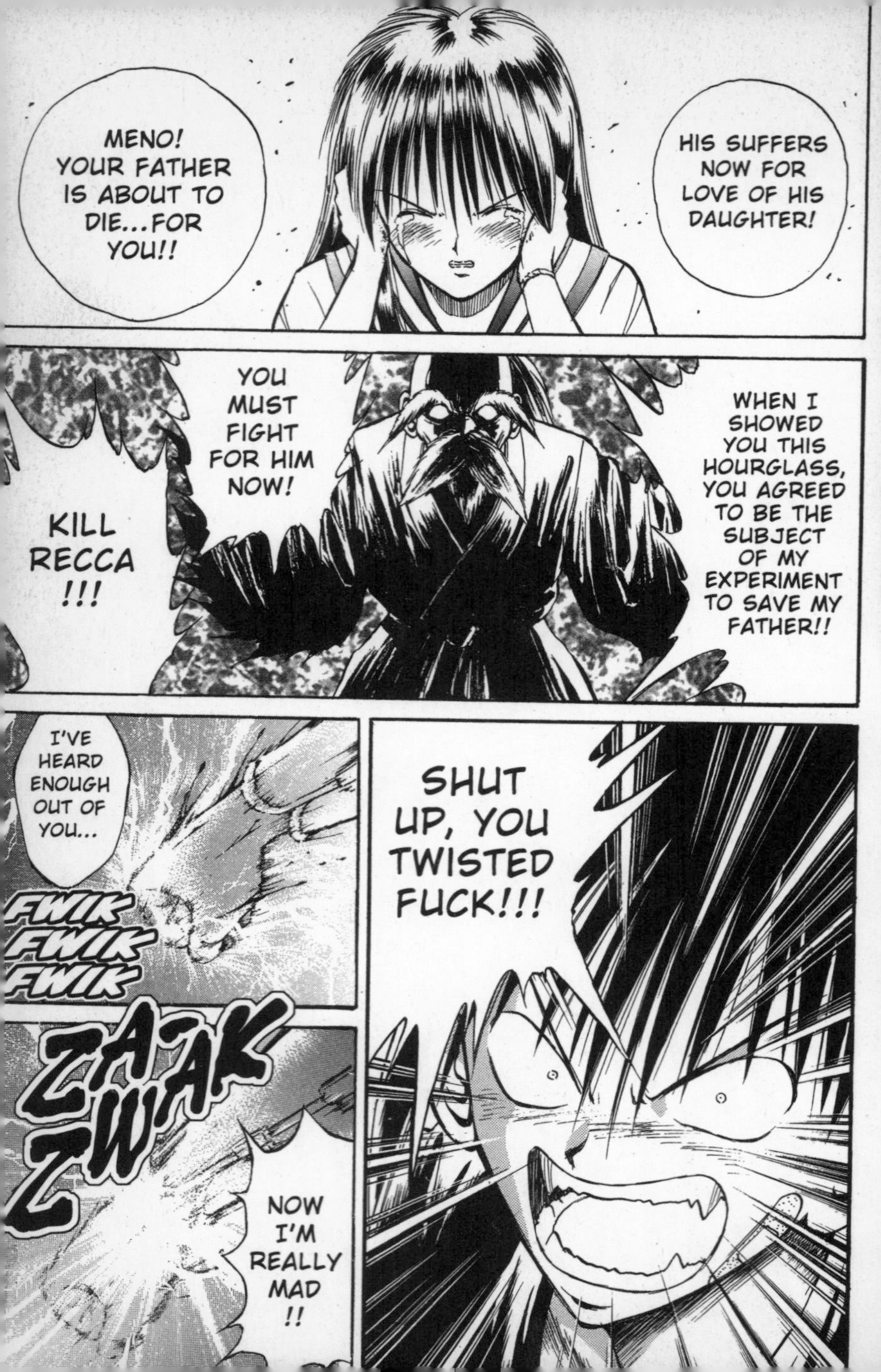
HIS SUFFERS NOW FOR LOVE OF HIS DAUGHTER!
MENO! YOUR FATHER IS ABOUT TO DIE...FOR YOU!!
WHEN I SHOWED YOU THIS HOURGLASS, YOU AGREED TO BE THE SUBJECT OF MY EXPERIMENT TO SAVE MY FATHER!!
YOU MUST FIGHT FOR HIM NOW!
KILL RECCA !!!
SHUT UP, YOU TWISTED FUCK!!!
I'VE HEARD ENOUGH OUT OF YOU...
FWIK FWIK FWIK
ZAAAK
ZWAK
NOW I'M REALLY MAD !!

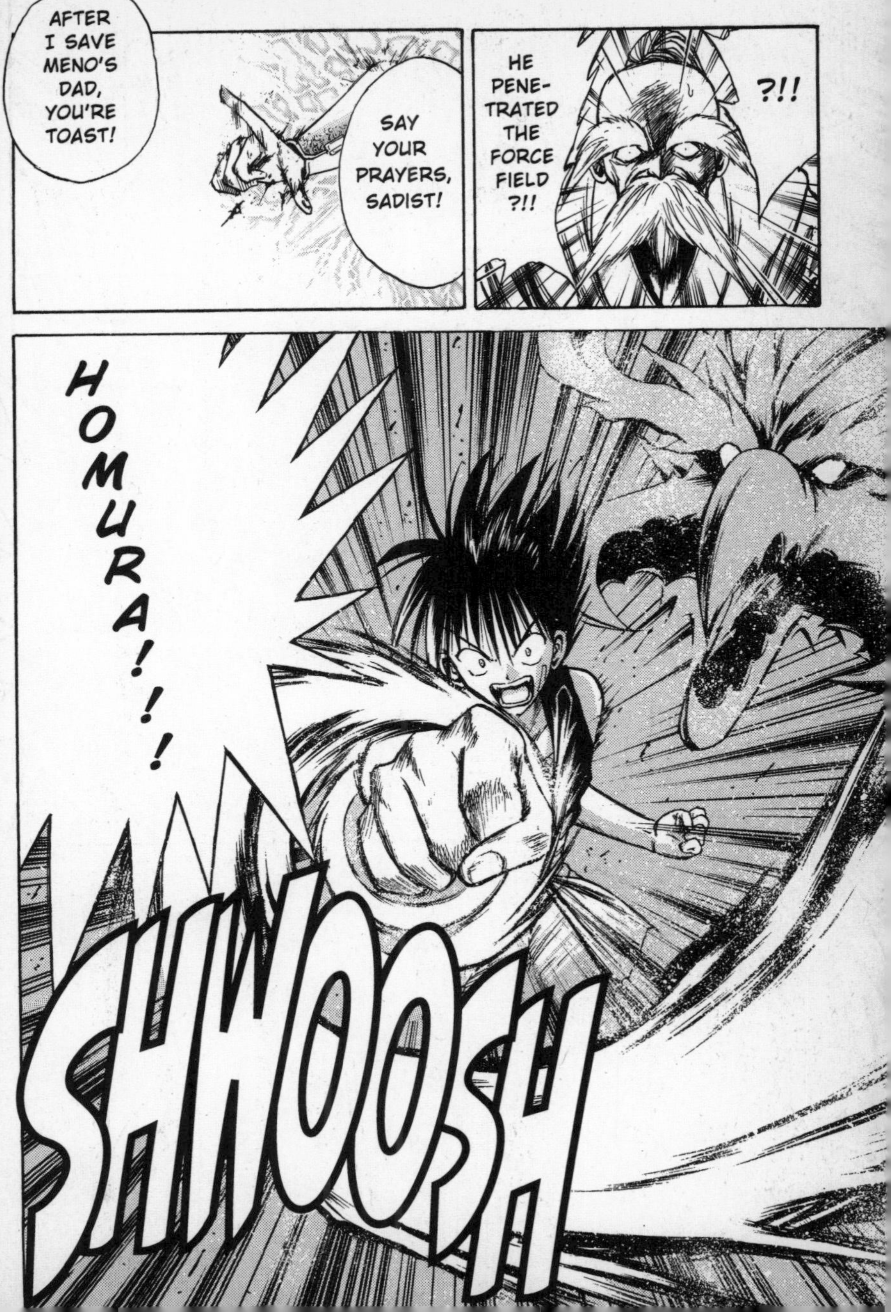
?!!
HE PENE-TRATED THE FORCE FIELD ?!!
SAY YOUR PRAYERS, SADIST!
AFTER I SAVE MENO'S DAD, YOU'RE TOAST!
HOMURA!!!
SHHOOSH

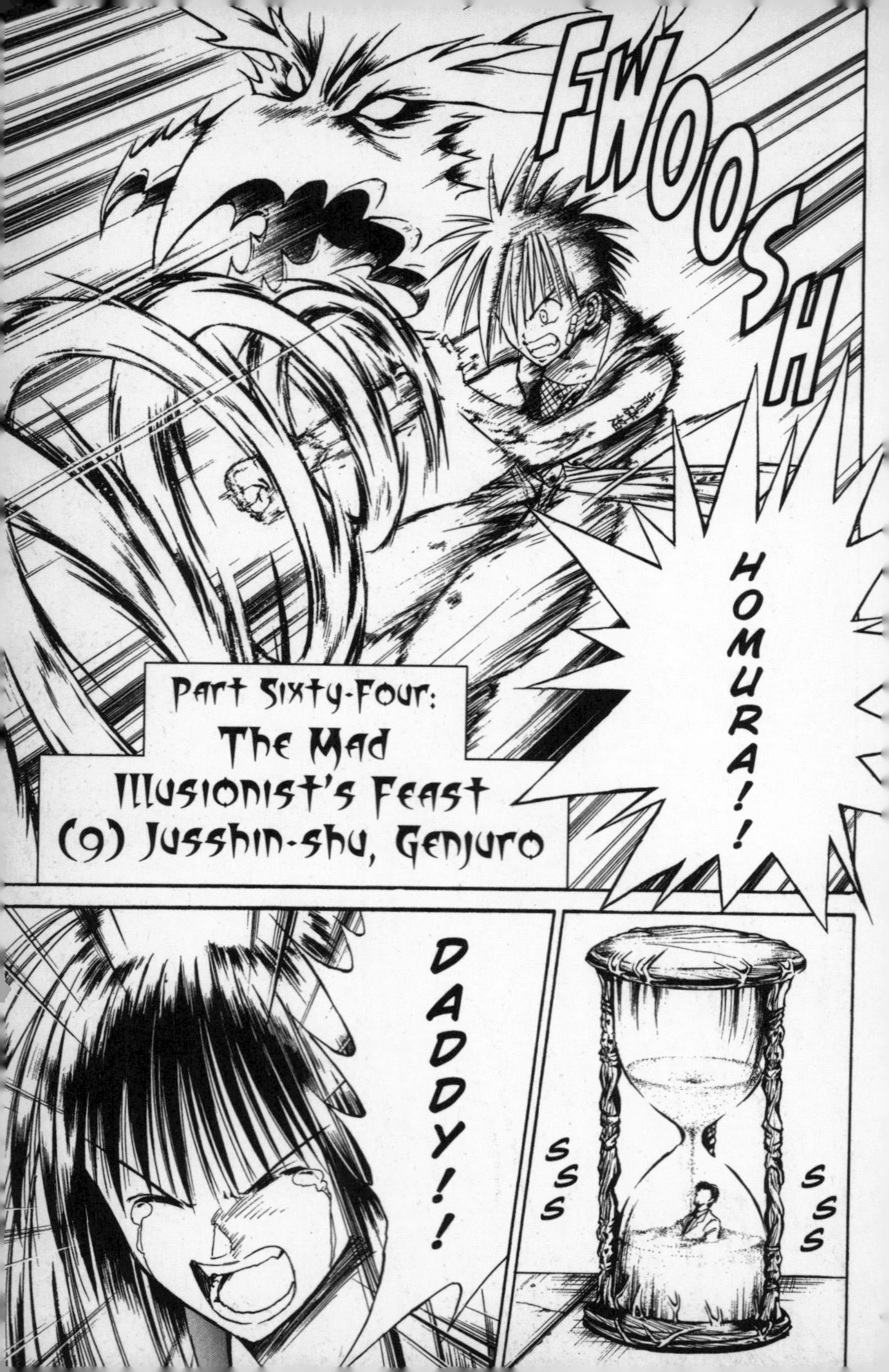
FWOOSH
HOMURA!!
Part Sixty-Four:
The Mad Illusionist's Feast
(9) Jusshin-shu, Genjuro
SSS
SSS
DADDY!!

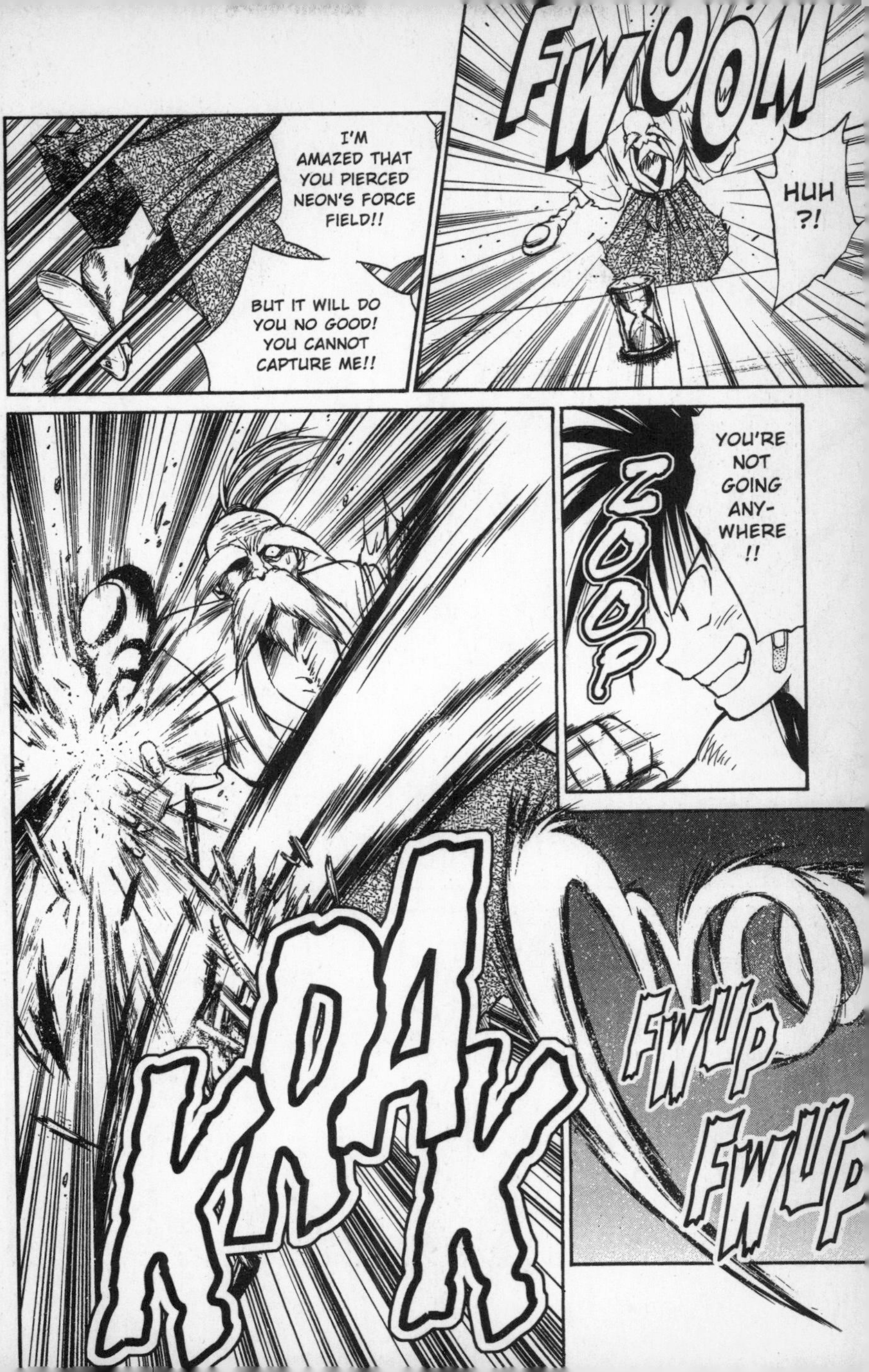
FWOOM
HUH ?!
I'M AMAZED THAT YOU PIERCED NEON'S FORCE FIELD!!
BUT IT WILL DO YOU NO GOOD! YOU CANNOT CAPTURE ME!!
ZOOP
YOU'RE NOT GOING ANY-WHERE !!
FWUP
FWUP
KRAK

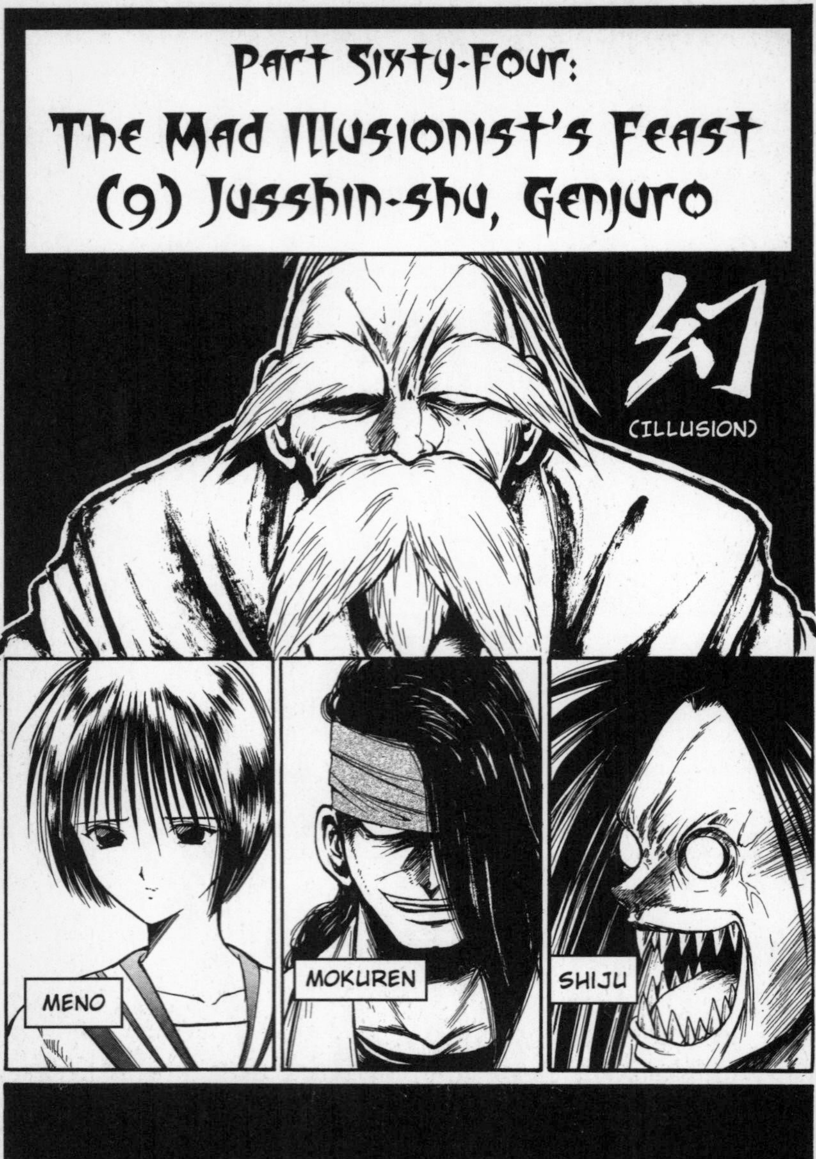
Part Sixty-Four:
The Mad Illusionist's Feast
(9) Jusshin-shu, Genjuro
幻
(ILLUSION)
SHIJU
MOKUREN
MENO

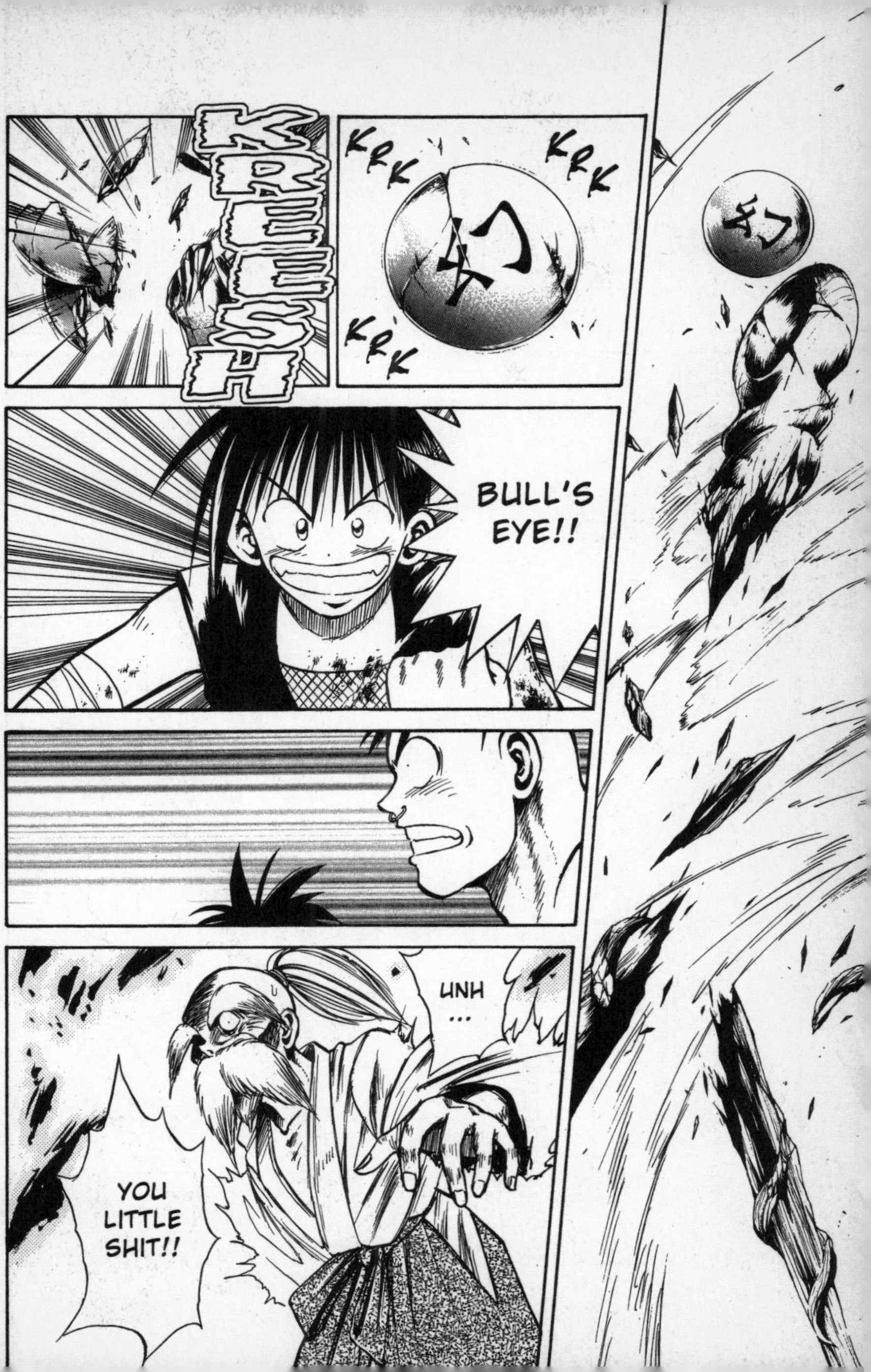
幻
KRK
KRK
KRK
幻
KRESH
BULL'S EYE!!
UNH ...
YOU LITTLE SHIT!!

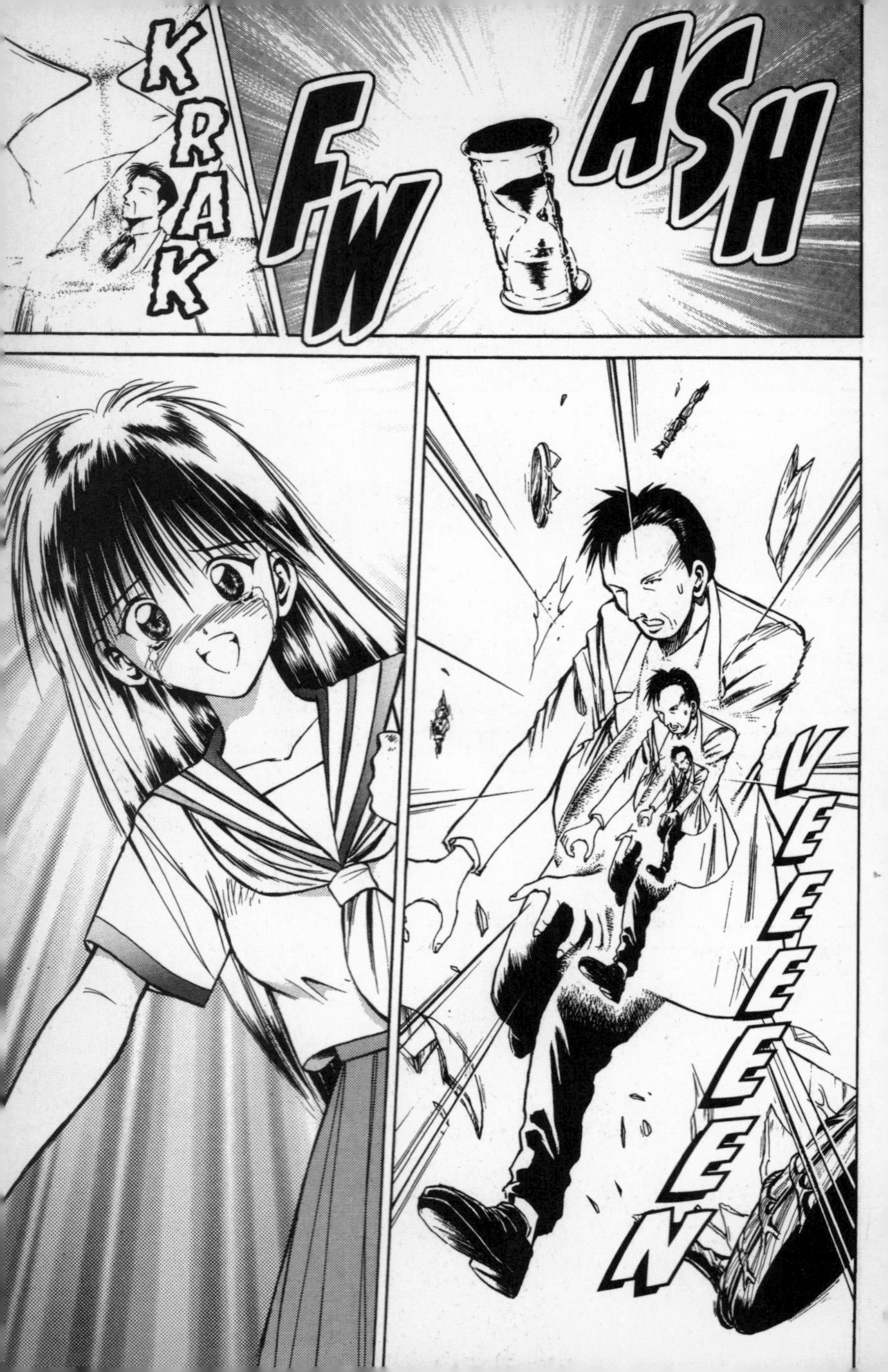
FWASH
KRAK
VEEEEEEN

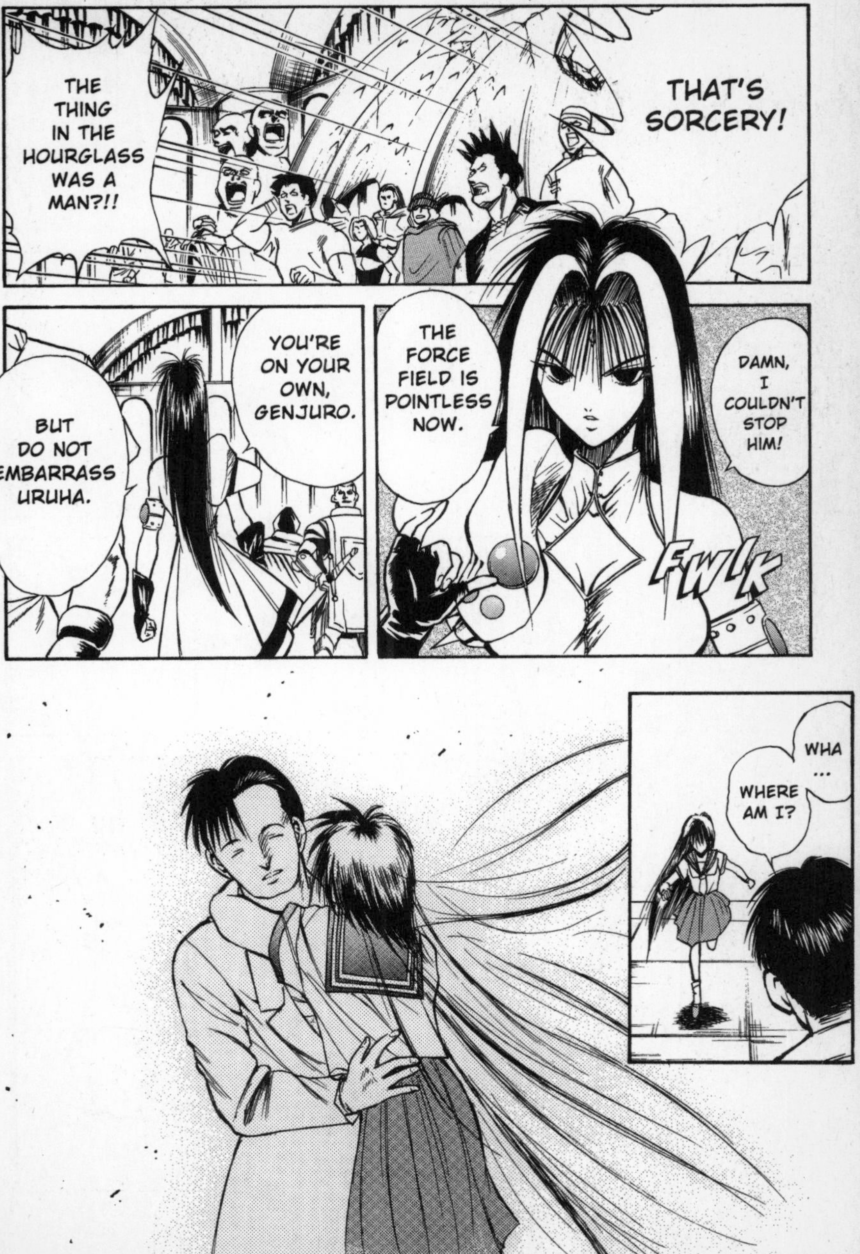
THAT'S SORCERY!
THE THING IN THE HOURGLASS WAS A MAN?!!
DAMN, I COULDN'T STOP HIM!
THE FORCE FIELD IS POINTLESS NOW.
FWIK
YOU'RE ON YOUR OWN, GENJURO.
BUT DO NOT EMBARRASS URUHA.
WHA ... WHERE AM I?

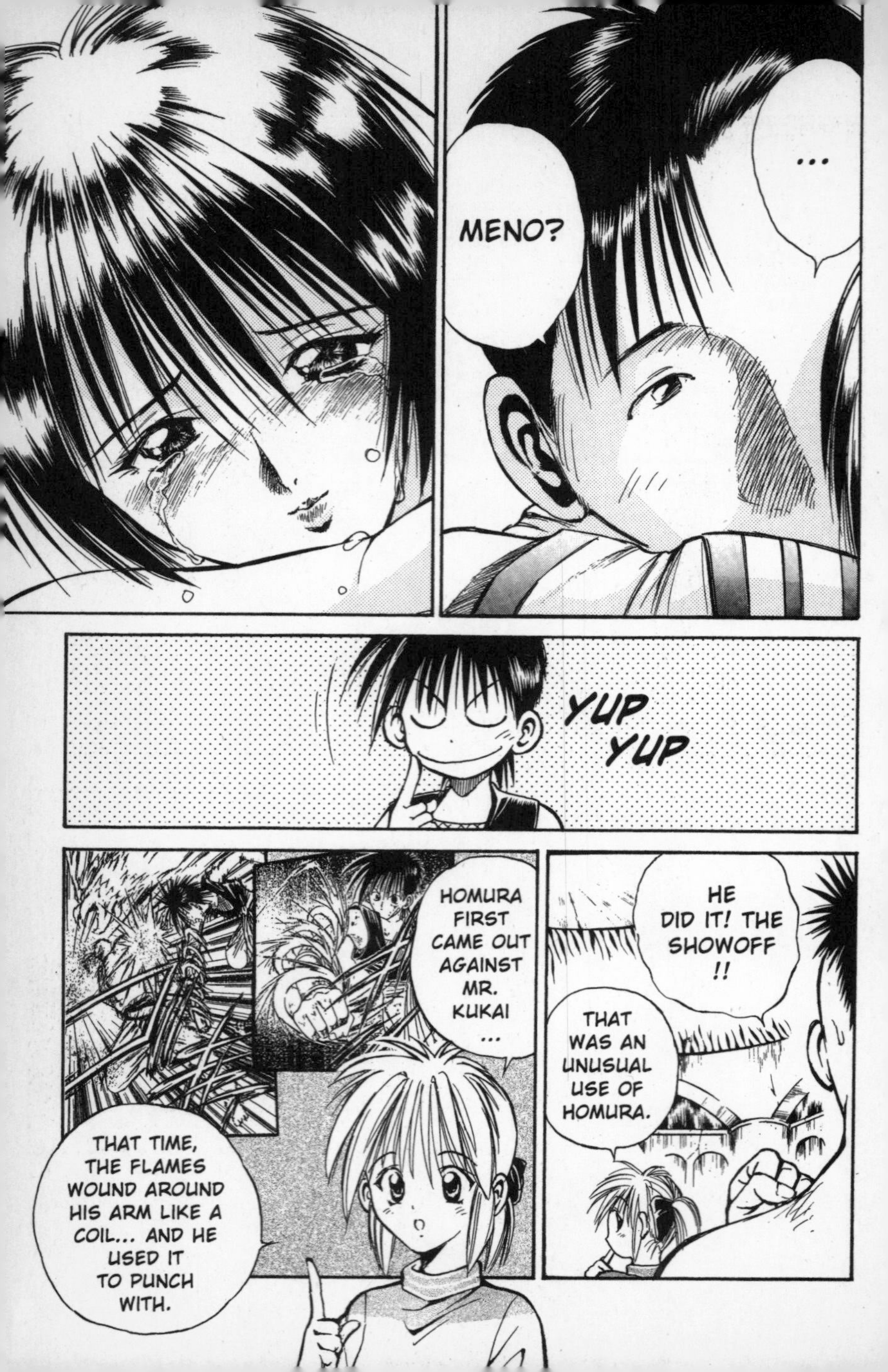

...
MENO?
YUP YUP
HE DID IT! THE SHOWOFF !!
THAT WAS AN UNUSUAL USE OF HOMURA.
HOMURA FIRST CAME OUT AGAINST MR. KUKAI ...
THAT TIME, THE FLAMES WOUND AROUND HIS ARM LIKE A COIL... AND HE USED IT TO PUNCH WITH.

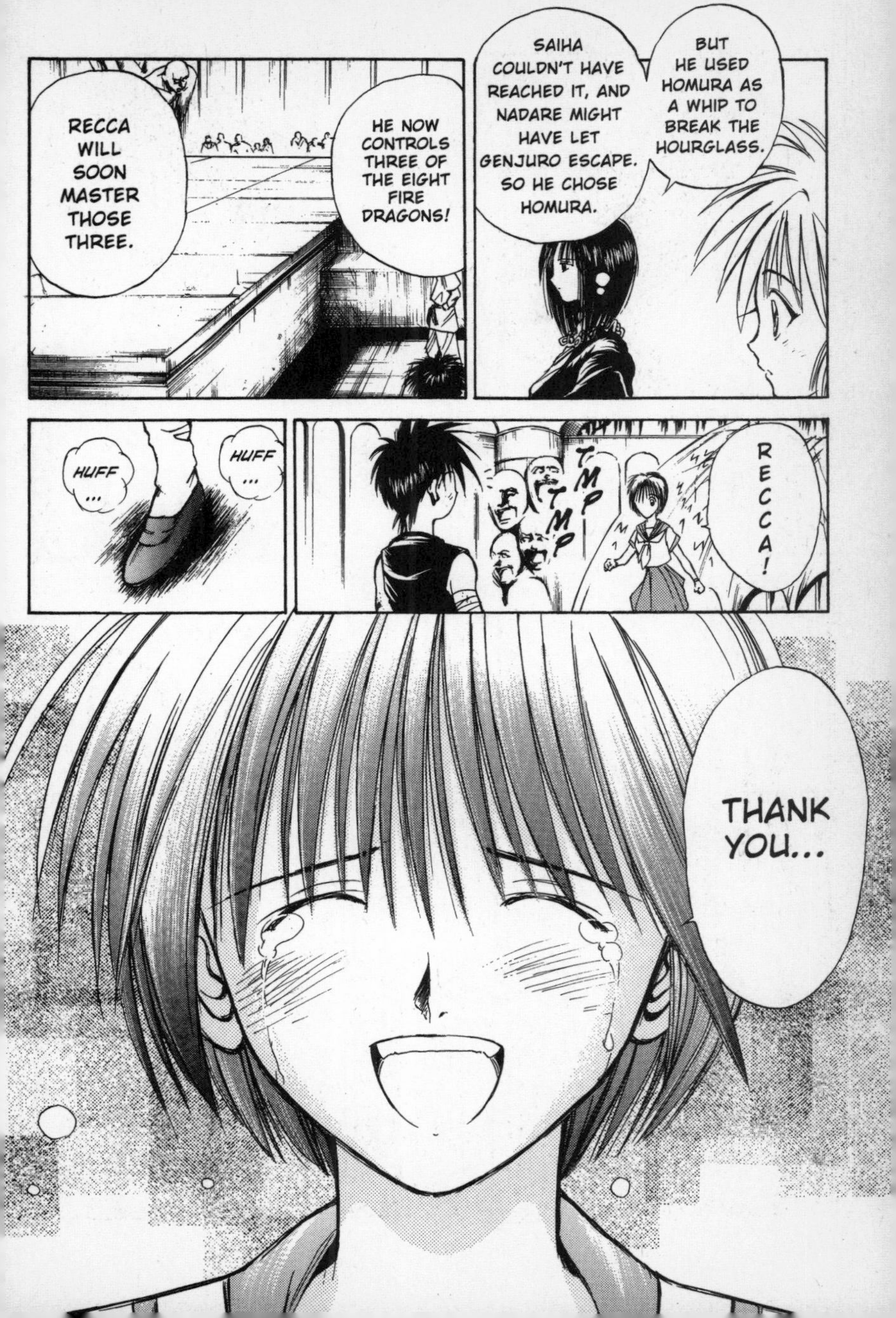
SAIHA COULDN'T HAVE REACHED IT, AND NADARE MIGHT HAVE LET GENJURO ESCAPE. SO HE CHOSE HOMURA.
BUT HE USED HOMURA AS A WHIP TO BREAK THE HOURGLASS.
HE NOW CONTROLS THREE OF THE EIGHT FIRE DRAGONS!
RECCA WILL SOON MASTER THOSE THREE.
RECCA!
TMP TMP
TMP
HUFF...
HUFF...
THANK YOU...

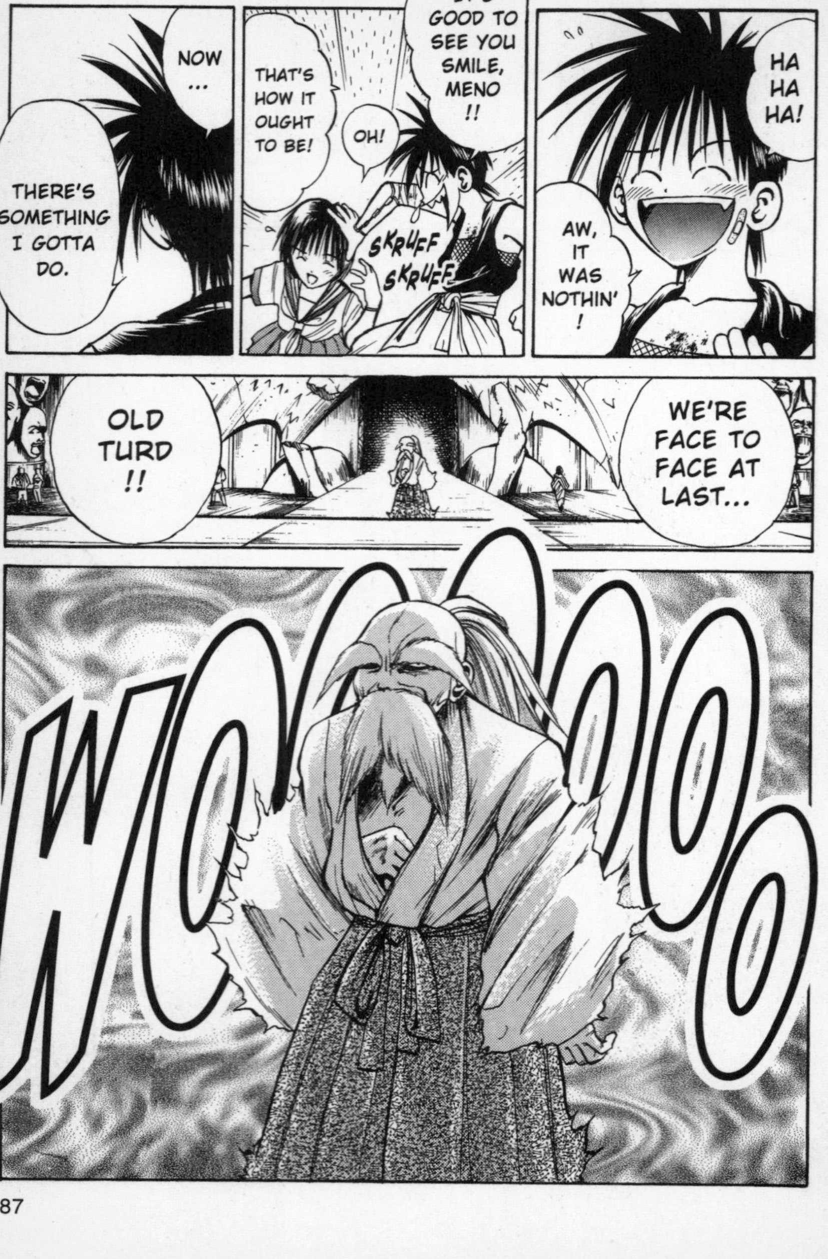
HA HA HA!
AW, IT WAS NOTHIN'!
IT'S GOOD TO SEE YOU SMILE, MENO!!
OH!
THAT'S HOW IT OUGHT TO BE!
SKRUFF SKRUFF
NOW...
THERE'S SOMETHING I GOTTA DO.
WE'RE FACE TO FACE AT LAST...
OLD TURD!!
WOOOOOOOO

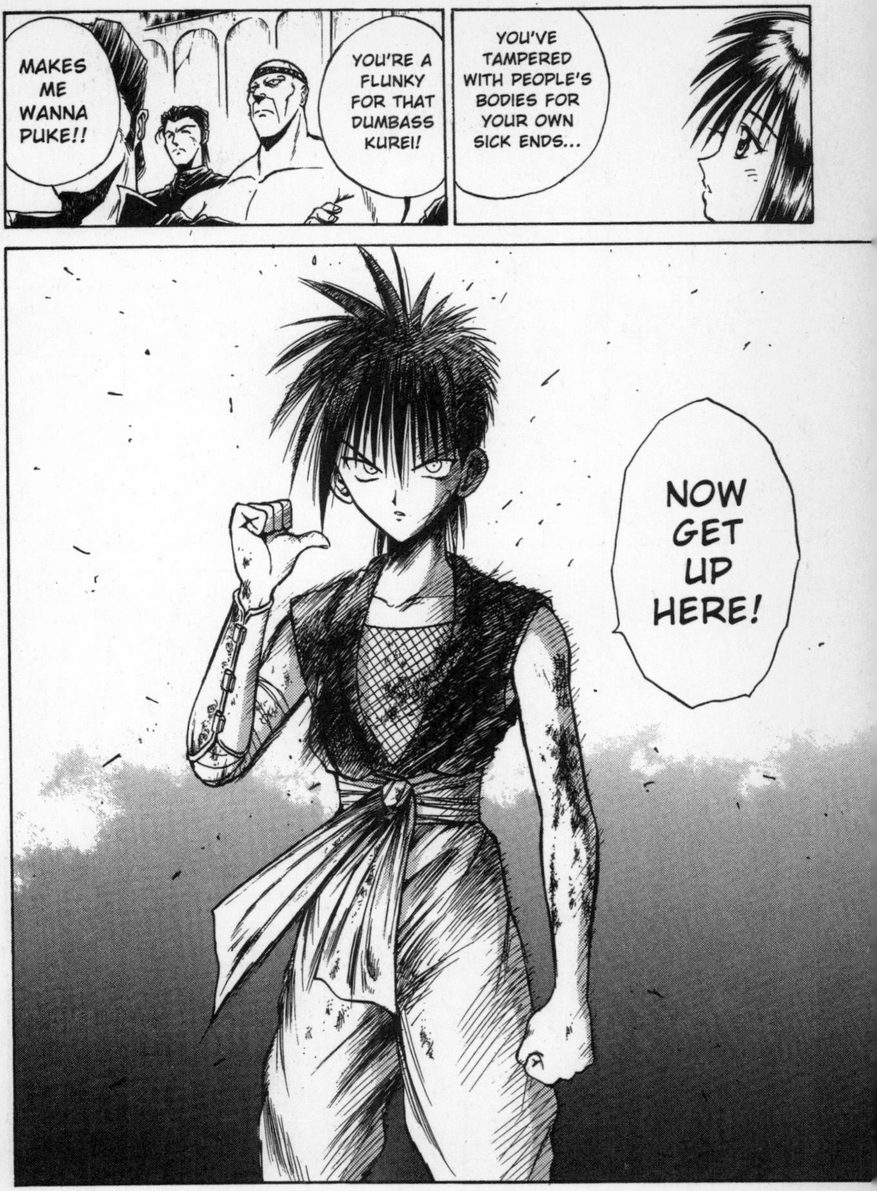
YOU'VE TAMPERED WITH PEOPLE'S BODIES FOR YOUR OWN SICK ENDS...
YOU'RE A FLUNKY FOR THAT DUMBASS KUREI!
MAKES ME WANNA PUKE!!
NOW GET UP HERE!

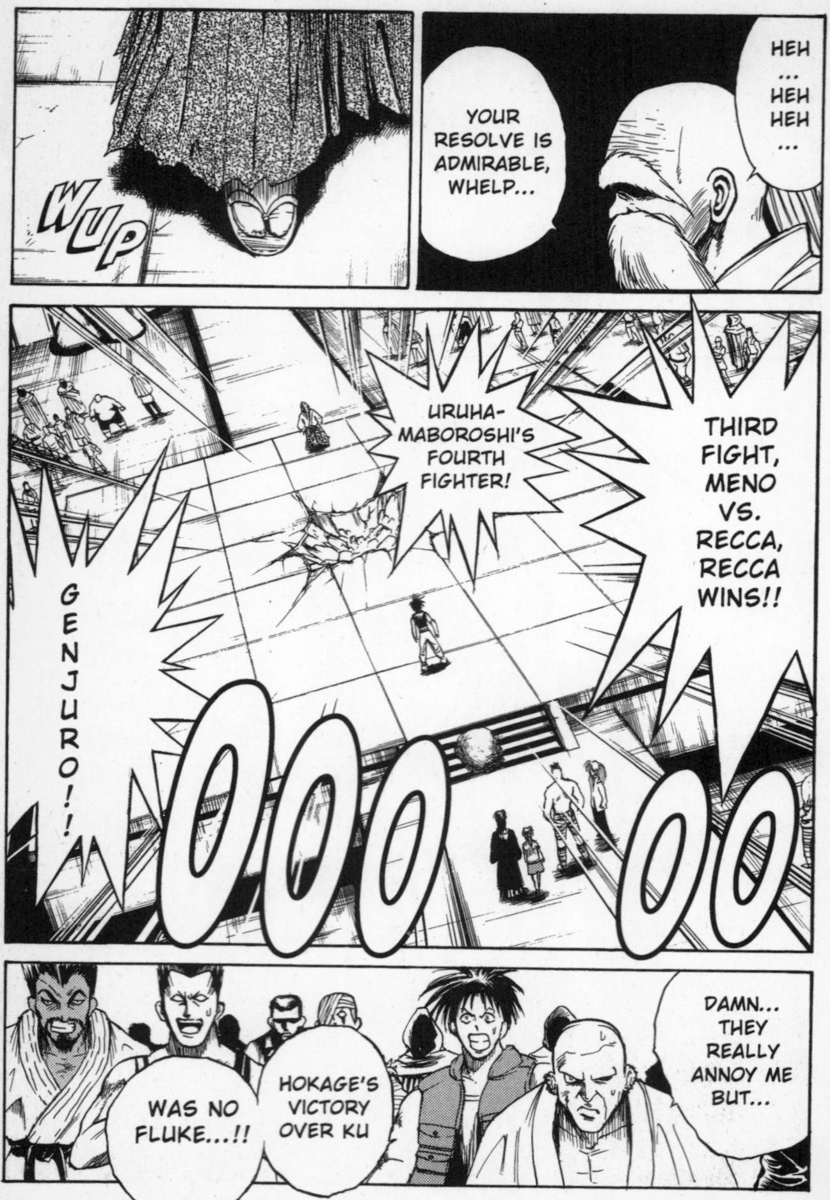

HEH ... HEH HEH ...
YOUR RESOLVE IS ADMIRABLE, WHELP...
WUP
THIRD FIGHT, MENO VS. RECCA, RECCA WINS!!
URUHA-MABOROSHI'S FOURTH FIGHTER!
GENJURO!!
OOOOO
DAMN... THEY REALLY ANNOY ME BUT...
HOKAGE'S VICTORY OVER KU
WAS NO FLUKE...!!

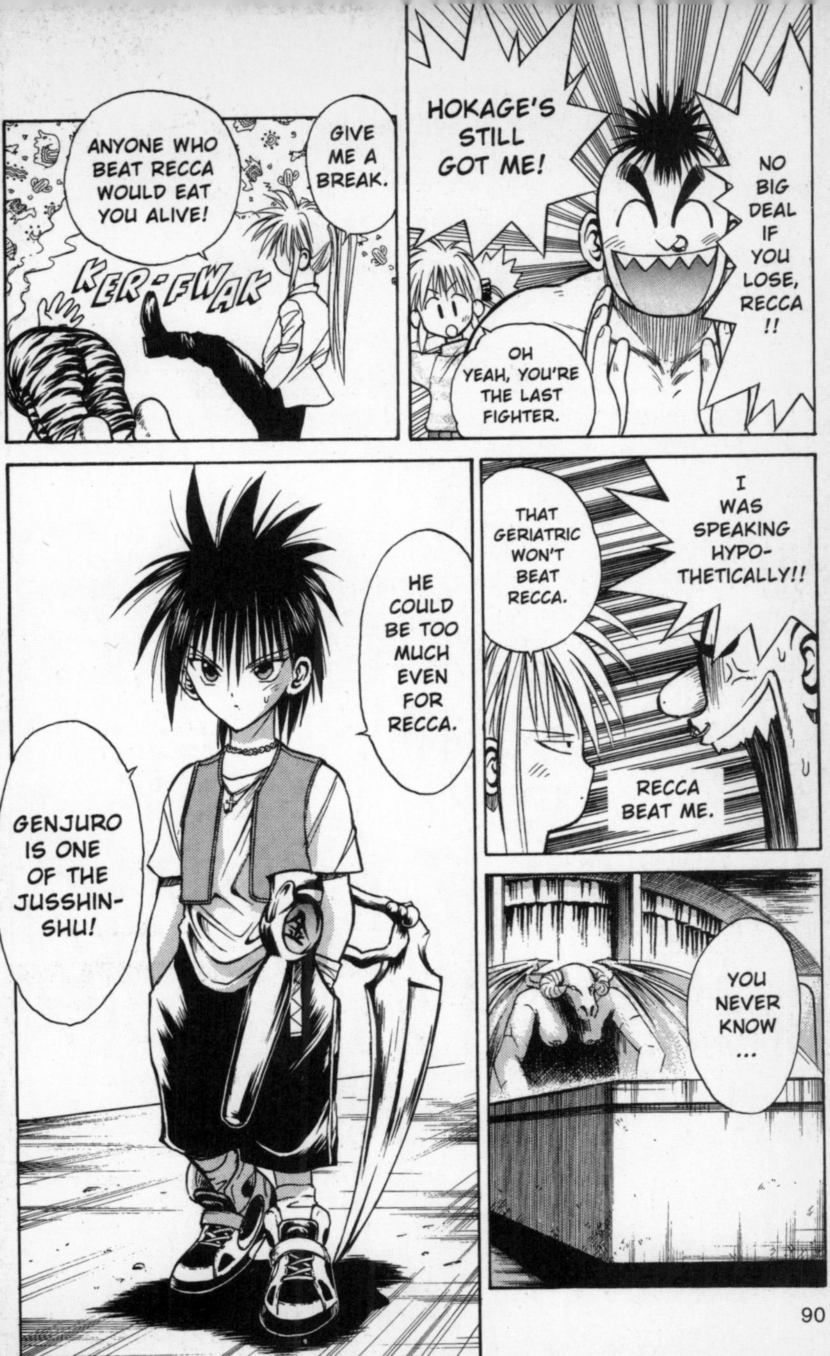

NO BIG DEAL IF YOU LOSE, RECCA!!
HOKAGE'S STILL GOT ME!
OH YEAH, YOU'RE THE LAST FIGHTER.
GIVE ME A BREAK.
ANYONE WHO BEAT RECCA WOULD EAT YOU ALIVE!
KER-FWAK
I WAS SPEAKING HYPO-THETICALLY!!
THAT GERIATRIC WON'T BEAT RECCA.
RECCA BEAT ME.
YOU NEVER KNOW ...
HE COULD BE TOO MUCH EVEN FOR RECCA.
GENJURO IS ONE OF THE JUSSHIN-SHU!

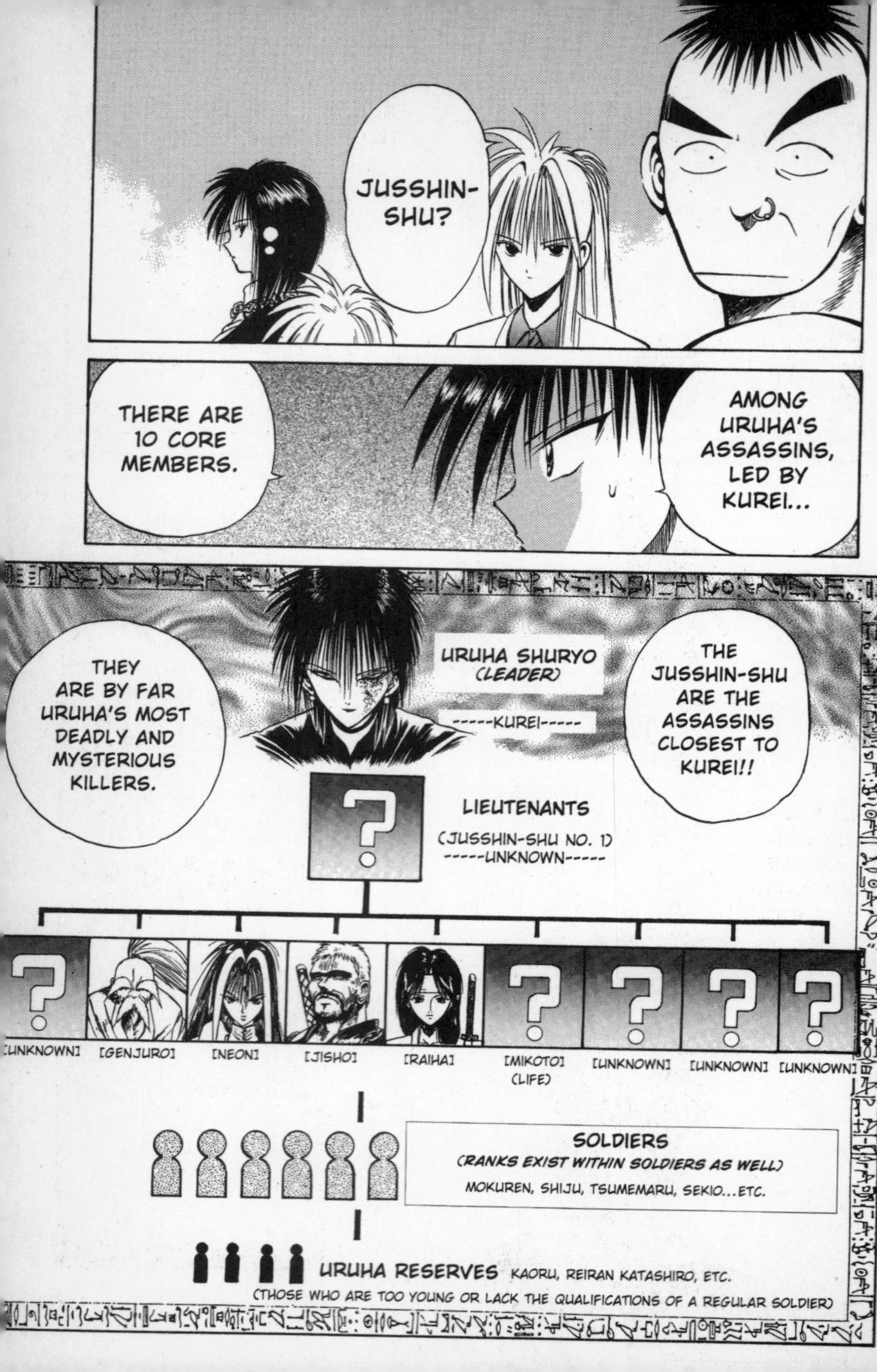
JUSSHIN-SHU?
AMONG URUHA'S ASSASSINS, LED BY KUREI...
THERE ARE 10 CORE MEMBERS.
THE JUSSHIN-SHU ARE THE ASSASSINS CLOSEST TO KUREI!!
THEY ARE BY FAR URUHA'S MOST DEADLY AND MYSTERIOUS KILLERS.
URUHA SHURYO (LEADER)
-----KUREI-----
LIEUTENANTS
(JUSSHIN-SHU NO. 1)
-----UNKNOWN-----
[UNKNOWN]
[GENJURO]
[NEON]
[JISHO]
[RAIHA]
[MIKOTO] (LIFE)
[UNKNOWN]
[UNKNOWN]
[UNKNOWN]
SOLDIERS
(RANKS EXIST WITHIN SOLDIERS AS WELL)
MOKUREN, SHIJU, TSUMEMARU, SEKIO...ETC.
URUHA RESERVES KAORU, REIRAN KATASHIRO, ETC.
(THOSE WHO ARE TOO YOUNG OR LACK THE QUALIFICATIONS OF A REGULAR SOLDIER)

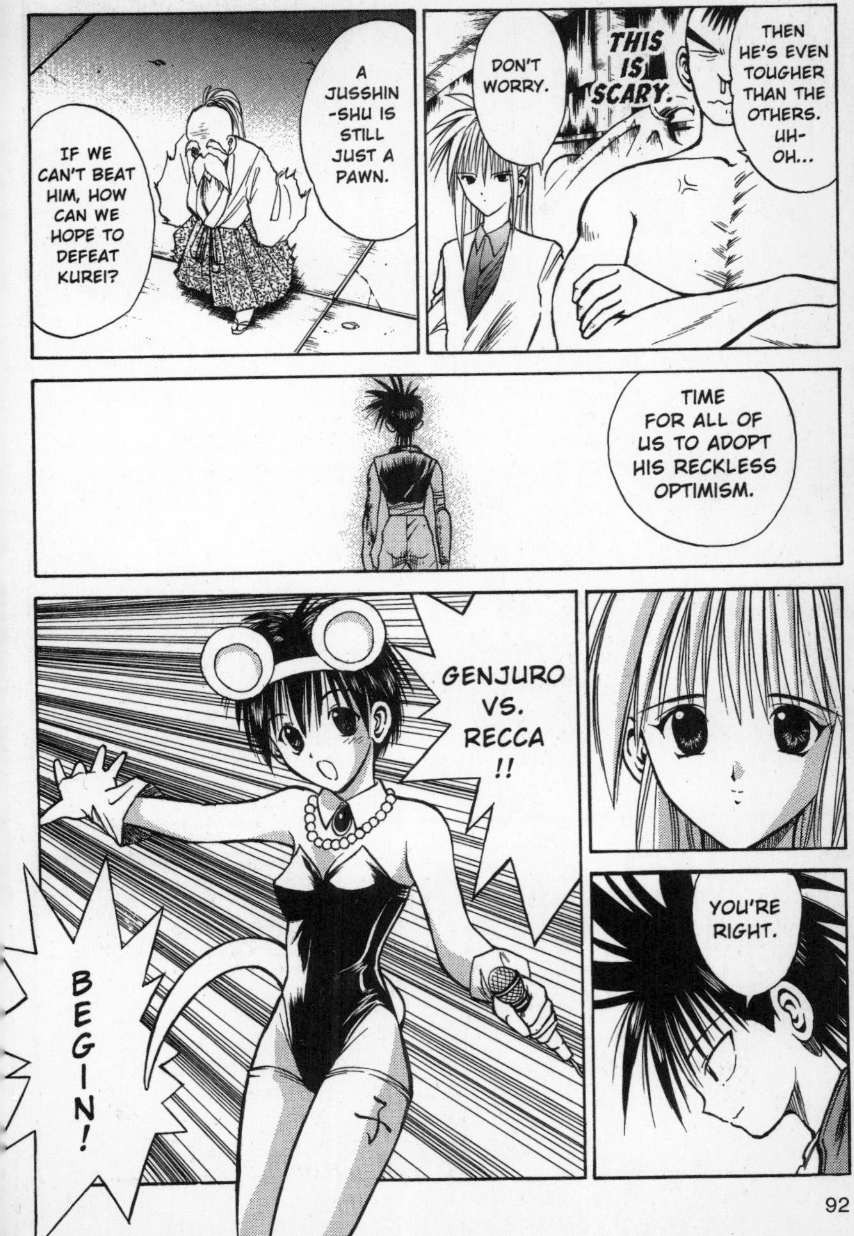
THEN HE'S EVEN TOUGHER THAN THE OTHERS. UH-OH...
THIS IS SCARY.
DON'T WORRY.
A JUSSHIN-SHU IS STILL JUST A PAWN.
IF WE CAN'T BEAT HIM, HOW CAN WE HOPE TO DEFEAT KUREI?
TIME FOR ALL OF US TO ADOPT HIS RECKLESS OPTIMISM.
YOU'RE RIGHT.
GENJURO VS. RECCA !!
BEGIN!

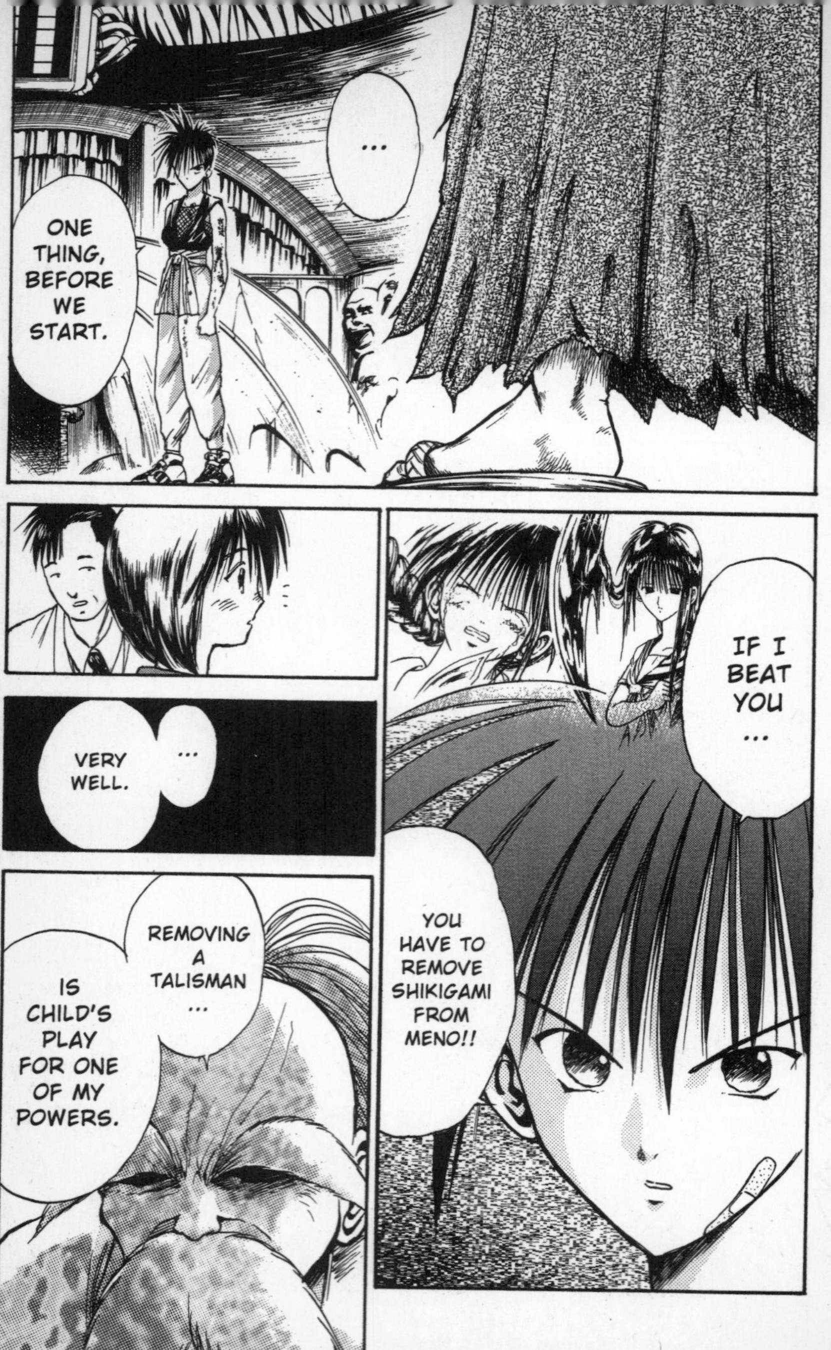
...
ONE THING, BEFORE WE START.
IF I BEAT YOU ...
YOU HAVE TO REMOVE SHIKIGAMI FROM MENO!!
...
VERY WELL.
REMOVING A TALISMAN ...
IS CHILD'S PLAY FOR ONE OF MY POWERS.

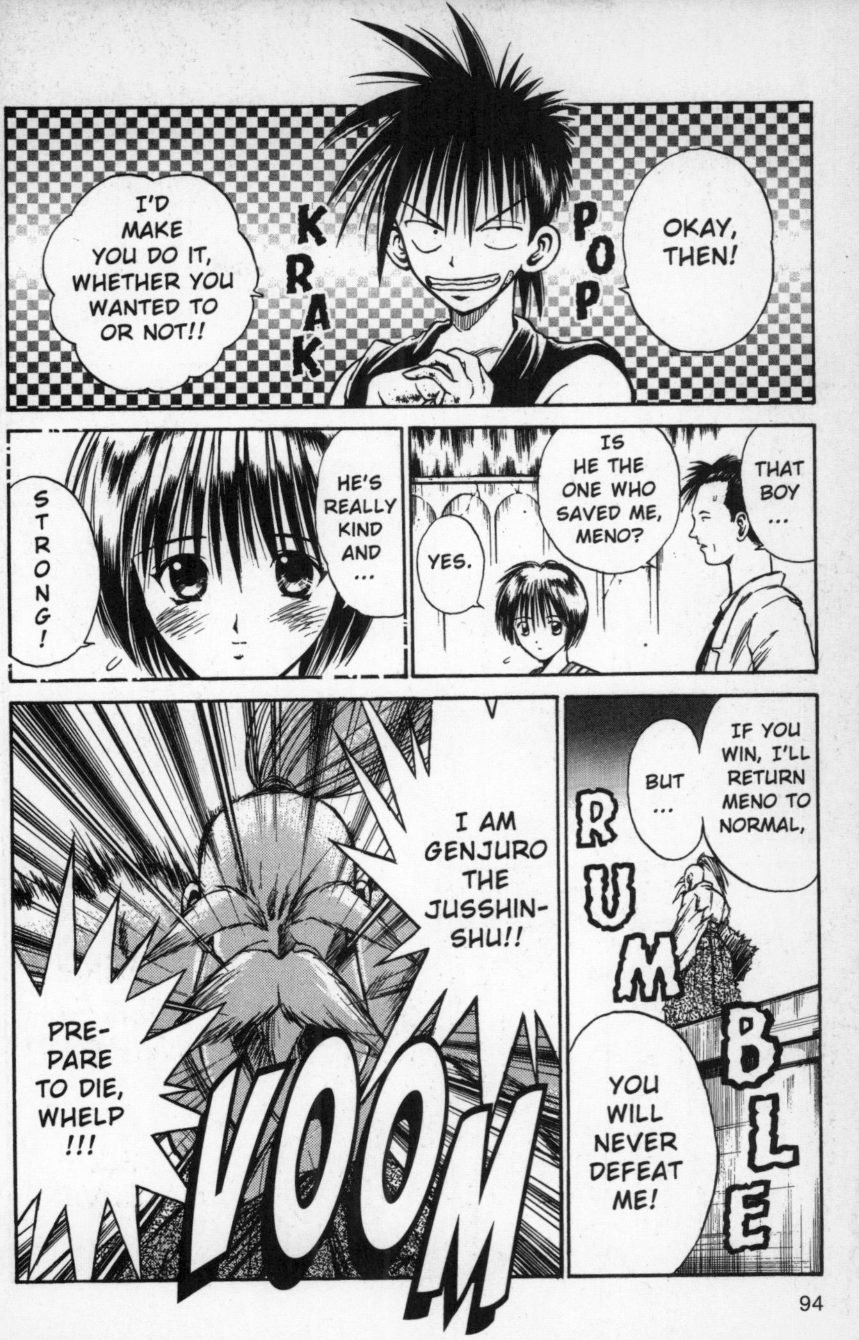
OKAY, THEN!
POP
KRAK
I'D MAKE YOU DO IT, WHETHER YOU WANTED TO OR NOT!!
THAT BOY ...
IS HE THE ONE WHO SAVED ME, MENO?
YES.
HE'S REALLY KIND AND ...
STRONG!
IF YOU WIN, I'LL RETURN MENO TO NORMAL,
BUT ...
RUMBLE
YOU WILL NEVER DEFEAT ME!
I AM GENJURO THE JUSSHIN-SHU!!
PRE-PARE TO DIE, WHELP!!!
VOOM

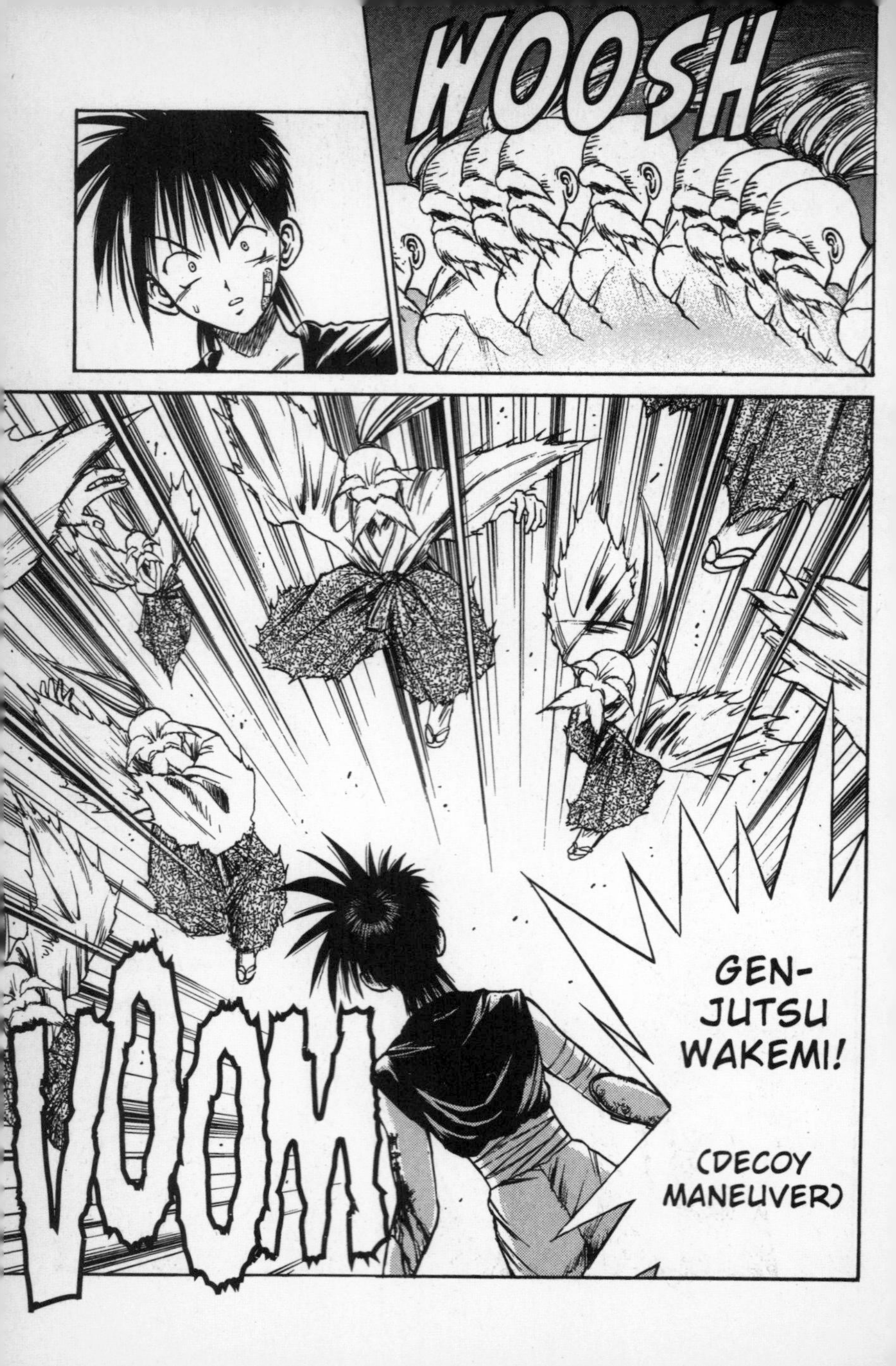
WOOSH
GEN-JUTSU WAKEMI!
(DECOY MANEUVER)
VOOM

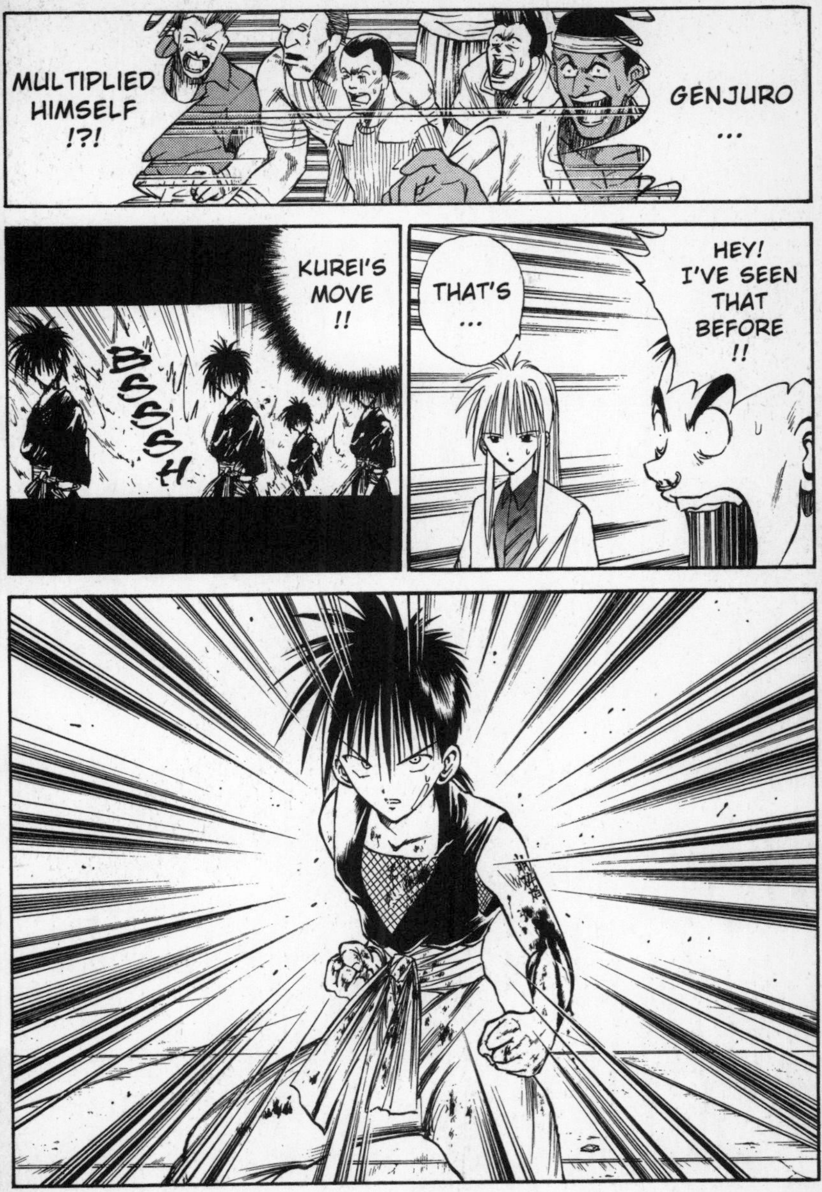
GENJURO ...
MULTIPLIED HIMSELF !?!
HEY! I'VE SEEN THAT BEFORE !!
THAT'S ...
KUREI'S MOVE !!
BSSSH

# Part Sixty-Five:
# The Mad Illusionist's Feast (10) Ambition

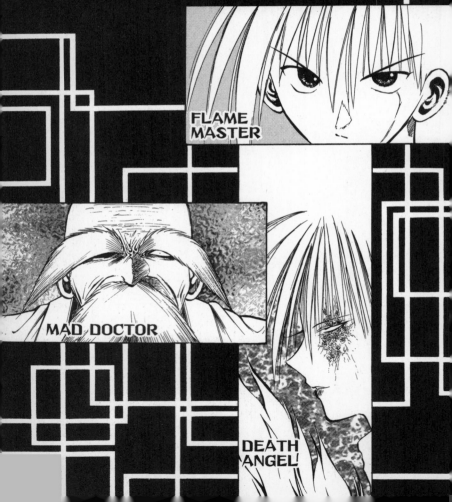

FLAME MASTER

MAD DOCTOR

DEATH ANGEL

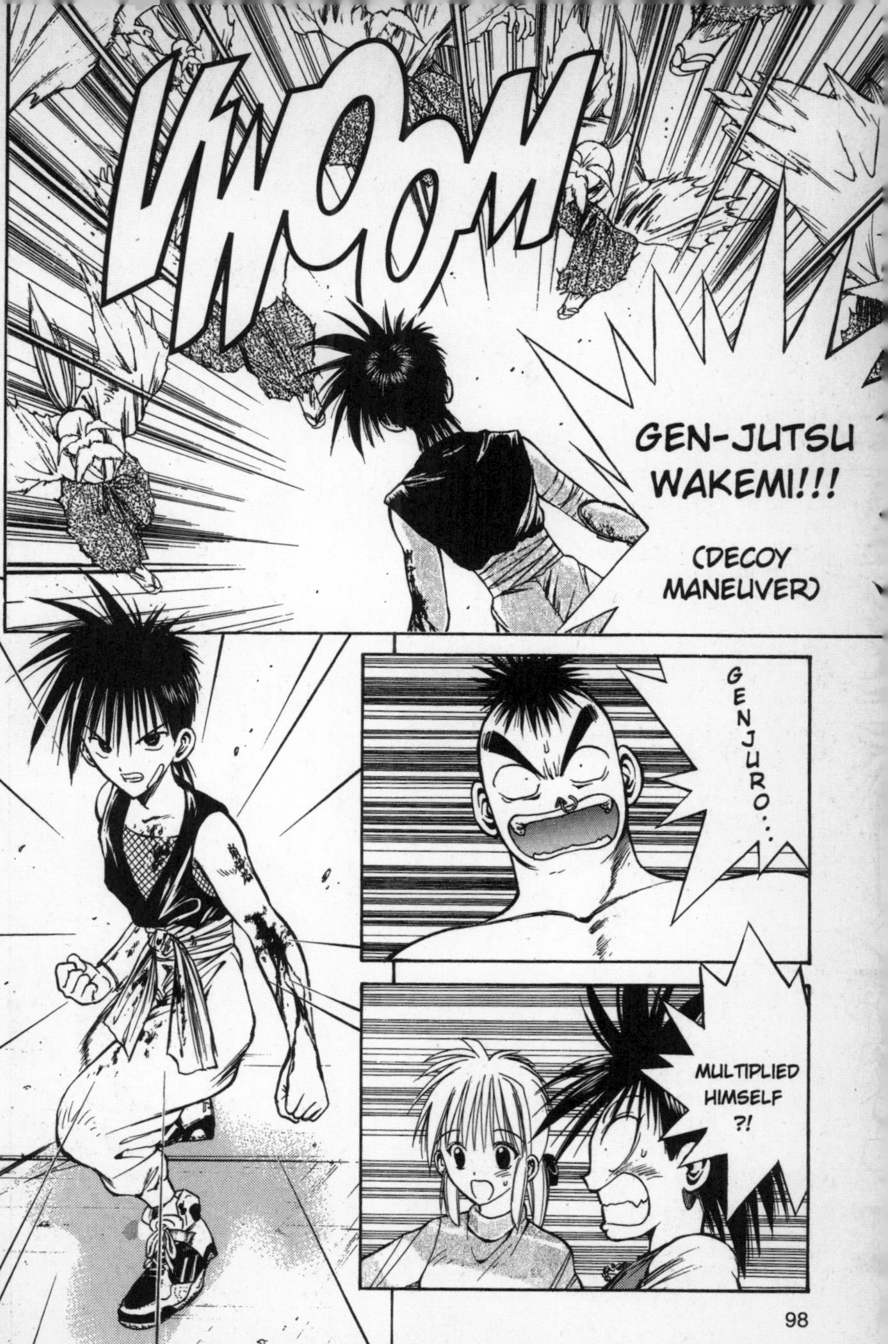
WHOOM
GEN-JUTSU WAKEMI!!!
(DECOY MANEUVER)
GENJURO...
MULTIPLIED HIMSELF ?!

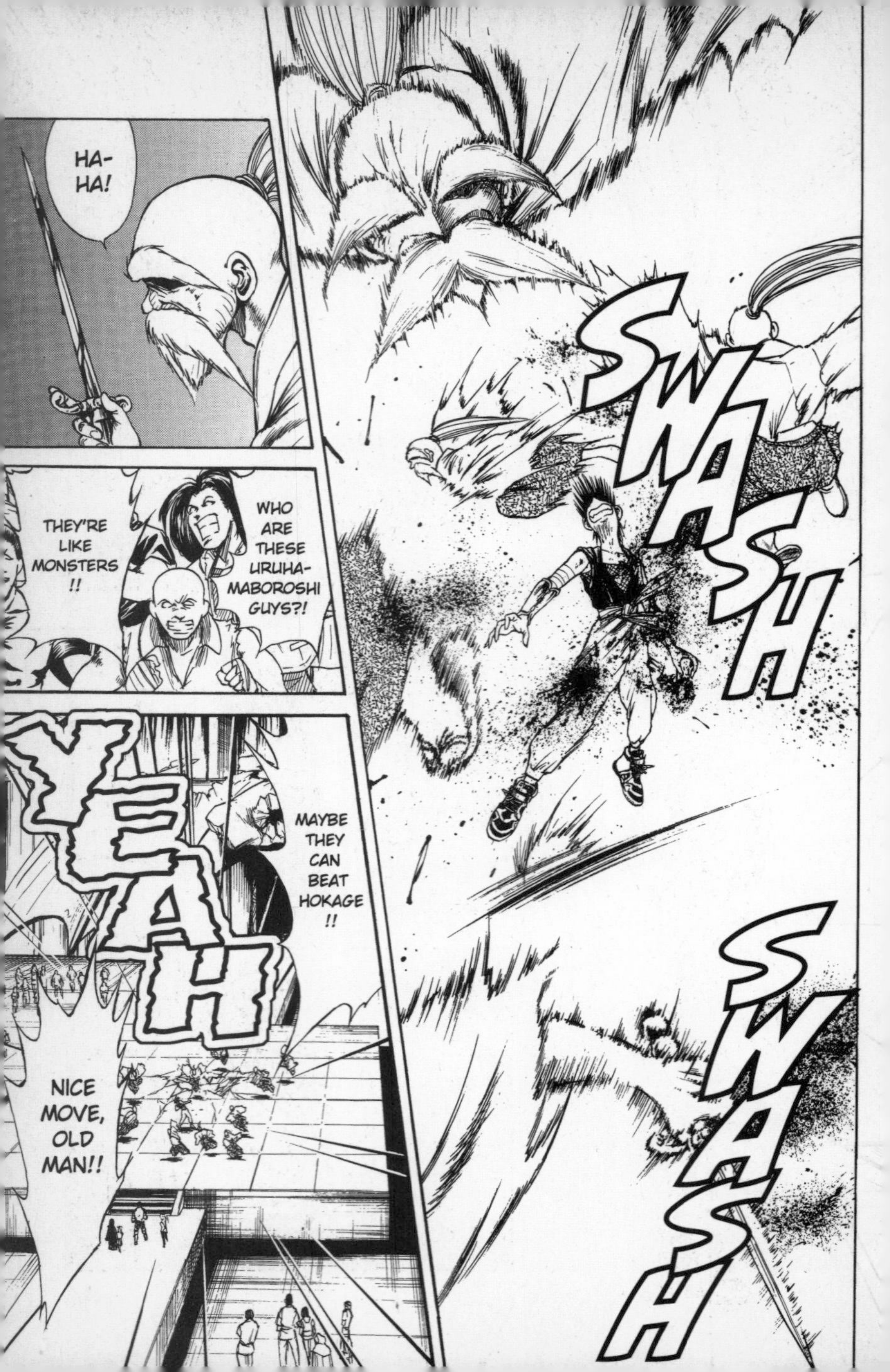
SMASH
SWASH
HA-HA!
WHO ARE THESE URUHA-MABOROSHI GUYS?!
THEY'RE LIKE MONSTERS !!
YEAH
MAYBE THEY CAN BEAT HOKAGE !!
NICE MOVE, OLD MAN!!

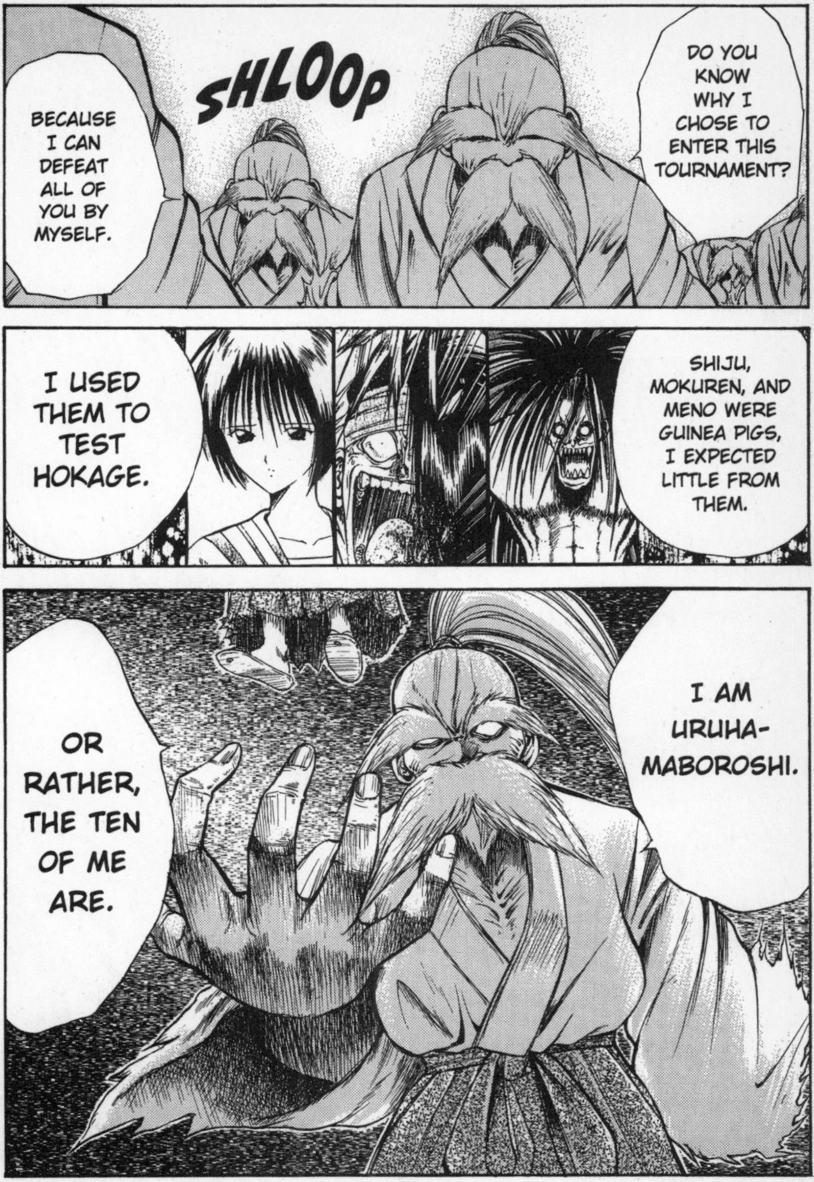
DO YOU KNOW WHY I CHOSE TO ENTER THIS TOURNAMENT?
SHLOOP
BECAUSE I CAN DEFEAT ALL OF YOU BY MYSELF.
SHIJU, MOKUREN, AND MENO WERE GUINEA PIGS, I EXPECTED LITTLE FROM THEM.
I USED THEM TO TEST HOKAGE.
I AM URUHA-MABOROSHI.
OR RATHER, THE TEN OF ME ARE.

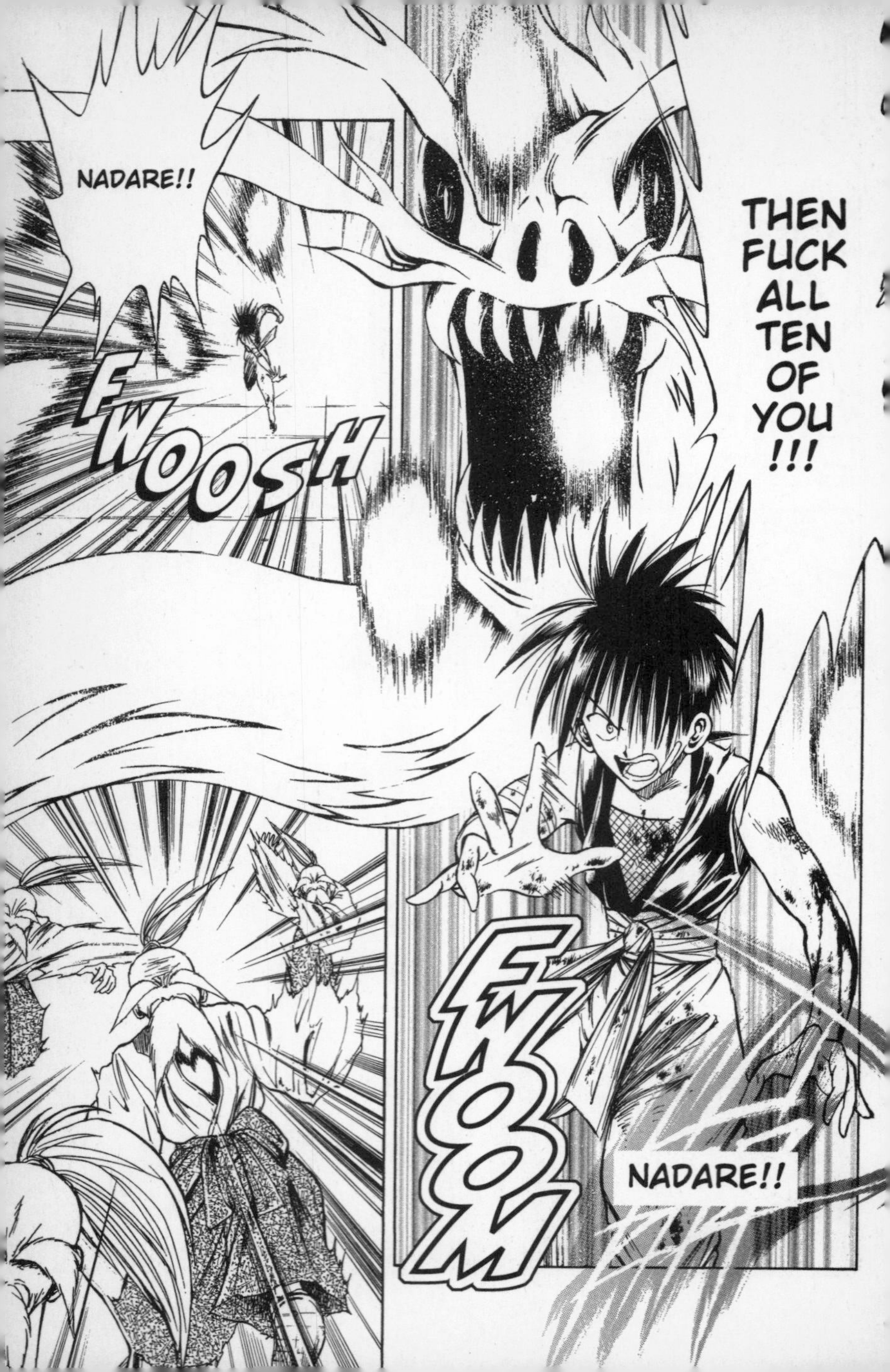
THEN FUCK ALL TEN OF YOU!!!
FWOOM
NADARE!!
NADARE!!
FWOOSH

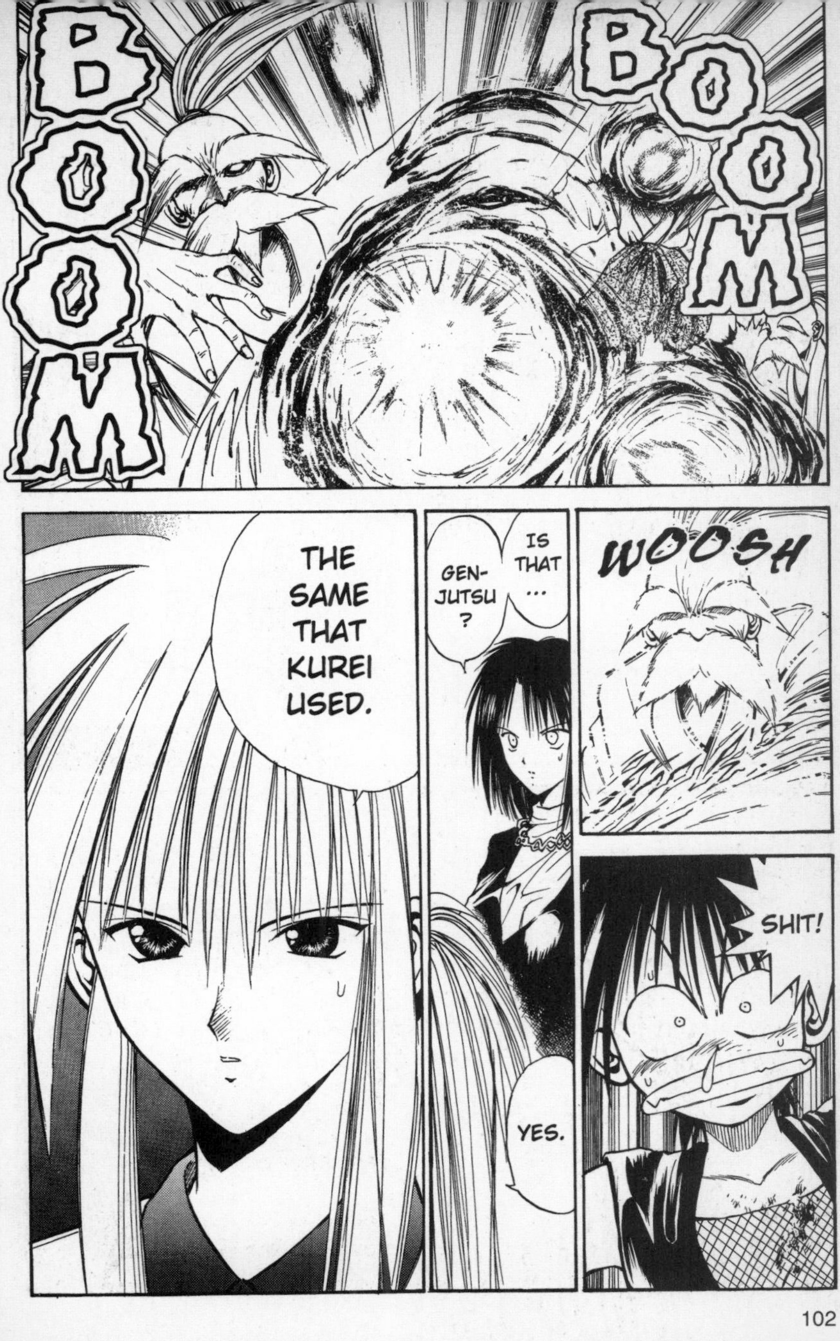
BOOM
BOOM
WOOSH
SHIT!
IS THAT ...
GENJUTSU?
YES.
THE SAME THAT KUREI USED.

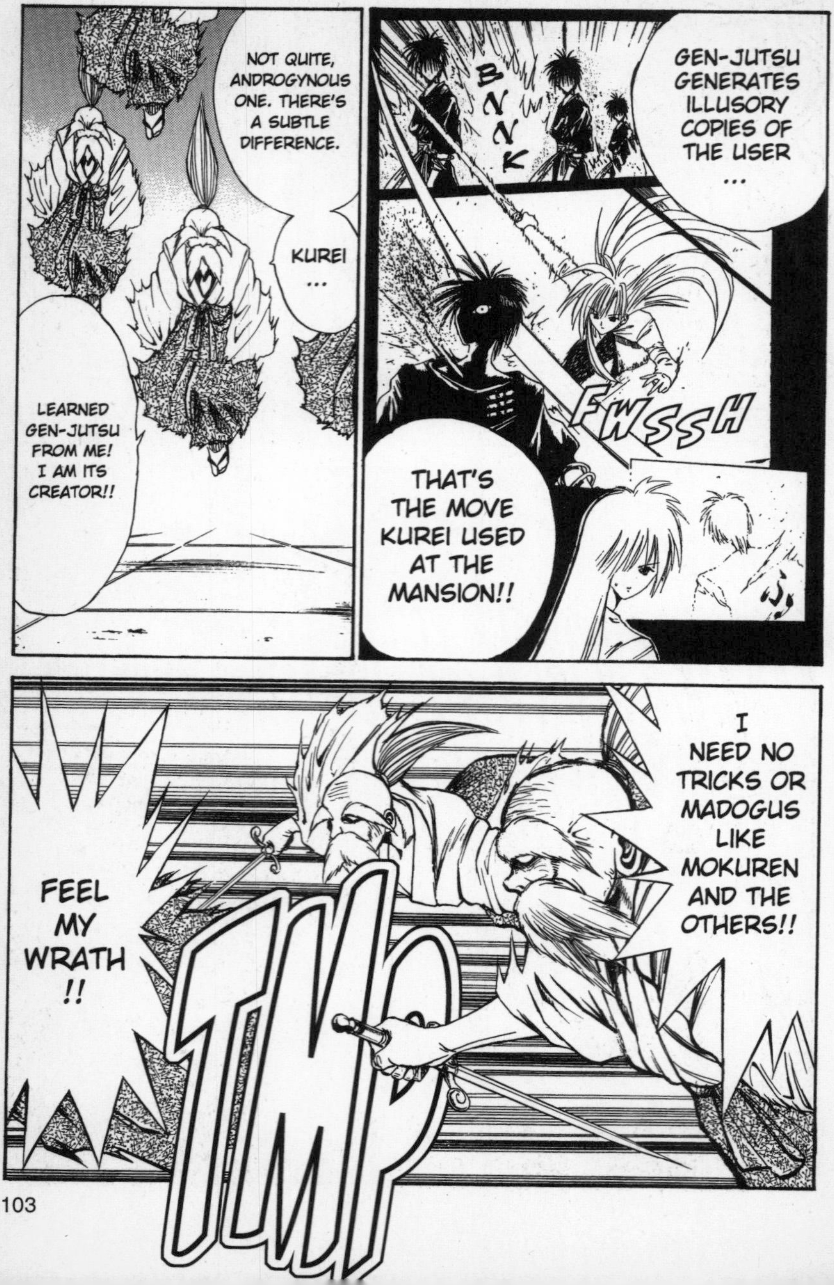
BNNK
GEN-JUTSU GENERATES ILLUSORY COPIES OF THE USER ...
FWSSH
THAT'S THE MOVE KUREI USED AT THE MANSION!!
NOT QUITE, ANDROGYNOUS ONE. THERE'S A SUBTLE DIFFERENCE.
KUREI ...
LEARNED GEN-JUTSU FROM ME! I AM ITS CREATOR!!
I NEED NO TRICKS OR MADOGUS LIKE MOKUREN AND THE OTHERS!!
FEEL MY WRATH !!
TMP

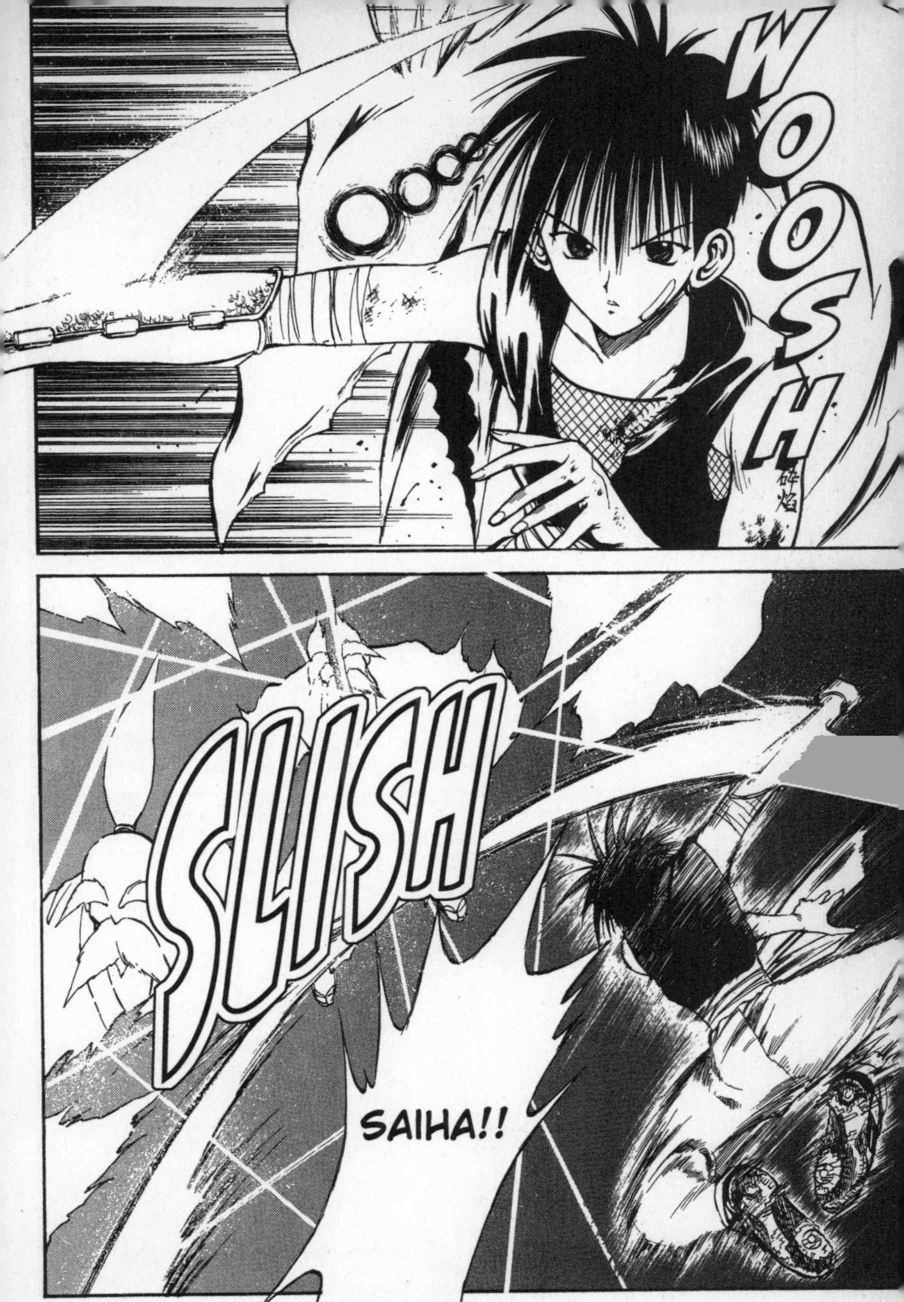
WOOOSH
砕焔
SLISH
SAIHA!!

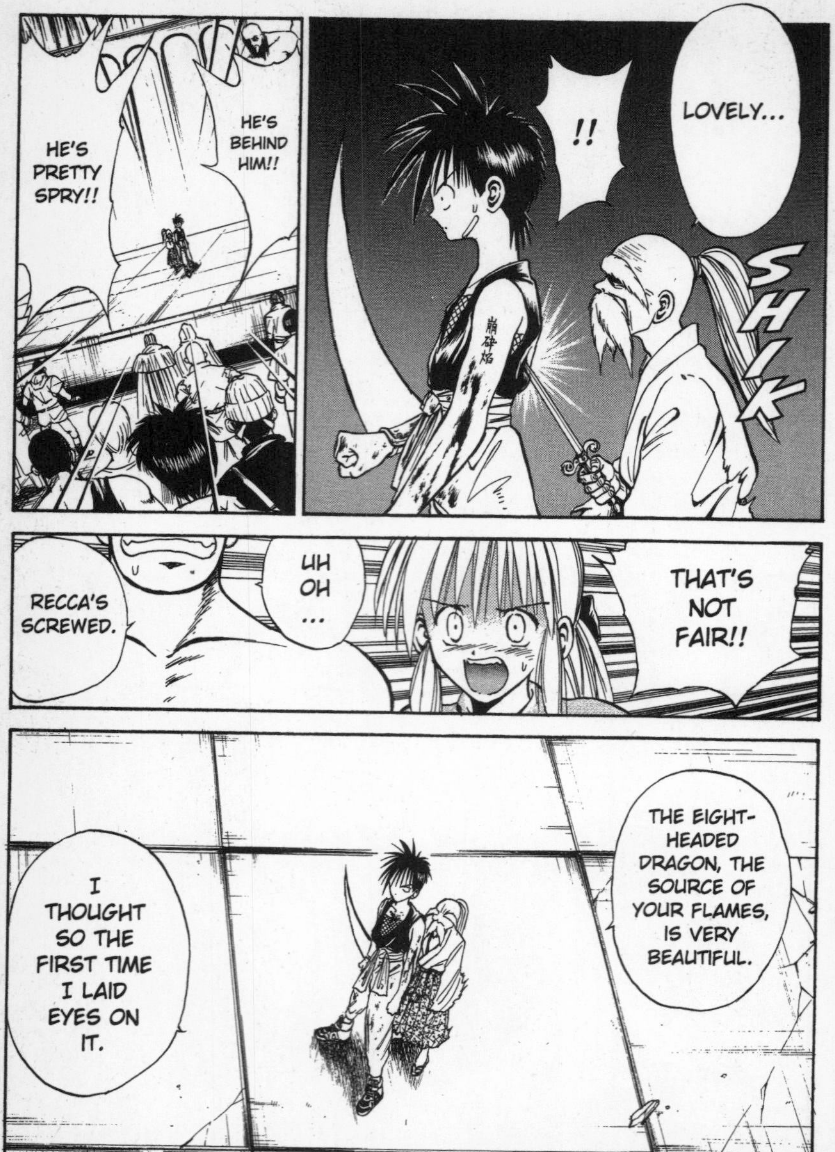
LOVELY...
!!
SHIK
崩砕焔
HE'S BEHIND HIM!!
HE'S PRETTY SPRY!!
THAT'S NOT FAIR!!
UH OH ...
RECCA'S SCREWED.
THE EIGHT-HEADED DRAGON, THE SOURCE OF YOUR FLAMES, IS VERY BEAUTIFUL.
I THOUGHT SO THE FIRST TIME I LAID EYES ON IT.

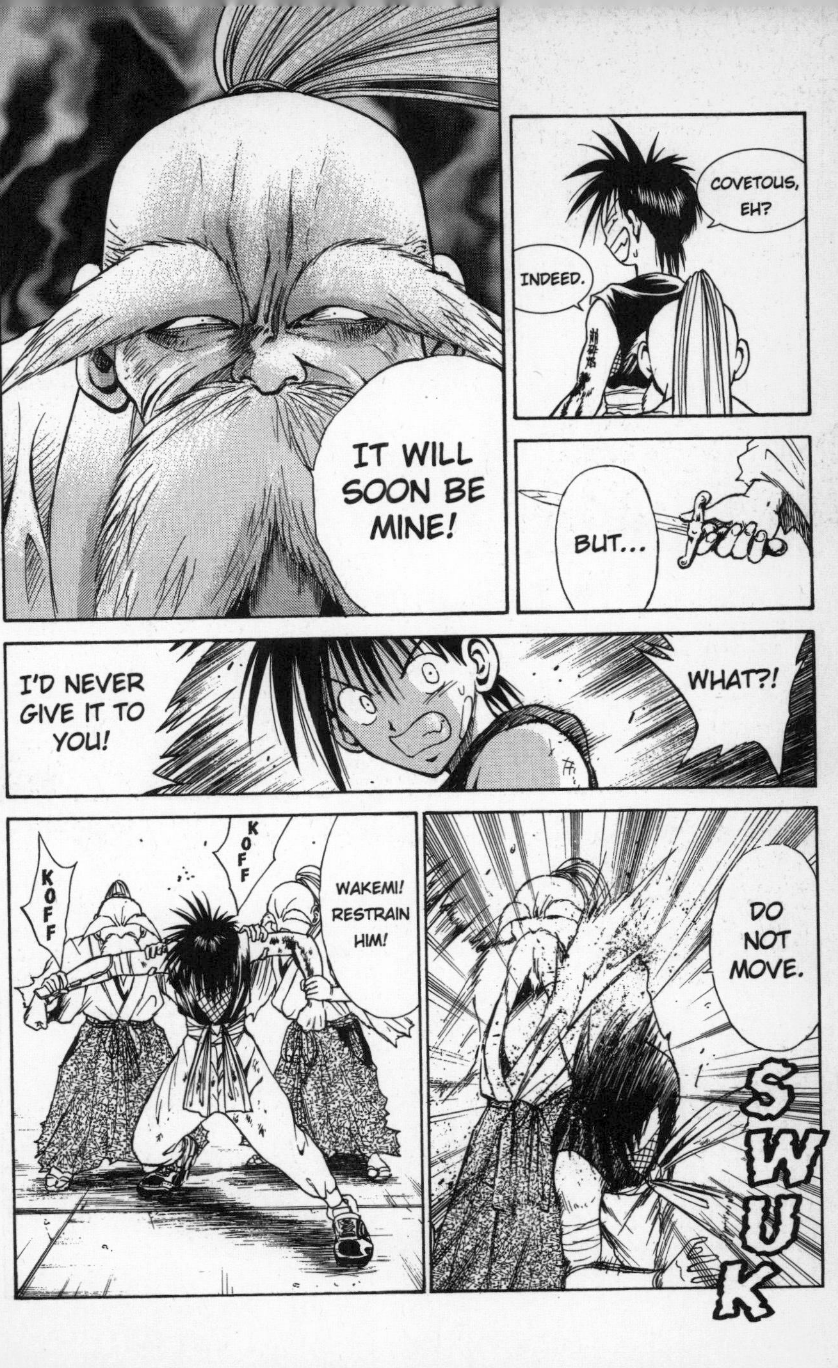
COVETOUS, EH?
INDEED.
BUT...
IT WILL SOON BE MINE!
WHAT?!
I'D NEVER GIVE IT TO YOU!
DO NOT MOVE.
SWUK
WAKEMI! RESTRAIN HIM!
KOFF
KOFF

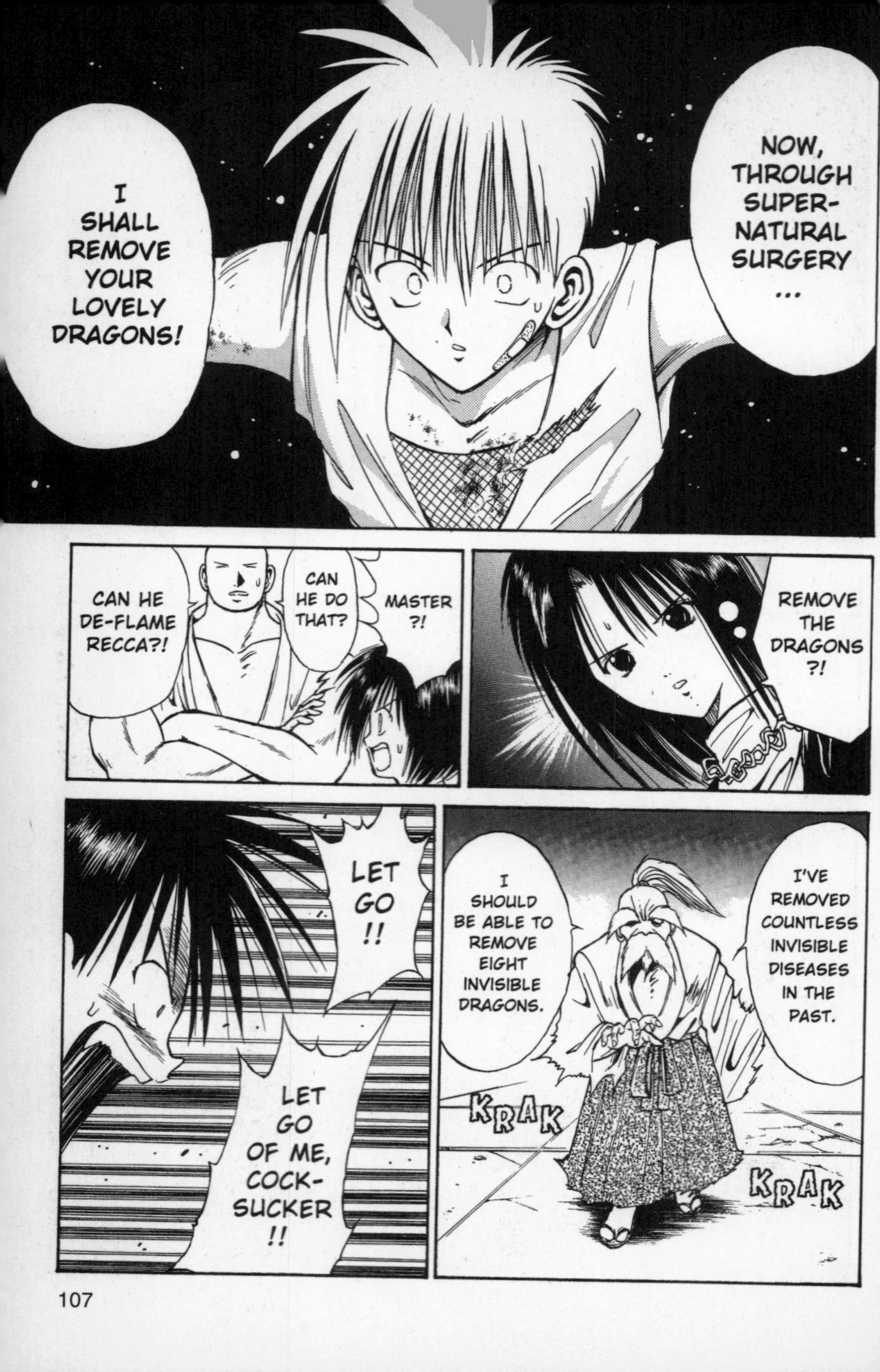
NOW, THROUGH SUPER-NATURAL SURGERY ...
I SHALL REMOVE YOUR LOVELY DRAGONS!
REMOVE THE DRAGONS ?!
MASTER ?!
CAN HE DO THAT?
CAN HE DE-FLAME RECCA?!
I'VE REMOVED COUNTLESS INVISIBLE DISEASES IN THE PAST.
I SHOULD BE ABLE TO REMOVE EIGHT INVISIBLE DRAGONS.
KRAK
KRAK
LET GO !!
LET GO OF ME, COCK-SUCKER !!

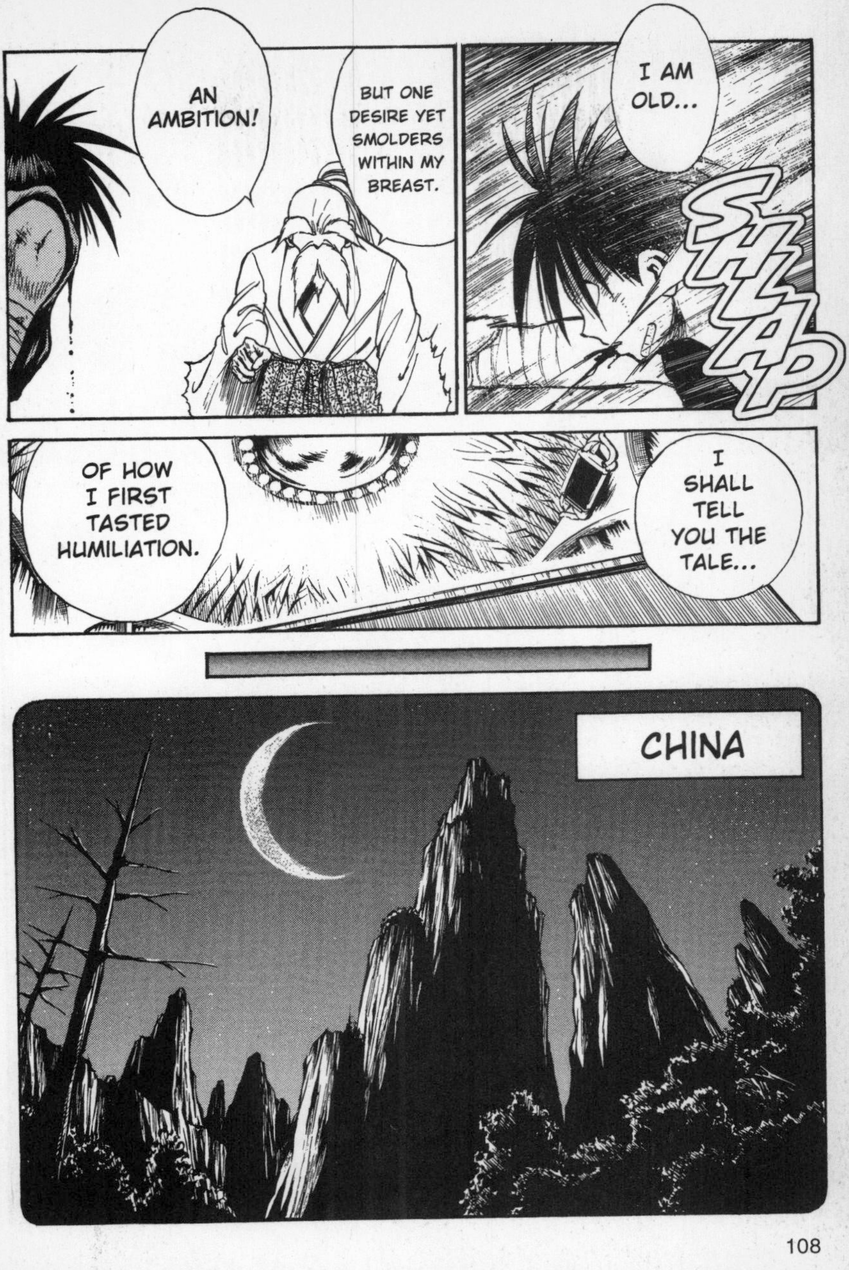
I AM OLD...
SHLAP
BUT ONE DESIRE YET SMOLDERS WITHIN MY BREAST.
AN AMBITION!
I SHALL TELL YOU THE TALE...
OF HOW I FIRST TASTED HUMILIATION.
CHINA

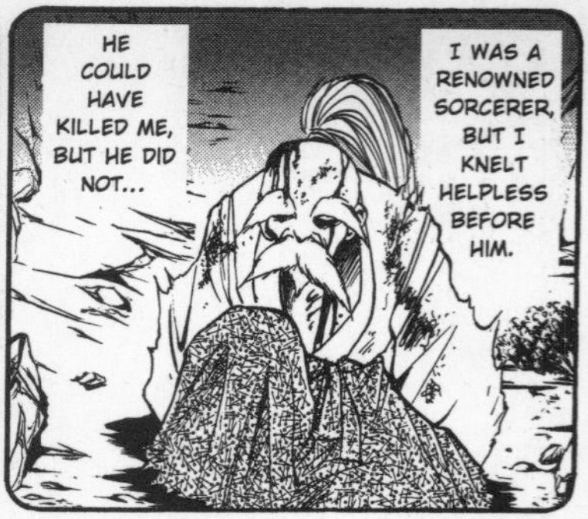
I WAS A RENOWNED SORCERER, BUT I KNELT HELPLESS BEFORE HIM.
HE COULD HAVE KILLED ME, BUT HE DID NOT...

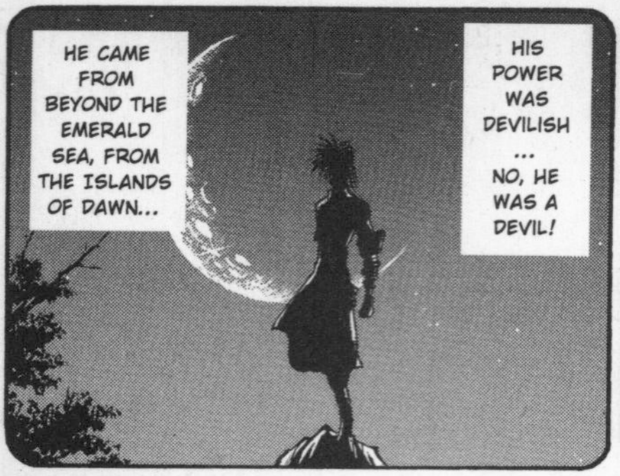
HIS POWER WAS DEVILISH ... NO, HE WAS A DEVIL!
HE CAME FROM BEYOND THE EMERALD SEA, FROM THE ISLANDS OF DAWN...

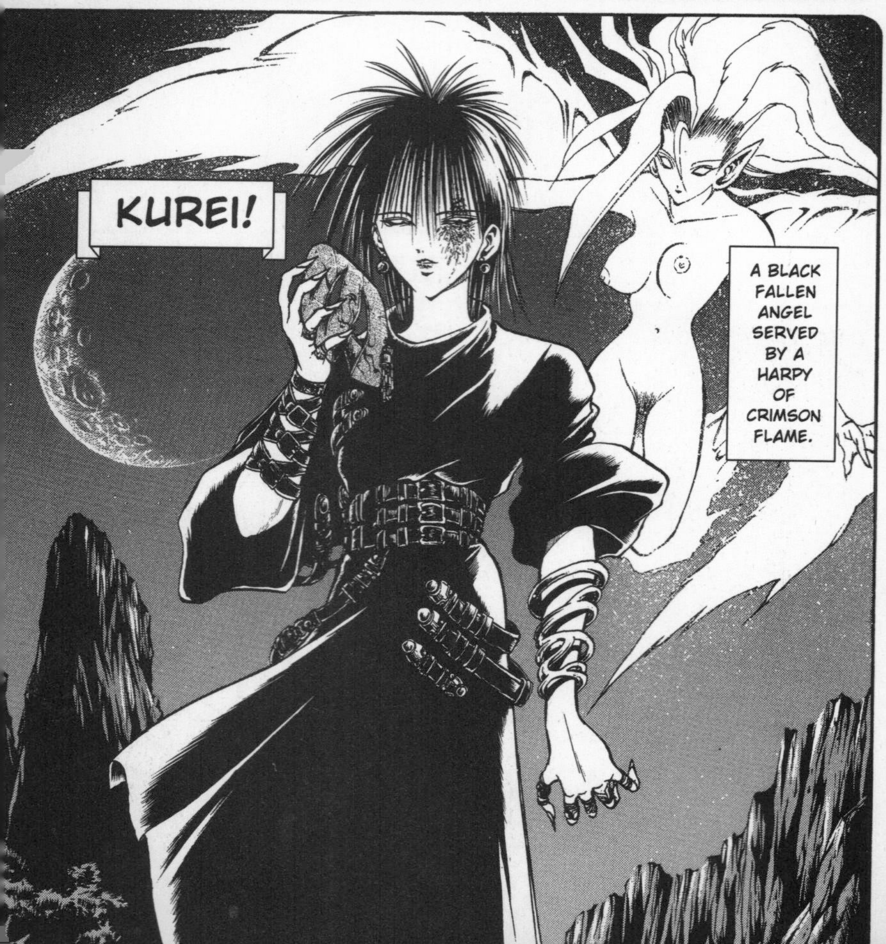
KUREI!
A BLACK FALLEN ANGEL SERVED BY A HARPY OF CRIMSON FLAME.

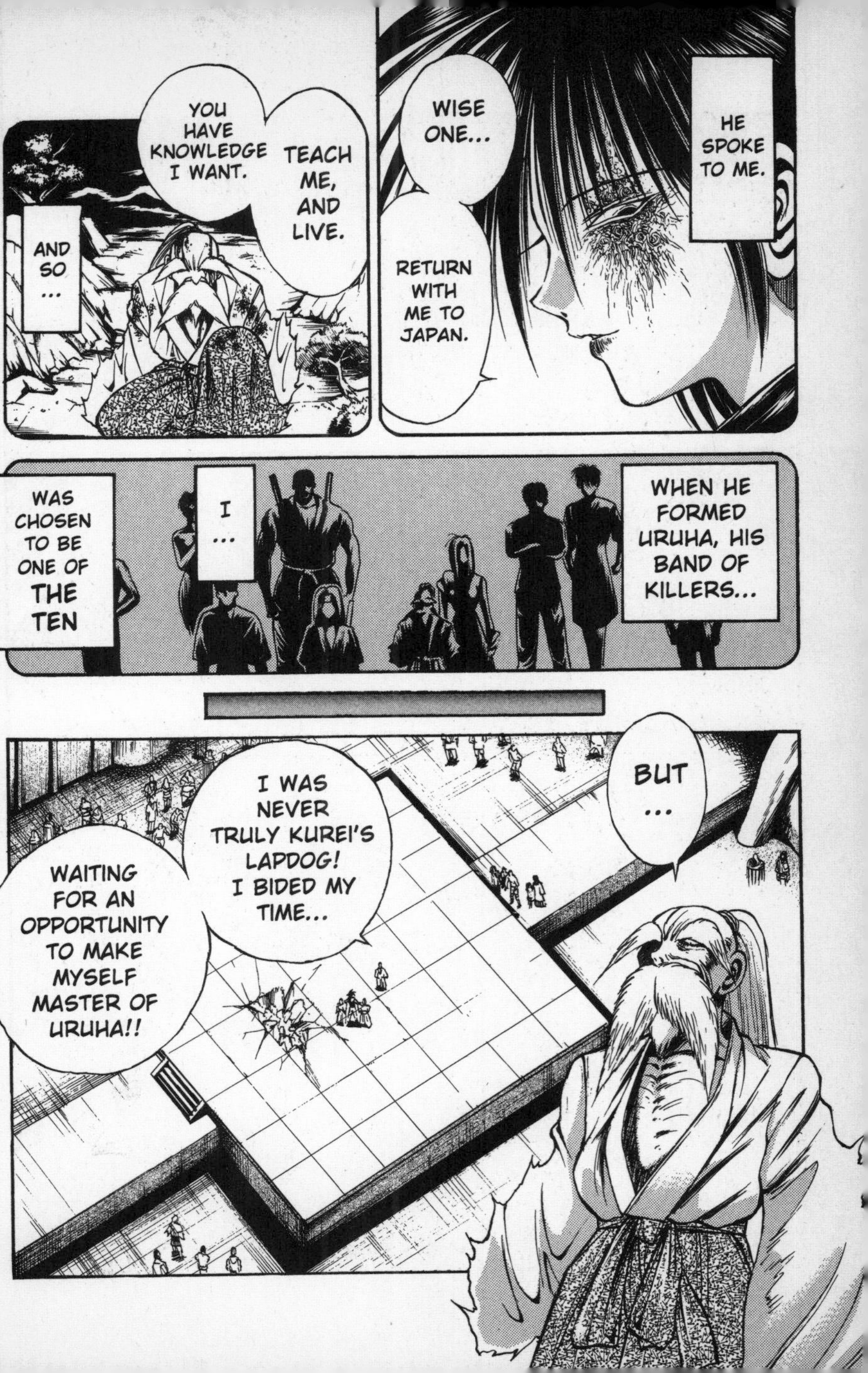
HE SPOKE TO ME.
WISE ONE...
RETURN WITH ME TO JAPAN.
YOU HAVE KNOWLEDGE I WANT.
TEACH ME, AND LIVE.
AND SO ...
WHEN HE FORMED URUHA, HIS BAND OF KILLERS...
I ...
WAS CHOSEN TO BE ONE OF THE TEN
BUT ...
I WAS NEVER TRULY KUREI'S LAPDOG! I BIDED MY TIME...
WAITING FOR AN OPPORTUNITY TO MAKE MYSELF MASTER OF URUHA!!

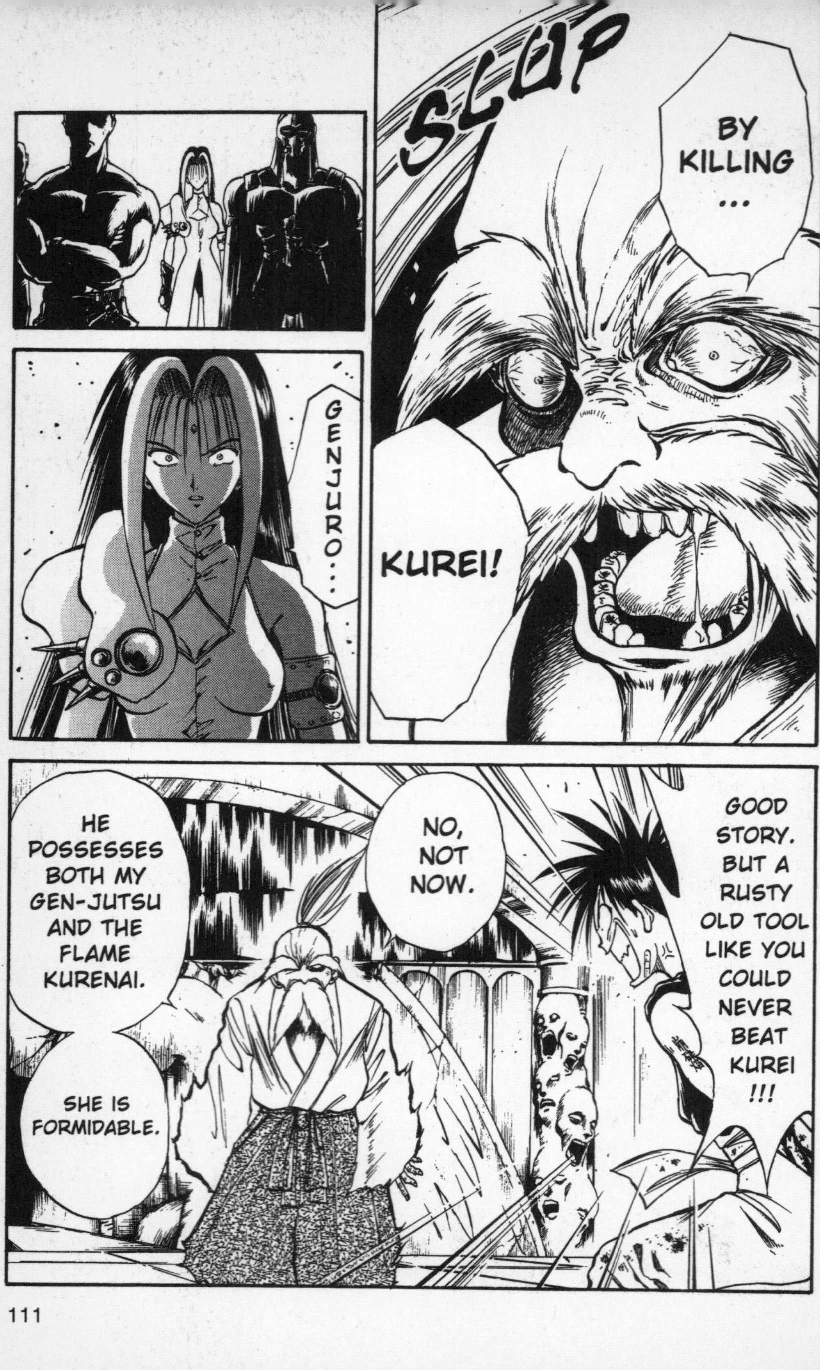
SLUP
BY KILLING ...
KUREI!
GENJURO...
GOOD STORY. BUT A RUSTY OLD TOOL LIKE YOU COULD NEVER BEAT KUREI !!!
NO, NOT NOW.
HE POSSESSES BOTH MY GEN-JUTSU AND THE FLAME KURENAI.
SHE IS FORMIDABLE.

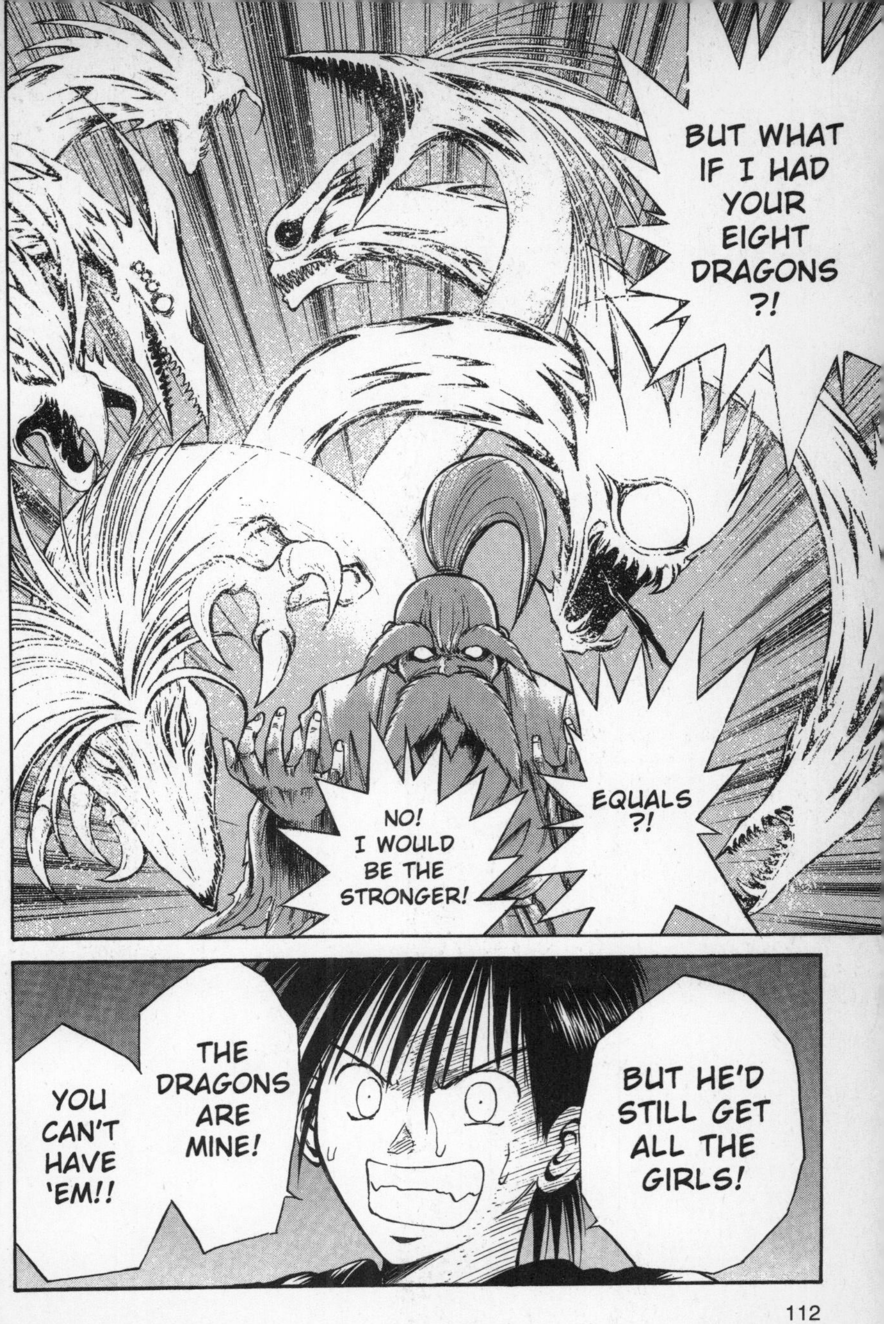
BUT WHAT IF I HAD YOUR EIGHT DRAGONS ?!
EQUALS ?!
NO! I WOULD BE THE STRONGER!
BUT HE'D STILL GET ALL THE GIRLS!
THE DRAGONS ARE MINE!
YOU CAN'T HAVE 'EM!!

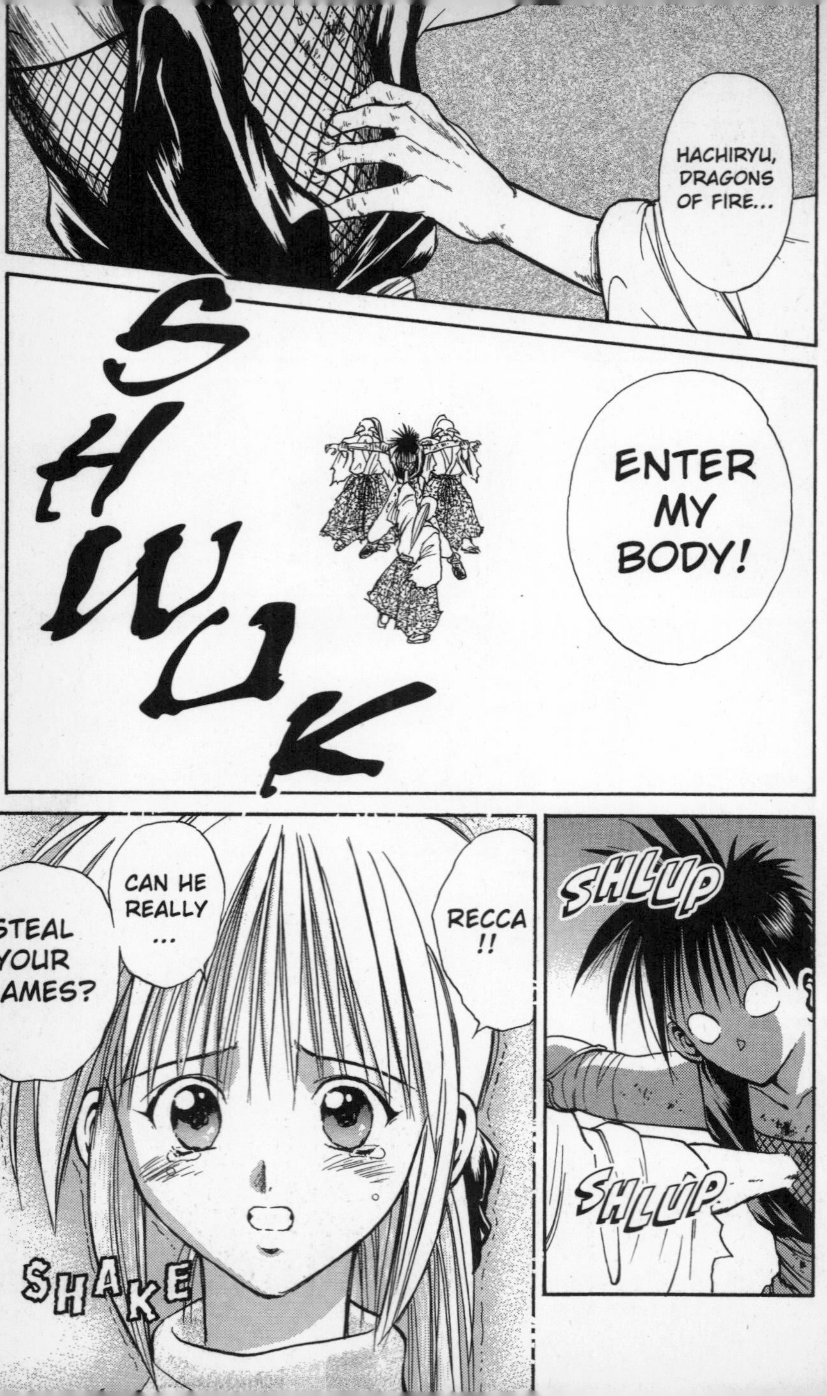
HACHIRYU, DRAGONS OF FIRE...
ENTER MY BODY!
SHWUK
SHLUP
SHLUP
RECCA !!
CAN HE REALLY ...
STEAL YOUR FLAMES?
SHAKE

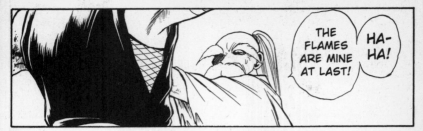

THE FLAMES ARE MINE AT LAST!

HA-HA!

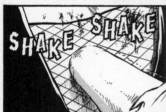

SHAKE SHAKE

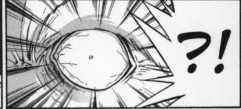

?!

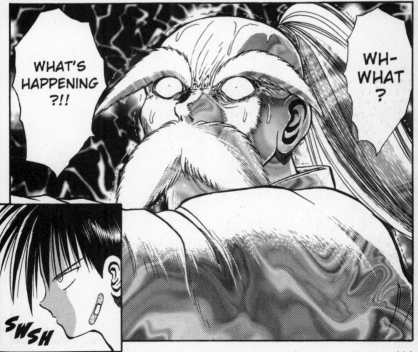

WHAT'S HAPPENING?!!

WH-WHAT?

SWSH

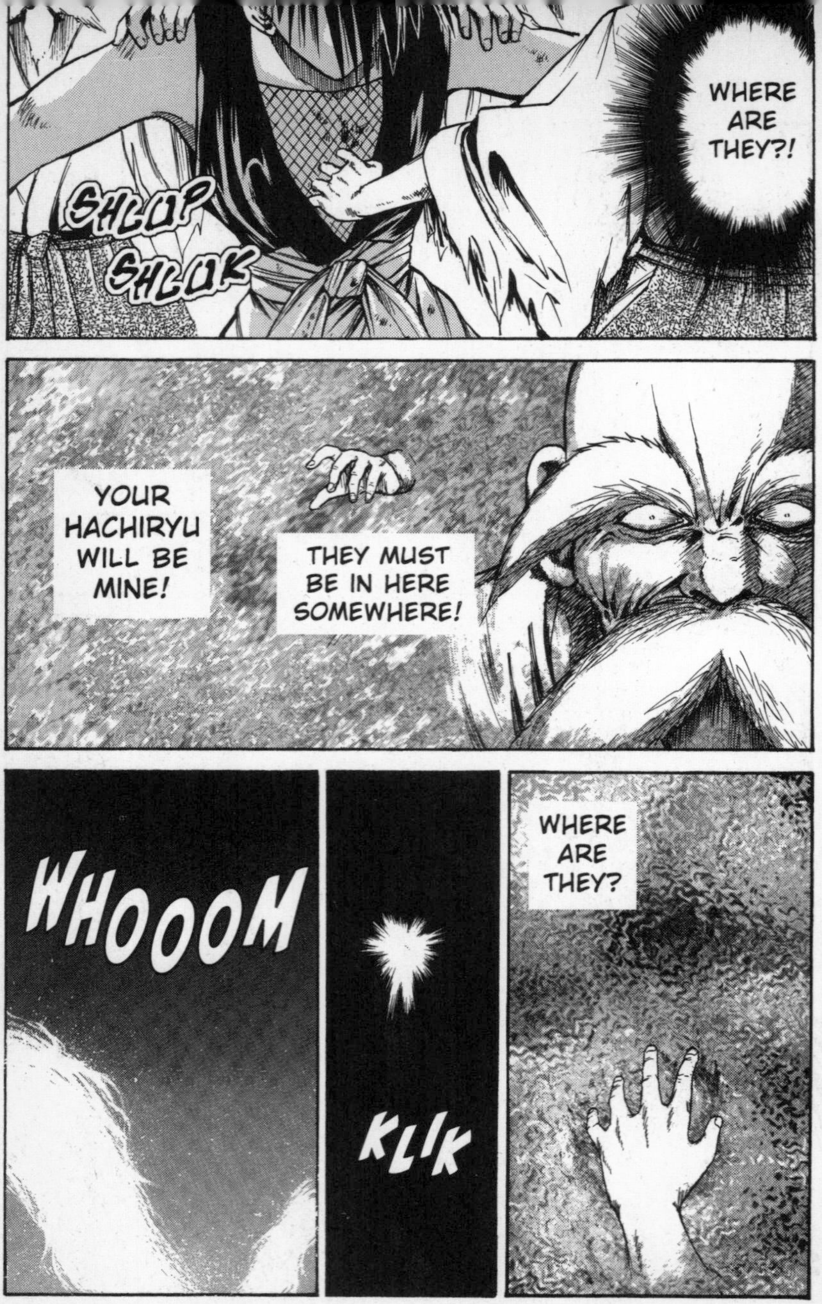
WHERE ARE THEY?!
SHLUP
SHLOK
THEY MUST BE IN HERE SOMEWHERE!
YOUR HACHIRYU WILL BE MINE!
WHERE ARE THEY?
KLIK
WHOOOM

## Part Sixty-Six: The Mad Illusionist's Feast (11) Setsuna Flashes

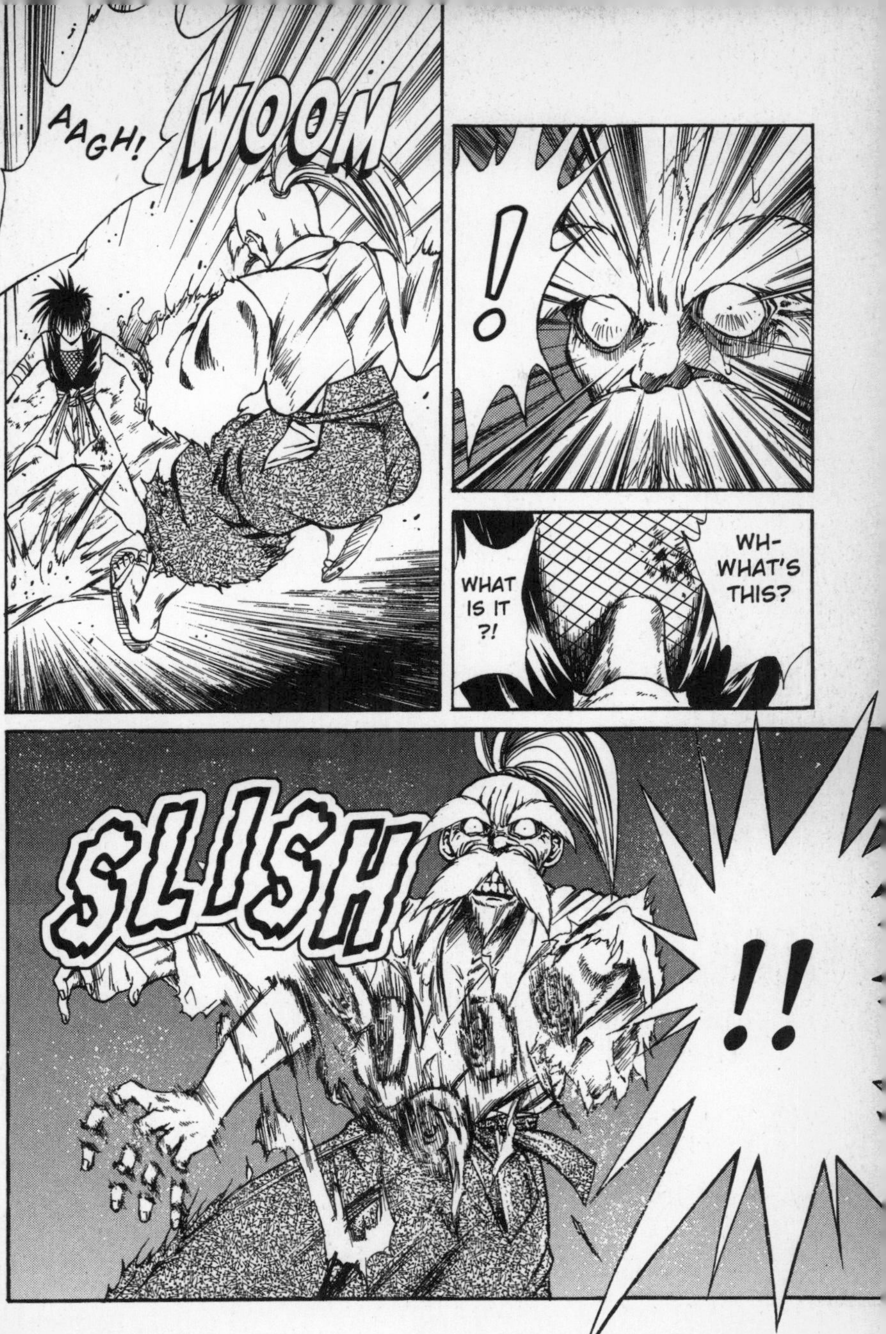
!
WH-WHAT'S THIS?
WHAT IS IT ?!
WOOM
AAGH!
SLISH
!!

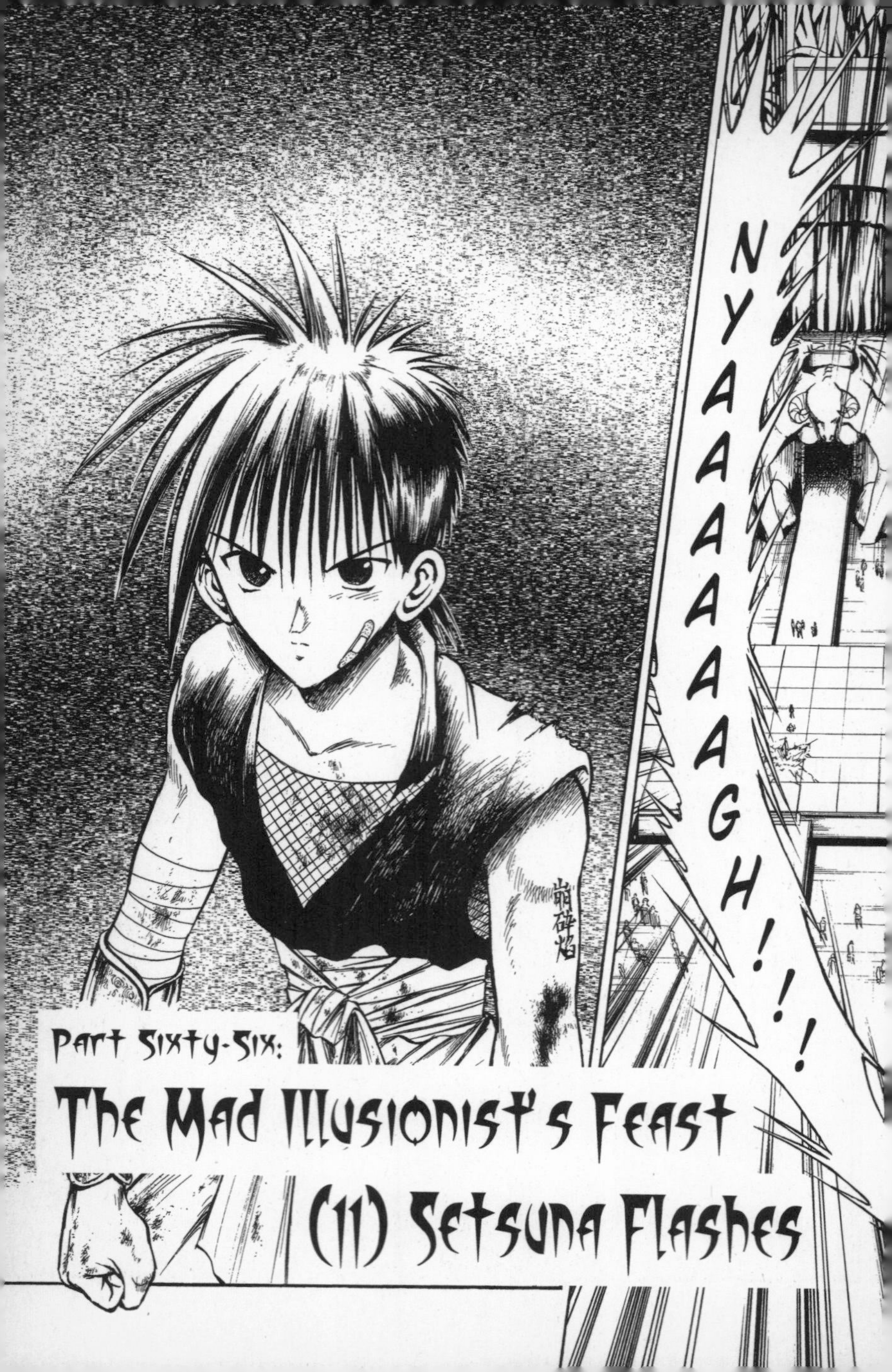
NYAAAAAAAGH!!!

## Part Sixty-Six:
# The Mad Illusionist's Feast (11) Setsuna Flashes

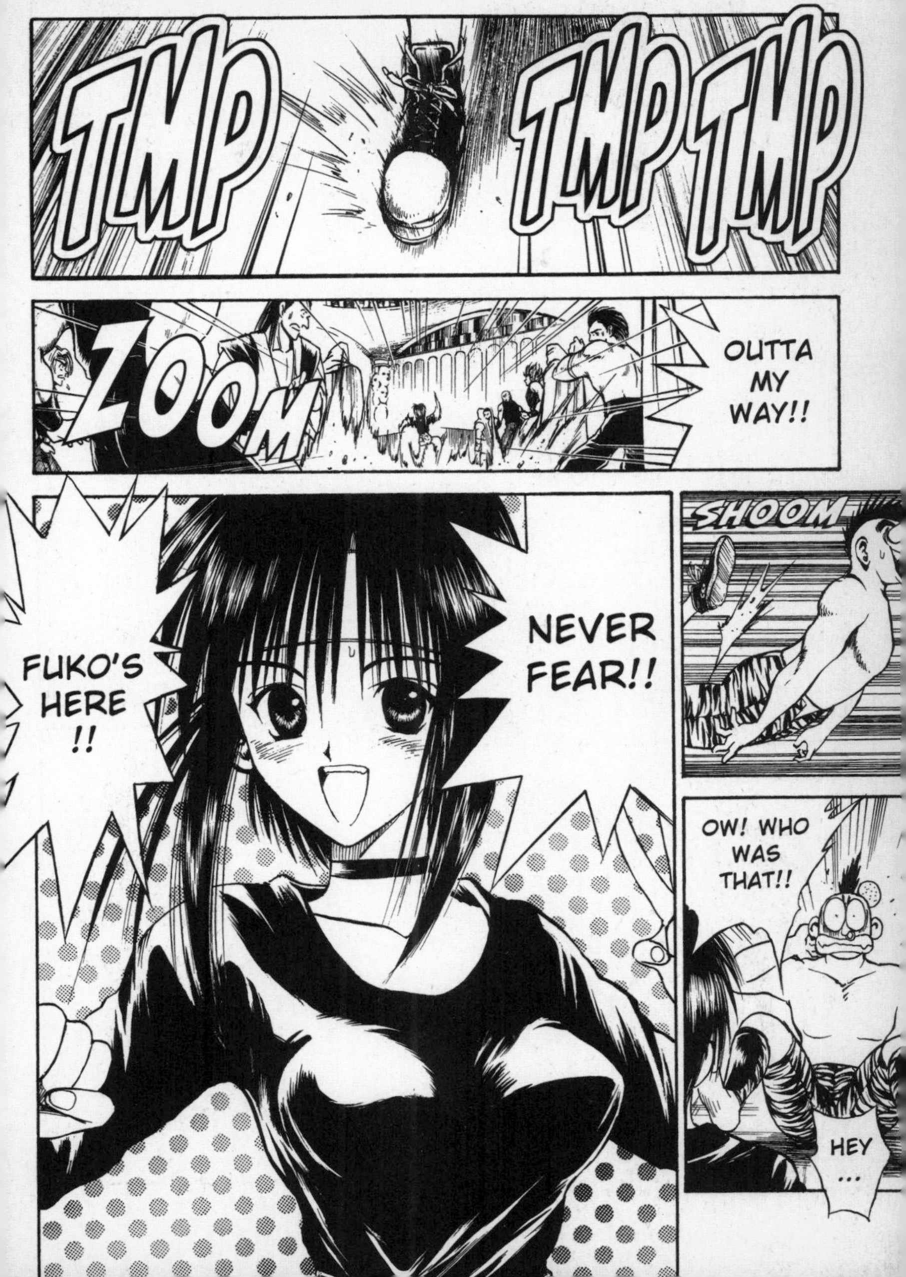
TMP TMP
TMP
OUTTA MY WAY!!
ZOOM
SHOOM
OW! WHO WAS THAT!!
HEY ...
NEVER FEAR!!
FUKO'S HERE !!

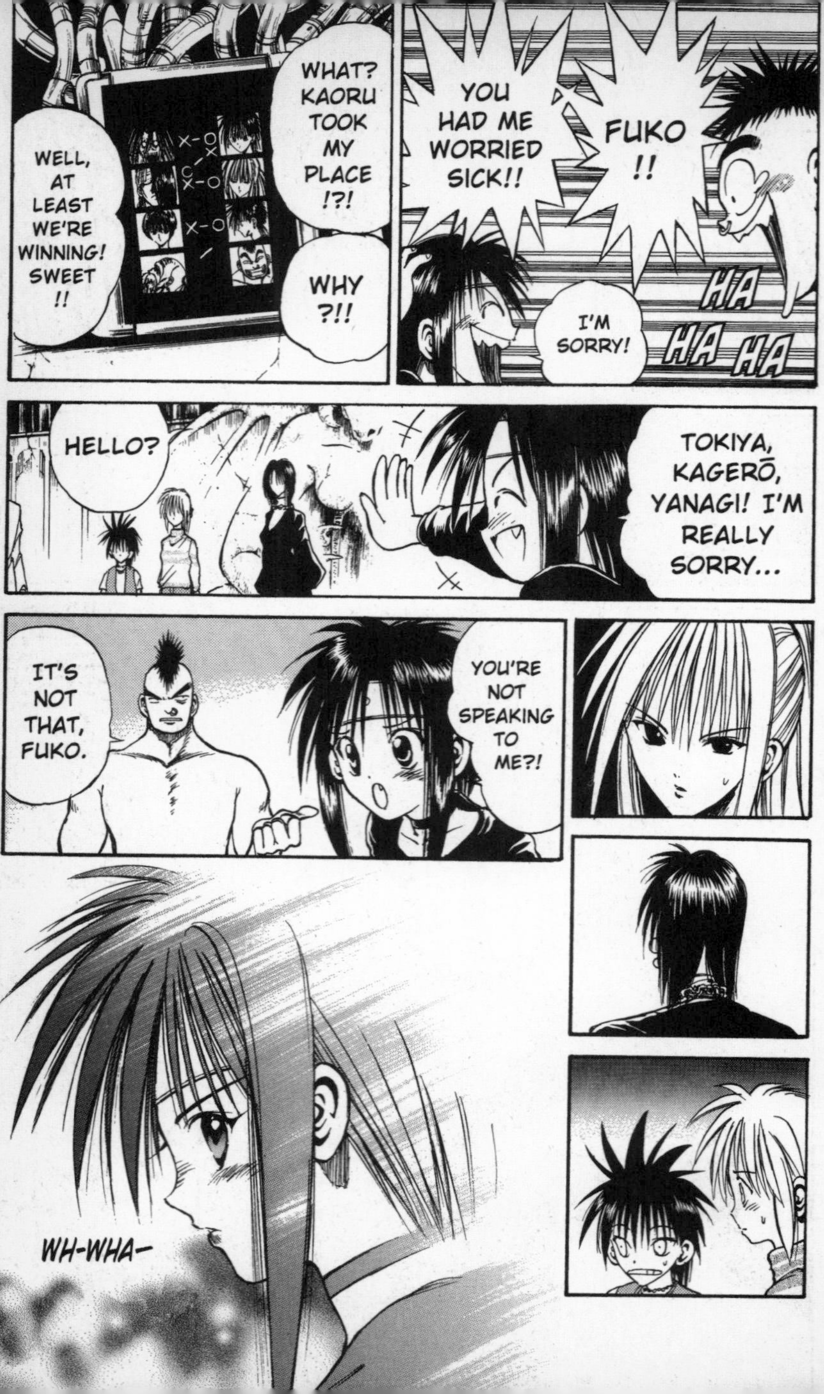
FUKO !!
YOU HAD ME WORRIED SICK!!
HA HA HA HA
I'M SORRY!
WHAT? KAORU TOOK MY PLACE !?!
WHY ?!!
WELL, AT LEAST WE'RE WINNING! SWEET !!
TOKIYA, KAGERŌ, YANAGI! I'M REALLY SORRY...
HELLO?
YOU'RE NOT SPEAKING TO ME?!
IT'S NOT THAT, FUKO.
WH-WHA-

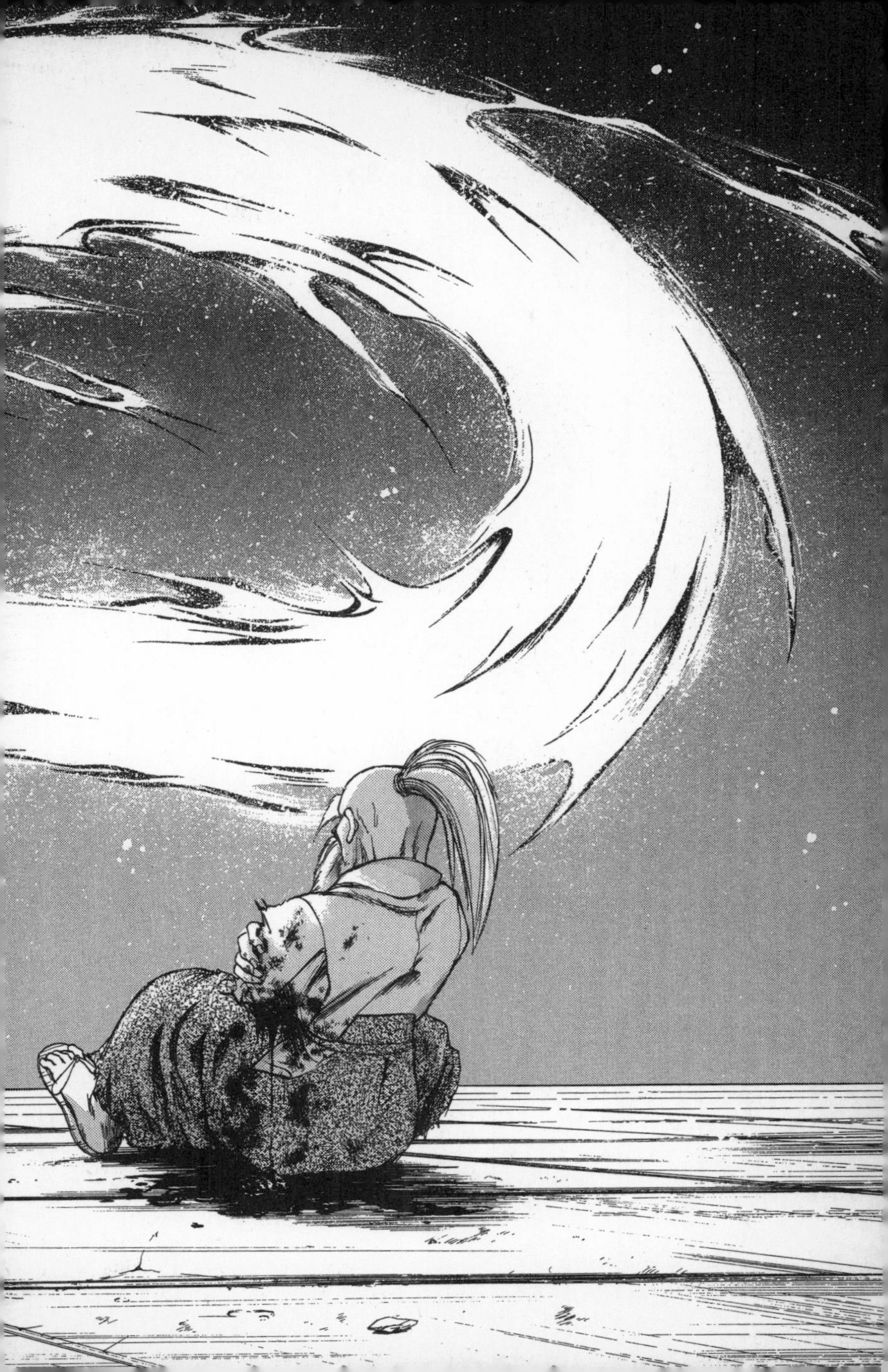

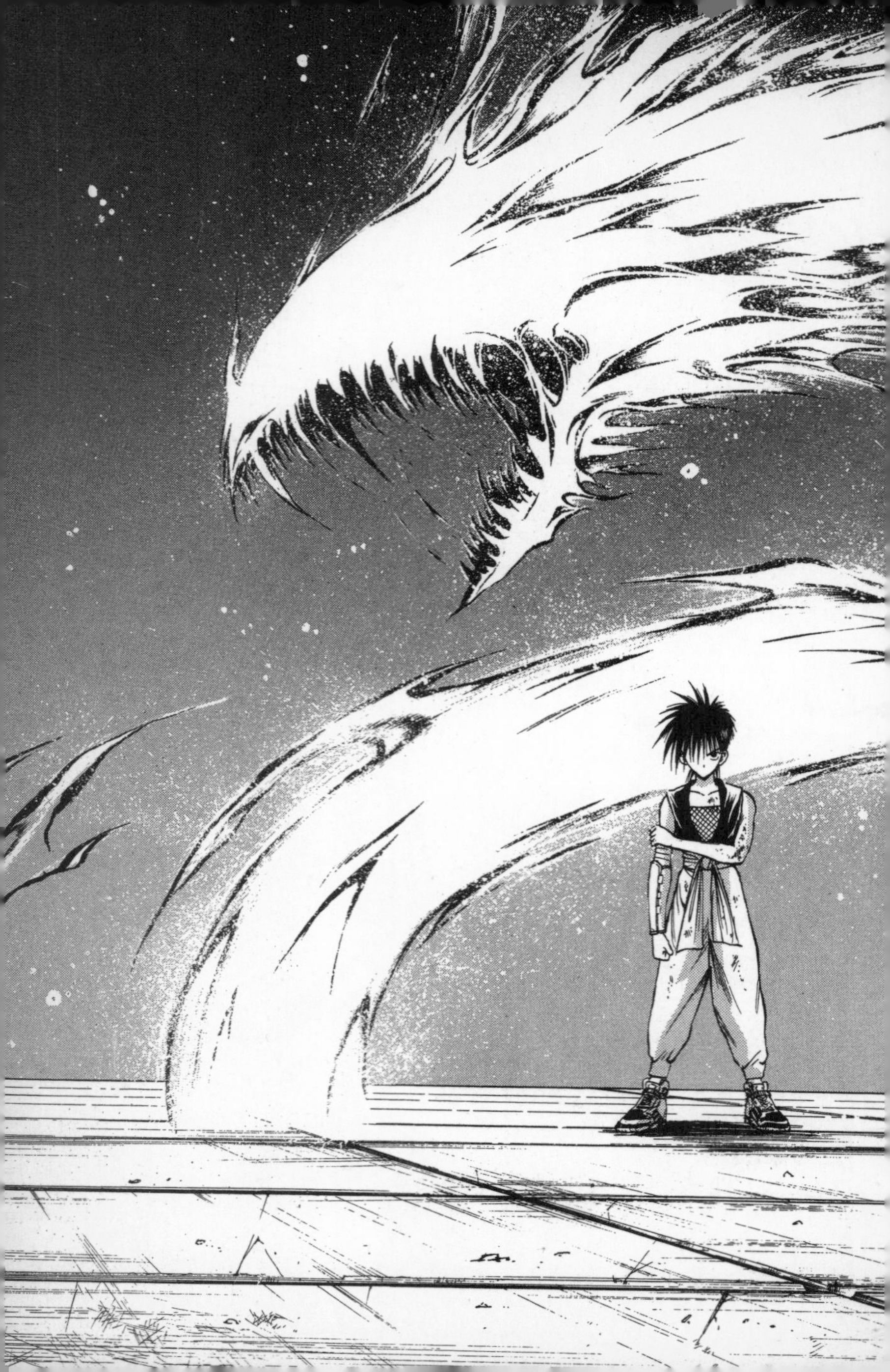

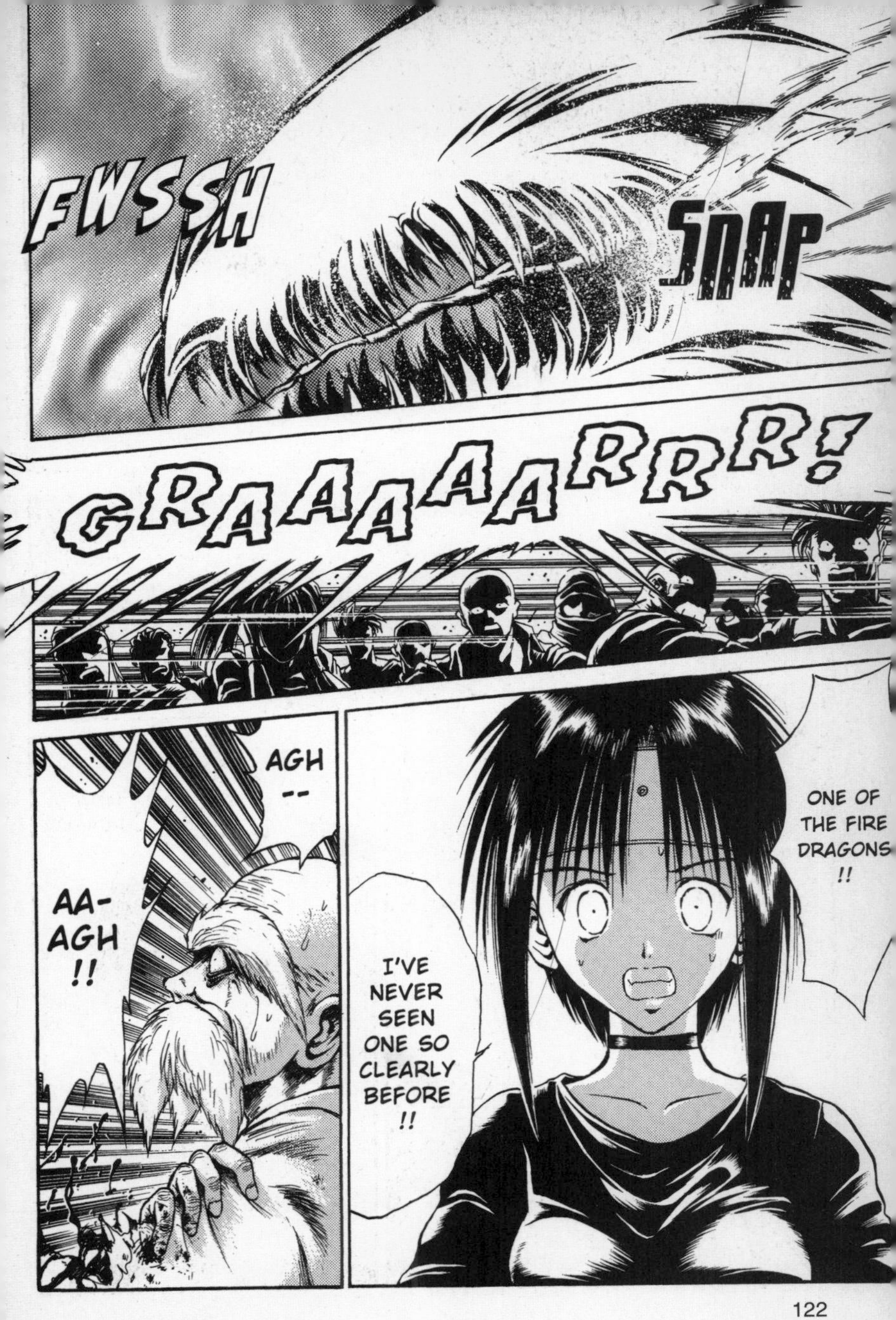
SNAP
FWSSH
GRAAAAARRR!
ONE OF THE FIRE DRAGONS!!
I'VE NEVER SEEN ONE SO CLEARLY BEFORE!!
AGH --
AA-AGH!!

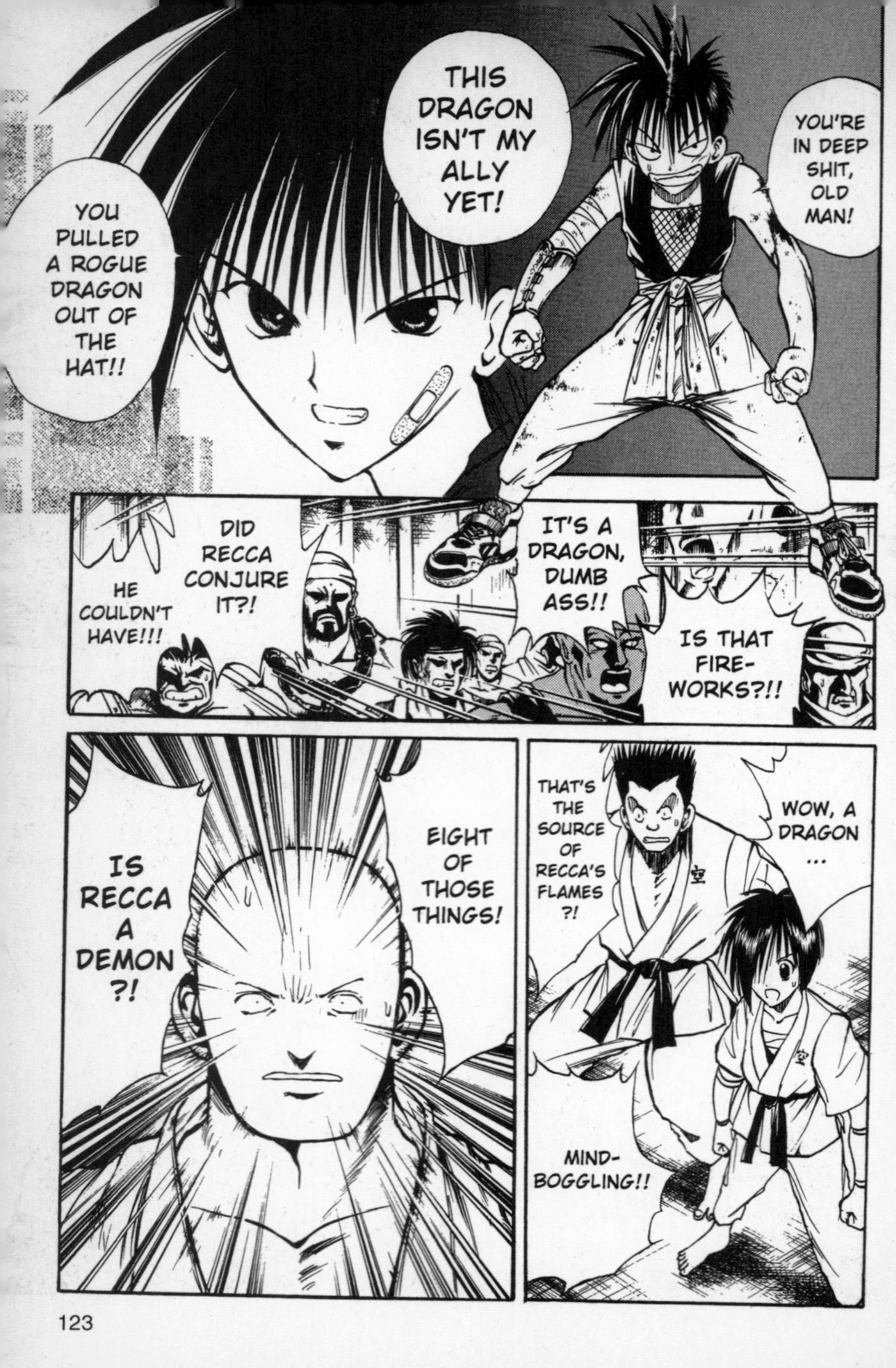
YOU'RE IN DEEP SHIT, OLD MAN!
THIS DRAGON ISN'T MY ALLY YET!
YOU PULLED A ROGUE DRAGON OUT OF THE HAT!!
IS THAT FIRE-WORKS?!!
IT'S A DRAGON, DUMB ASS!!
DID RECCA CONJURE IT?!
HE COULDN'T HAVE!!!
WOW, A DRAGON ...
THAT'S THE SOURCE OF RECCA'S FLAMES ?!
MIND-BOGGLING!!
EIGHT OF THOSE THINGS!
IS RECCA A DEMON ?!

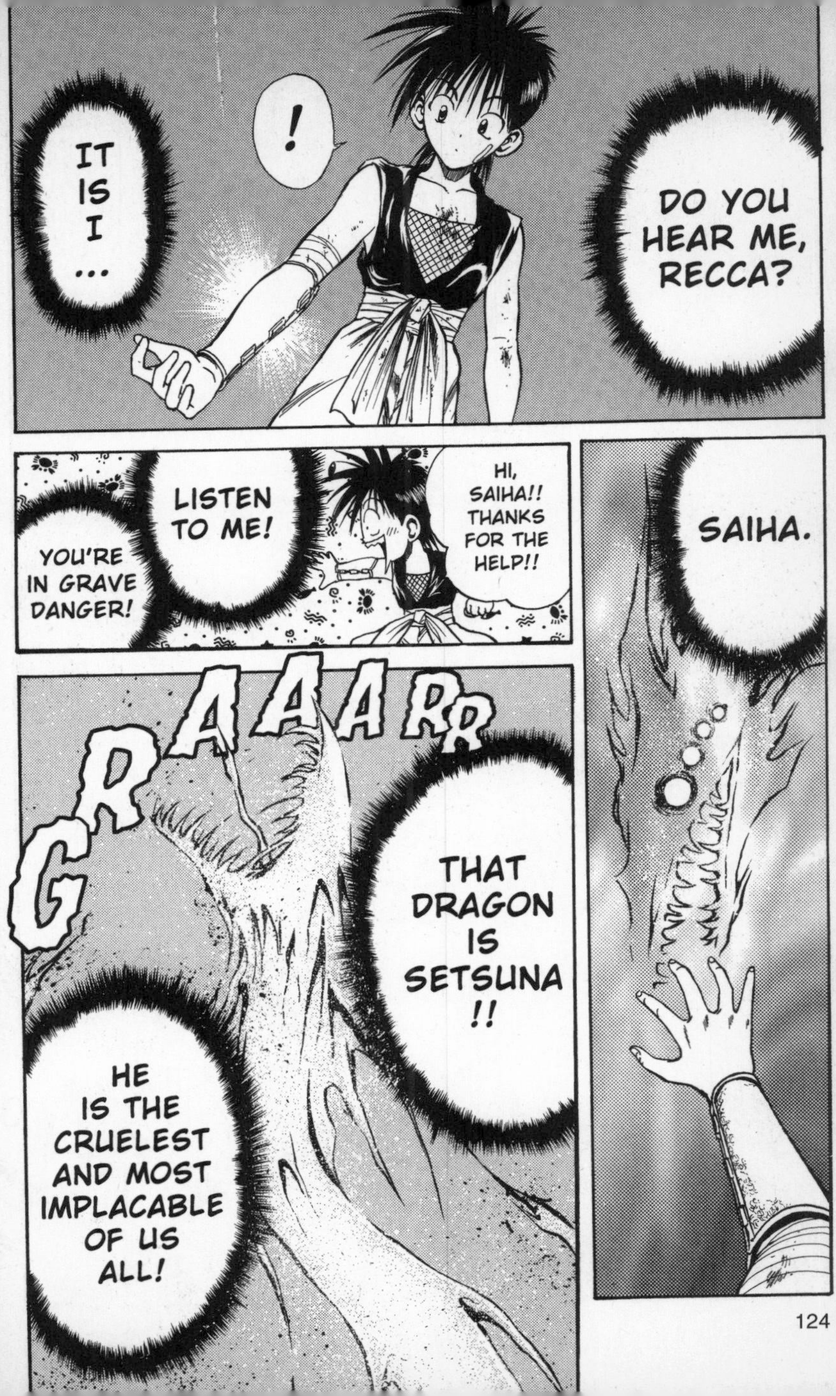

DO YOU HEAR ME, RECCA?
!
IT IS I ...
SAIHA.
HI, SAIHA!! THANKS FOR THE HELP!!
LISTEN TO ME!
YOU'RE IN GRAVE DANGER!
GRAAARR
THAT DRAGON IS SETSUNA!!
HE IS THE CRUELEST AND MOST IMPLACABLE OF US ALL!

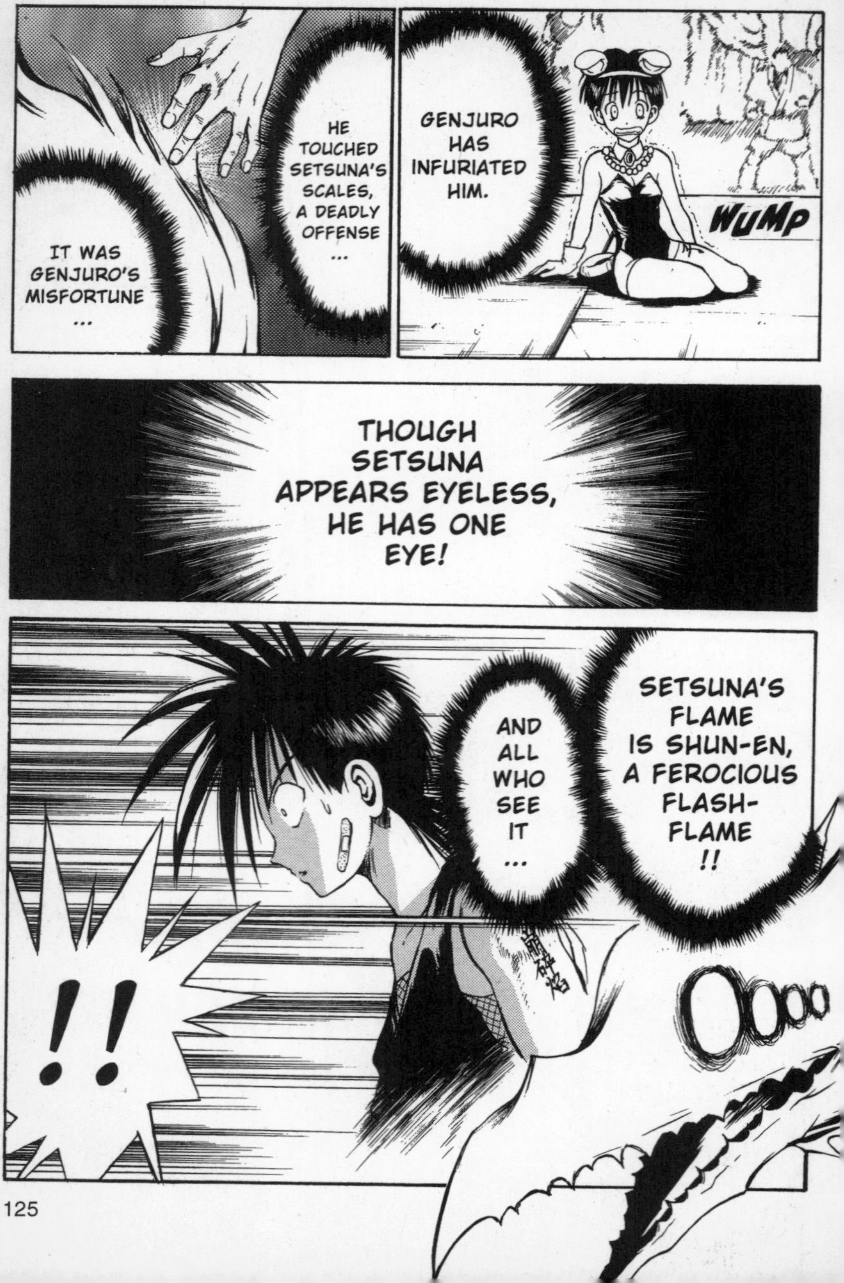
GENJURO HAS INFURIATED HIM.
WUMP
HE TOUCHED SETSUNA'S SCALES, A DEADLY OFFENSE ...
IT WAS GENJURO'S MISFORTUNE ...
THOUGH SETSUNA APPEARS EYELESS, HE HAS ONE EYE!
SETSUNA'S FLAME IS SHUN-EN, A FEROCIOUS FLASH-FLAME !!
AND ALL WHO SEE IT ...
!!
Oooo

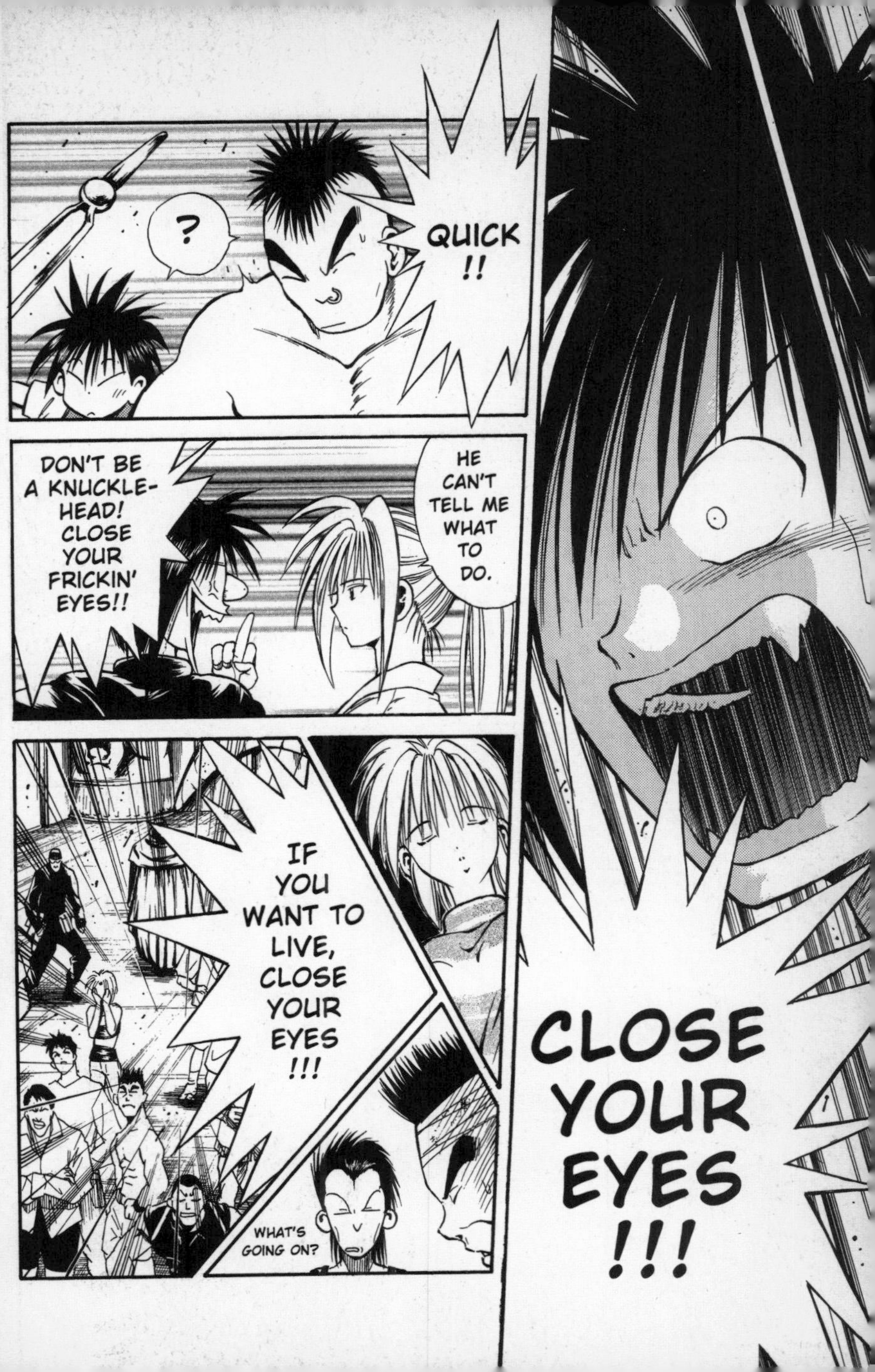
CLOSE YOUR EYES !!!
QUICK !!
?
HE CAN'T TELL ME WHAT TO DO.
DON'T BE A KNUCKLE-HEAD! CLOSE YOUR FRICKIN' EYES!!
IF YOU WANT TO LIVE, CLOSE YOUR EYES !!!
WHAT'S GOING ON?

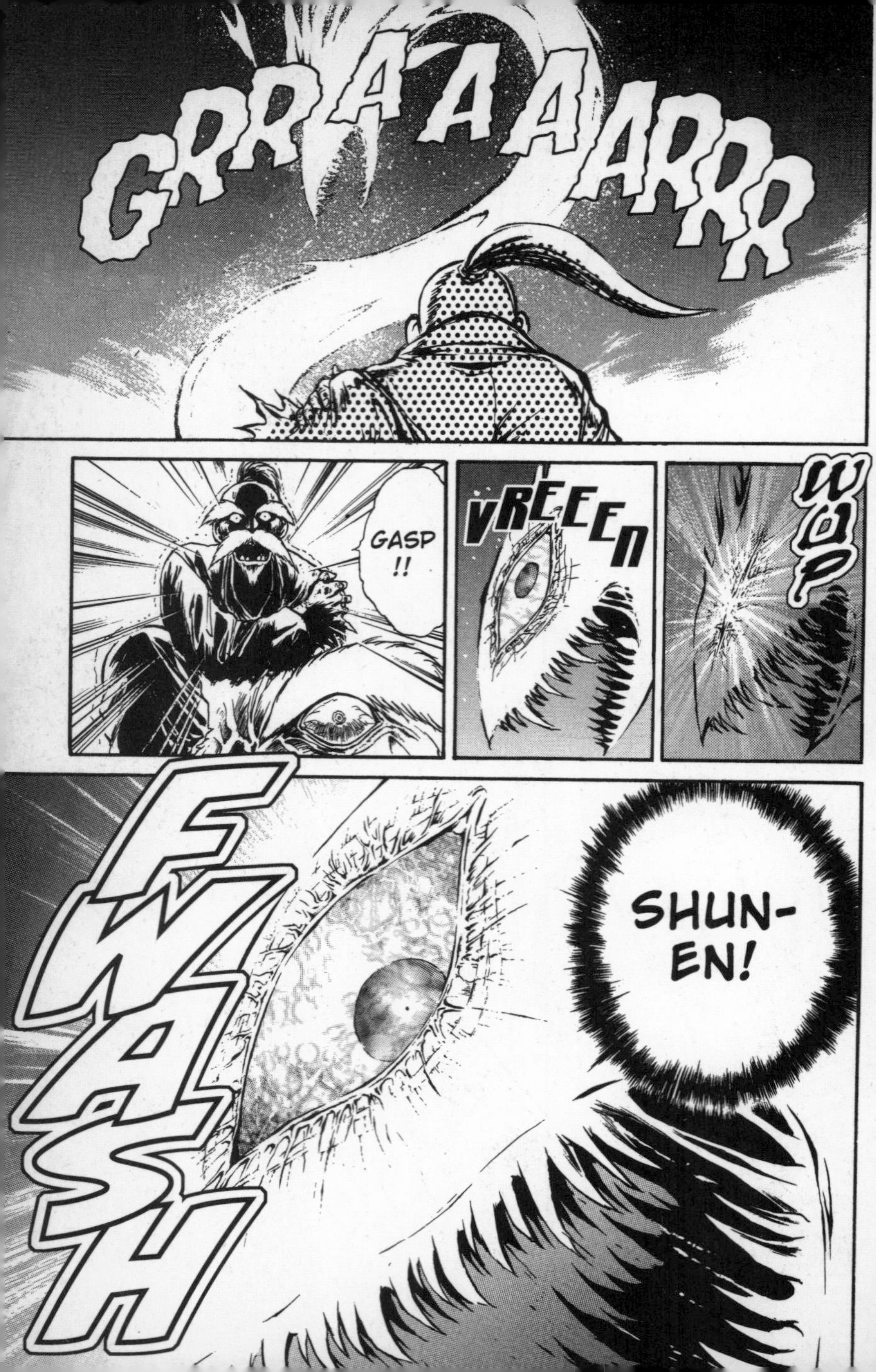
GRRAAAARRR
WOP
VREEEN
GASP !!
SHUN-EN!
FWASH

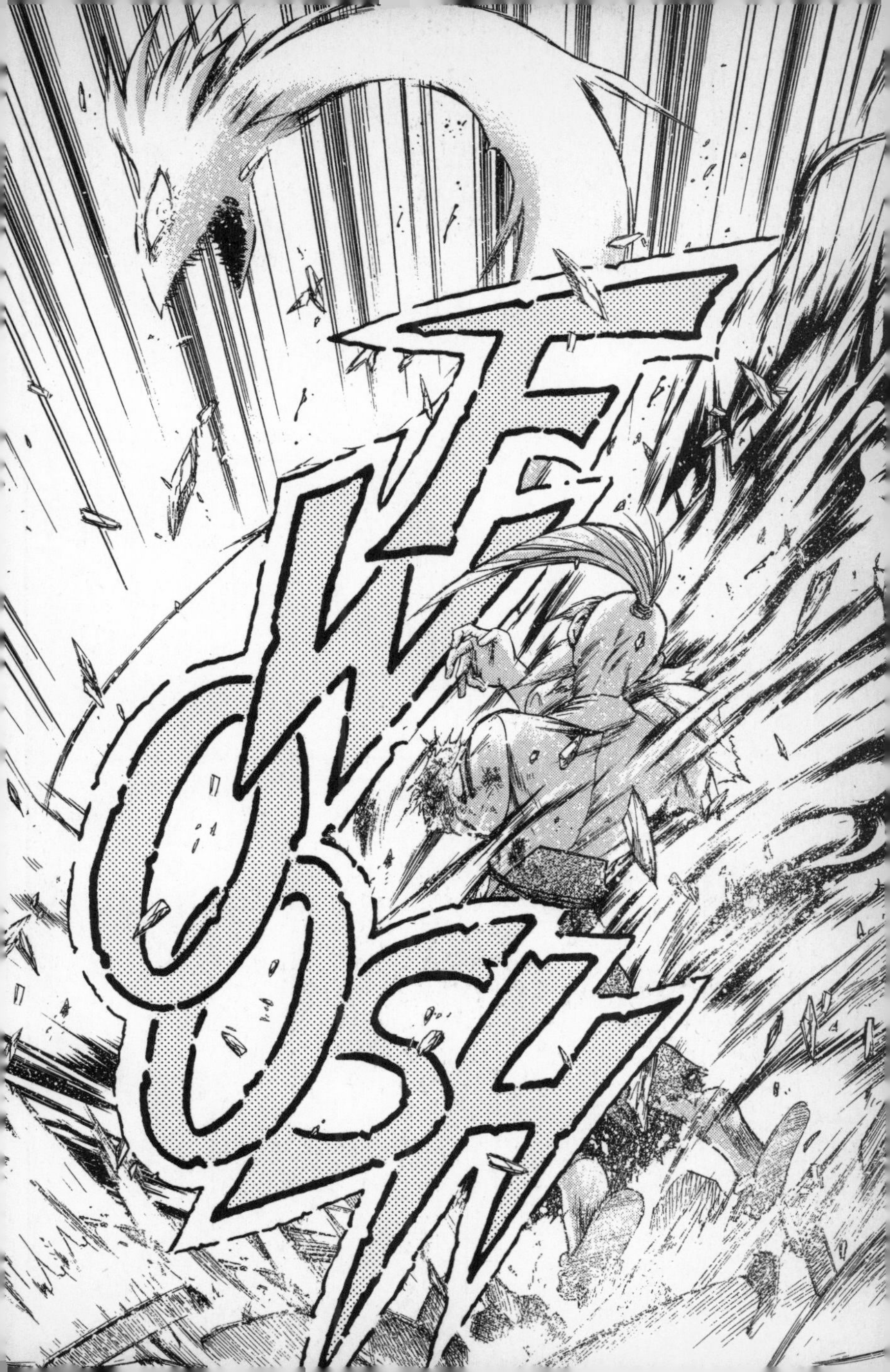
FWOOSH

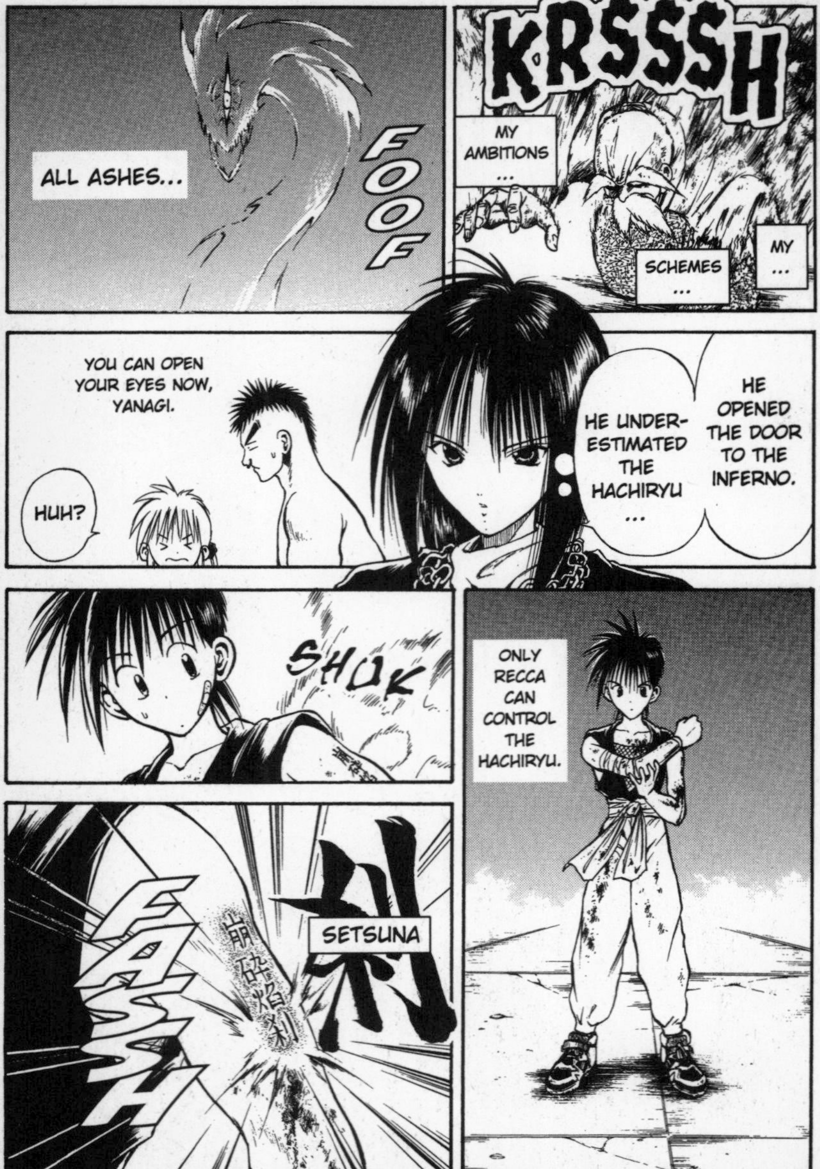
KRSSSH
MY AMBITIONS ...
MY ...
SCHEMES ...
ALL ASHES...
FOOF
HE OPENED THE DOOR TO THE INFERNO.
HE UNDER-ESTIMATED THE HACHIRYU ...
YOU CAN OPEN YOUR EYES NOW, YANAGI.
HUH?
ONLY RECCA CAN CONTROL THE HACHIRYU.
SHOK
刹
SETSUNA
崩砕焔刹
FLASH

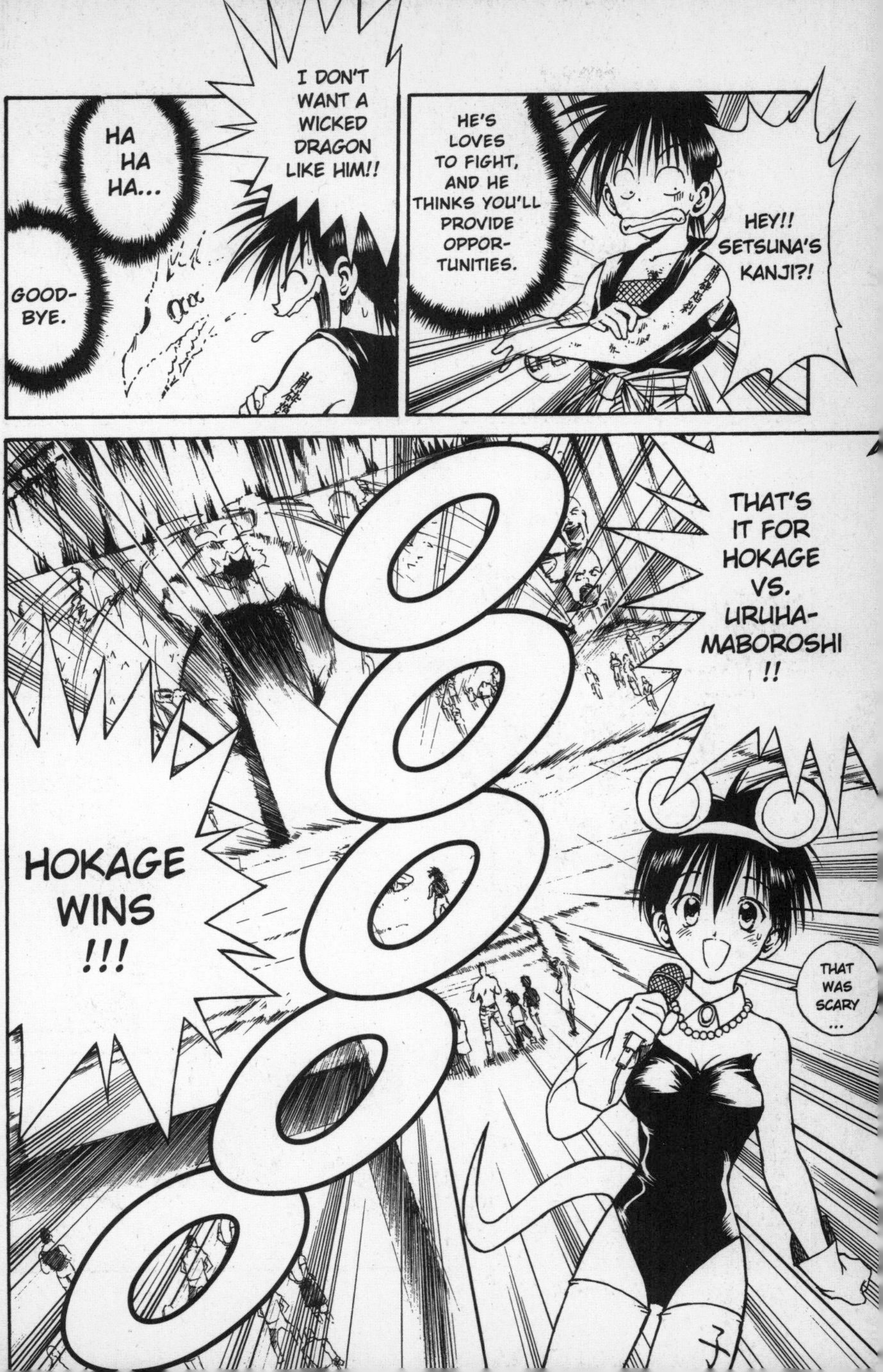
HEY!! SETSUNA'S KANJI?!
HE'S LOVES TO FIGHT, AND HE THINKS YOU'LL PROVIDE OPPOR-TUNITIES.
I DON'T WANT A WICKED DRAGON LIKE HIM!!
HA HA HA...
GOOD-BYE.
THAT'S IT FOR HOKAGE VS. URUHA-MABOROSHI !!
THAT WAS SCARY ...
HOKAGE WINS !!!

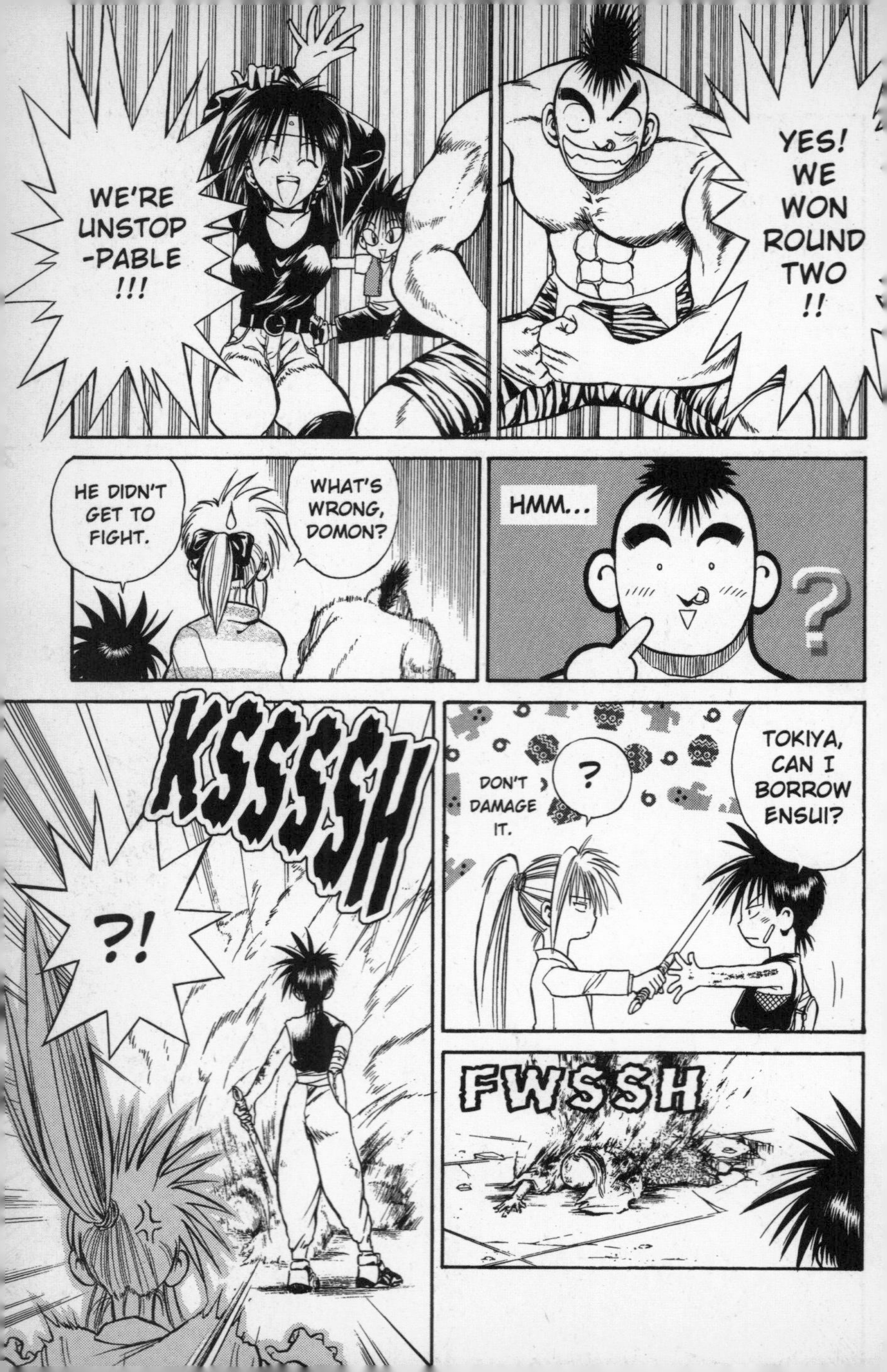
YES! WE WON ROUND TWO !!
WE'RE UNSTOP-PABLE !!!
HMM...
?
WHAT'S WRONG, DOMON?
HE DIDN'T GET TO FIGHT.
TOKIYA, CAN I BORROW ENSUI?
?
DON'T DAMAGE IT.
FWSSH
KSSSSH
?!

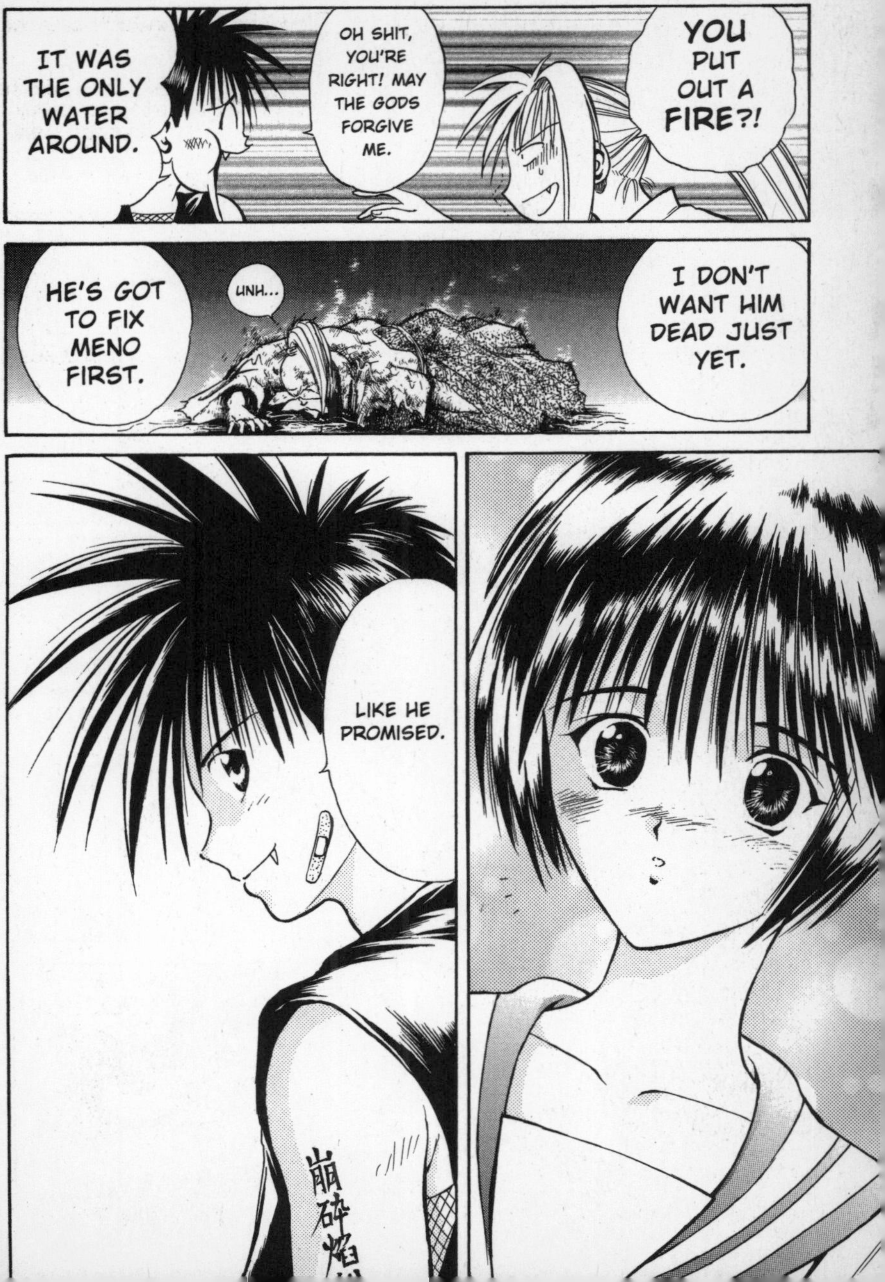
YOU PUT OUT A FIRE?!
OH SHIT, YOU'RE RIGHT! MAY THE GODS FORGIVE ME.
IT WAS THE ONLY WATER AROUND.
I DON'T WANT HIM DEAD JUST YET.
UNH...
HE'S GOT TO FIX MENO FIRST.
LIKE HE PROMISED.

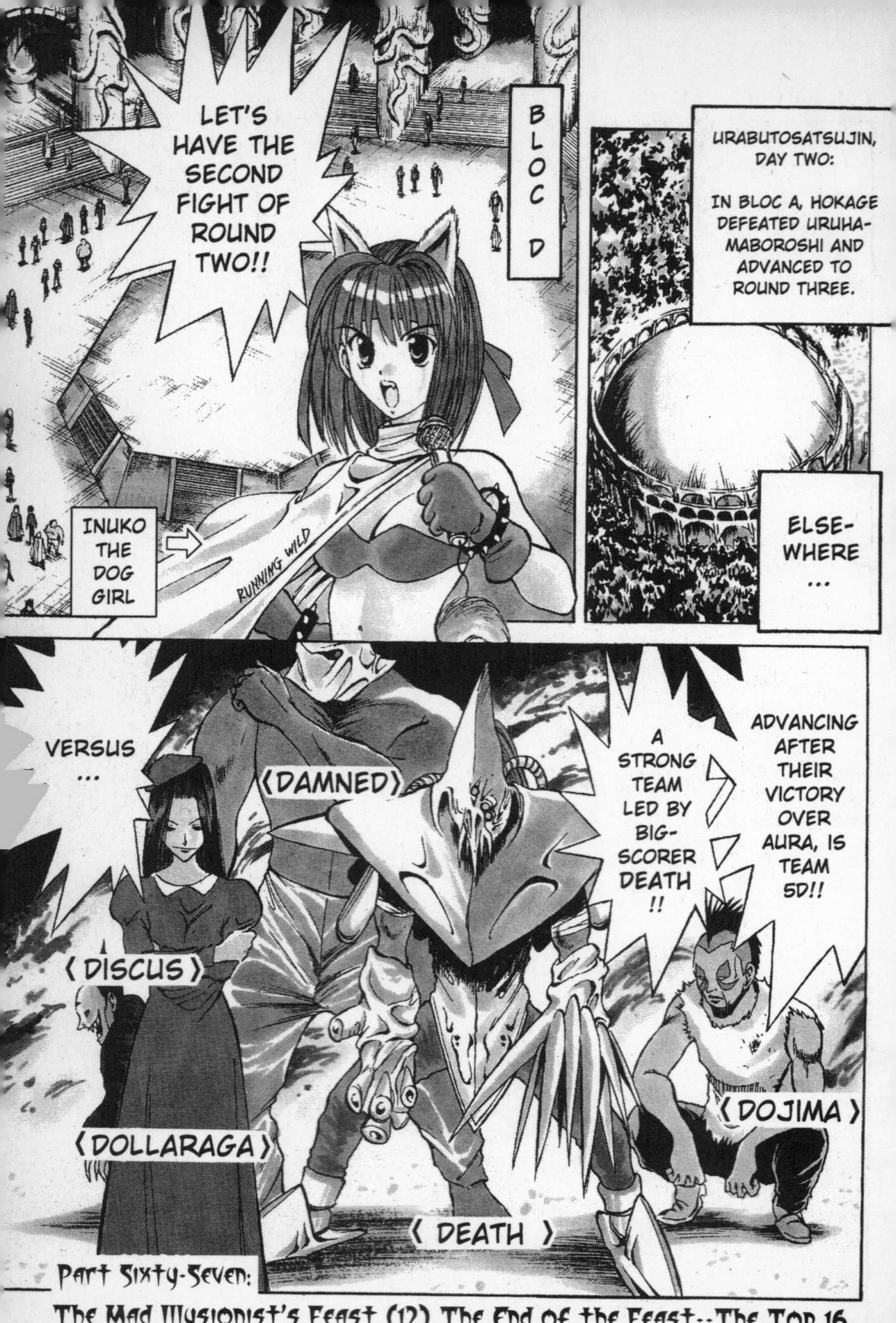
URABUTOSATSUJIN, DAY TWO:
IN BLOC A, HOKAGE DEFEATED URUHA-MABOROSHI AND ADVANCED TO ROUND THREE.
ELSE-WHERE ...
BLOC D
LET'S HAVE THE SECOND FIGHT OF ROUND TWO!!
INUKO THE DOG GIRL
RUNNING WILD
ADVANCING AFTER THEIR VICTORY OVER AURA, IS TEAM SD!!
A STRONG TEAM LED BY BIG-SCORER DEATH !!
VERSUS ...
《DAMNED》
《DISCUS》
《DOJIMA》
《DOLLARAGA》
《DEATH》

## Part Sixty-Seven:

## The Mad Illusionist's Feast (12) The End of the Feast--The Top 16

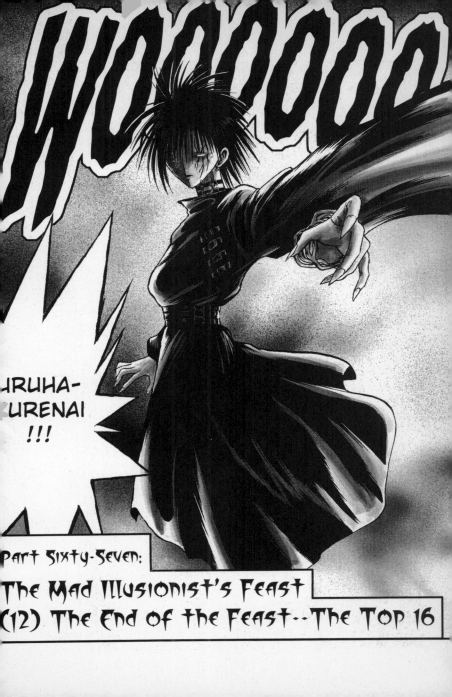

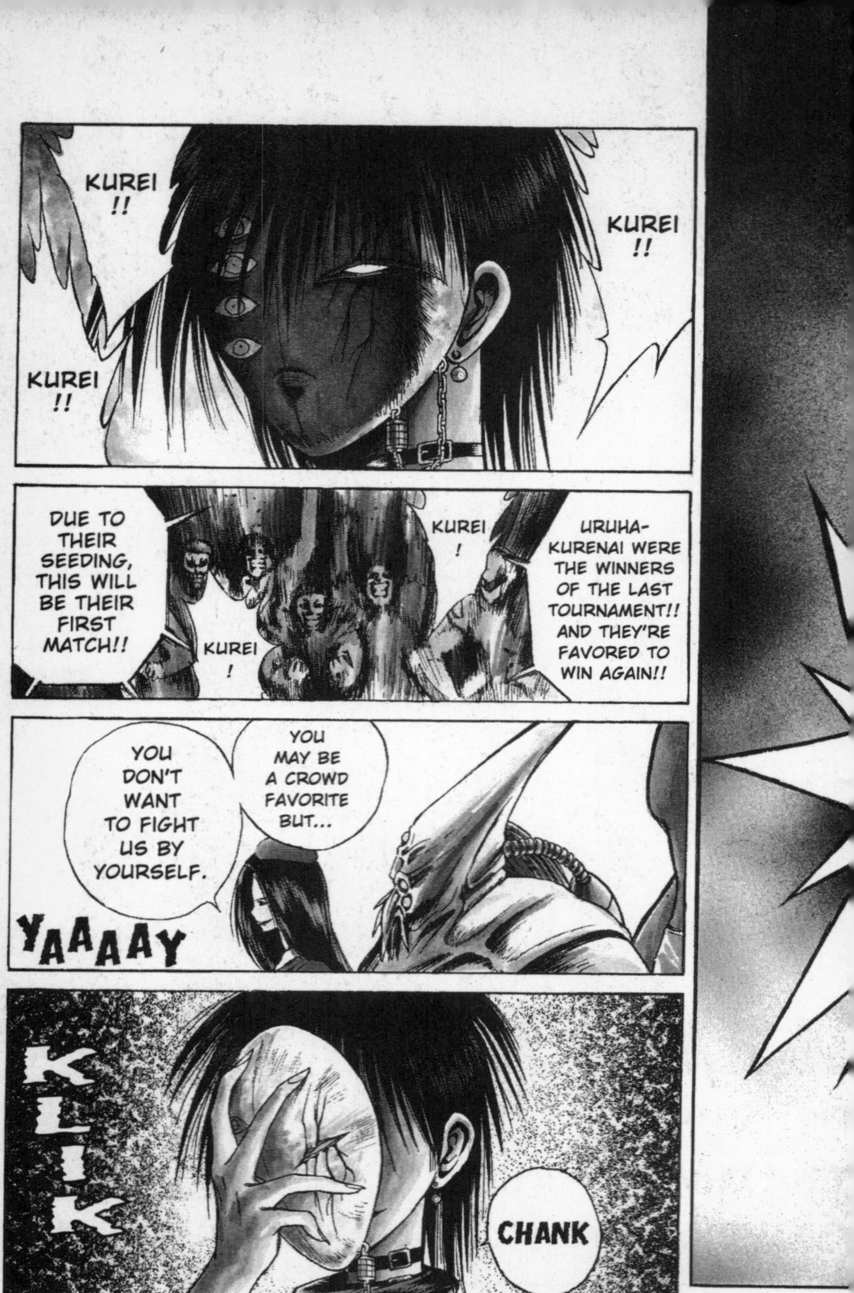
KUREI !!
KUREI !!
KUREI !!
URUHA-KURENAI WERE THE WINNERS OF THE LAST TOURNAMENT!! AND THEY'RE FAVORED TO WIN AGAIN!!
KUREI !
KUREI !
DUE TO THEIR SEEDING, THIS WILL BE THEIR FIRST MATCH!!
YOU MAY BE A CROWD FAVORITE BUT...
YOU DON'T WANT TO FIGHT US BY YOURSELF.
YAAAAY
CHANK
KLIK

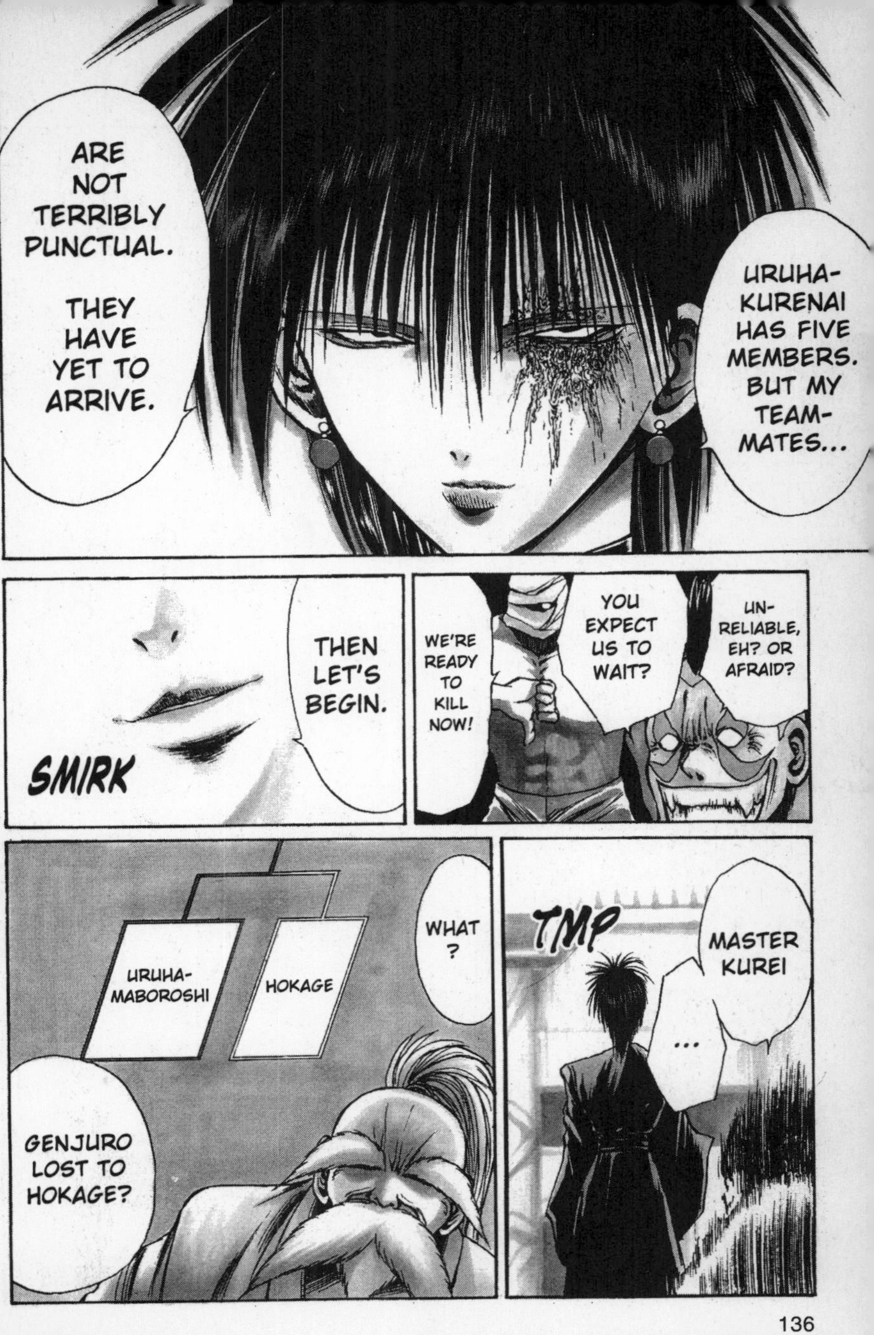
URUHA-KURENAI HAS FIVE MEMBERS. BUT MY TEAM-MATES...
ARE NOT TERRIBLY PUNCTUAL.
THEY HAVE YET TO ARRIVE.
UN-RELIABLE, EH? OR AFRAID?
YOU EXPECT US TO WAIT?
WE'RE READY TO KILL NOW!
THEN LET'S BEGIN.
SMIRK
MASTER KUREI
TMP
...
WHAT ?
HOKAGE
URUHA-MABOROSHI
GENJURO LOST TO HOKAGE?

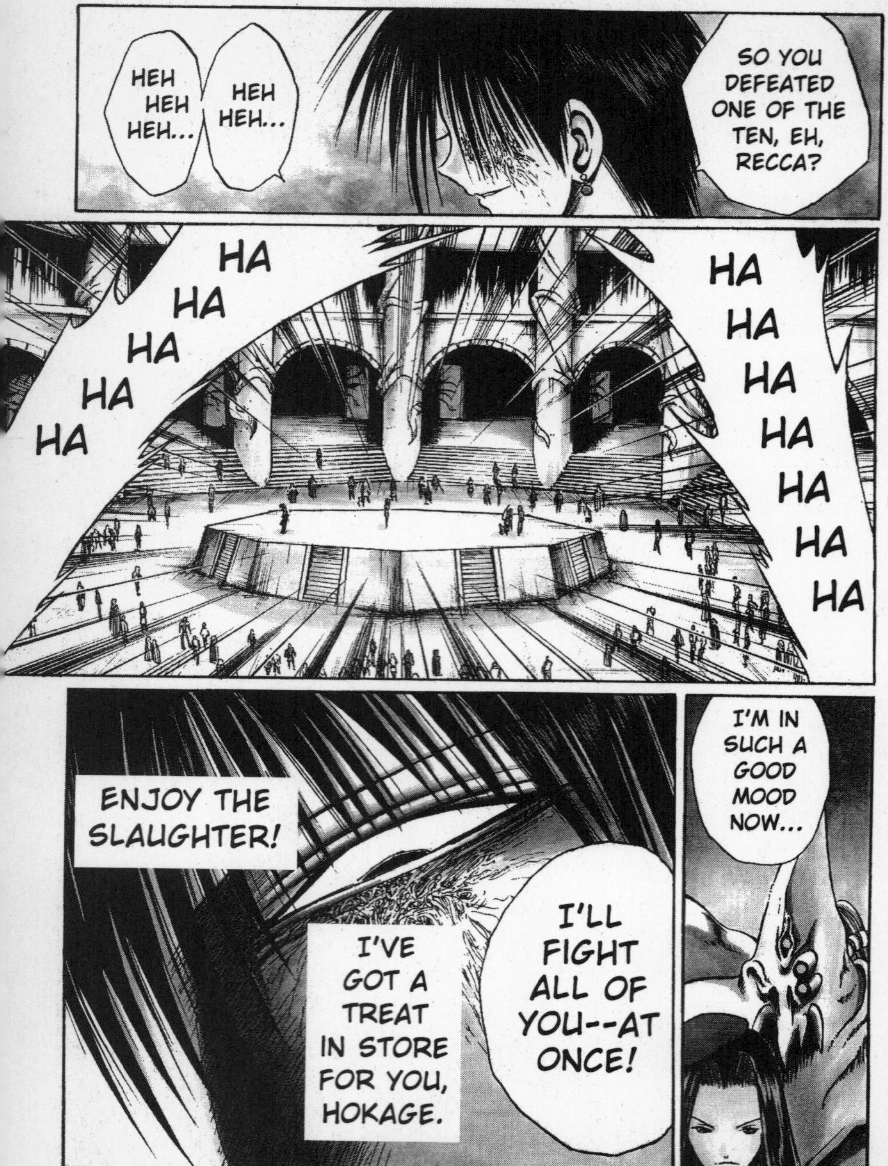
SO YOU DEFEATED ONE OF THE TEN, EH, RECCA?
HEH HEH...
HEH HEH HEH...
HA HA HA HA HA HA HA
HA HA HA HA HA
I'M IN SUCH A GOOD MOOD NOW...
I'VE GOT A TREAT IN STORE FOR YOU, HOKAGE.
I'LL FIGHT ALL OF YOU--AT ONCE!
ENJOY THE SLAUGHTER!

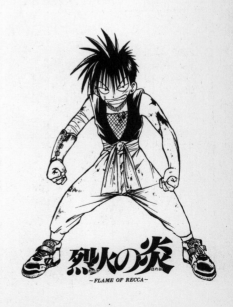

烈火の炎
~FLAME OF RECCA~

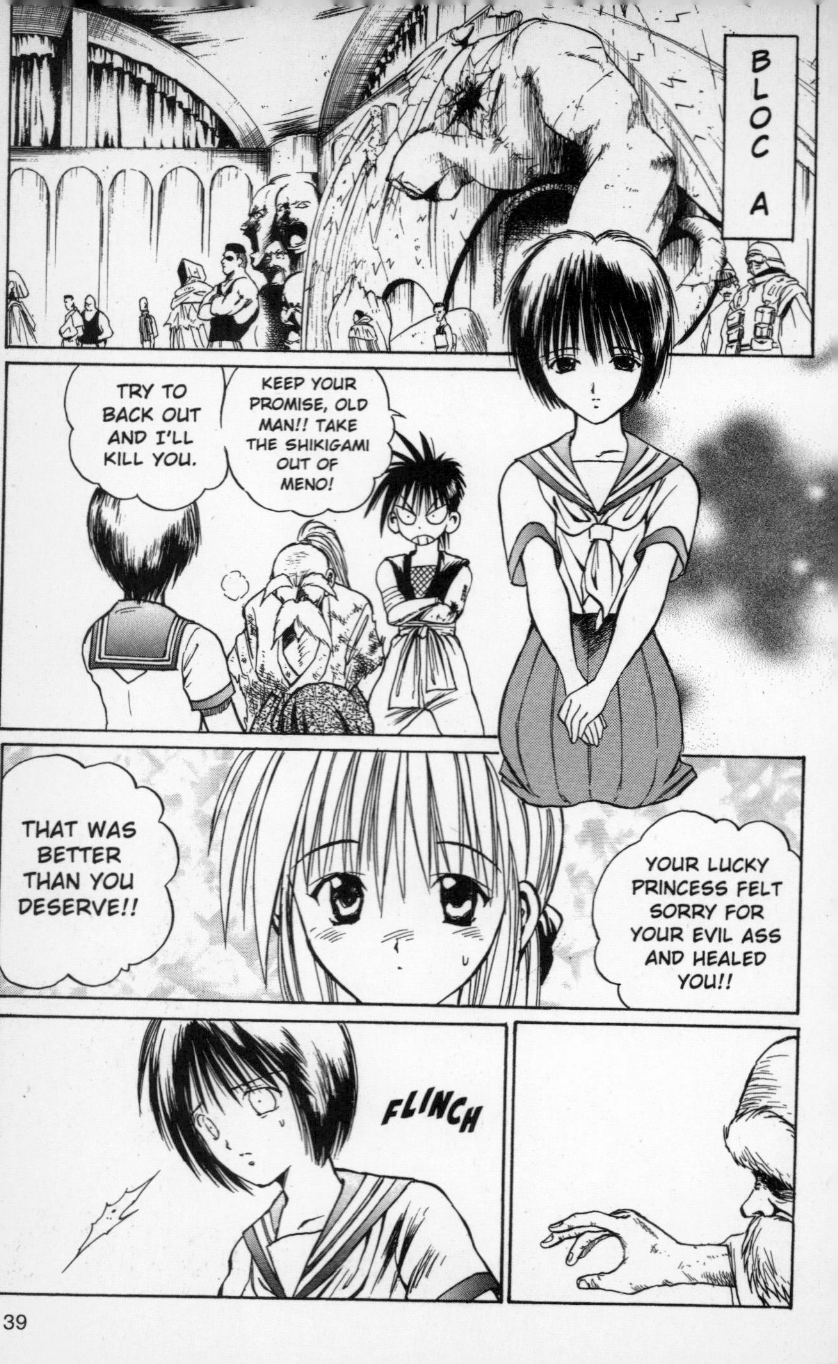
BLOC A
KEEP YOUR PROMISE, OLD MAN!! TAKE THE SHIKIGAMI OUT OF MENO!
TRY TO BACK OUT AND I'LL KILL YOU.
YOUR LUCKY PRINCESS FELT SORRY FOR YOUR EVIL ASS AND HEALED YOU!!
THAT WAS BETTER THAN YOU DESERVE!!
FLINCH

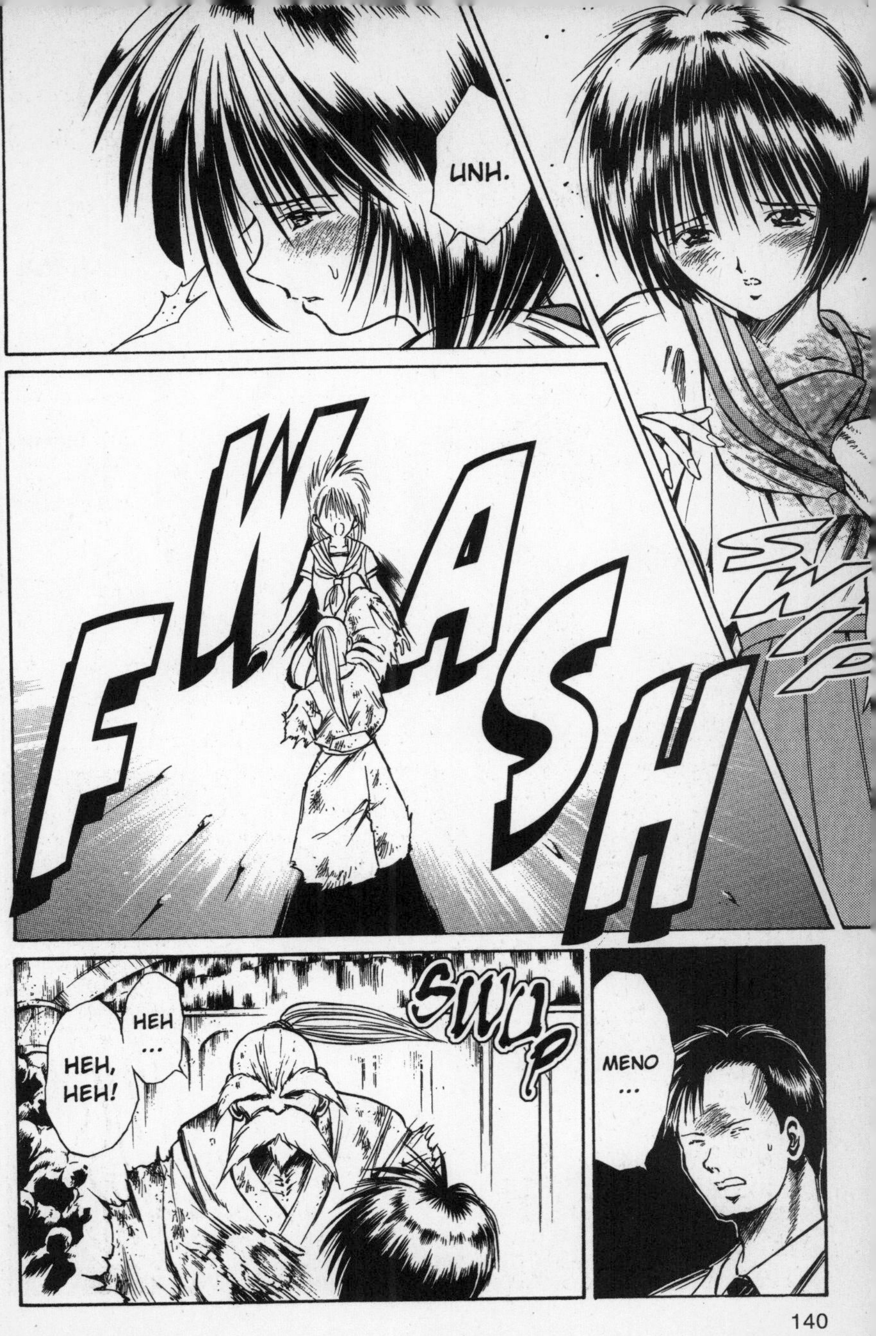
SWIP
UNH.
FWASH
MENO ...
SWUP
HEH ...
HEH, HEH!

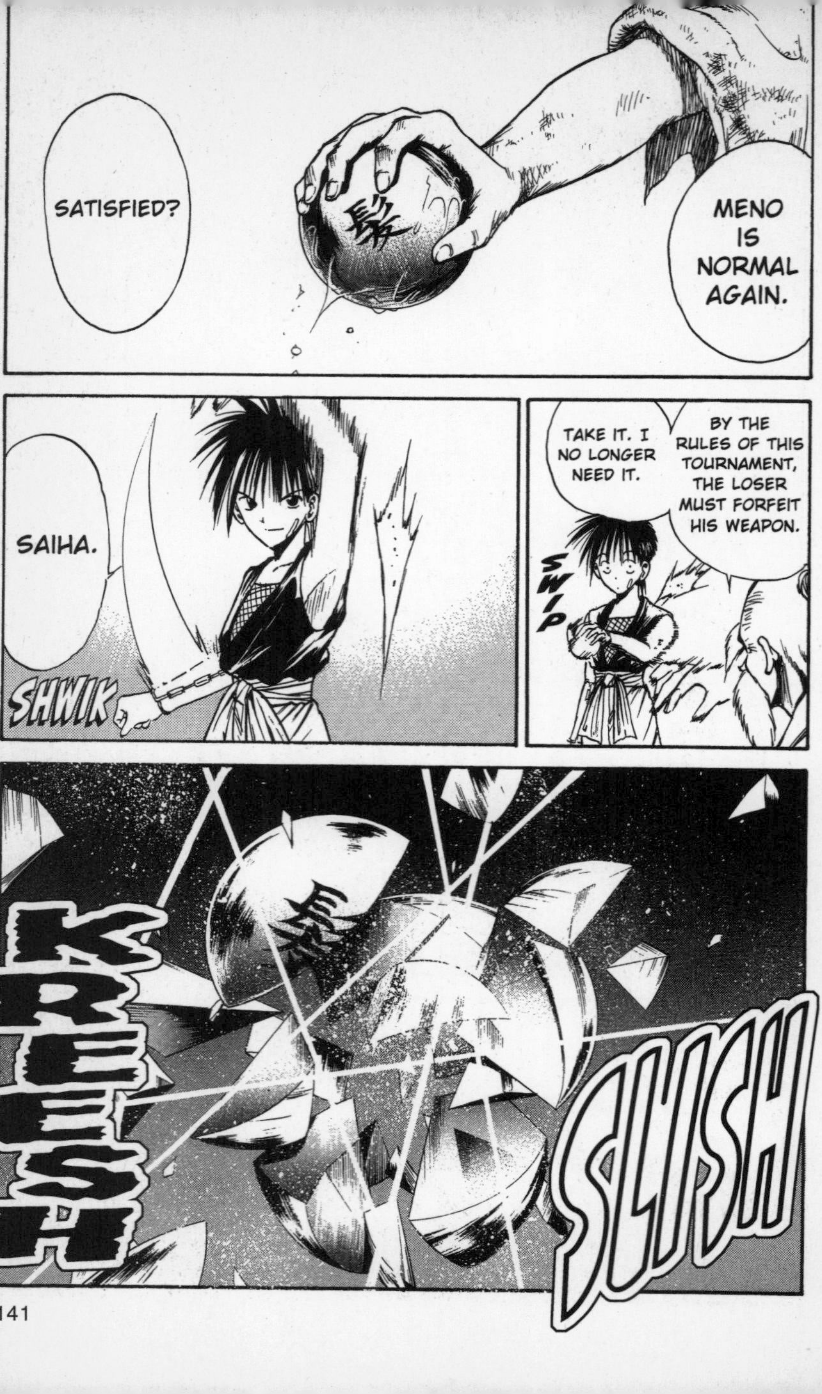
MENO IS NORMAL AGAIN.
髪
SATISFIED?
BY THE RULES OF THIS TOURNAMENT, THE LOSER MUST FORFEIT HIS WEAPON.
TAKE IT. I NO LONGER NEED IT.
SWIP
SAIHA.
SHWIK
SLISH
KRESH

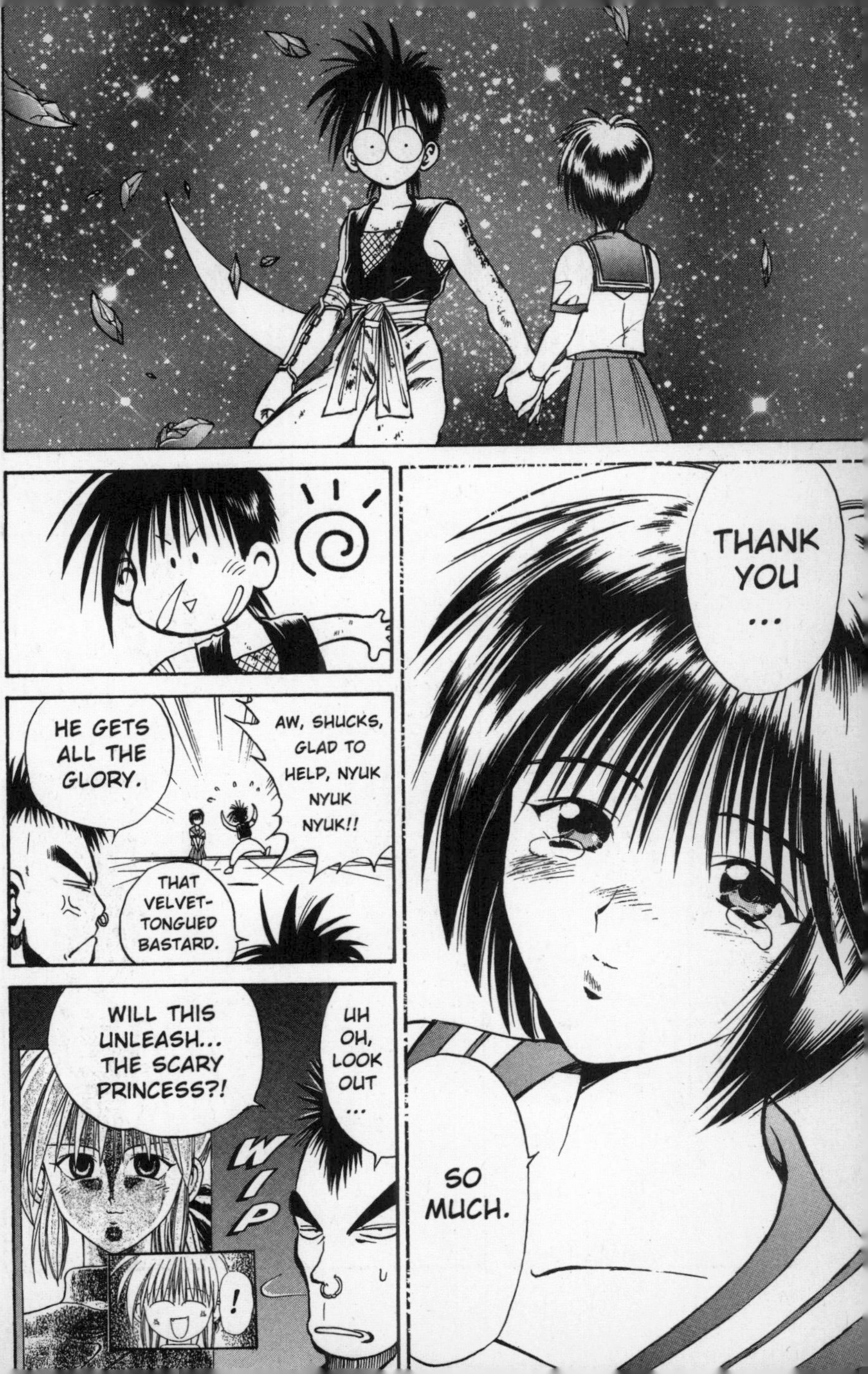
THANK YOU ...
SO MUCH.
AW, SHUCKS, GLAD TO HELP, NYUK NYUK NYUK!!
HE GETS ALL THE GLORY.
THAT VELVET-TONGUED BASTARD.
UH OH, LOOK OUT ...
WILL THIS UNLEASH... THE SCARY PRINCESS?!
WIP
!

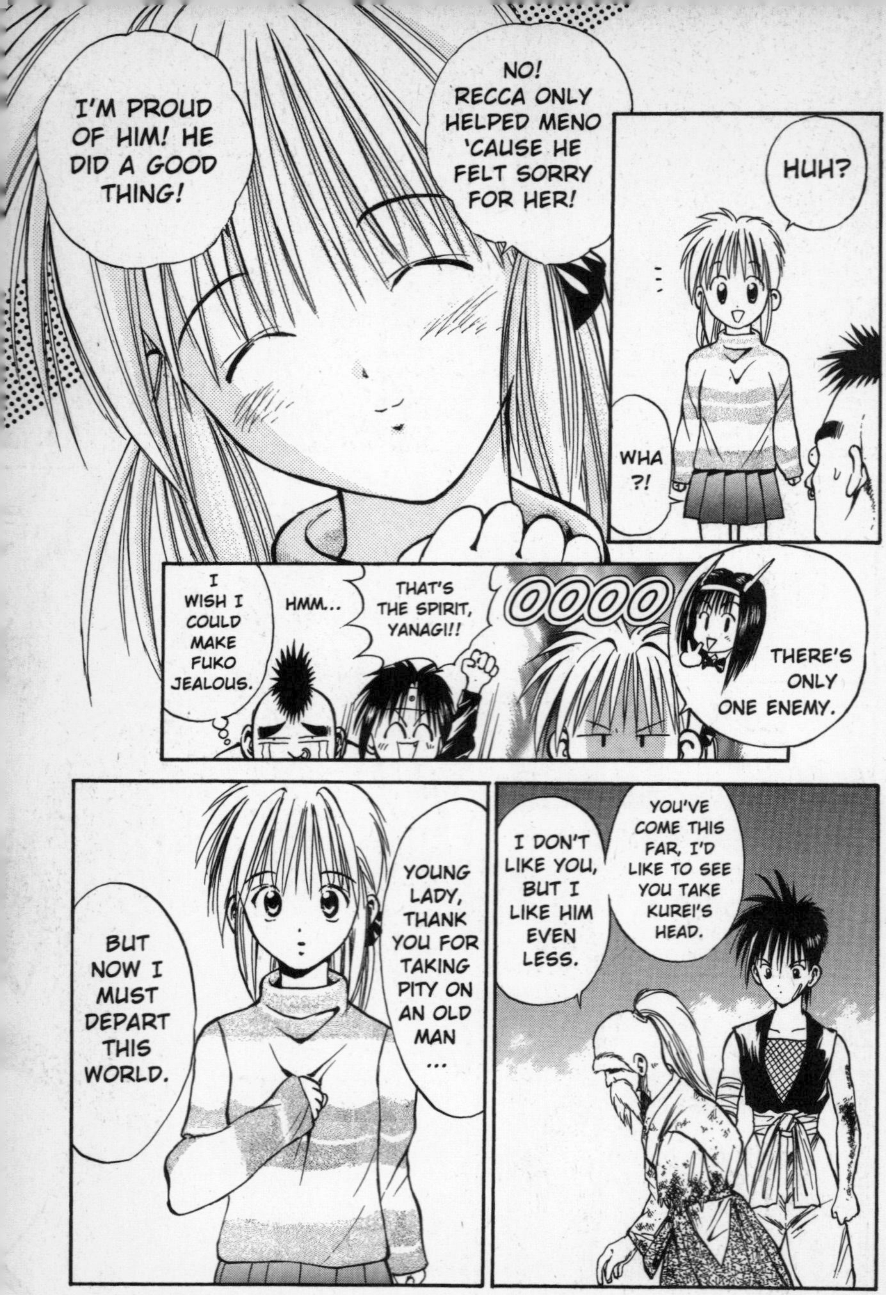

HUH?
WHA ?!
NO! RECCA ONLY HELPED MENO 'CAUSE HE FELT SORRY FOR HER!
I'M PROUD OF HIM! HE DID A GOOD THING!
THERE'S ONLY ONE ENEMY.
OOOO
THAT'S THE SPIRIT, YANAGI!!
HMM...
I WISH I COULD MAKE FUKO JEALOUS.
YOU'VE COME THIS FAR, I'D LIKE TO SEE YOU TAKE KUREI'S HEAD.
I DON'T LIKE YOU, BUT I LIKE HIM EVEN LESS.
YOUNG LADY, THANK YOU FOR TAKING PITY ON AN OLD MAN ...
BUT NOW I MUST DEPART THIS WORLD.

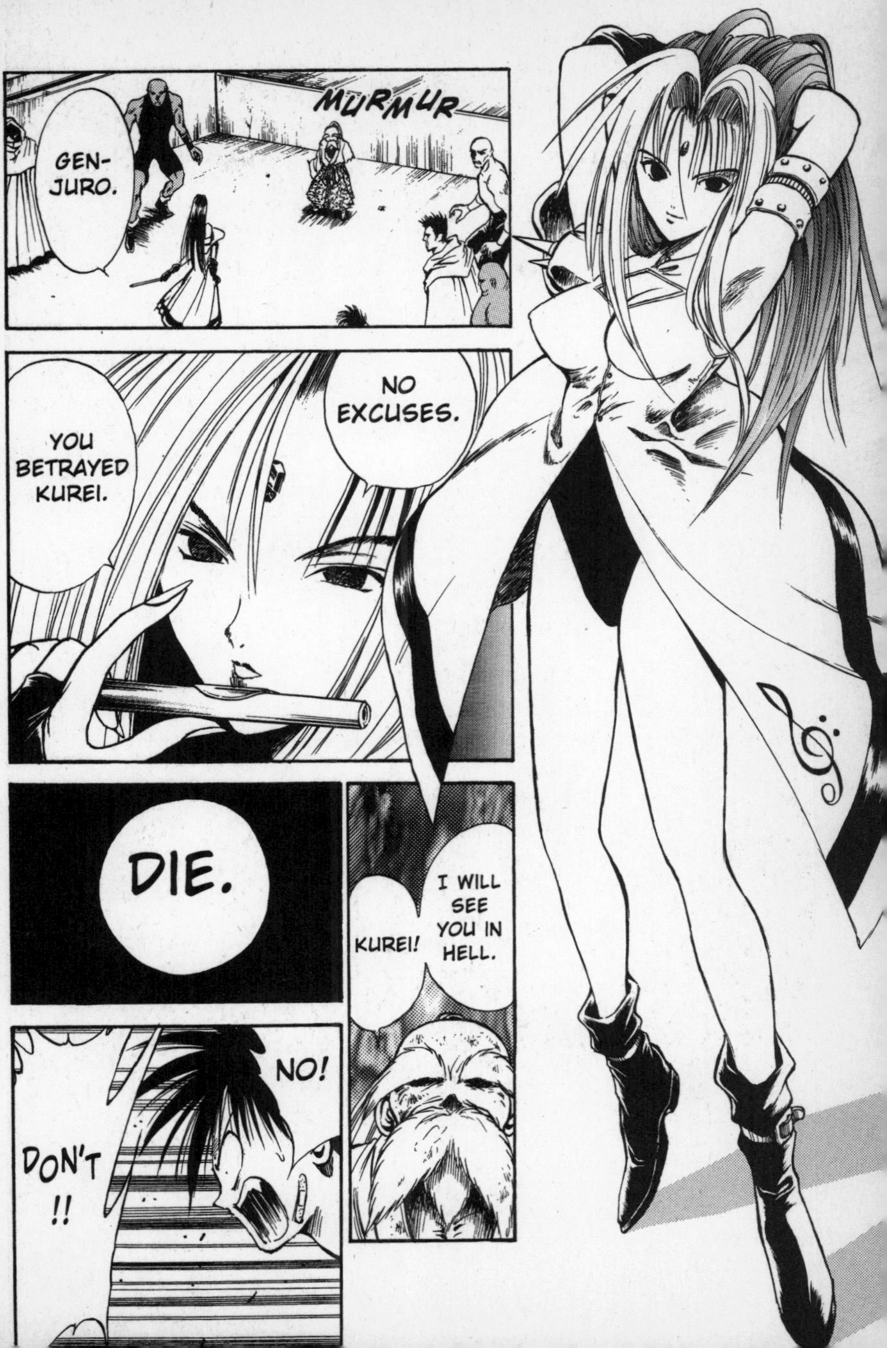
MURMUR
GEN-JURO.
NO EXCUSES.
YOU BETRAYED KUREI.
I WILL SEE YOU IN HELL.
KUREI!
DIE.
NO!
DON'T !!

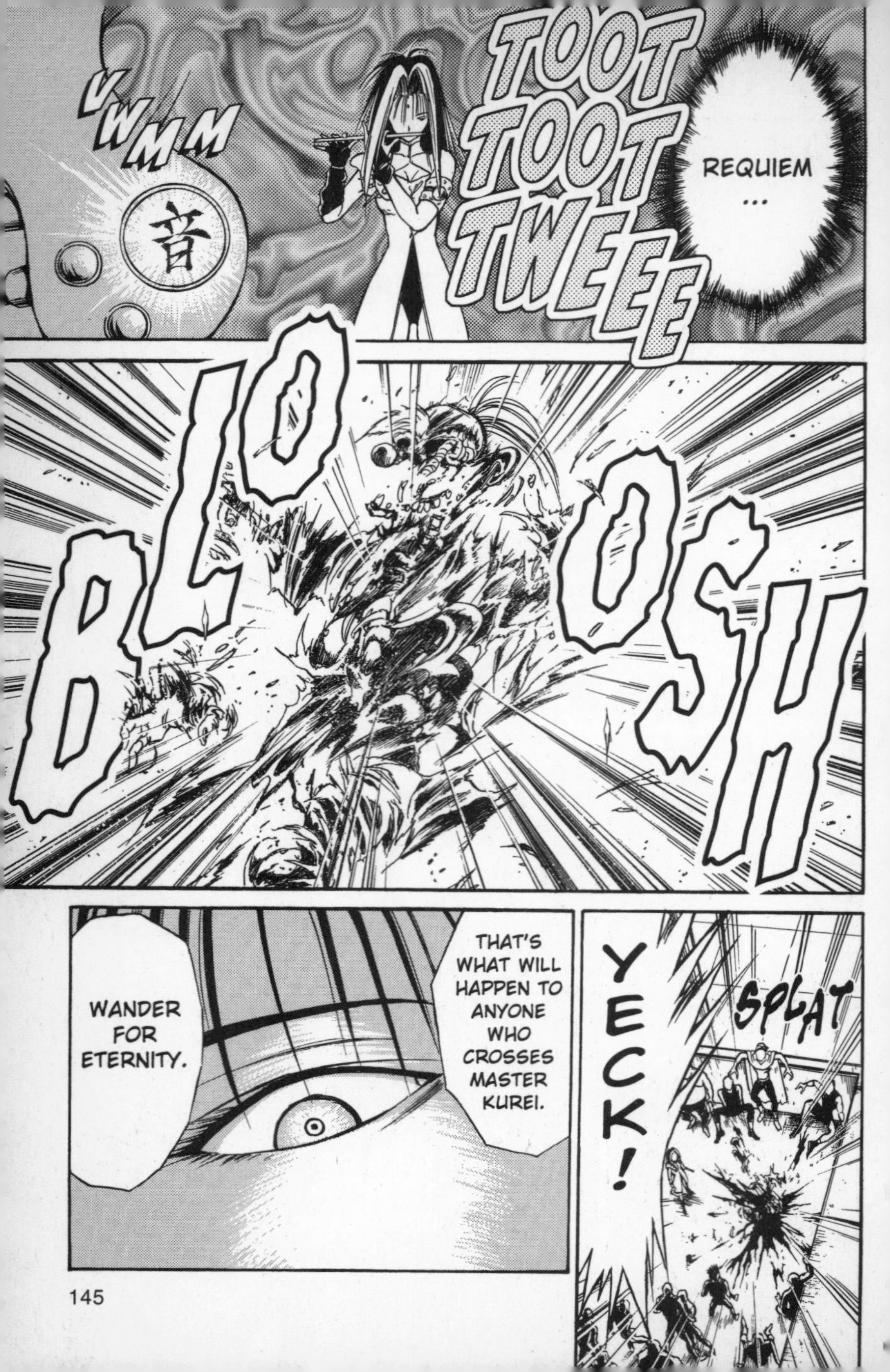
REQUIEM ...
TOOT TOOT TWEEE
VWMMM
音
BLOOSH
YECK!
SPLAT
THAT'S WHAT WILL HAPPEN TO ANYONE WHO CROSSES MASTER KUREI.
WANDER FOR ETERNITY.

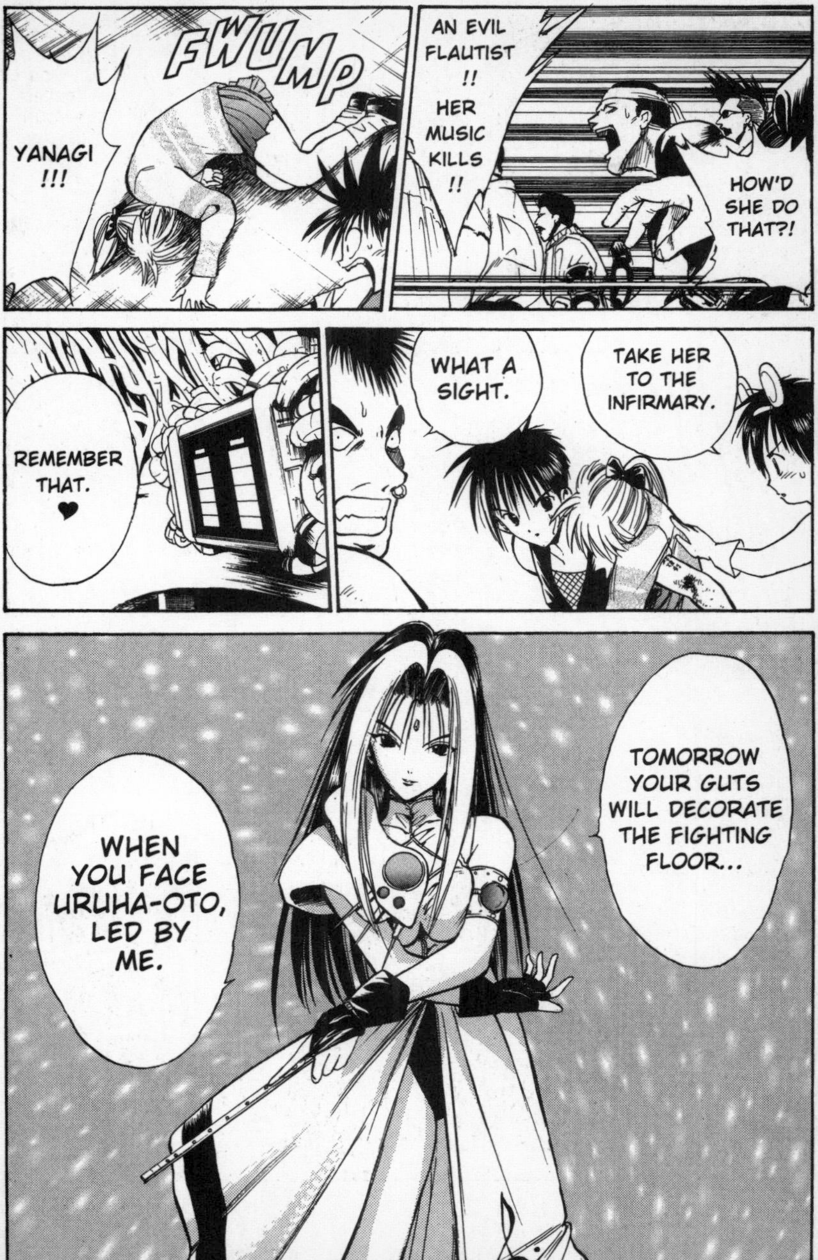
HOW'D SHE DO THAT?!
AN EVIL FLAUTIST !!
HER MUSIC KILLS !!
FWUMP
YANAGI !!!
TAKE HER TO THE INFIRMARY.
WHAT A SIGHT.
REMEMBER THAT. ♥
TOMORROW YOUR GUTS WILL DECORATE THE FIGHTING FLOOR...
WHEN YOU FACE URUHA-OTO, LED BY ME.

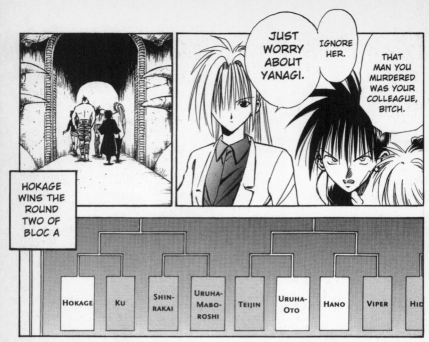

THAT MAN YOU MURDERED WAS YOUR COLLEAGUE, BITCH.
IGNORE HER.
JUST WORRY ABOUT YANAGI.
HOKAGE WINS THE ROUND TWO OF BLOC A
Hokage
Ku
Shin-rakai
Uruha-Maboroshi
Teijin
Uruha-Oto
Hano
Viper
Hid
AND FOLLOWING THEIR LEAD ...

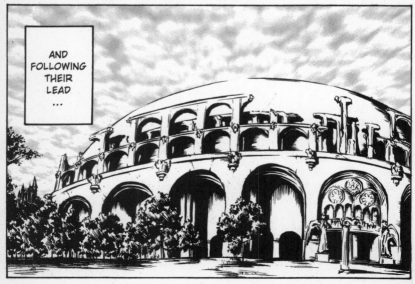

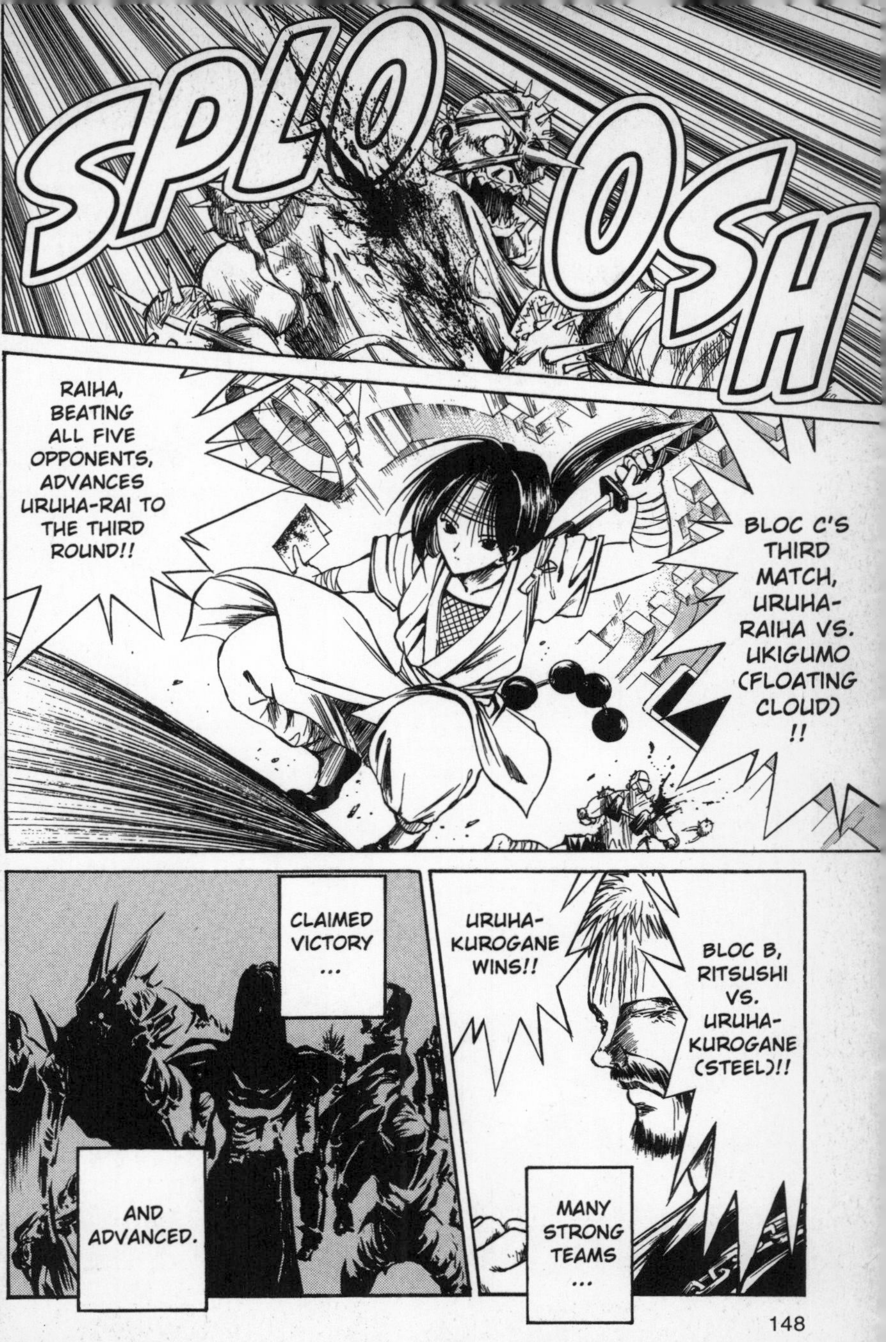
SPLOOSH
BLOC C'S THIRD MATCH, URUHA-RAIHA VS. UKIGUMO (FLOATING CLOUD)!!
RAIHA, BEATING ALL FIVE OPPONENTS, ADVANCES URUHA-RAI TO THE THIRD ROUND!!
BLOC B, RITSUSHI VS. URUHA-KUROGANE (STEEL)!!
URUHA-KUROGANE WINS!!
MANY STRONG TEAMS ...
CLAIMED VICTORY ...
AND ADVANCED.

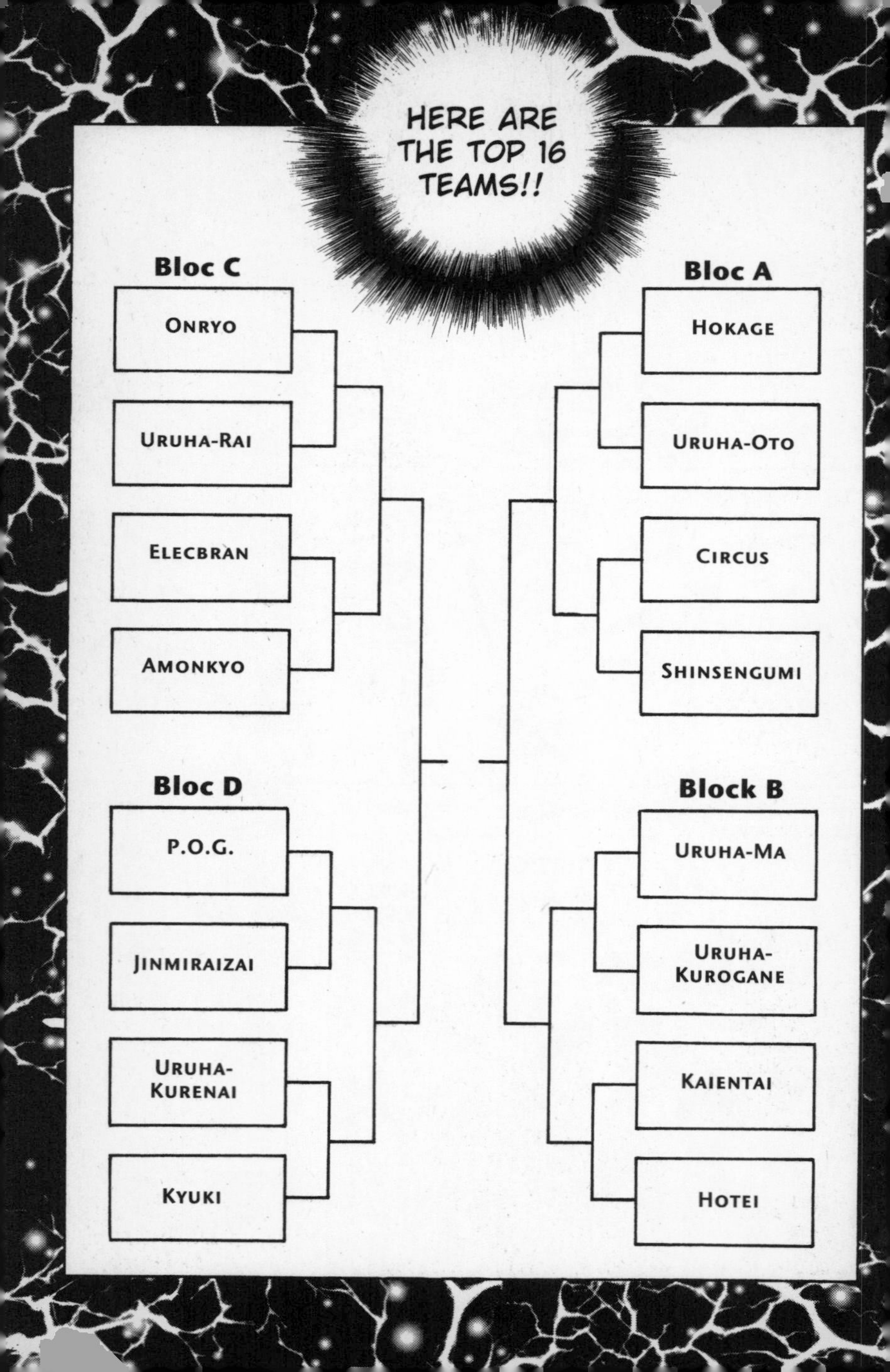
HERE ARE THE TOP 16 TEAMS!!
Bloc A
Hokage
Uruha-Oto
Circus
Shinsengumi
Block B
Uruha-Ma
Uruha-Kurogane
Kaientai
Hotei
Bloc C
Onryo
Uruha-Rai
Elecbran
Amonkyo
Bloc D
P.O.G.
Jinmiraizai
Uruha-Kurenai
Kyuki

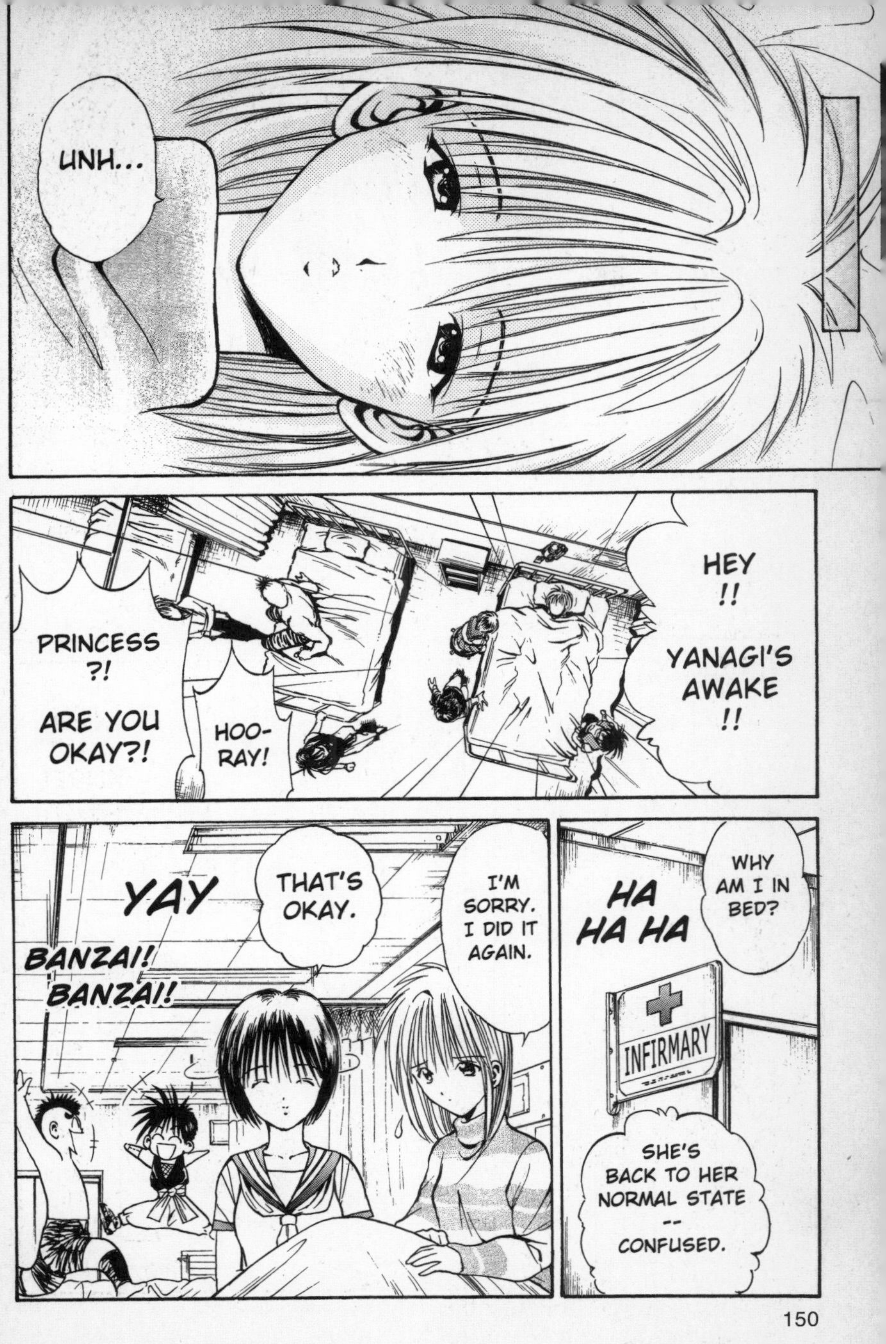
UNH...
HEY!! YANAGI'S AWAKE!!
HOO-RAY!
PRINCESS?! ARE YOU OKAY?!
WHY AM I IN BED?
HA HA HA
INFIRMARY
SHE'S BACK TO HER NORMAL STATE -- CONFUSED.
I'M SORRY. I DID IT AGAIN.
THAT'S OKAY.
YAY
BANZAI! BANZAI!

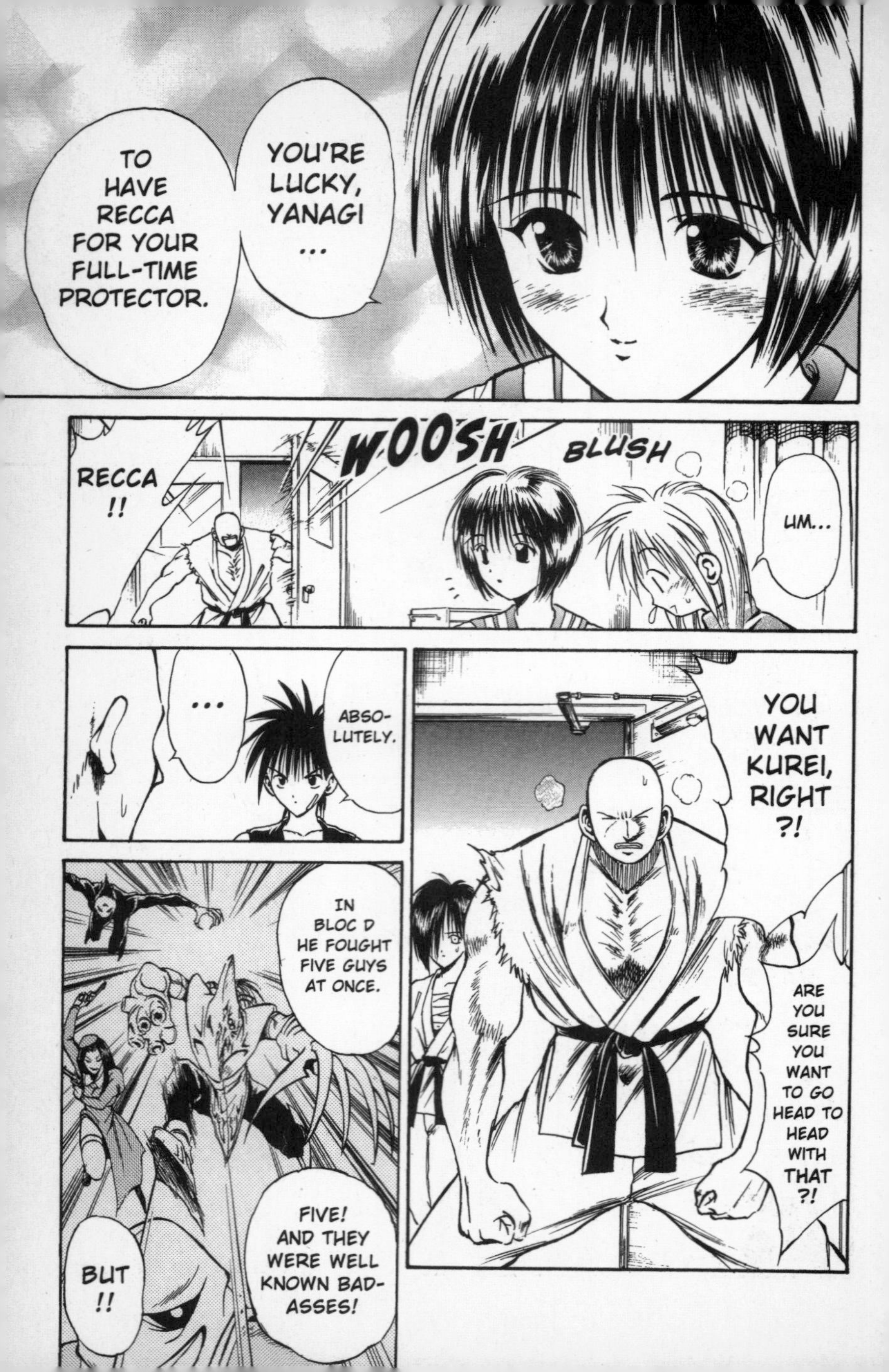
YOU'RE LUCKY, YANAGI ...
TO HAVE RECCA FOR YOUR FULL-TIME PROTECTOR.
UM...
BLUSH
WOOSH
RECCA !!
YOU WANT KUREI, RIGHT ?!
ARE YOU SURE YOU WANT TO GO HEAD TO HEAD WITH THAT ?!
ABSO-LUTELY.
...
IN BLOC D HE FOUGHT FIVE GUYS AT ONCE.
FIVE! AND THEY WERE WELL KNOWN BAD-ASSES!
BUT !!

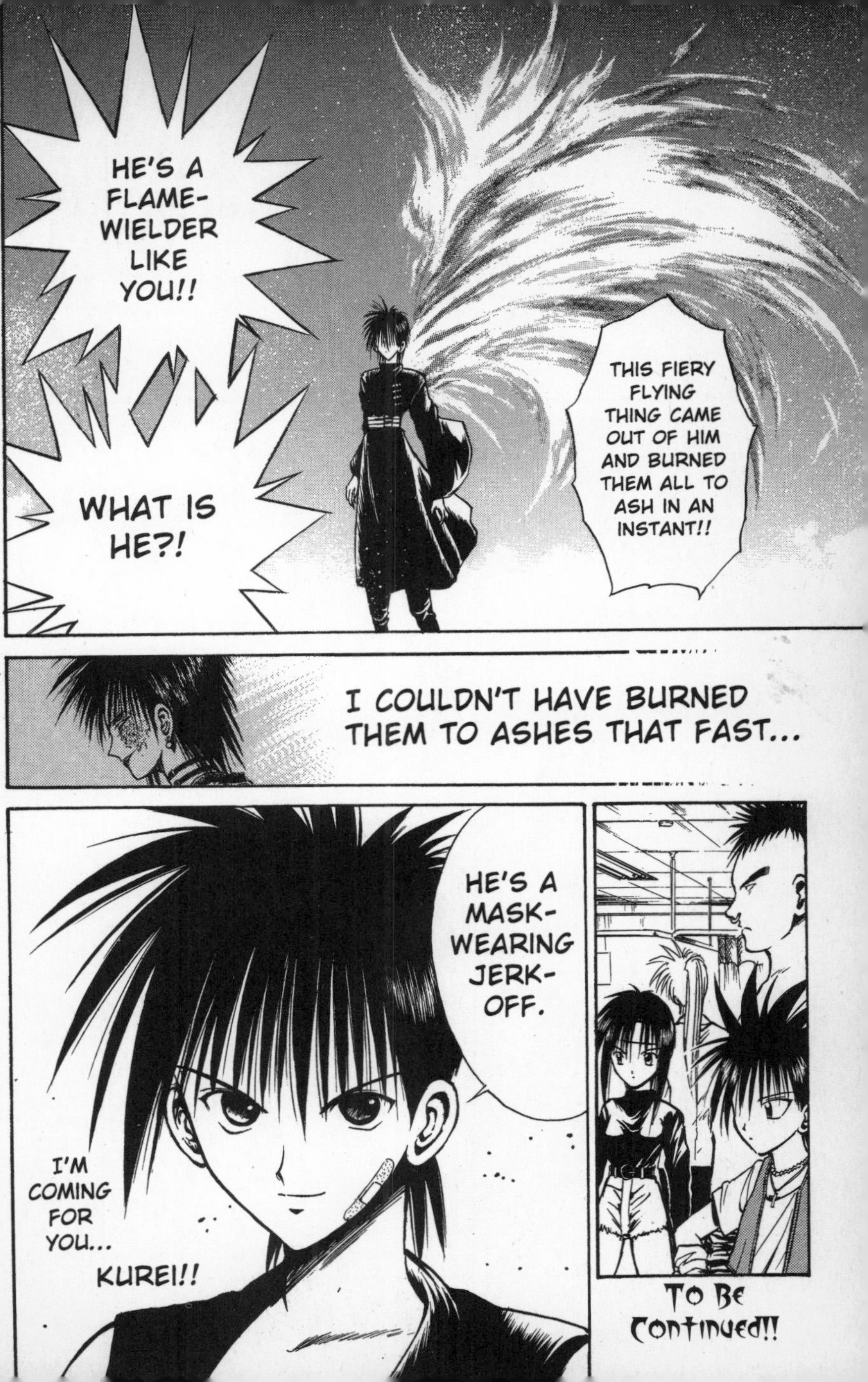
THIS FIERY FLYING THING CAME OUT OF HIM AND BURNED THEM ALL TO ASH IN AN INSTANT!!
HE'S A FLAME-WIELDER LIKE YOU!!
WHAT IS HE?!
I COULDN'T HAVE BURNED THEM TO ASHES THAT FAST...
TO BE CONTINUED!!
HE'S A MASK-WEARING JERK-OFF.
...
..
I'M COMING FOR YOU... KUREI!!

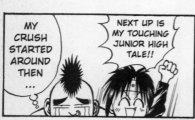

NEXT UP IS MY TOUCHING JUNIOR HIGH TALE!!
MY CRUSH STARTED AROUND THEN ...

烈火の炎

~FLAME OF RECCA~

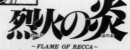

# Flame of Recca--Flashback
# One Windy Night

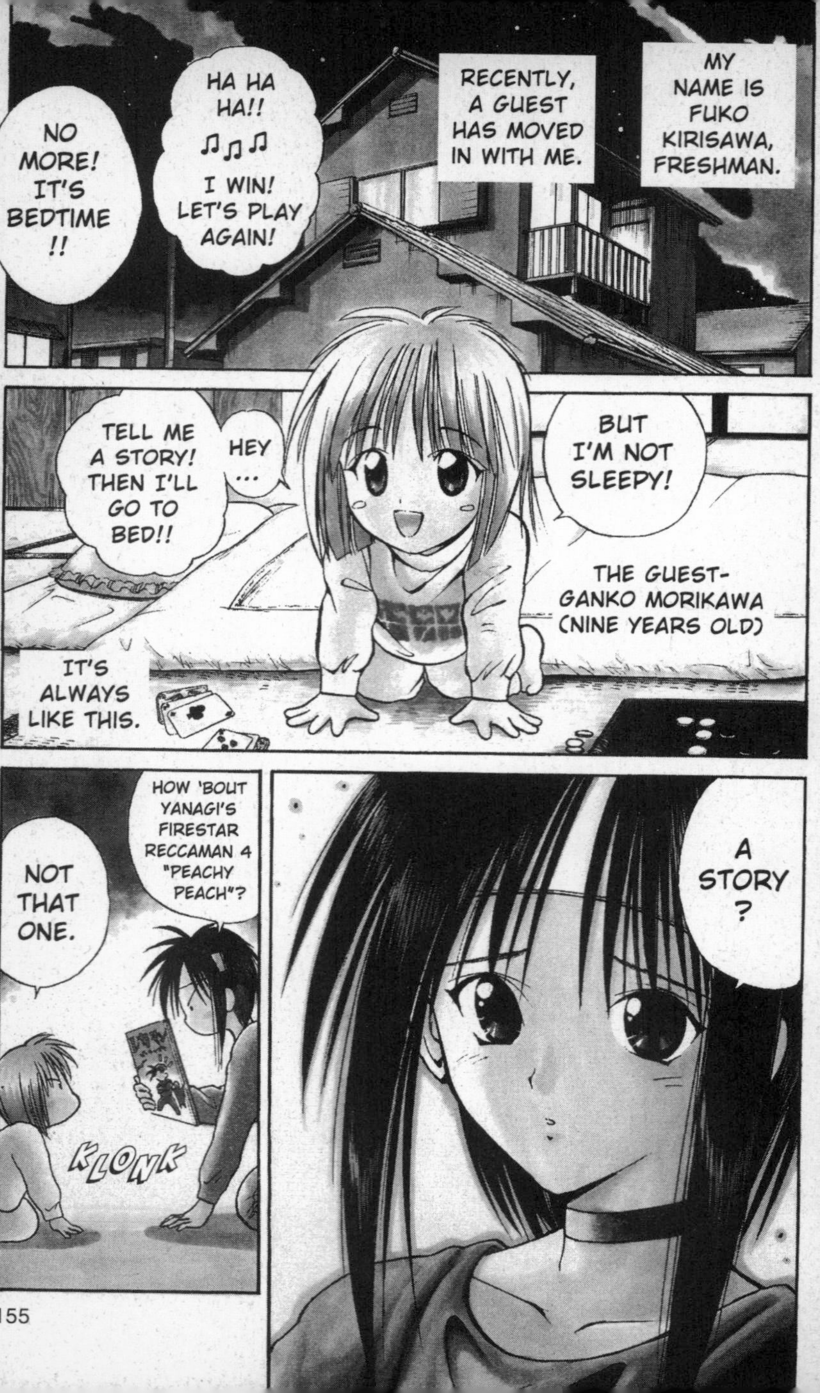
MY NAME IS FUKO KIRISAWA, FRESHMAN.
RECENTLY, A GUEST HAS MOVED IN WITH ME.
HA HA HA!! ♫♫♫
I WIN! LET'S PLAY AGAIN!
NO MORE! IT'S BEDTIME !!
BUT I'M NOT SLEEPY!
THE GUEST- GANKO MORIKAWA (NINE YEARS OLD)
HEY ...
TELL ME A STORY! THEN I'LL GO TO BED!!
IT'S ALWAYS LIKE THIS.
A STORY ?
HOW 'BOUT YANAGI'S FIRESTAR RECCAMAN 4 "PEACHY PEACH"?
NOT THAT ONE.
KLONK

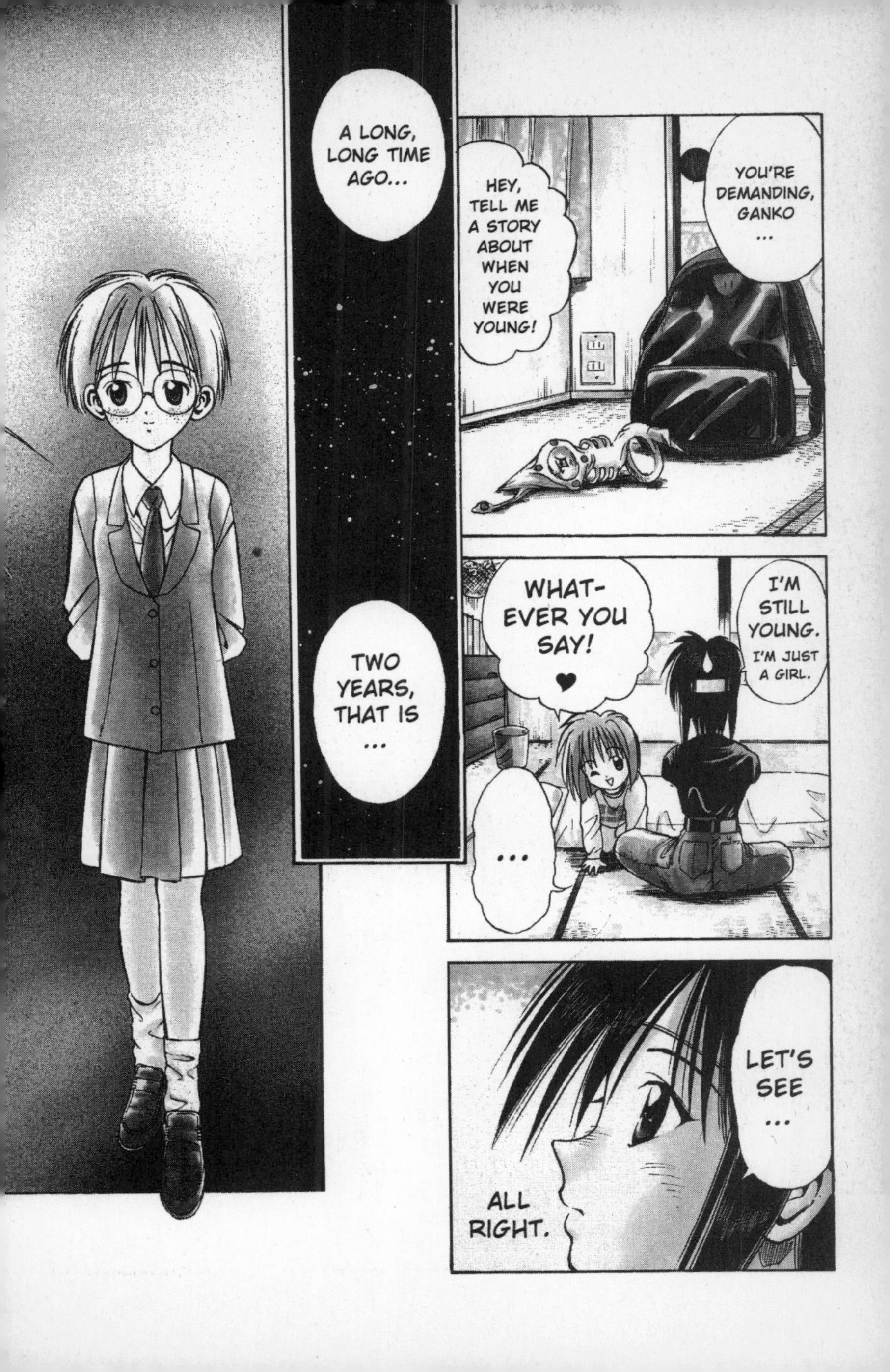
YOU'RE DEMANDING, GANKO ...
HEY, TELL ME A STORY ABOUT WHEN YOU WERE YOUNG!
I'M STILL YOUNG. I'M JUST A GIRL.
WHAT-EVER YOU SAY! ♥
...
LET'S SEE ...
ALL RIGHT.
A LONG, LONG TIME AGO...
TWO YEARS, THAT IS ...

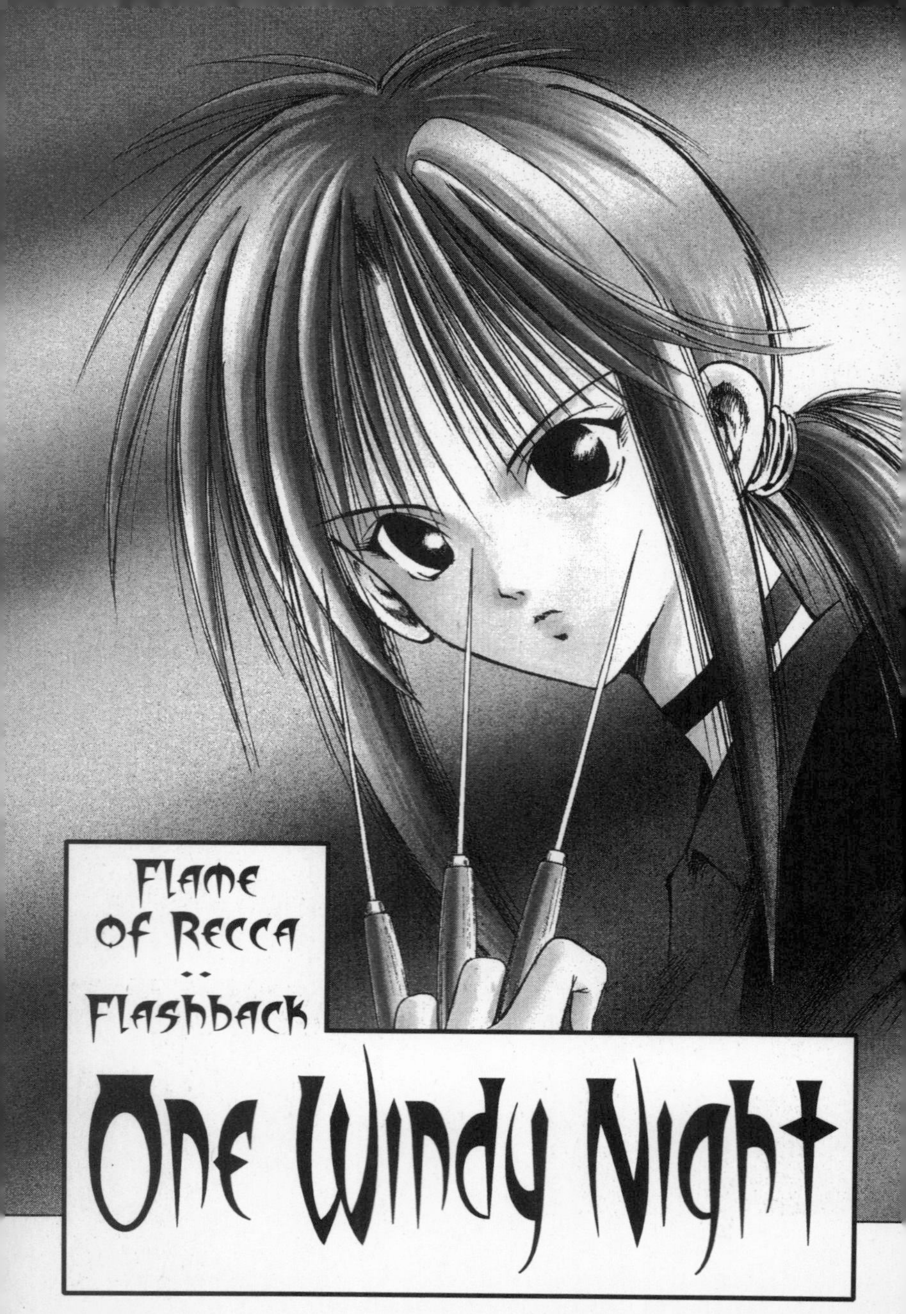
FLAME OF RECCA
--
FLASHBACK
ONE WINDY NIGHT

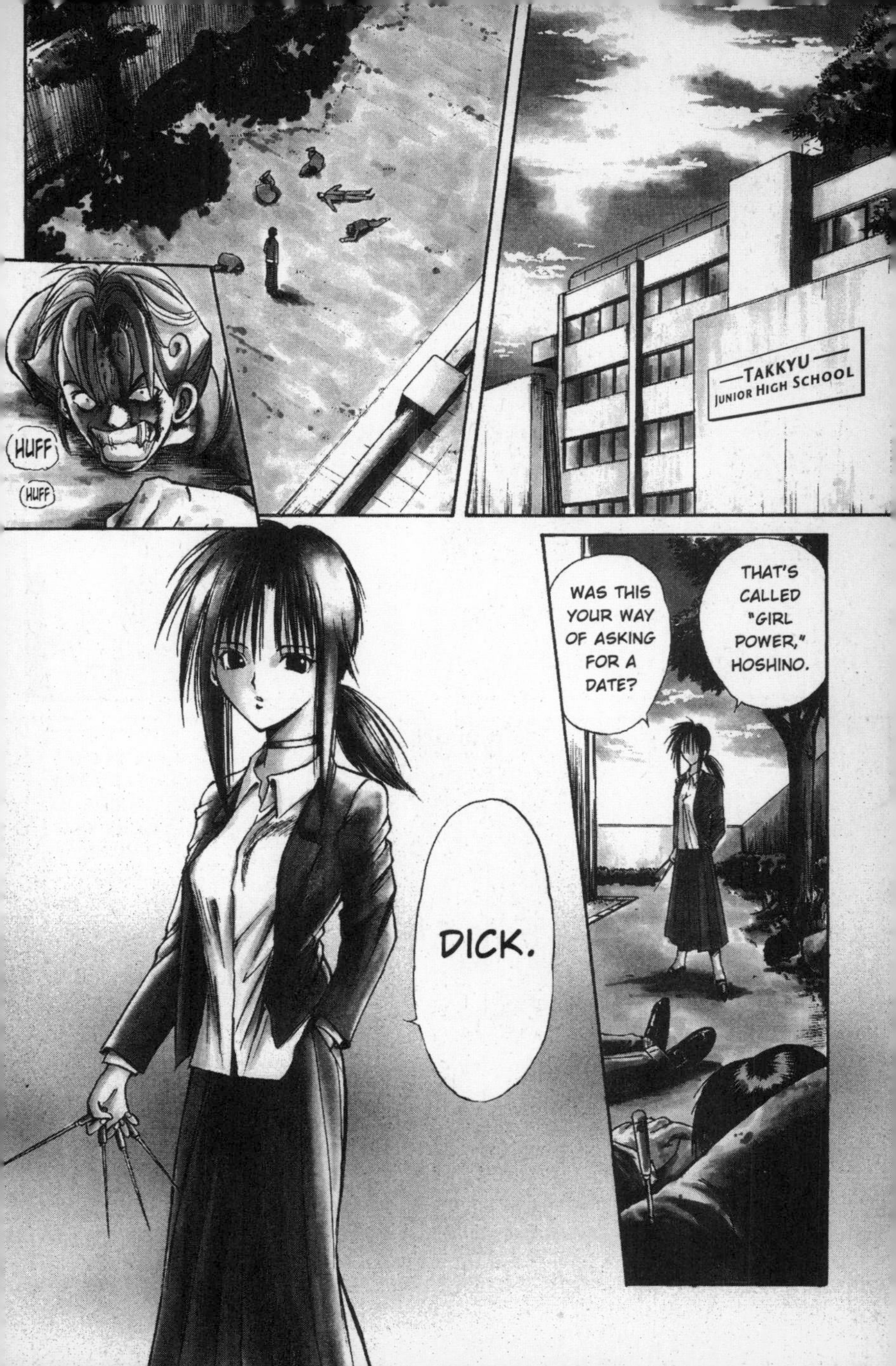

—TAKKYU—
JUNIOR HIGH SCHOOL
HUFF
HUFF
THAT'S CALLED "GIRL POWER," HOSHINO.
WAS THIS YOUR WAY OF ASKING FOR A DATE?
DICK.

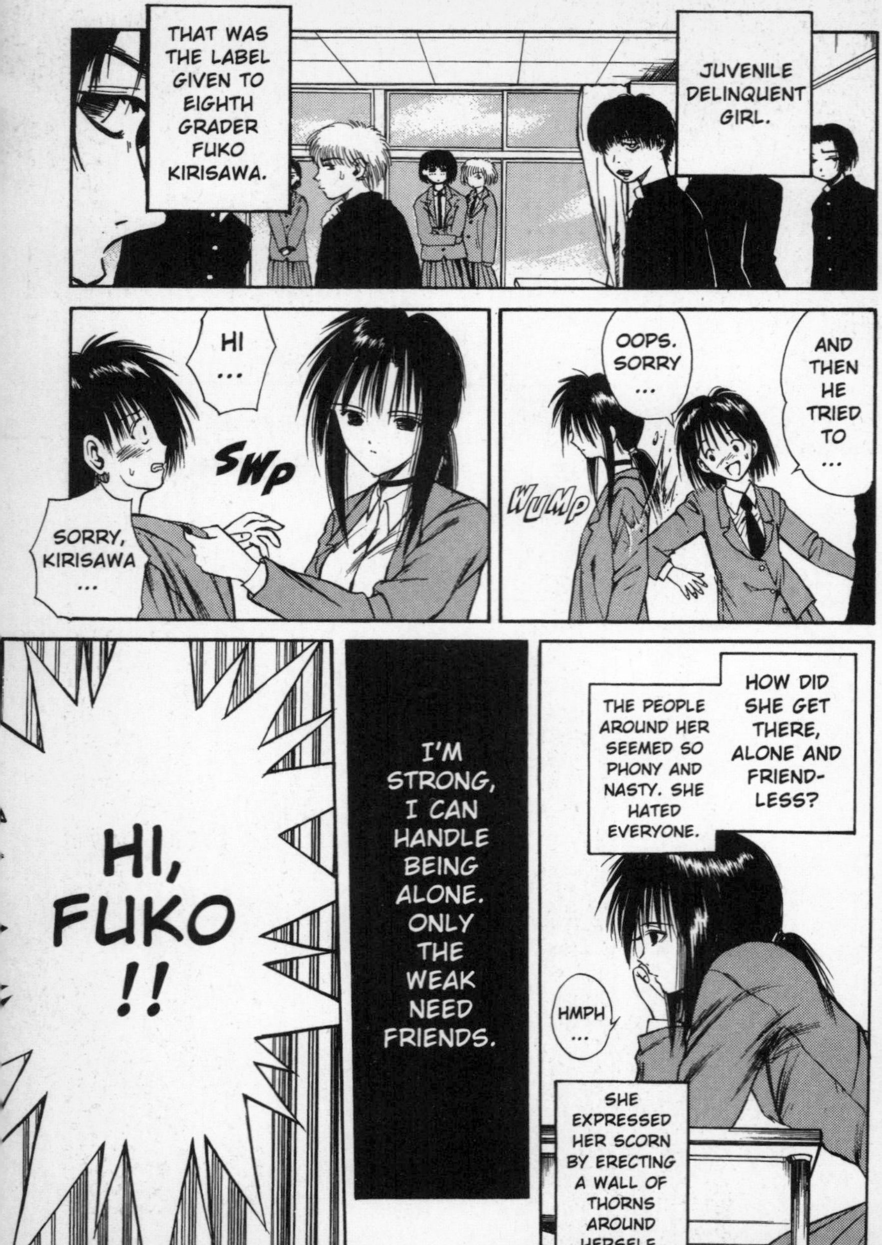
JUVENILE DELINQUENT GIRL.
THAT WAS THE LABEL GIVEN TO EIGHTH GRADER FUKO KIRISAWA.
AND THEN HE TRIED TO ...
OOPS. SORRY ...
WUMP
HI ...
SWP
SORRY, KIRISAWA ...
HOW DID SHE GET THERE, ALONE AND FRIEND-LESS?
THE PEOPLE AROUND HER SEEMED SO PHONY AND NASTY. SHE HATED EVERYONE.
HMPH ...
SHE EXPRESSED HER SCORN BY ERECTING A WALL OF THORNS AROUND HERSELF.
I'M STRONG, I CAN HANDLE BEING ALONE. ONLY THE WEAK NEED FRIENDS.
HI, FUKO !!

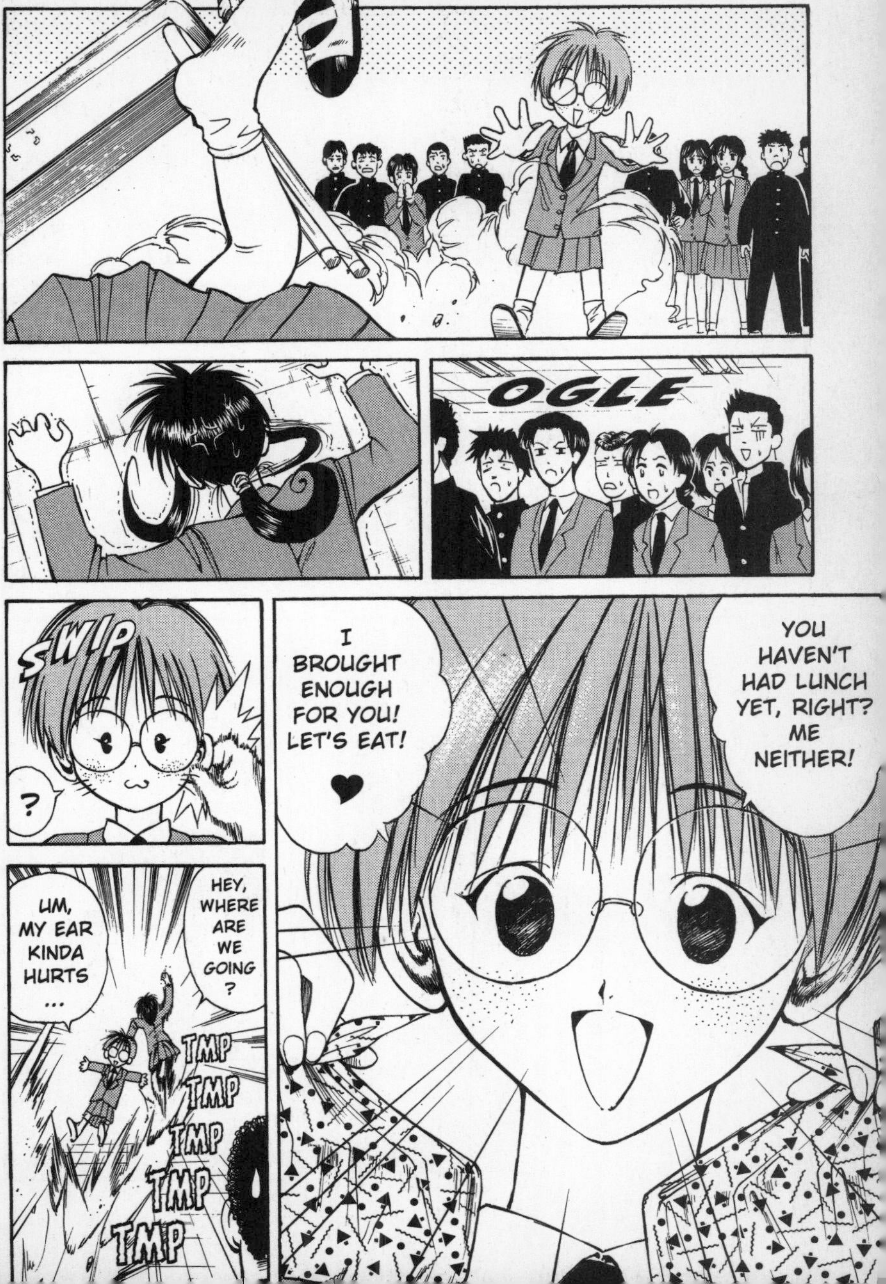
OGLE
YOU HAVEN'T HAD LUNCH YET, RIGHT? ME NEITHER!
I BROUGHT ENOUGH FOR YOU! LET'S EAT! ♥
SWIP
?
HEY, WHERE ARE WE GOING?
UM, MY EAR KINDA HURTS...
TMP
TMP
TMP
TMP
TMP

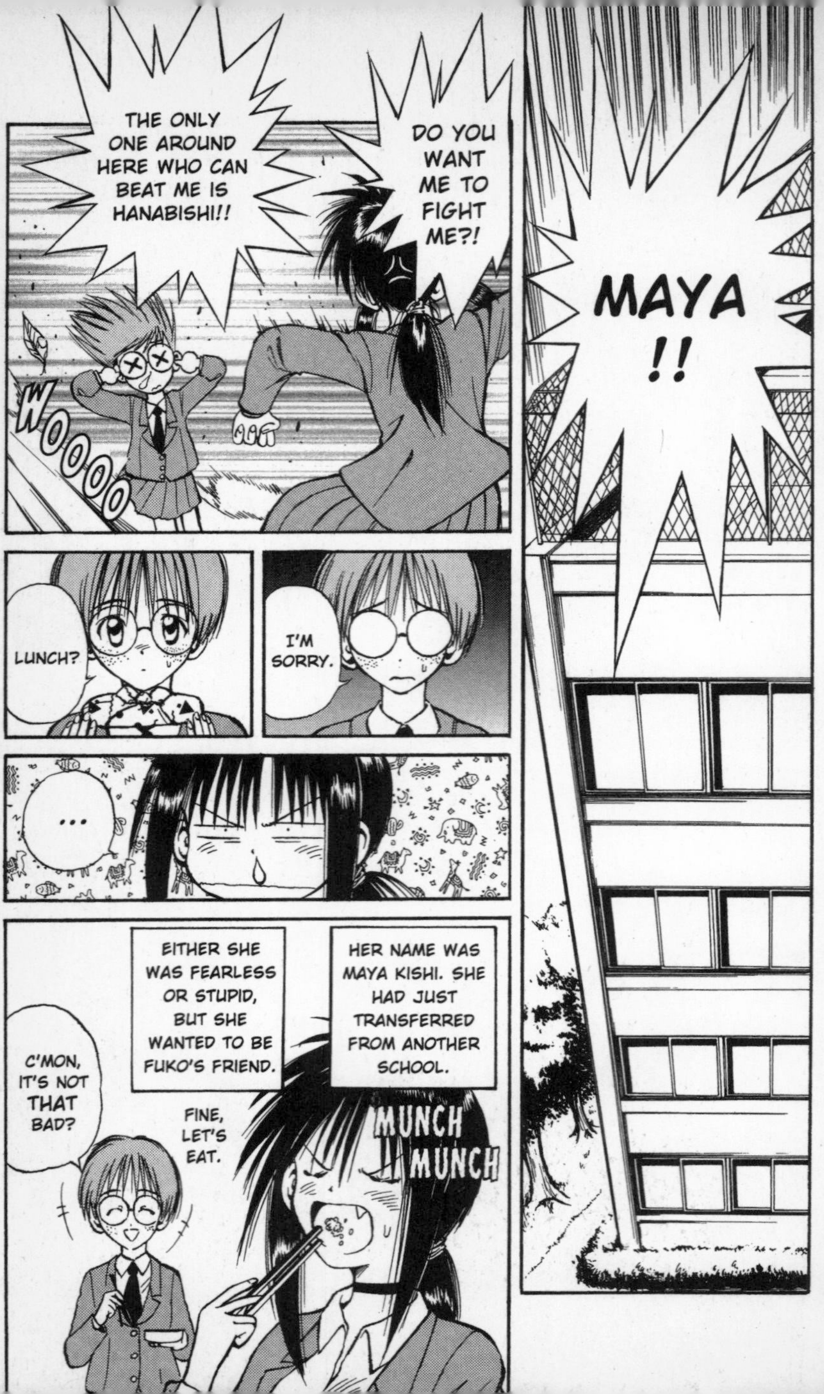
MAYA !!
DO YOU WANT ME TO FIGHT ME?!
THE ONLY ONE AROUND HERE WHO CAN BEAT ME IS HANABISHI!!
WOOOO
I'M SORRY.
LUNCH?
...
HER NAME WAS MAYA KISHI. SHE HAD JUST TRANSFERRED FROM ANOTHER SCHOOL.
EITHER SHE WAS FEARLESS OR STUPID, BUT SHE WANTED TO BE FUKO'S FRIEND.
MUNCH MUNCH
FINE, LET'S EAT.
C'MON, IT'S NOT THAT BAD?

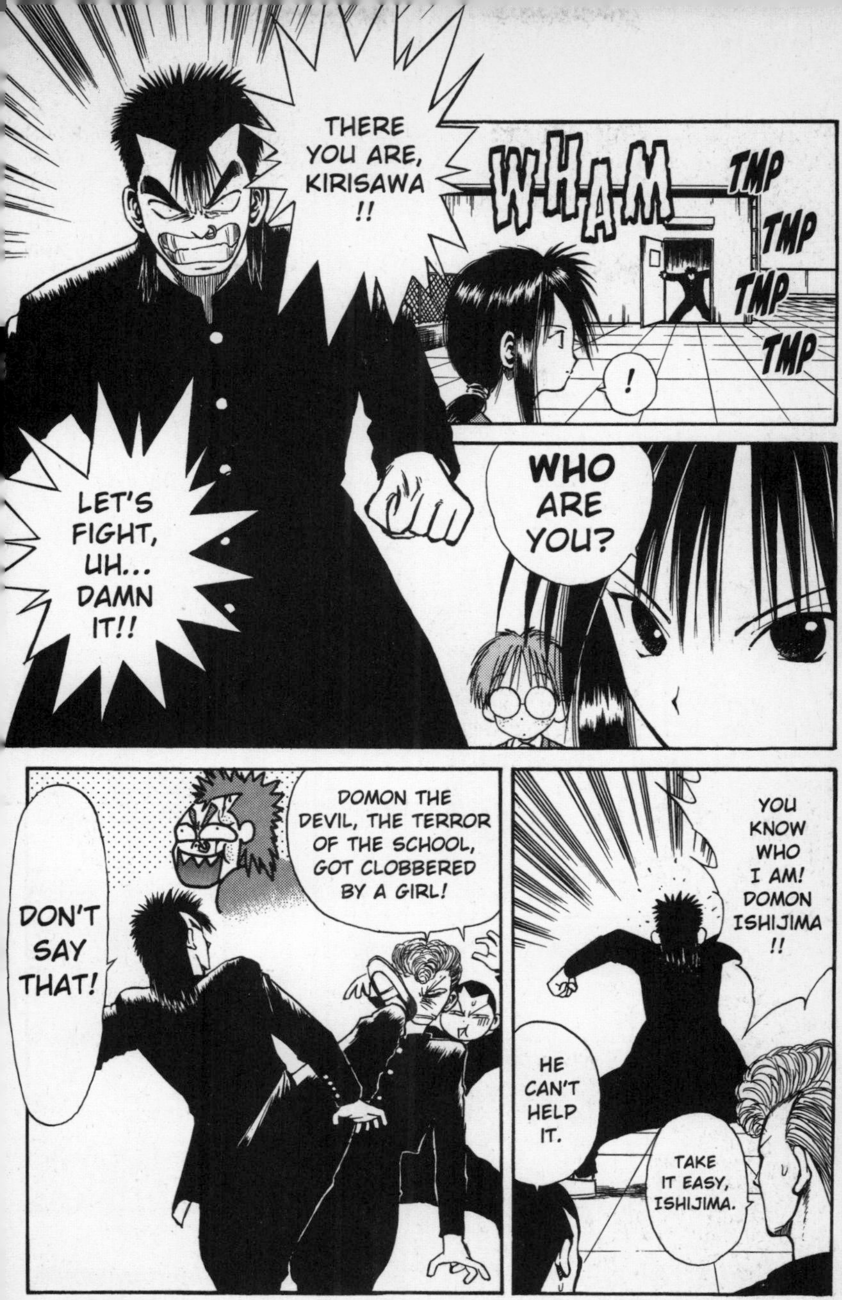
WHAM
TMP TMP TMP TMP
THERE YOU ARE, KIRISAWA!!
!
WHO ARE YOU?
LET'S FIGHT, UH... DAMN IT!!
YOU KNOW WHO I AM! DOMON ISHIJIMA!!
HE CAN'T HELP IT.
TAKE IT EASY, ISHIJIMA.
DOMON THE DEVIL, THE TERROR OF THE SCHOOL, GOT CLOBBERED BY A GIRL!
DON'T SAY THAT!

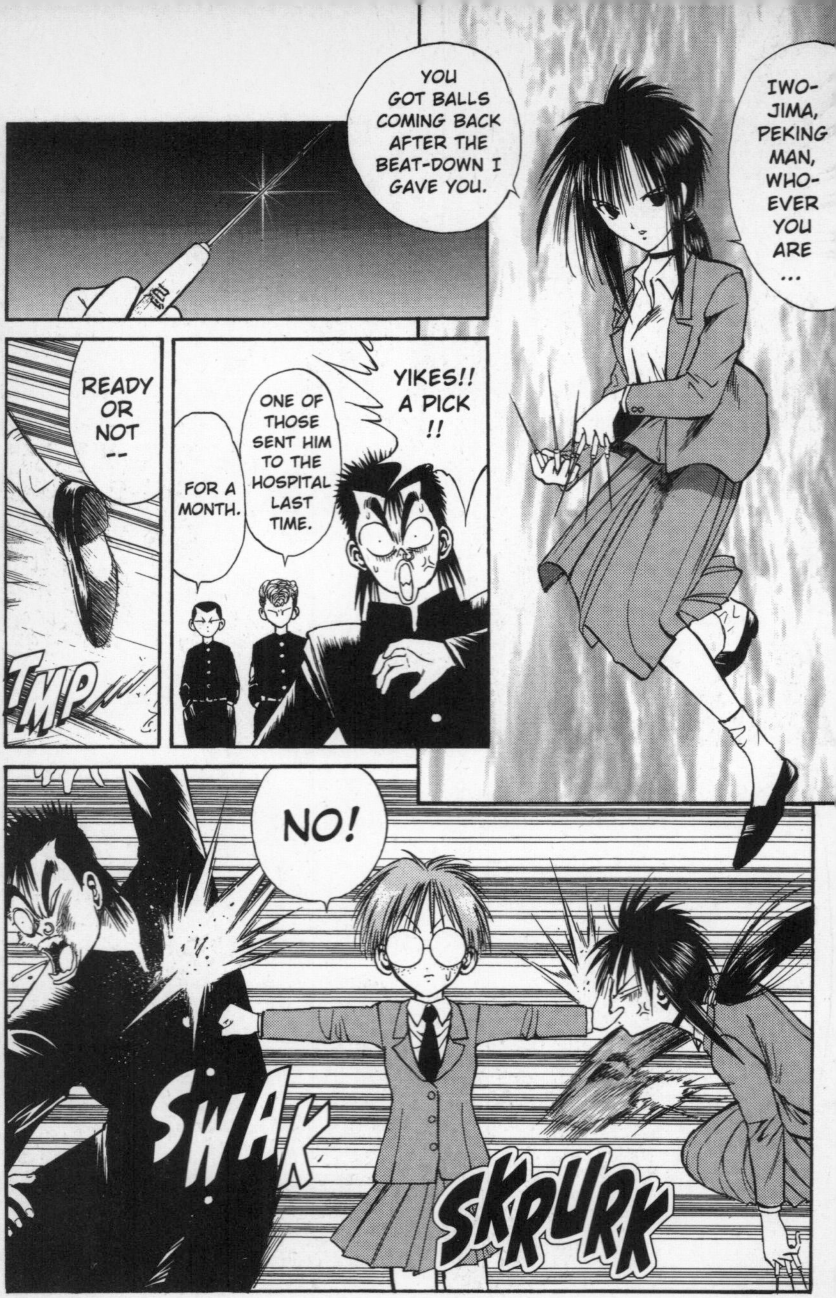
IWO-JIMA, PEKING MAN, WHO-EVER YOU ARE ...
YOU GOT BALLS COMING BACK AFTER THE BEAT-DOWN I GAVE YOU.
YIKES!! A PICK !!
ONE OF THOSE SENT HIM TO THE HOSPITAL LAST TIME.
FOR A MONTH.
READY OR NOT --
TMP
NO!
SKRURK
SWAK

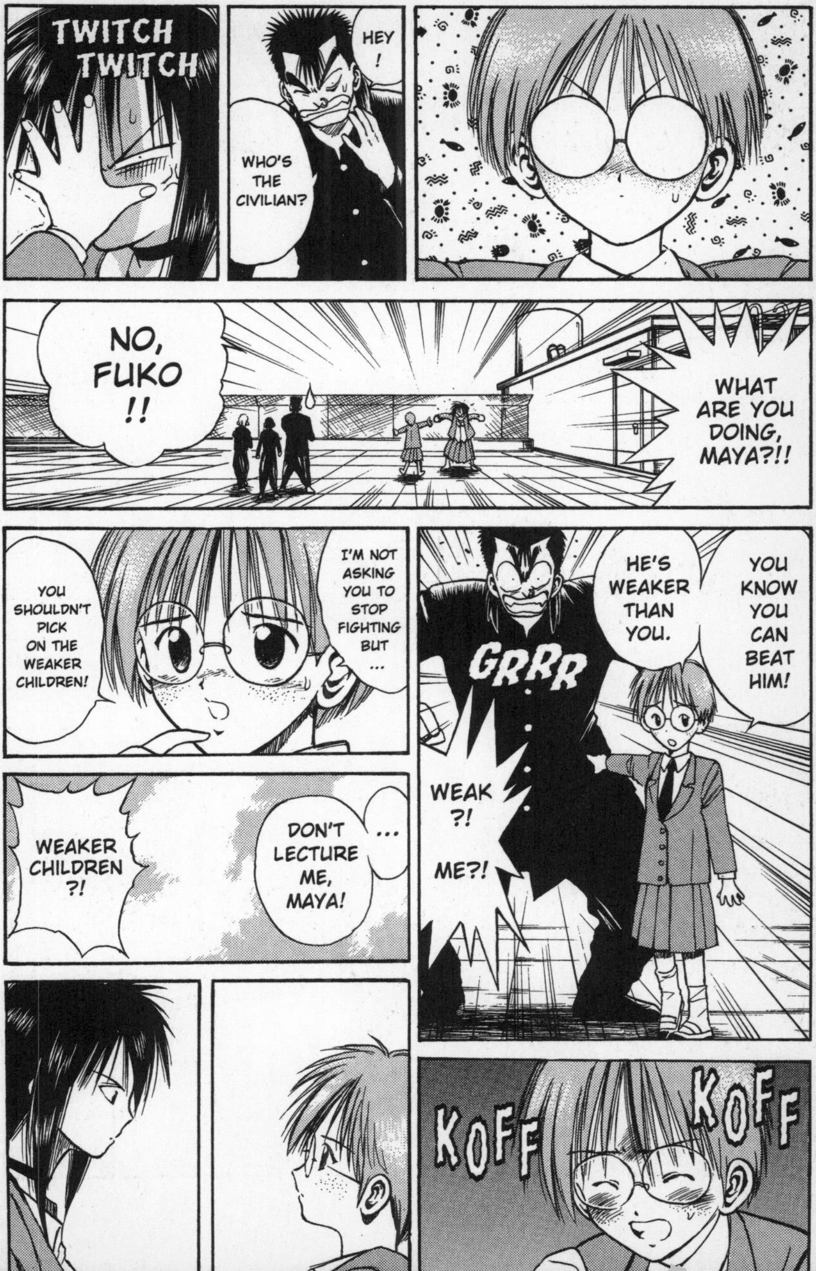
HEY!
WHO'S THE CIVILIAN?
TWITCH TWITCH
WHAT ARE YOU DOING, MAYA?!!
NO, FUKO!!
YOU KNOW YOU CAN BEAT HIM!
HE'S WEAKER THAN YOU.
GRRR
WEAK?!
ME?!
I'M NOT ASKING YOU TO STOP FIGHTING BUT ...
YOU SHOULDN'T PICK ON THE WEAKER CHILDREN!
...
DON'T LECTURE ME, MAYA!
WEAKER CHILDREN?!
KOFF KOFF

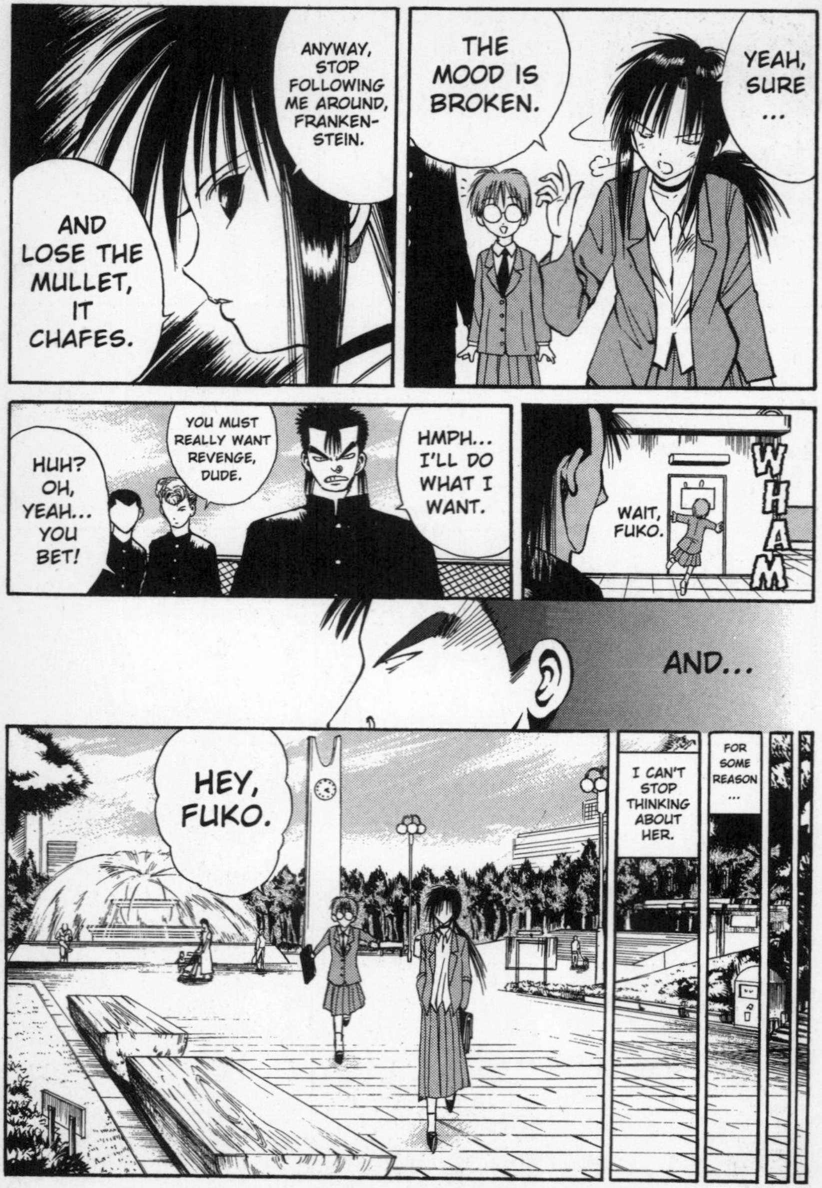
YEAH, SURE ...
THE MOOD IS BROKEN.
ANYWAY, STOP FOLLOWING ME AROUND, FRANKEN-STEIN.
AND LOSE THE MULLET, IT CHAFES.
WAIT, FUKO.
WHAM
HMPH... I'LL DO WHAT I WANT.
YOU MUST REALLY WANT REVENGE, DUDE.
HUH? OH, YEAH... YOU BET!
AND...
FOR SOME REASON ...
I CAN'T STOP THINKING ABOUT HER.
HEY, FUKO.

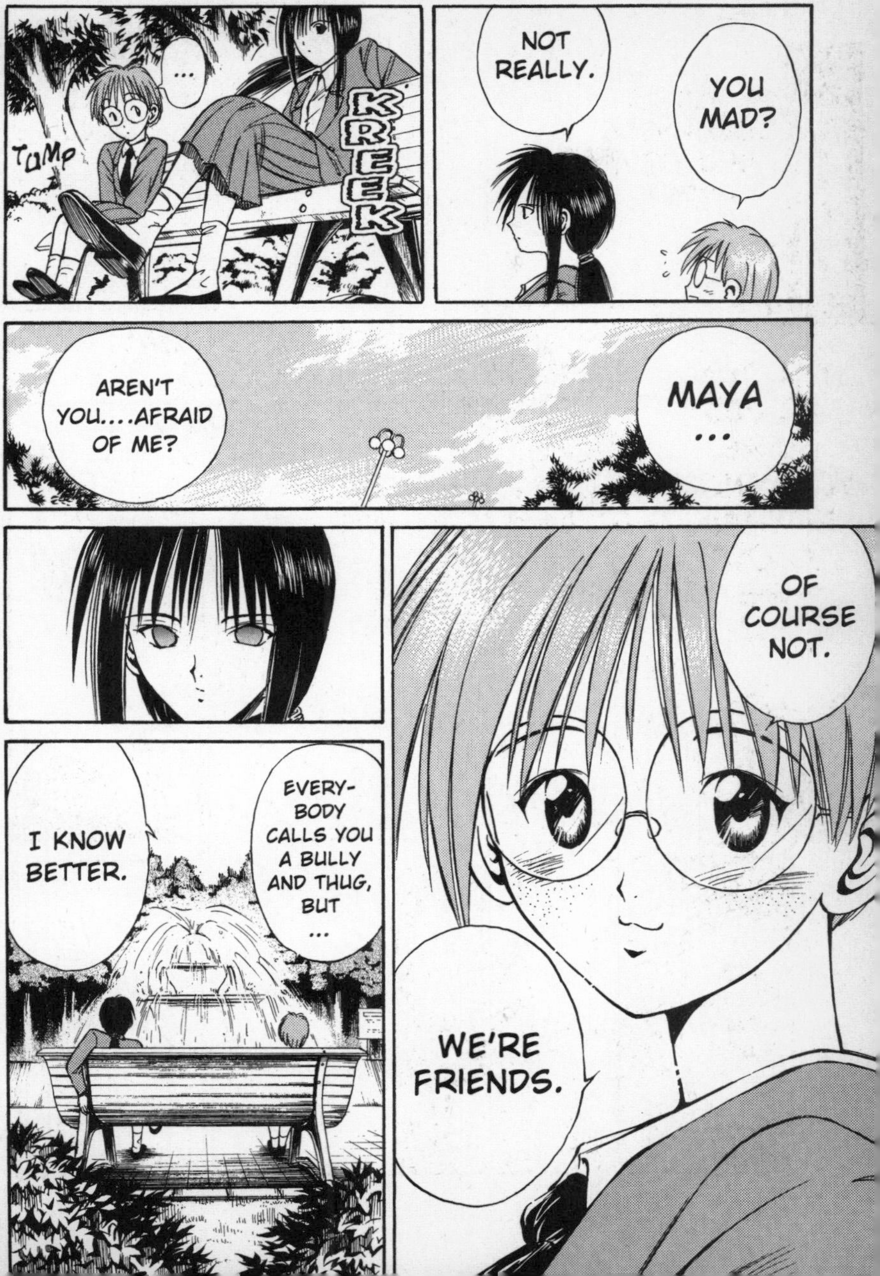
YOU MAD?
NOT REALLY.
...
KREEK
TUMP
MAYA ...
AREN'T YOU....AFRAID OF ME?
OF COURSE NOT.
WE'RE FRIENDS.
EVERY-BODY CALLS YOU A BULLY AND THUG, BUT ...
I KNOW BETTER.

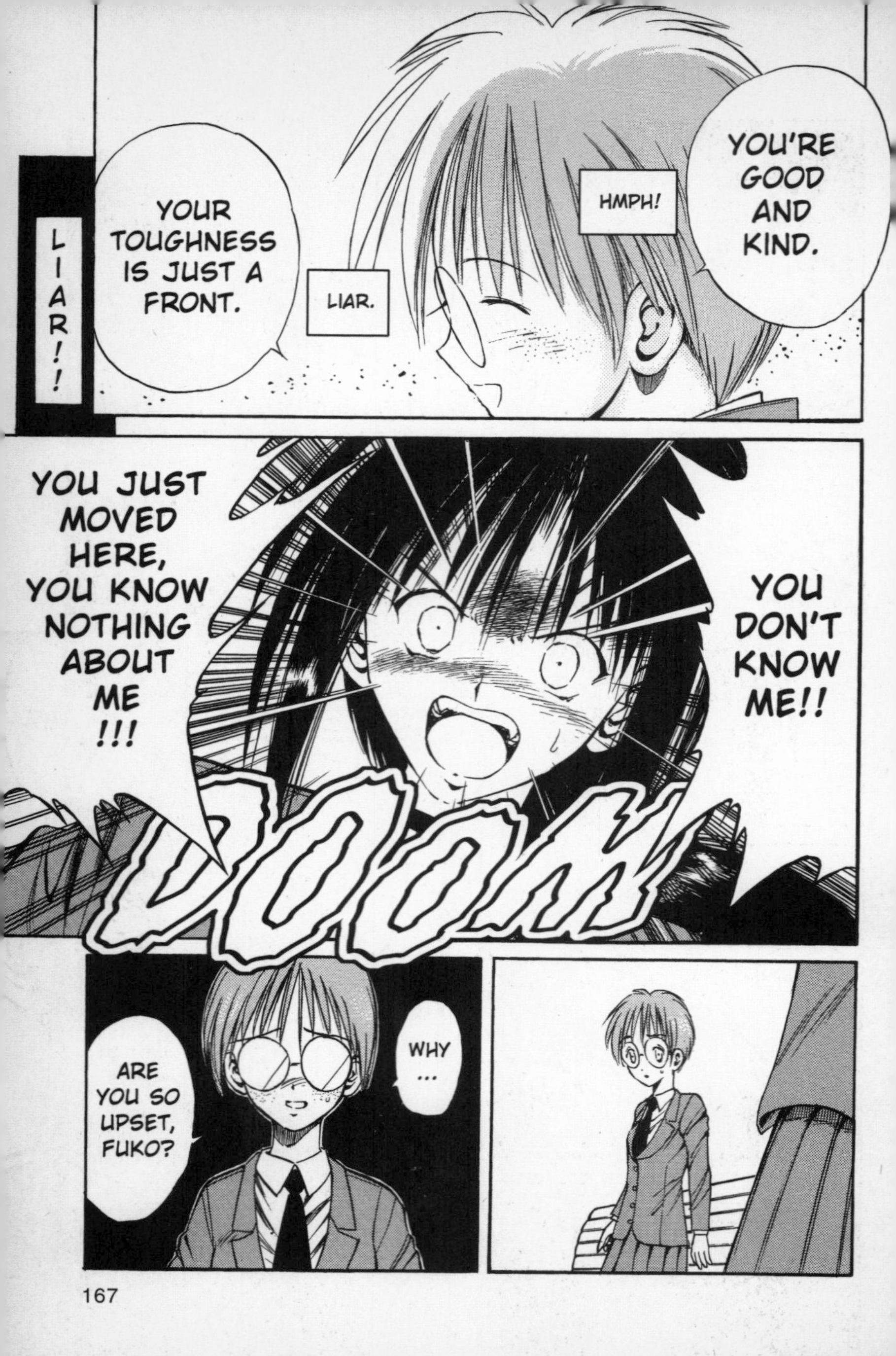
YOU'RE GOOD AND KIND.
HMPH!
LIAR.
YOUR TOUGHNESS IS JUST A FRONT.
LIAR!!
YOU DON'T KNOW ME!!
YOU JUST MOVED HERE, YOU KNOW NOTHING ABOUT ME!!!
VOOM
WHY ...
ARE YOU SO UPSET, FUKO?

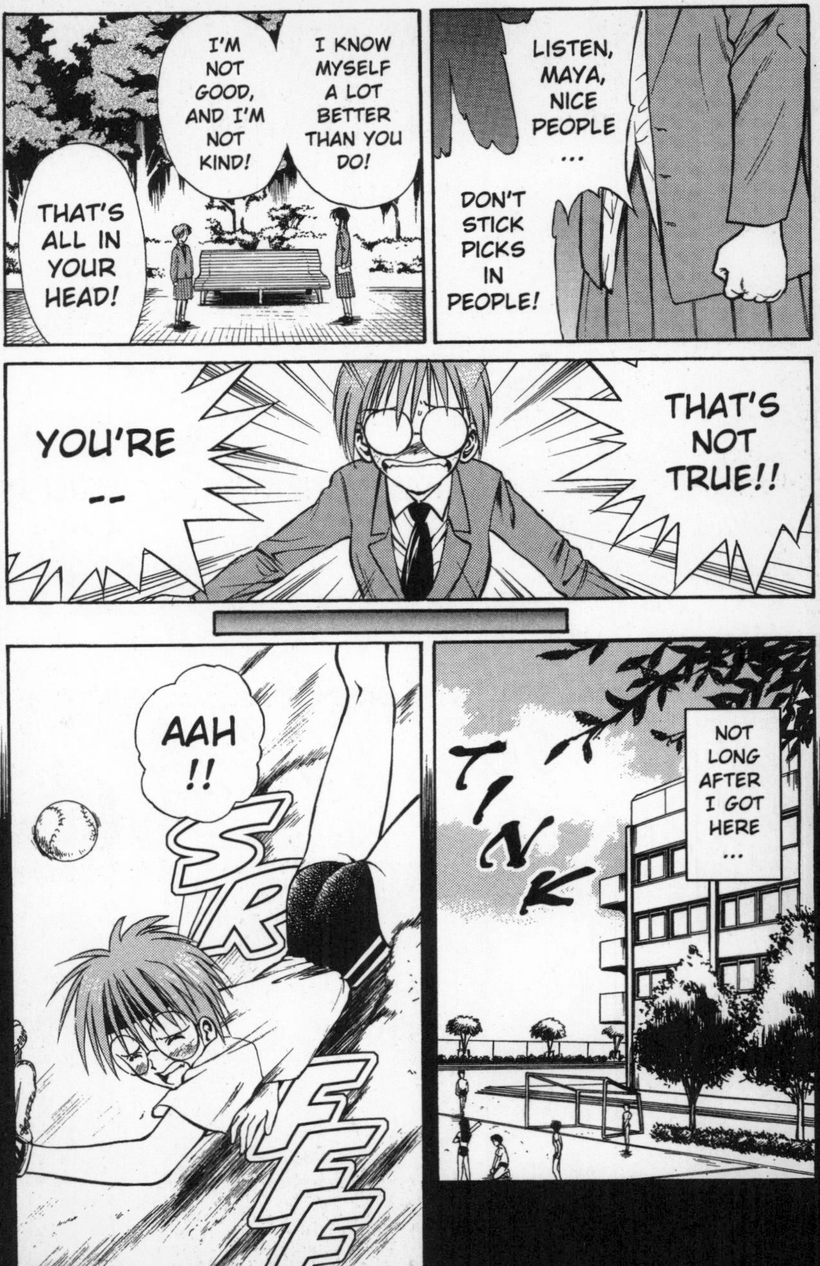
LISTEN, MAYA, NICE PEOPLE ...
DON'T STICK PICKS IN PEOPLE!
I KNOW MYSELF A LOT BETTER THAN YOU DO!
I'M NOT GOOD, AND I'M NOT KIND!
THAT'S ALL IN YOUR HEAD!
THAT'S NOT TRUE!!
YOU'RE --
NOT LONG AFTER I GOT HERE ...
TIN
AAH !!

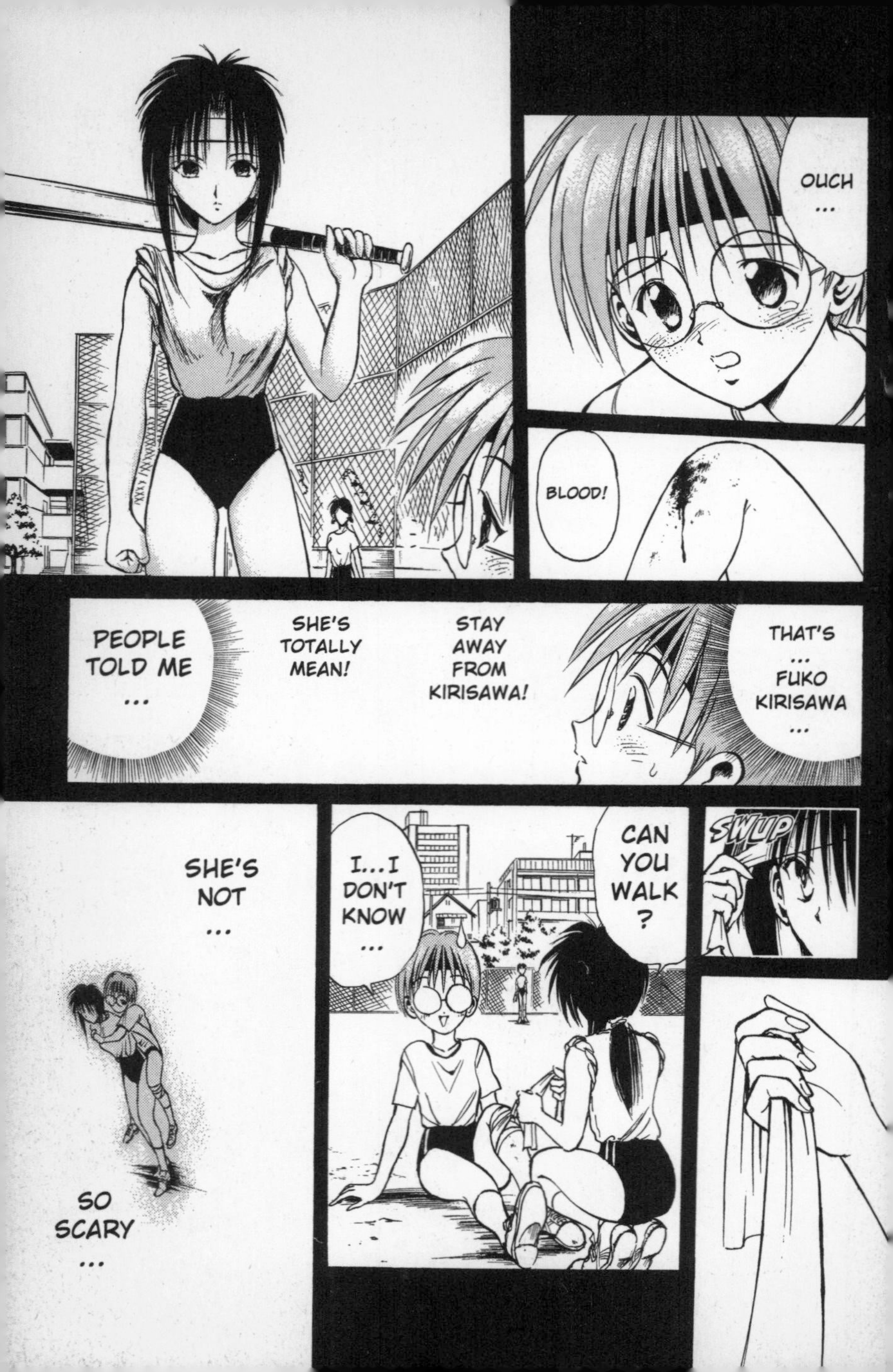
OUCH ...
BLOOD!
THAT'S ... FUKO KIRISAWA ...
STAY AWAY FROM KIRISAWA!
SHE'S TOTALLY MEAN!
PEOPLE TOLD ME ...
SWUP
CAN YOU WALK ?
I...I DON'T KNOW ...
SHE'S NOT ...
SO SCARY ...

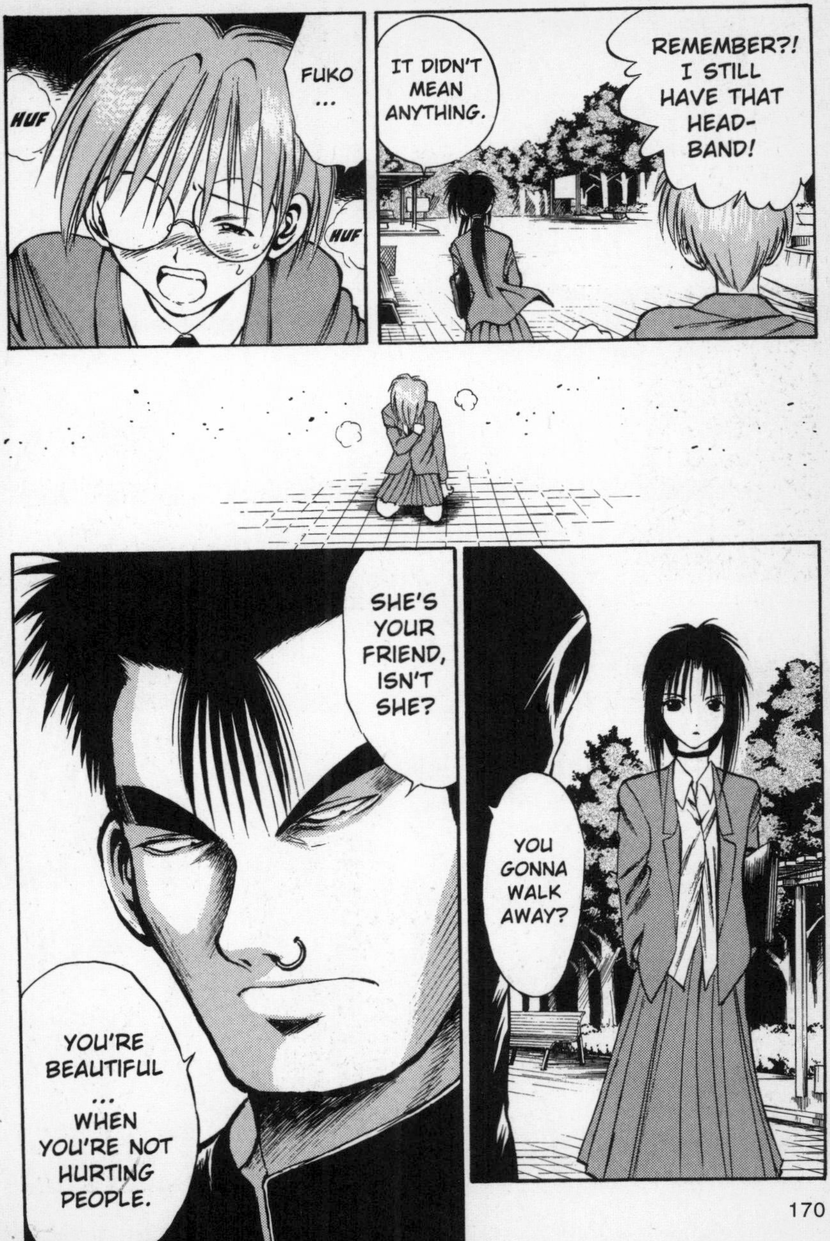
REMEMBER?! I STILL HAVE THAT HEAD-BAND!
IT DIDN'T MEAN ANYTHING.
FUKO ...
HUF
HUF
YOU GONNA WALK AWAY?
SHE'S YOUR FRIEND, ISN'T SHE?
YOU'RE BEAUTIFUL ... WHEN YOU'RE NOT HURTING PEOPLE.

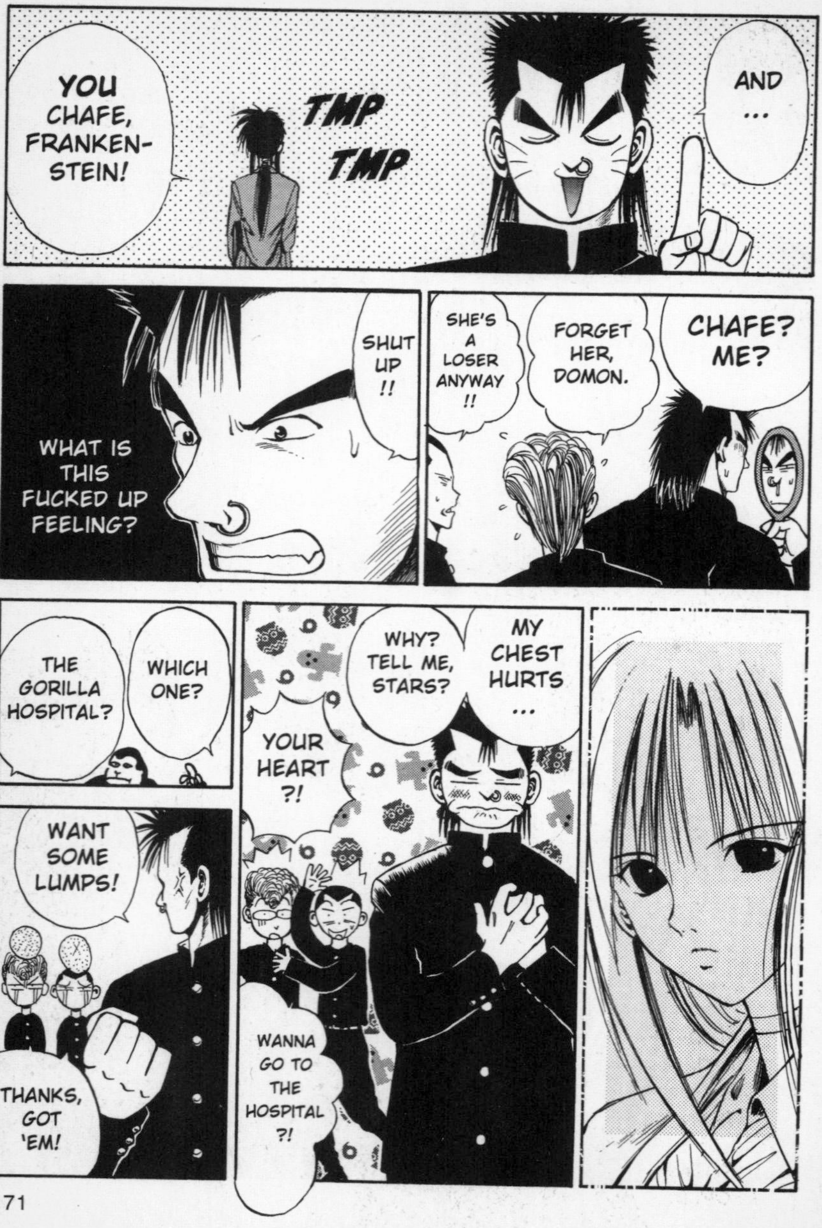
AND ...
TMP TMP
YOU CHAFE, FRANKEN-STEIN!
CHAFE? ME?
FORGET HER, DOMON.
SHE'S A LOSER ANYWAY !!
SHUT UP !!
WHAT IS THIS FUCKED UP FEELING?
MY CHEST HURTS ...
WHY? TELL ME, STARS?
YOUR HEART ?!
WANNA GO TO THE HOSPITAL ?!
WHICH ONE?
THE GORILLA HOSPITAL?
WANT SOME LUMPS!
THANKS, GOT 'EM!

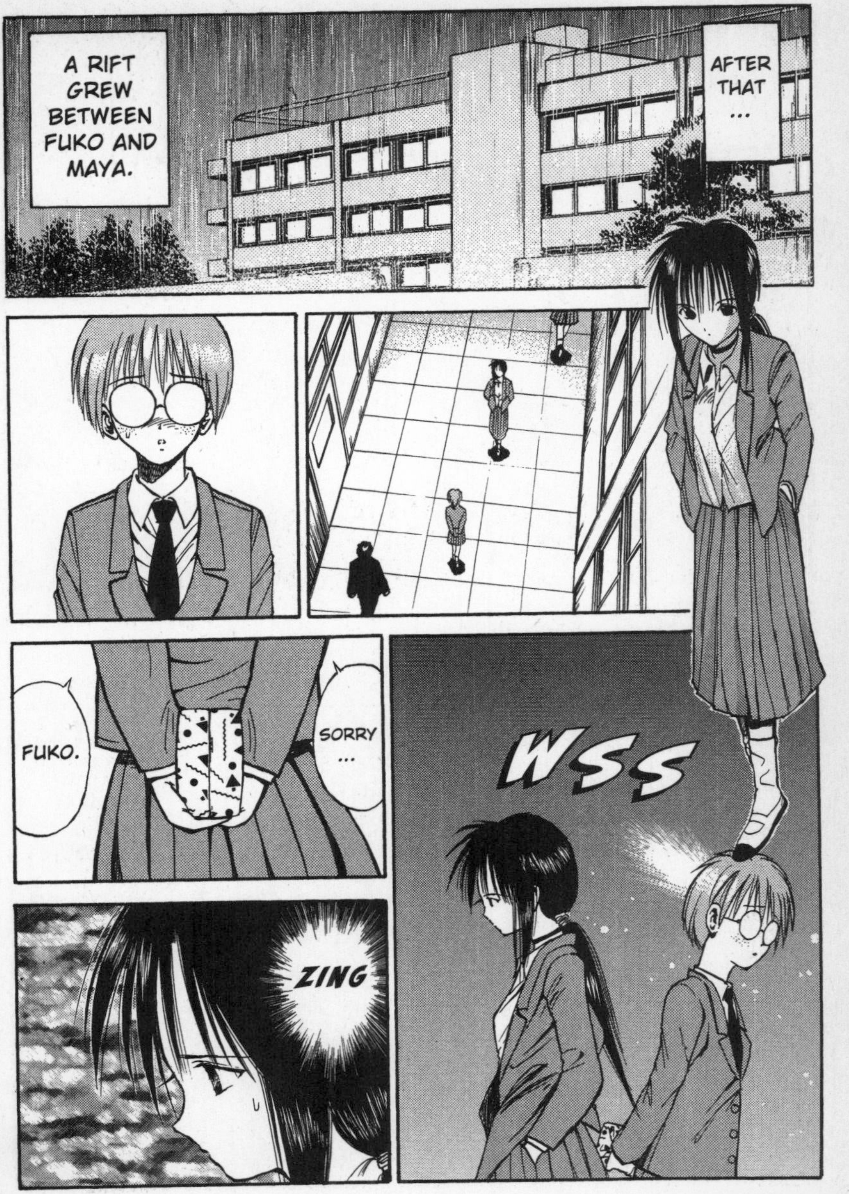
AFTER THAT ...
A RIFT GREW BETWEEN FUKO AND MAYA.
WSS
SORRY ...
FUKO.
ZING

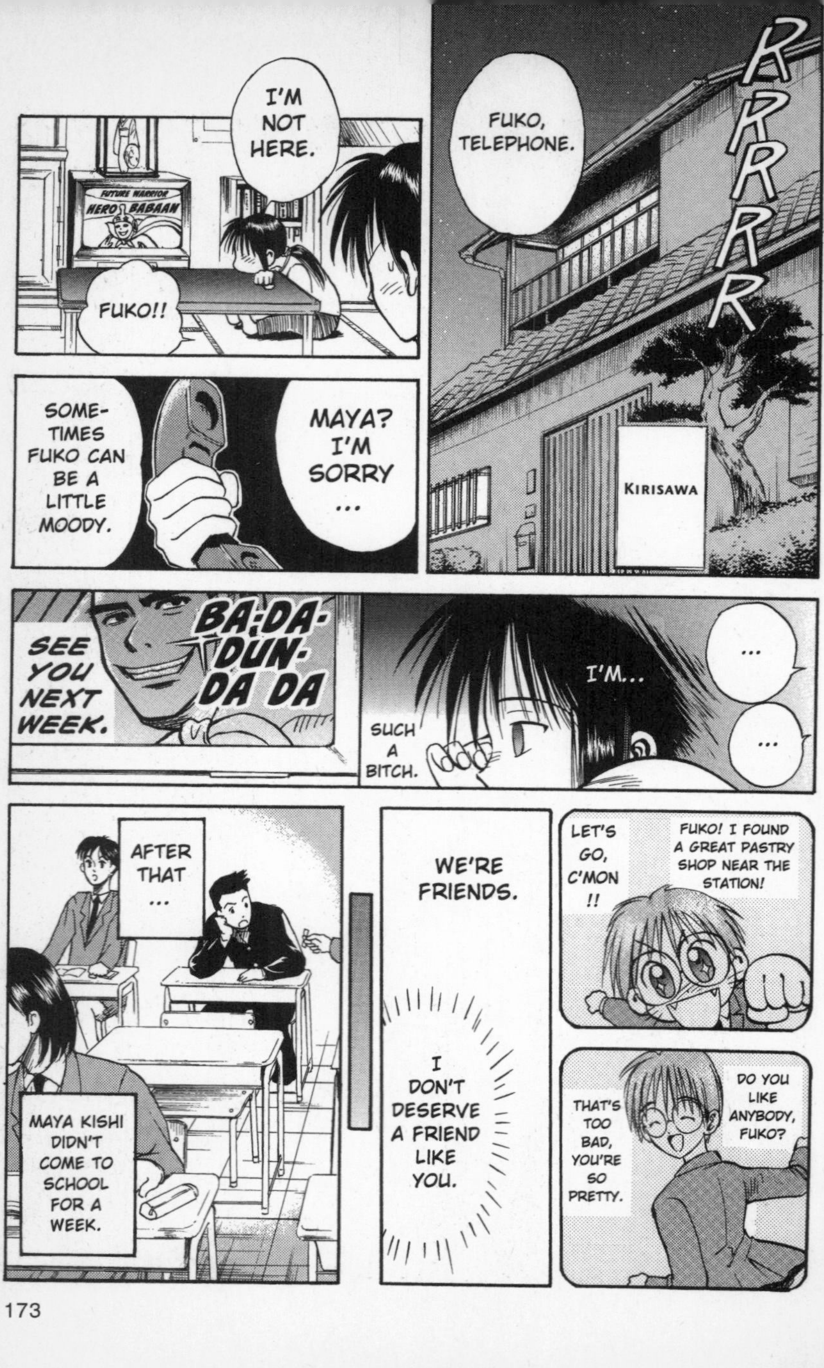
RRRRR
FUKO, TELEPHONE.
KIRISAWA
FUTURE WARRIOR HERO BABAAN
I'M NOT HERE.
FUKO!!
MAYA? I'M SORRY ...
SOMETIMES FUKO CAN BE A LITTLE MOODY.
...
...
I'M...
SUCH A BITCH.
BA-DA-DUN-DA DA
SEE YOU NEXT WEEK.
FUKO! I FOUND A GREAT PASTRY SHOP NEAR THE STATION!
LET'S GO, C'MON !!
DO YOU LIKE ANYBODY, FUKO?
THAT'S TOO BAD, YOU'RE SO PRETTY.
WE'RE FRIENDS.
I DON'T DESERVE A FRIEND LIKE YOU.
AFTER THAT ...
MAYA KISHI DIDN'T COME TO SCHOOL FOR A WEEK.

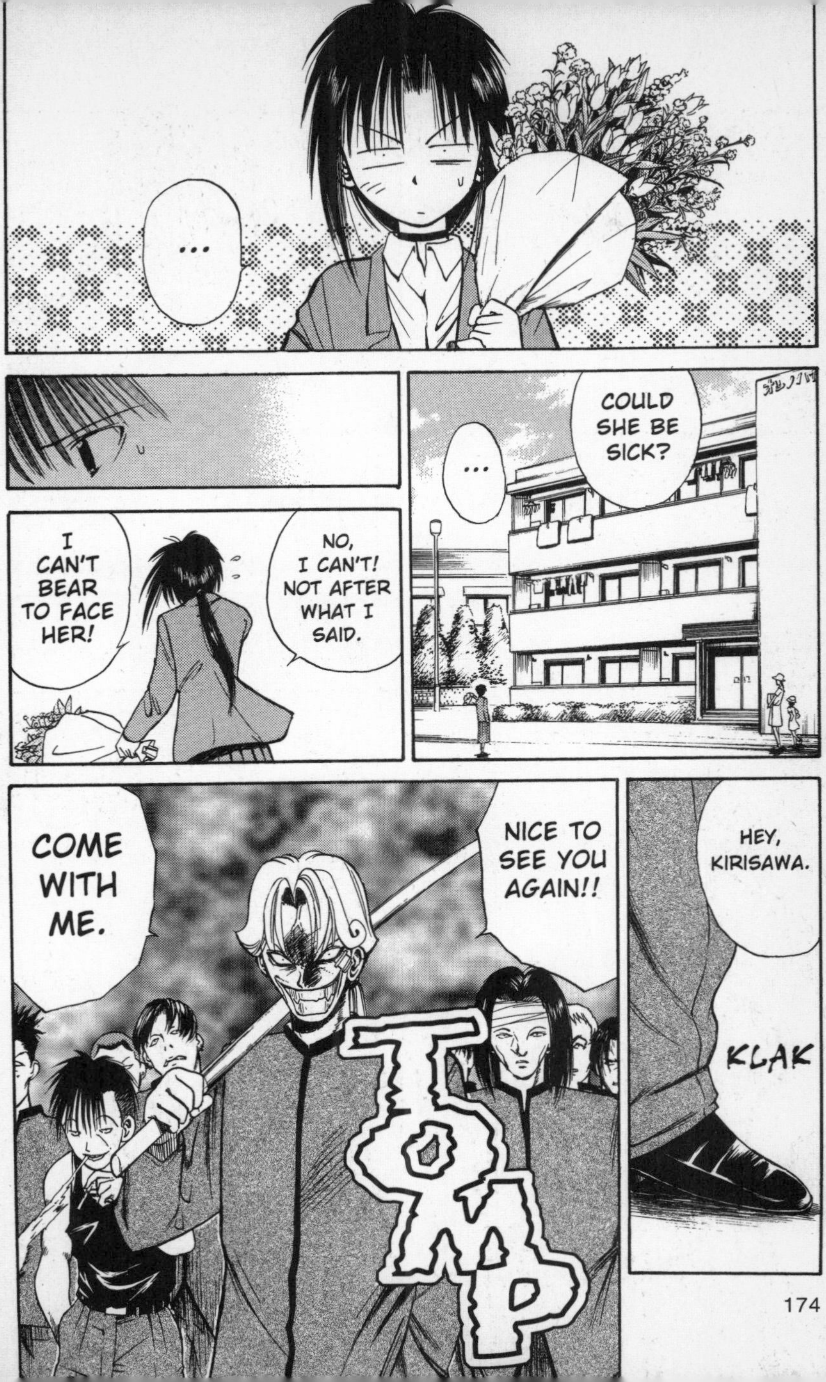
...
COULD SHE BE SICK?
...
NO, I CAN'T! NOT AFTER WHAT I SAID.
I CAN'T BEAR TO FACE HER!
HEY, KIRISAWA.
KLAK
NICE TO SEE YOU AGAIN!!
COME WITH ME.
TAP

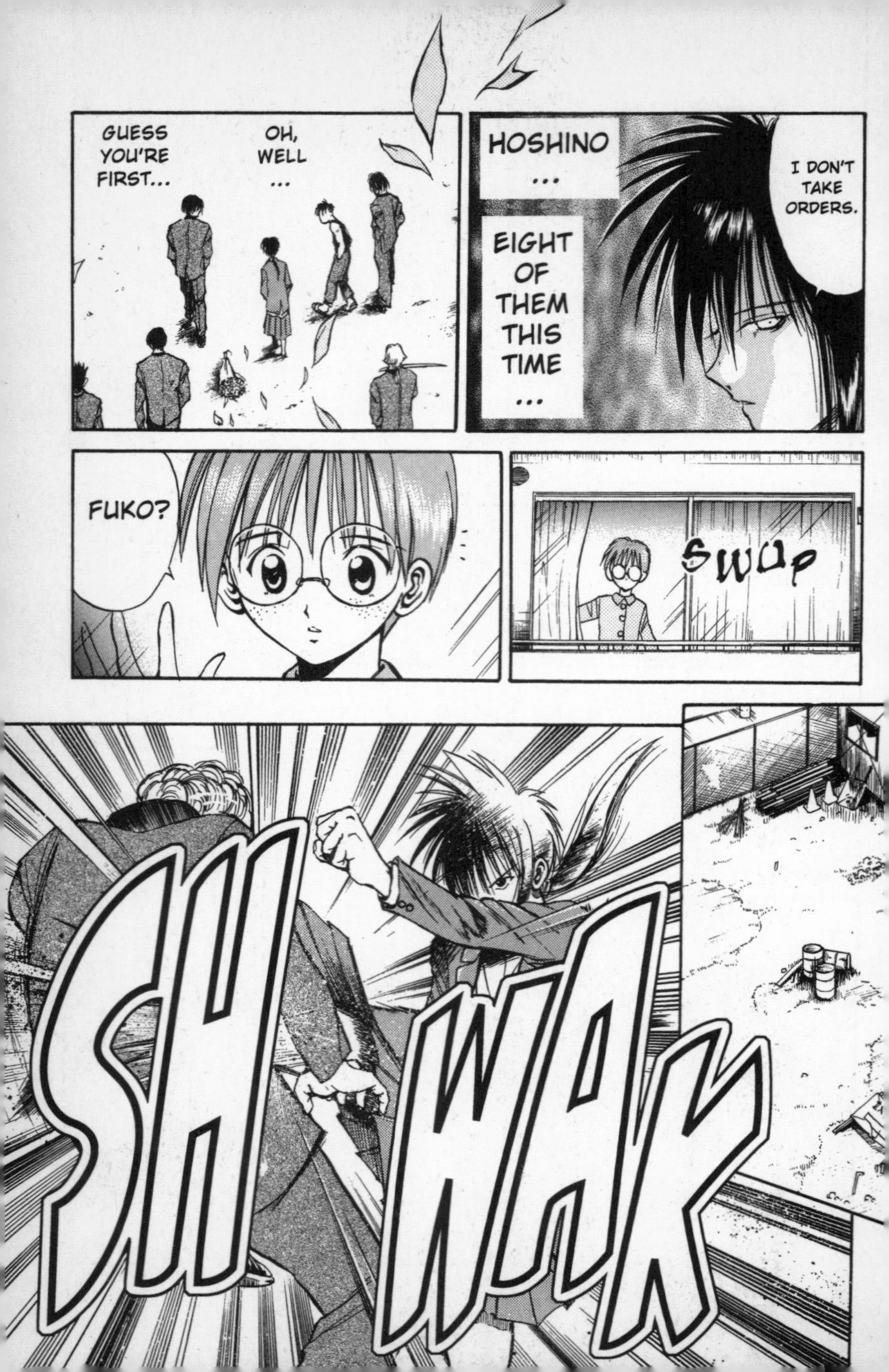
HOSHINO ...
EIGHT OF THEM THIS TIME ...
I DON'T TAKE ORDERS.
OH, WELL ...
GUESS YOU'RE FIRST...
SWUP
FUKO?
SHWAK

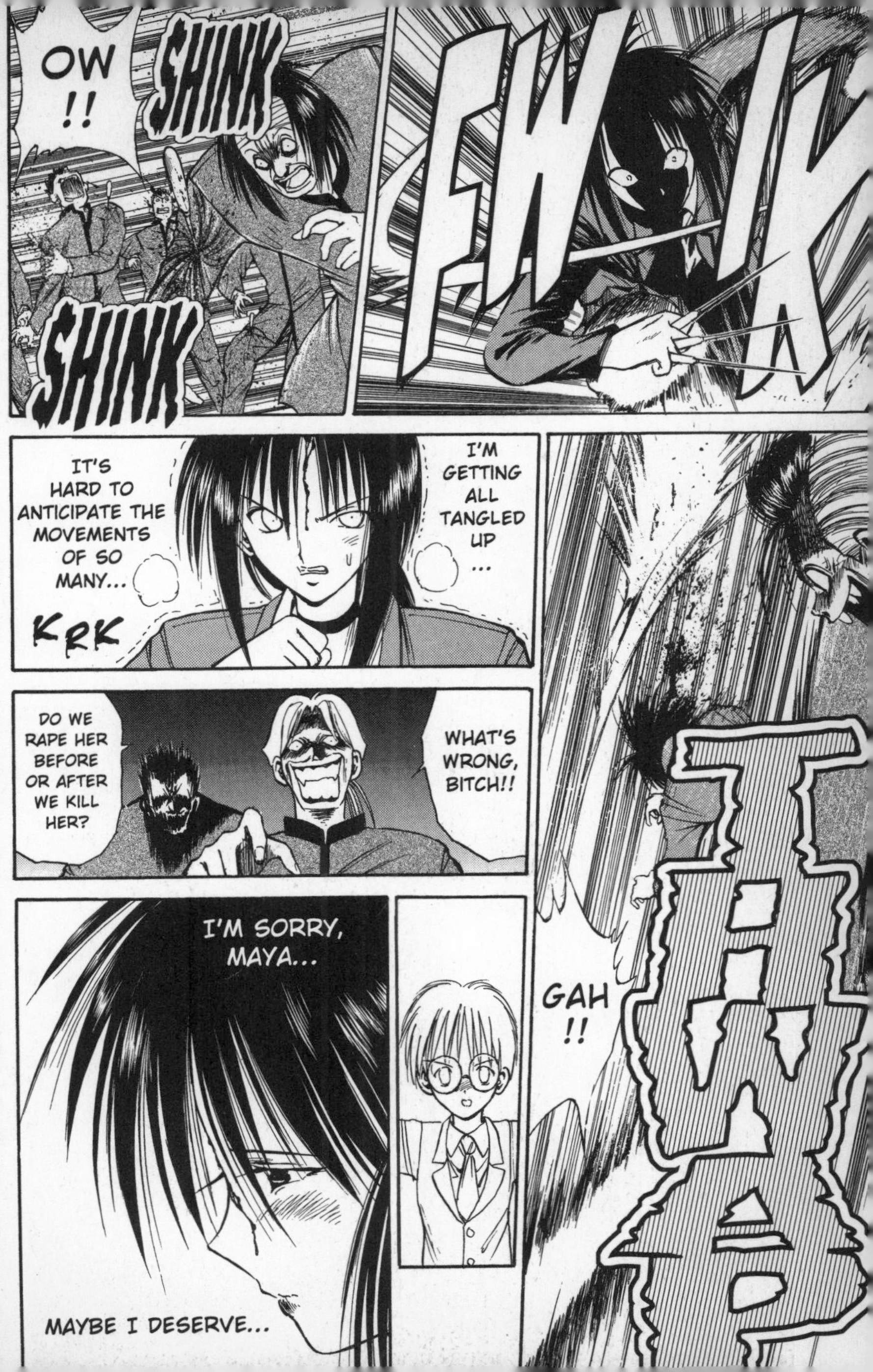
OW !!
SHINK
SHINK
GAH !!
I'M GETTING ALL TANGLED UP ...
IT'S HARD TO ANTICIPATE THE MOVEMENTS OF SO MANY...
KRK
WHAT'S WRONG, BITCH!!
DO WE RAPE HER BEFORE OR AFTER WE KILL HER?
I'M SORRY, MAYA...
MAYBE I DESERVE...

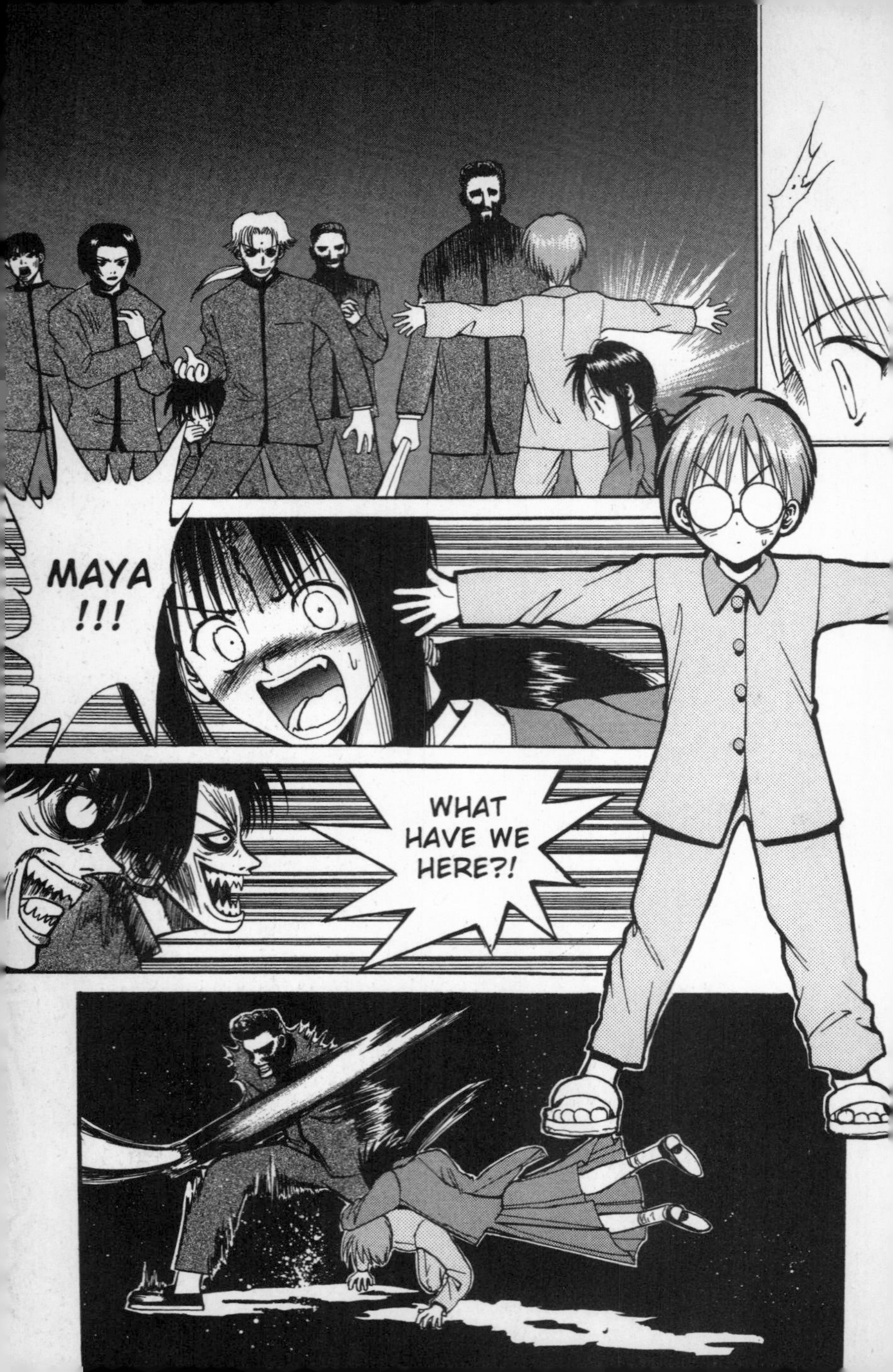
MAYA !!!
WHAT HAVE WE HERE?!

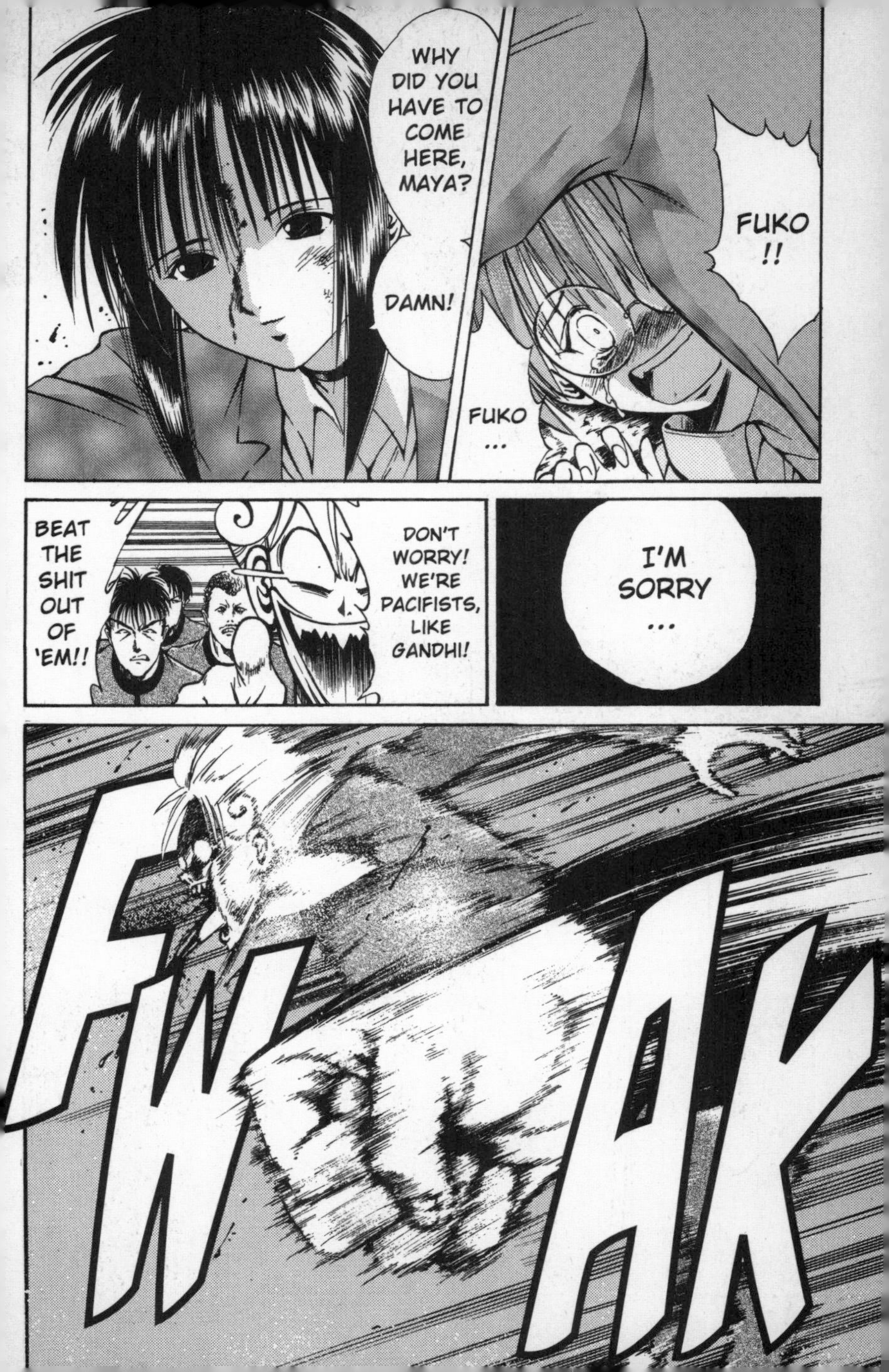
FUKO !!
FUKO ...
WHY DID YOU HAVE TO COME HERE, MAYA?
DAMN!
I'M SORRY ...
DON'T WORRY! WE'RE PACIFISTS, LIKE GANDHI!
BEAT THE SHIT OUT OF 'EM!!

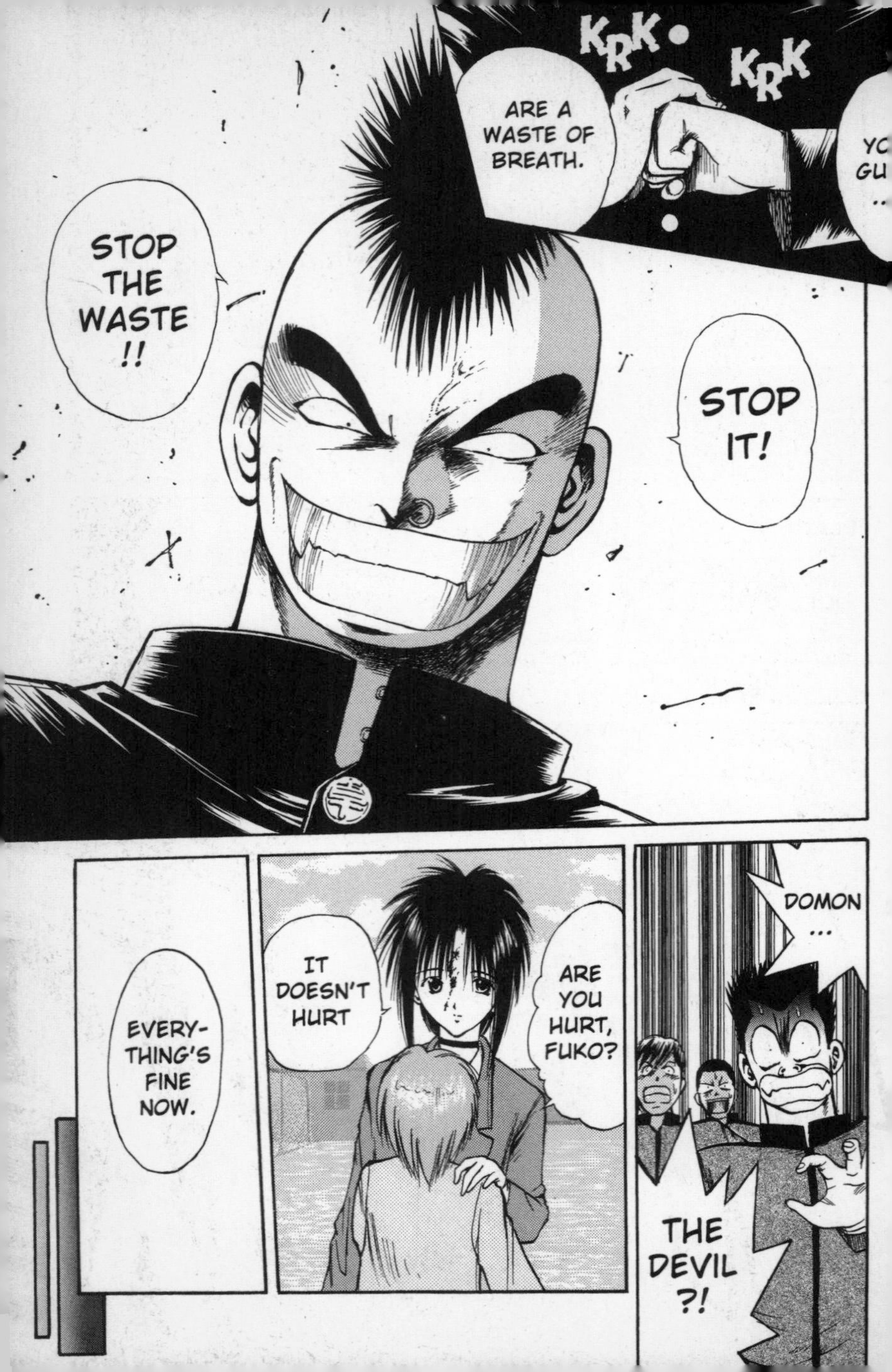
KRK • KRK
ARE A WASTE OF BREATH.
STOP IT!
STOP THE WASTE !!
DOMON ...
THE DEVIL ?!
ARE YOU HURT, FUKO?
IT DOESN'T HURT
EVERY-THING'S FINE NOW.

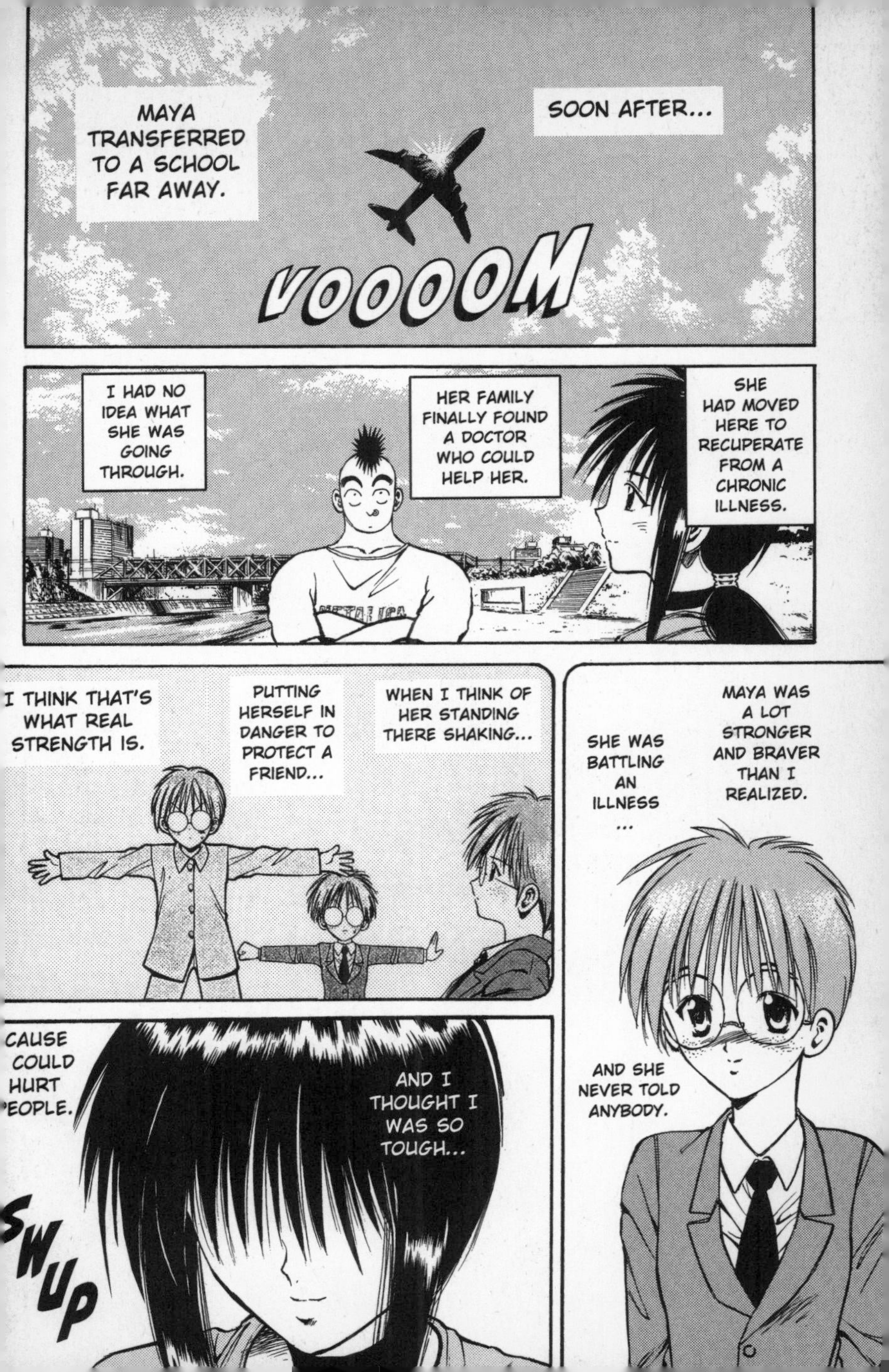
SOON AFTER...
MAYA TRANSFERRED TO A SCHOOL FAR AWAY.
VOOOOM
SHE HAD MOVED HERE TO RECUPERATE FROM A CHRONIC ILLNESS.
HER FAMILY FINALLY FOUND A DOCTOR WHO COULD HELP HER.
I HAD NO IDEA WHAT SHE WAS GOING THROUGH.
MAYA WAS A LOT STRONGER AND BRAVER THAN I REALIZED.
SHE WAS BATTLING AN ILLNESS ...
AND SHE NEVER TOLD ANYBODY.
WHEN I THINK OF HER STANDING THERE SHAKING...
PUTTING HERSELF IN DANGER TO PROTECT A FRIEND...
I THINK THAT'S WHAT REAL STRENGTH IS.
AND I THOUGHT I WAS SO TOUGH...
CAUSE COULD HURT EOPLE.
SWUP

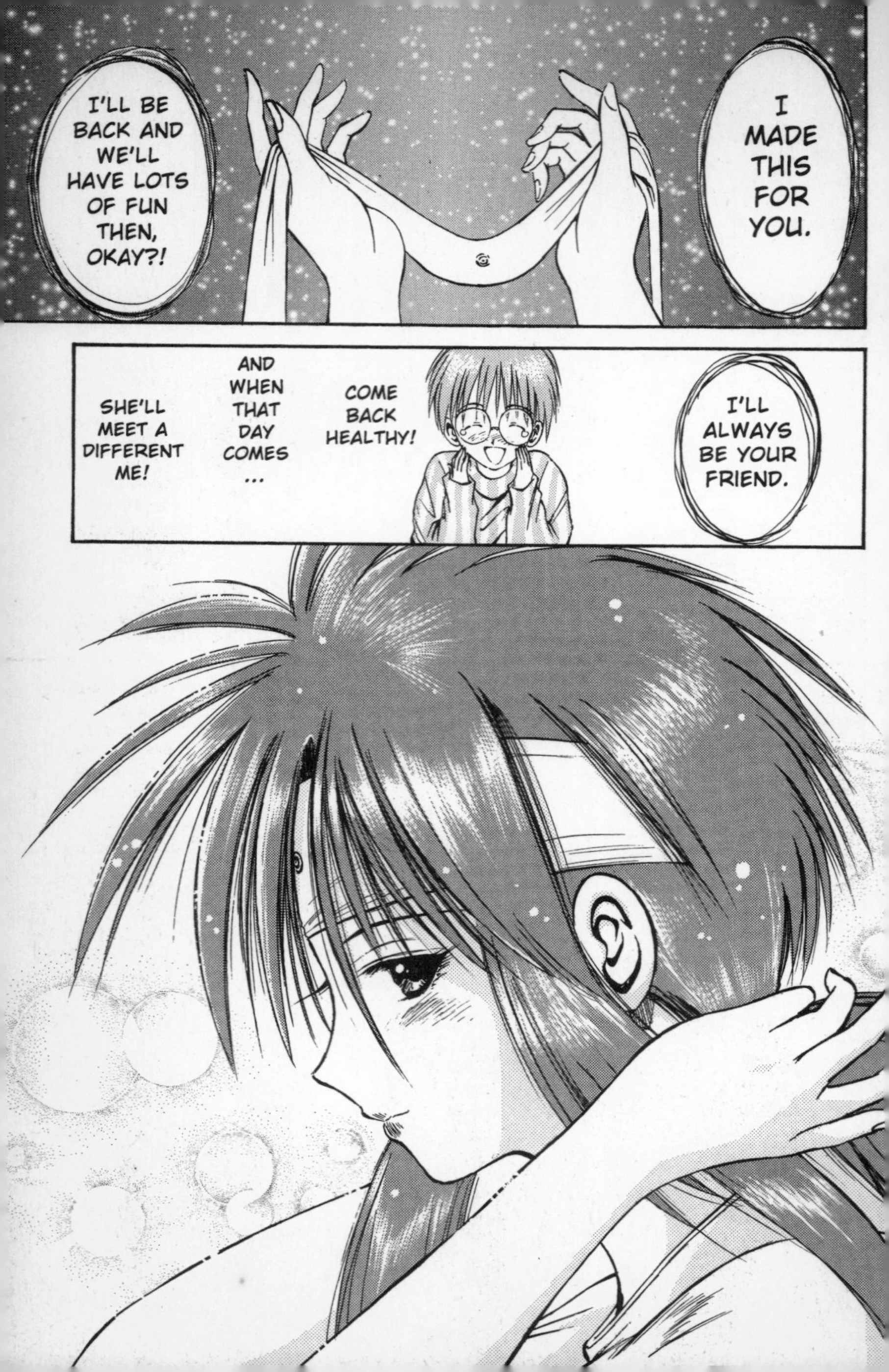
I MADE THIS FOR YOU.
I'LL BE BACK AND WE'LL HAVE LOTS OF FUN THEN, OKAY?!
I'LL ALWAYS BE YOUR FRIEND.
COME BACK HEALTHY!
AND WHEN THAT DAY COMES ...
SHE'LL MEET A DIFFERENT ME!

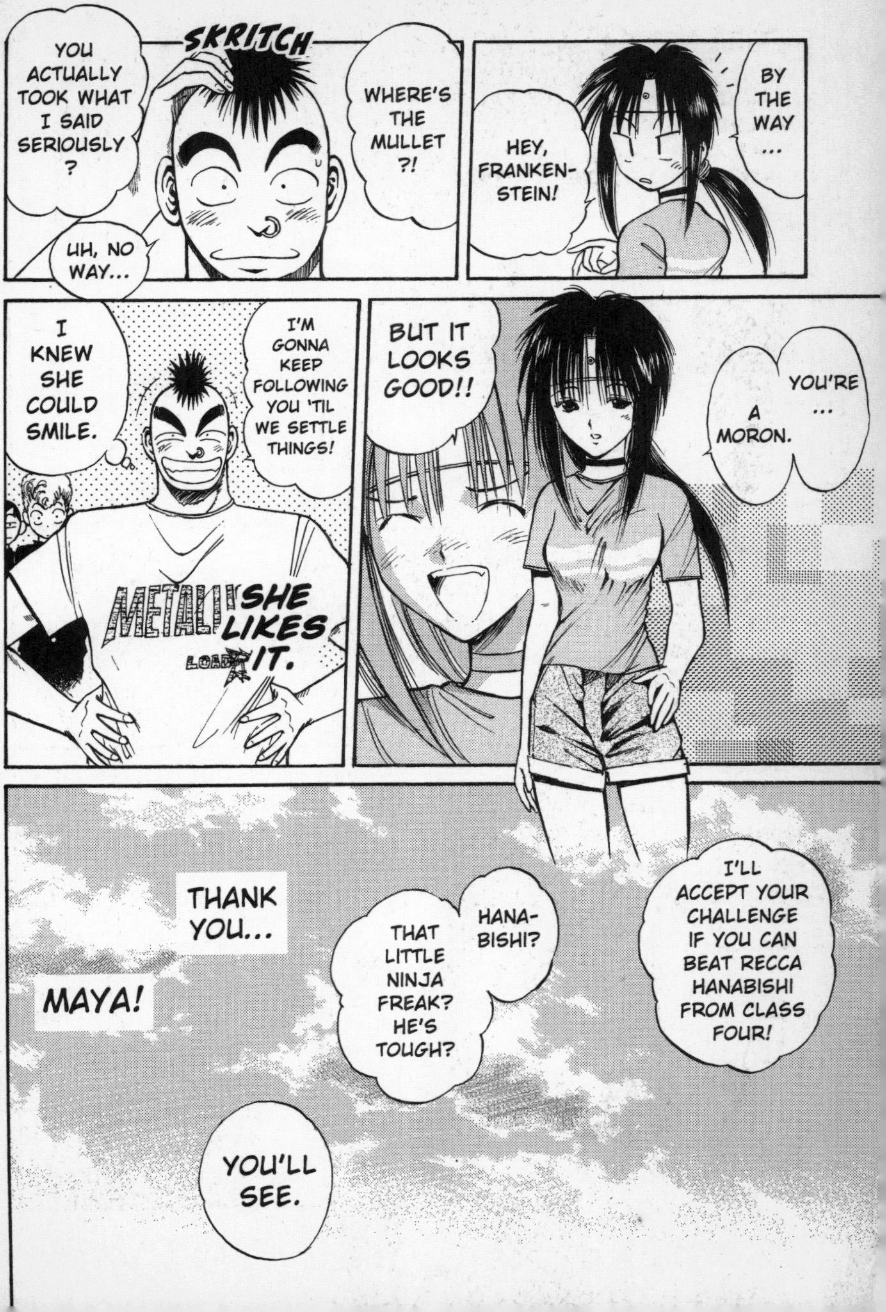
BY THE WAY ...
HEY, FRANKENSTEIN!
WHERE'S THE MULLET ?!
SKRITCH
YOU ACTUALLY TOOK WHAT I SAID SERIOUSLY ?
UH, NO WAY...
YOU'RE ... A MORON.
BUT IT LOOKS GOOD!!
I'M GONNA KEEP FOLLOWING YOU 'TIL WE SETTLE THINGS!
I KNEW SHE COULD SMILE.
SHE LIKES IT.
I'LL ACCEPT YOUR CHALLENGE IF YOU CAN BEAT RECCA HANABISHI FROM CLASS FOUR!
HANABISHI?
THAT LITTLE NINJA FREAK? HE'S TOUGH?
THANK YOU...
MAYA!
YOU'LL SEE.

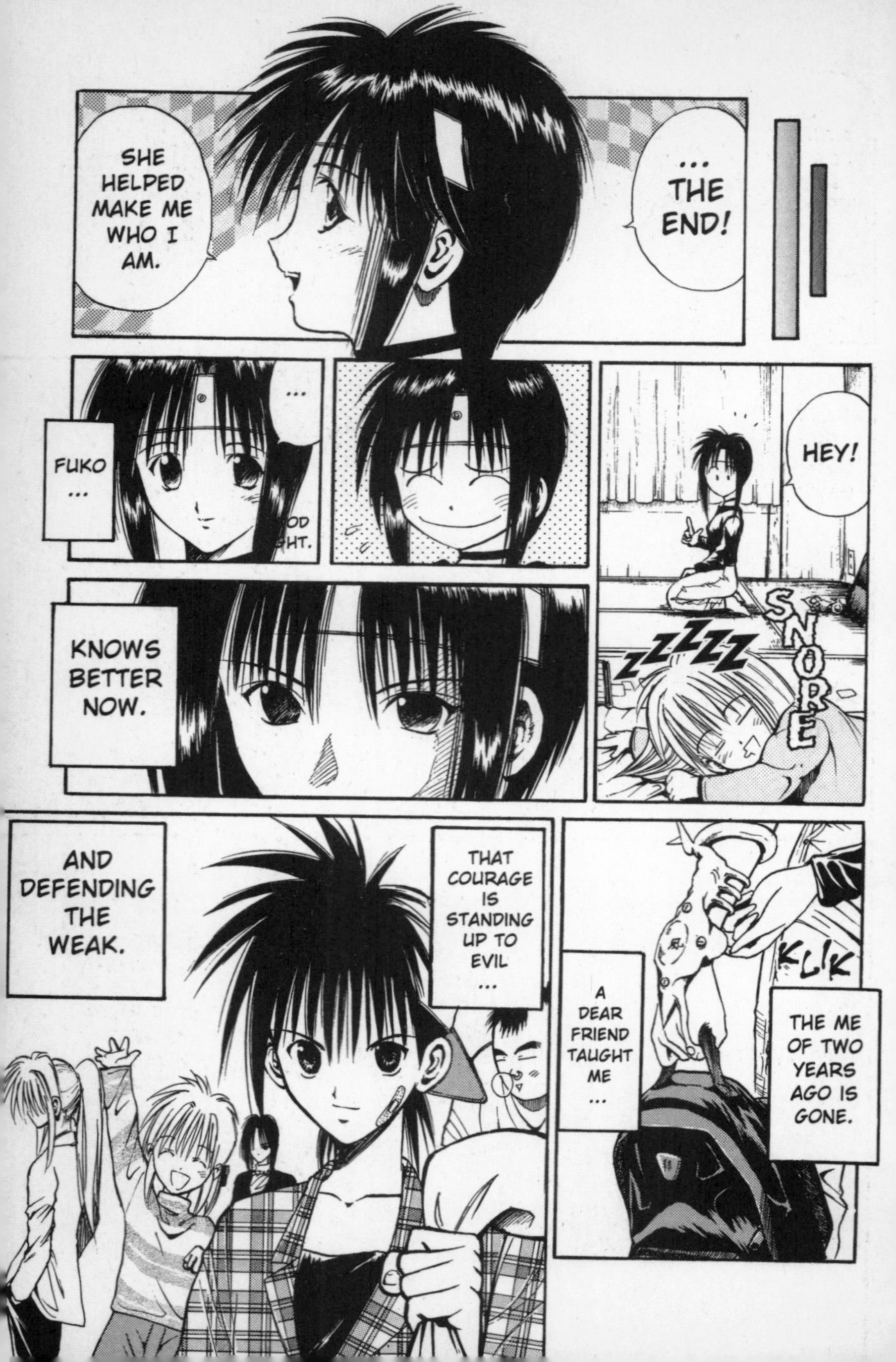
... THE END!
SHE HELPED MAKE ME WHO I AM.
HEY!
ZZZZZ
SNORE
...
FUKO ...
KNOWS BETTER NOW.
KLIK
THE ME OF TWO YEARS AGO IS GONE.
A DEAR FRIEND TAUGHT ME ...
THAT COURAGE IS STANDING UP TO EVIL ...
AND DEFENDING THE WEAK.

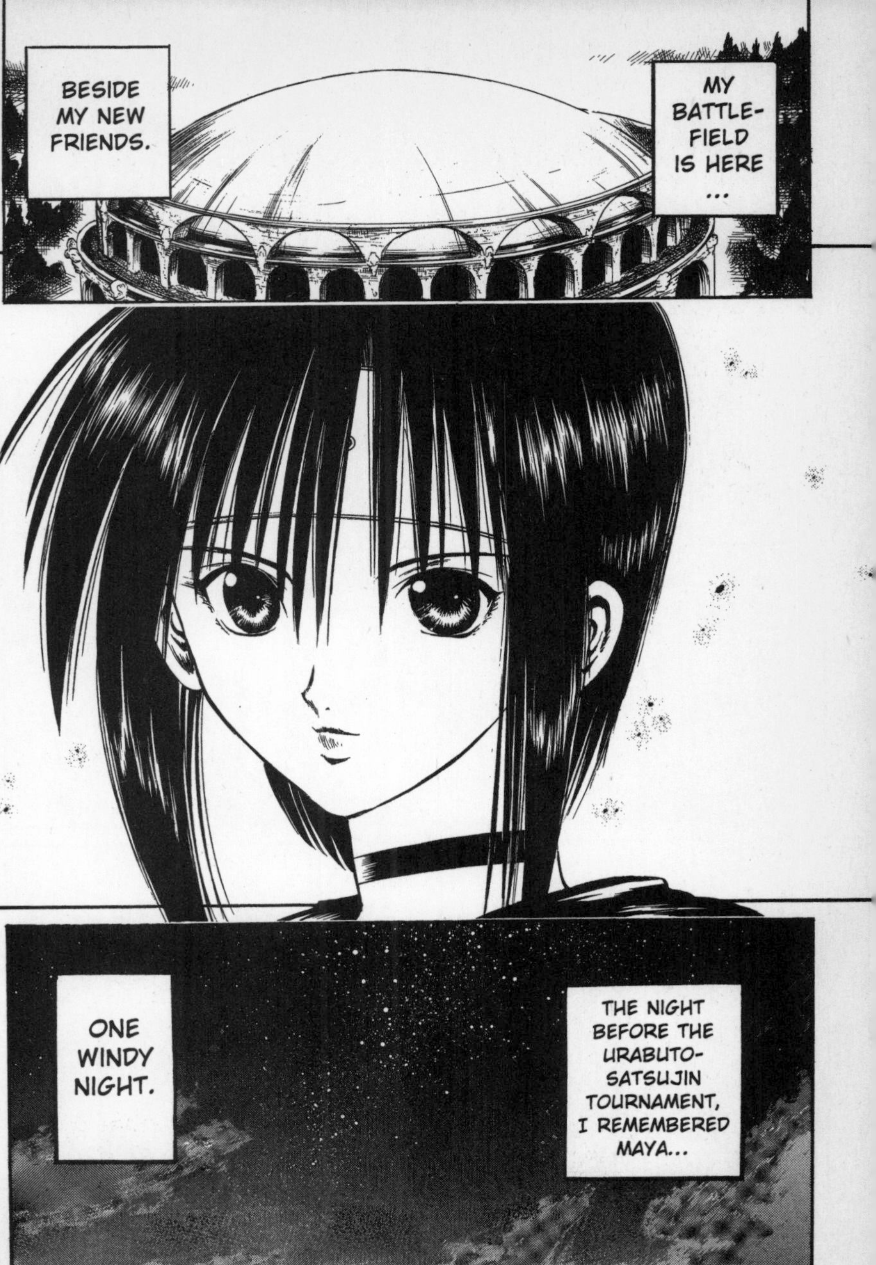
MY BATTLE-FIELD IS HERE ...
BESIDE MY NEW FRIENDS.
THE NIGHT BEFORE THE URABUTO-SATSUJIN TOURNAMENT, I REMEMBERED MAYA...
ONE WINDY NIGHT.

The End

## Author's Note:

WHEN MY EDITOR CAME TO ME WITH THE IDEA OF A FLASHBACK, IT WASN'T RECCA OR TOKIYA I THOUGHT OF, BUT FUKO KIRISAWA. FUKO IS ONE OF MY FAVORITE CHARACTERS, SHE'S ALWAYS UP TO SOMETHING.

INCIDENTALLY, I THINK FUKO CUT HER HAIR BECAUSE SHE FELT BAD FOR WHAT SHE DID TO DOMON.

YIPPEE ♪

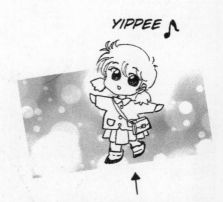

↑
FUKO, FOUR YEARS OLD
(JUST KIDDING!)

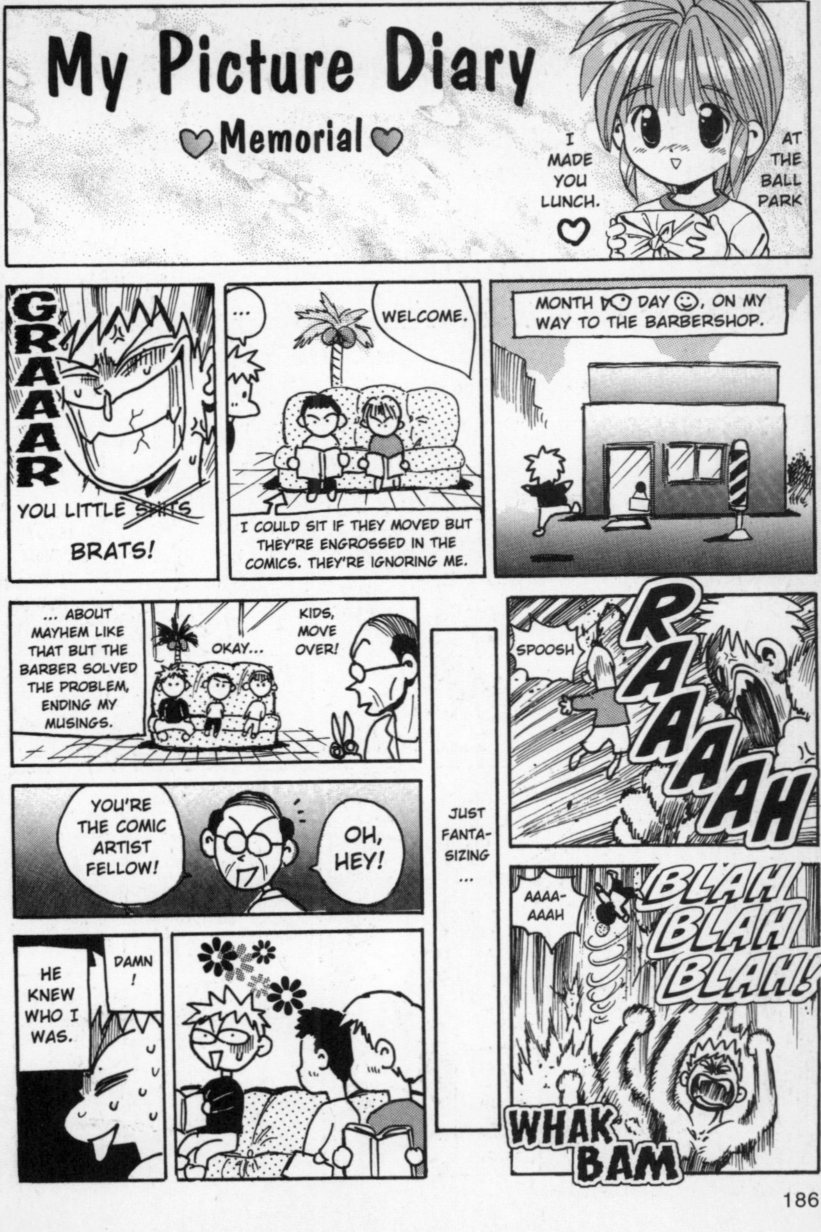
My Picture Diary
♥Memorial♥
AT THE BALL PARK
I MADE YOU LUNCH. ♡
MONTH DAY, ON MY WAY TO THE BARBERSHOP.
WELCOME.
...
I COULD SIT IF THEY MOVED BUT THEY'RE ENGROSSED IN THE COMICS. THEY'RE IGNORING ME.
GRAAAR
YOU LITTLE ~~SHITS~~
BRATS!
RAAAAAH
SPOOSH
BLAH BLAH BLAH!
AAAA-AAAH
WHAK BAM
JUST FANTA-SIZING ...
KIDS, MOVE OVER!
OKAY...
... ABOUT MAYHEM LIKE THAT BUT THE BARBER SOLVED THE PROBLEM, ENDING MY MUSINGS.
OH, HEY!
YOU'RE THE COMIC ARTIST FELLOW!
DAMN !
HE KNEW WHO I WAS.

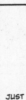

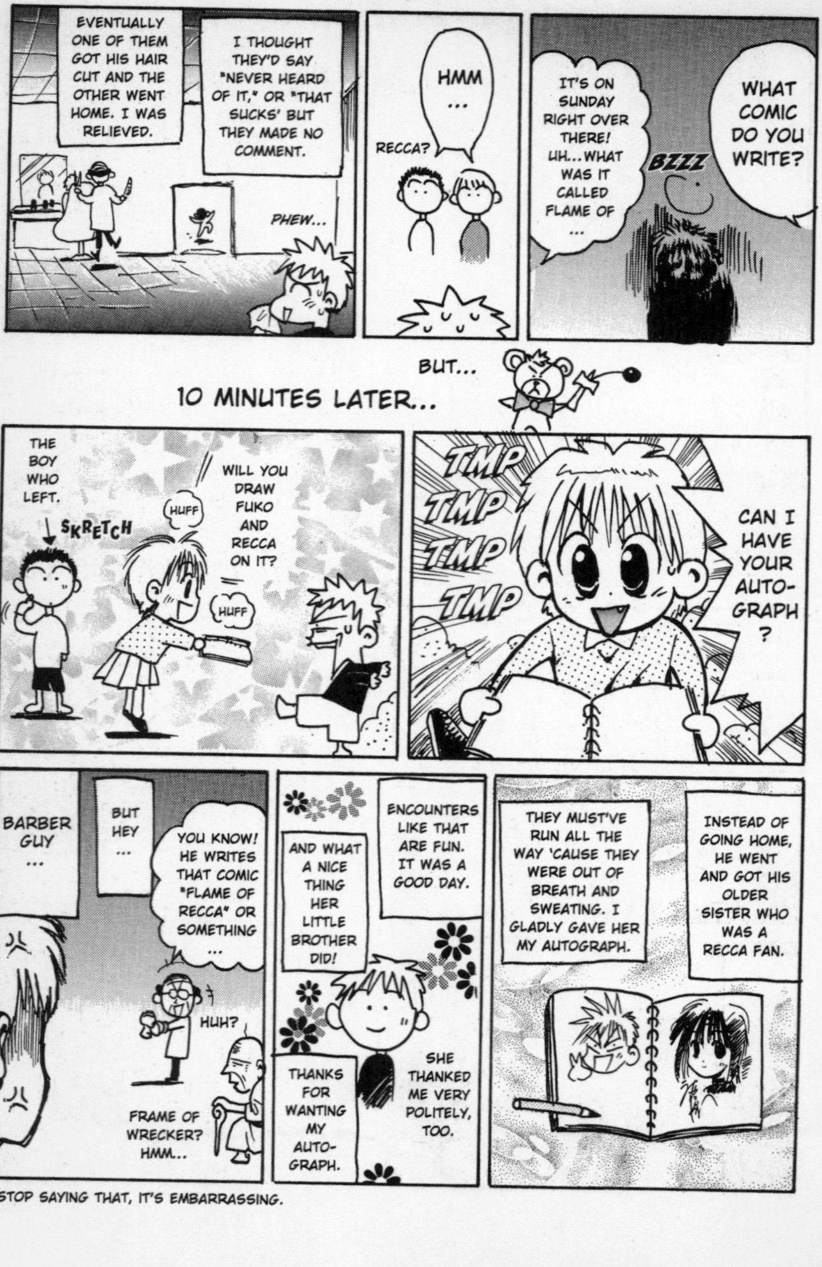
WHAT COMIC DO YOU WRITE?
IT'S ON SUNDAY RIGHT OVER THERE! UH...WHAT WAS IT CALLED FLAME OF ...
BZZZ
HMM ...
RECCA?
I THOUGHT THEY'D SAY "NEVER HEARD OF IT," OR "THAT SUCKS' BUT THEY MADE NO COMMENT.
EVENTUALLY ONE OF THEM GOT HIS HAIR CUT AND THE OTHER WENT HOME. I WAS RELIEVED.
PHEW...
BUT...
10 MINUTES LATER...
TMP
TMP
TMP
TMP
CAN I HAVE YOUR AUTO-GRAPH ?
WILL YOU DRAW FUKO AND RECCA ON IT?
HUFF
HUFF
THE BOY WHO LEFT.
SKRETCH
INSTEAD OF GOING HOME, HE WENT AND GOT HIS OLDER SISTER WHO WAS A RECCA FAN.
THEY MUST'VE RUN ALL THE WAY 'CAUSE THEY WERE OUT OF BREATH AND SWEATING. I GLADLY GAVE HER MY AUTOGRAPH.
ENCOUNTERS LIKE THAT ARE FUN. IT WAS A GOOD DAY.
AND WHAT A NICE THING HER LITTLE BROTHER DID!
SHE THANKED ME VERY POLITELY, TOO.
THANKS FOR WANTING MY AUTO-GRAPH.
YOU KNOW! HE WRITES THAT COMIC "FLAME OF RECCA" OR SOMETHING ...
BUT HEY ...
BARBER GUY ...
HUH?
FRAME OF WRECKER? HMM...

STOP SAYING THAT, IT'S EMBARRASSING.

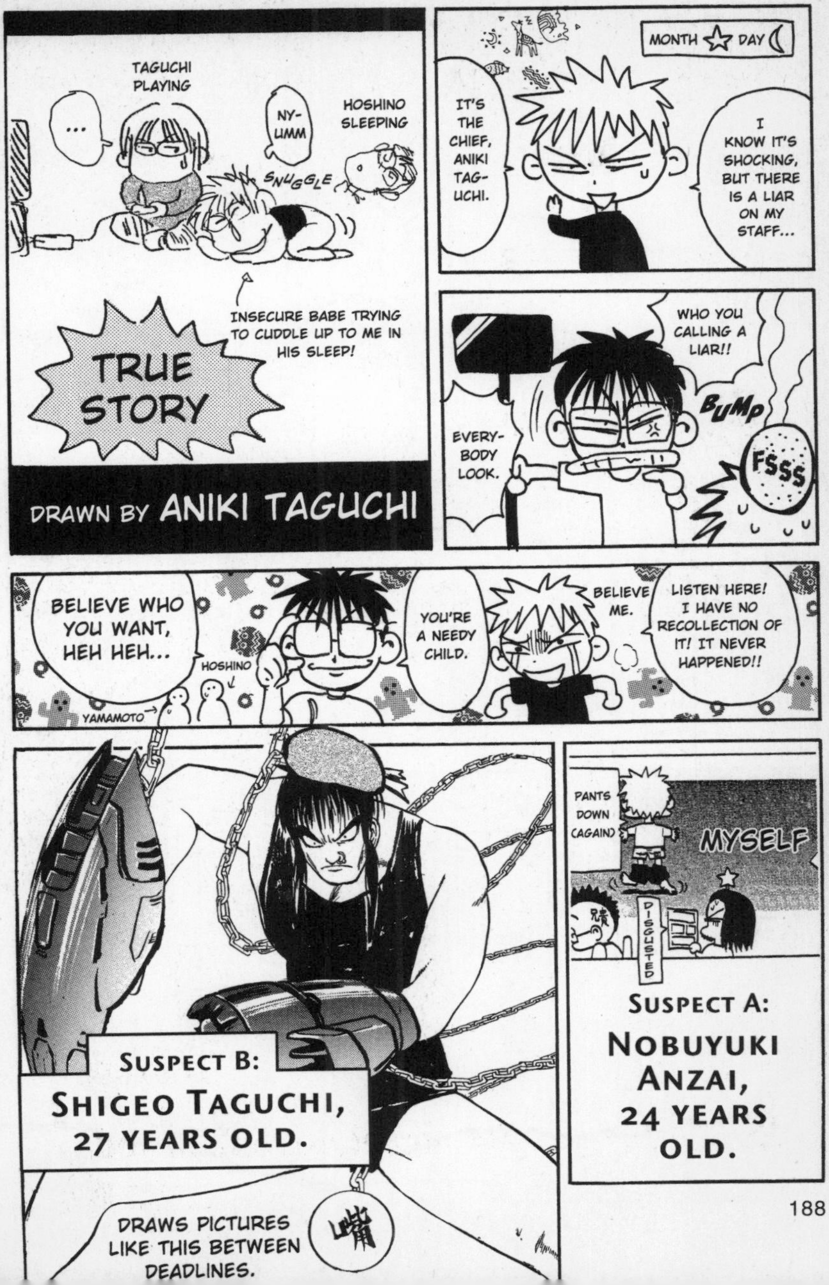
MONTH ☆ DAY
I KNOW IT'S SHOCKING, BUT THERE IS A LIAR ON MY STAFF...
IT'S THE CHIEF, ANIKI TAGUCHI.
WHO YOU CALLING A LIAR!!
BUMP
FSSS
EVERYBODY LOOK.
HOSHINO SLEEPING
NY-UMM
TAGUCHI PLAYING
...
SNUGGLE
INSECURE BABE TRYING TO CUDDLE UP TO ME IN HIS SLEEP!
TRUE STORY
DRAWN BY ANIKI TAGUCHI
LISTEN HERE! I HAVE NO RECOLLECTION OF IT! IT NEVER HAPPENED!!
BELIEVE ME.
YOU'RE A NEEDY CHILD.
BELIEVE WHO YOU WANT, HEH HEH...
HOSHINO
YAMAMOTO
PANTS DOWN (AGAIN)
MYSELF
DISGUSTED
SUSPECT A:
NOBUYUKI ANZAI, 24 YEARS OLD.
SUSPECT B:
SHIGEO TAGUCHI, 27 YEARS OLD.
DRAWS PICTURES LIKE THIS BETWEEN DEADLINES.

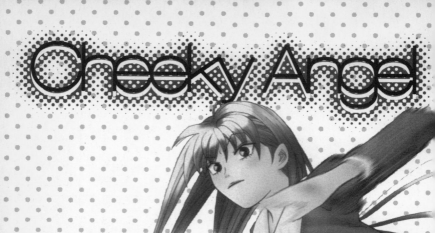
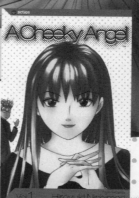

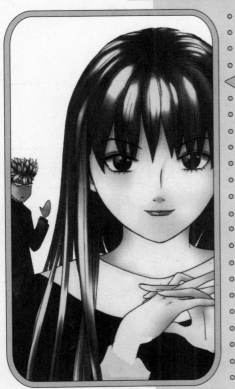

# COMPLETE OUR SURVEY AND LET US KNOW WHAT YOU THINK!

☑ Please do NOT send me information about VIZ products, news and events, special offers, or other information.

☐ Please do NOT send me information from VIZ's trusted business partners.

**Name:** Lauren Ybarra

**Address:** _____

**City:** _____ **State:** _____ **Zip:** _____

**E-mail:** _____

☐ Male ☑ Female   **Date of Birth** (mm/dd/yyyy): 4 / 29 / 1903 ( Under 13? Parental consent required )

## What race/ethnicity do you consider yourself? (please check one)

☐ Asian/Pacific Islander   ☐ Black/African American   ☐ Hispanic/Latino

☐ Native American/Alaskan Native   ☐ White/Caucasian   ☐ Other: _____

## What VIZ product did you purchase? (check all that apply and indicate title purchased)

☐ DVD/VHS _____

☐ Graphic Novel _____

☐ Magazines _____

☐ Merchandise _____

## Reason for purchase: (check all that apply)

☐ Special offer   ☑ Favorite title   ☐ Gift

☐ Recommendation   ☐ Other _____

## Where did you make your purchase? (please check one)

☐ Comic store   ☑ Bookstore   ☐ Mass/Grocery Store

☐ Newsstand   ☐ Video/Video Game Store   ☐ Other: _____

☐ Online (site: _____ )

## What other VIZ properties have you purchased/own? _____

_____

**How many anime and/or manga titles have you purchased in the last year? How many were VIZ titles?** **(please check one from each column)**

| ANIME | MANGA | VIZ |
|---|---|---|
| ☐ None | ☐ None | ☐ None |
| ☐ 1-4 | ☐ 1-4 | ☐ 1-4 |
| ☐ 5-10 | ☐ 5-10 | ☐ 5-10 |
| ☐ 11+ | ☐ 11+ | ☐ 11+ |

**I find the pricing of VIZ products to be:** **(please check one)**

☐ Cheap ☐ Reasonable ☐ Expensive

**What genre of manga and anime would you like to see from VIZ?** **(please check two)**

☐ Adventure ☐ Comic Strip ☐ Science Fiction ☐ Fighting

☐ Horror ☐ Romance ☐ Fantasy ☐ Sports

**What do you think of VIZ's new look?**

☐ Love It ☐ It's OK ☐ Hate It ☐ Didn't Notice ☐ No Opinion



**Which do you prefer?** **(please check one)**

☐ Reading right-to-left

☐ Reading left-to-right

**Which do you prefer?** **(please check one)**

☐ Sound effects in English

☐ Sound effects in Japanese with English captions

☐ Sound effects in Japanese only with a glossary at the back

**THANK YOU! Please send the completed form to:**

VIZ

NJW Research
42 Catharine St.
Poughkeepsie, NY 12601

**All information provided will be used for internal purposes only. We promise not to sell or otherwise divulge your information.**